The Transgender Phenomenon

The Transgender Phenomenon

Richard Ekins and Dave King

SAGE Publications

London ● Thousand Oaks ● New Delhi

First published 2006

SAGE Publications Ltd
1 Oliver's Yard
55 City Road
London EC1Y 1SP

SAGE Publications Inc
2455 Teller Road
Thousand Oaks, California 91320

SAGE Publications India Pvt Ltd
B-42 Panchsheel Enclave
Post Box 4109
New Delhi 110 017

British Library Cataloguing in Publication data

A catalogue record for this book is available
from the British Library

ISBN 0 7619 7163 7   978 0 7619 7163 4
     0 7619 7164 5   978 0 7619 7164 1

Library of Congress control number: 2006920988

Typeset by C&M Digitals (P) Ltd., Chennai, India
Printed on paper from sustainable resources
Printed and bound in Great Britain by Athenaeum Press, Gateshead

For Wendy, Denise and James
In memory of Nicholas Dodge (1943–2004)

I am accustoming myself to regarding every sexual act
as a process in which four individuals are involved.
We have a lot to discuss on this topic.

From a letter on 1 August 1899 by
Sigmund Freud to Wilhelm Fliess

Contents

List of Figures

Preface

The newspaper headline, 'What is a man? Parliament may have to decide', appeared in the UK *Manchester Guardian* on 19 March 1954, amidst the massive press coverage of the story of Roberta (formerly Robert) Cowell. In 2004, the UK Parliament finally decided and passed the Gender Recognition Act which according to Lord Filkin, Minister at the Department for Constitutional Affairs, 'allows transsexual people who have taken decisive steps to live fully and permanently in the acquired gender to gain legal recognition in that gender' (Filkin, 1993).

Even as the story of Roberta Cowell was breaking in England, Dr Harry Benjamin, with the help of American 'sex change' ex-GI Christine Jorgensen, was fashioning a story of the 'transsexual' that was to become the dominant medical story for the half century that followed. Jorgensen had travelled to Denmark to have her male genitalia removed by a medical team who, in 1951, told a story of relieving the distress of a troubled homosexual (Hamburger and Sprechler, 1951; Hertoft and Sørensen, 1979). In 1953, following the fusion of Jorgensen's personal story with Benjamin's developing medical story, the seeds were sown for the modern tale of the transsexual conceptualized as a problem of gender identity quite separate from that of sexual orientation.

At around the same time in Los Angeles, a man named Arnold Lowman was giving a lot of thought to why he liked to dress in women's clothes and was adopting the name of Virginia Prince. Prince's story of the male heterosexual transvestite, as adopted in the Euro-American world, spawned a host of supportive and commercial ventures so that today male cross-dressers can find welcoming venues across the globe, on any night of the week (Lee, 2005).

These fragments are illustrative of the two stories that became dominant in the realm of human experience that is today considered under the heading of 'transgender'. More recently, however, a new story has emerged. It is a story that has emerged within a transgender community built upon the foundations provided by the stories of Harry Benjamin and Virginia Prince. It is a story of diversity, of 'blending genders', of 'gender outlaws': a 'beyond the binary' view of transgender. As US transgender activist Dallas Denny put it in 1996 (Denny, 1996: 4): 'the ways of thinking given us by Harry Benjamin and Virginia Prince no longer provide a good "fit" for all of us . . . It's no secret that we are in the midst of turmoil and change. A "beyond the binary" view of transgender is emerging.'

Implicit within all these stories are tales of the interrelations between personal transgender narratives and medical, legal, media, and transgender community stories; variously dominant, contested, and socially distributed in time and place. We prefer the gerund 'transgendering' to the noun and adjective 'transgender' because of its focus not on *types* of people, but on behaviour and social *process*. Transgendering, for us, refers to the idea of moving across (transferring) from one pre-existing gender category to another (either temporarily or permanently); to the idea of living in between genders; and to the idea of living 'beyond gender' altogether. It also refers to the social process within which competing transgendering stories and attendant identities and ideologies emerge, develop, and wax and wane in influence, in time and place.

Tales of transgendering take many forms. This book sets forth a sociological framework within which it is possible to map the emergence of the maximum diversity of such tales and to consider the diverse interrelations between their origins, developments and consequences. In particular, it examines the emergence of diverse conceptualizations of transgender phenomena in terms of their relationship with the binary gender divide in contemporary Euro-American societies, with reference to problems of conceptualization, theorization, identity and social worlds.

Acknowledgements

This book draws upon the personal and professional life experiences of untold individuals who variously identify with the term transgender, and of untold individuals, who, for whatever reasons, find themselves working within the transgender community whether as academics, independent scholars, professionals or activists. We thank them all.

Our theory and research methodology entail maintaining contact with many of our informants over the entire period of our research – a period that now extends over 30 years.

It is quite impossible to pay the proper respect to our informants in an acknowledgements entry in a single book. For this book, however, we have drawn especially on the time, experience and expertise of selected informants. We owe a special debt of gratitude to Holly Boswell, Sissy Diana, Christie Elan-Cane, Anne Lawrence, Millie, Debra Rose, Del LaGrace Volcano, Rachael Webb, and Stephen Whittle.

Of our academic and professional mentors who do not identify as transgendered, we are especially grateful to Ken Plummer and Friedemann Pfäfflin, whose particular combinations of humanity, integrity, and commitment to rigorous science have long been an inspiration to us.

We are also very grateful to Peter Farrer, Alice Purnell and Barbara Ross for the help and support they have given us over many years.

Finally, we particularly thank Wendy Saunderson for providing vital intellectual and emotional support, thereby enabling the completion of this book.

ONE Telling Transgendering Tales

Beginnings

The story of our research begins in the mid-1970s in the United Kingdom at a time when there was little or no sociological interest in what was then conceptualized as 'transvestism' and 'transsexuality'. Today, by contrast, 'transgender' provides a focal point for cutting-edge theoretical work in cultural and gender studies and cutting-edge gender activism. In the same 30-year period, transgendering has moved from the peripheries of 'deviance' and 'perversion' in Euro-American societies to the centre of mainstream celebrity. As we write, the Portuguese transsexual Nadia Almada has recently won the UK reality TV show *Big Brother 5* and is among the hottest 'celebs' featured on the covers of the major celebrity magazine weeklies:

> Now we've taken her to our hearts because she isn't afraid to show her insecurities. Despite her thick mascara and lip gloss, she's refreshingly real. AND she wears heels to do the housework. That makes her our kind of woman. (Johnson, 2004: 3)

Within a few weeks, the focus of attention has switched from 'Nadia: "Why I Had My Sex Change"' (*Closer*, 2004a) to more pressing concerns of celebrity womanhood: 'Nadia's Agony: "I've Lost My Virginity to a Love Cheat"' (*Closer*, 2004b); 'Nadia: My Agony Over Secret Boyfriend' (*Star: The World's Greatest Celeb Weekly*, 2004); 'Nadia Loses a Stone in 4 Weeks' (*Heat*, 2004).

In the same 30-year period since we began our research, our focus of interest has extended from the United Kingdom, to North America, Europe, South Africa and Australasia. In addition, we have observed in this time how Western discourses of transgenderism have been increasingly exported to many other parts of the world and are usurping or heavily influencing more traditional indigenous notions of gender and 'transgender' phenomena (Teh, 2001; 2002; Winter, 2002; Winter and Udomsak, 2002).

Dave's story

Although as an undergraduate I had read US sociologist Garfinkel's (1967) study of 'Agnes', it was the British sociologists Carol Riddell and Mike Brake who provided the inspiration for my interest in developing a sociology of transgender. Carol Riddell, then a lecturer at the University of Lancaster, England, presented an unpublished paper in 1972 to the National Deviancy Conference 10, entitled 'Transvestism and the Tyranny of Gender'. For Riddell (1972), transvestites and transsexuals, along with gay men and lesbians, were the casualties of a gender role system that performs important functions for capitalism. In particular, she argued that the medical profession was acting as an agent of 'capitalist family and gender relations': 'In no way is the T.V. [transvestite] encouraged to develop his/her inclinations, to express them publicly and to politicise them into a rejection of the system which produced the need for them' (ibid.: 10).

Riddell's recommendation was for transvestites and transsexuals to join 'with other sexually persecuted minorities, particularly homosexuals, in confrontation with the police, the legal profession, the psychiatrists, the capitalist nuclear family, capitalist gender roles, capitalist attitudes, and fundamentally the capitalist system itself' (ibid.: 12). Mike Brake, then a lecturer at the University of Kent, England, had intentions of publishing Riddell's article in a book he was editing at the time but, unfortunately, his plan did not materialize and it remains unpublished.

Two years later, in 1974, Mike Brake presented his own more nuanced thoughts on the matter in a conference paper entitled 'I May Be Queer, but At Least I am a Man' (Brake, 1976). Brake made the point, as relevant today as it was then, that:

> [MTF] Transvestites and transsexuals polarize the problems of gay activism. At one level they are accused of sexism because of their concern with traditional femininity, but it must be remembered that the masters are not supposed to dress as slaves, and men who dress as women are giving up their power as men. Their oppression is similar to that experienced by gay men and all women. (ibid.: 187)

These comments by Brake on the politics of transgender seem to be the first published thoughts by a British sociologist on transvestism and transsexualism. It was not a topic Brake returned to and when my research story began in the mid-1970s, I was determined to make a serious study of transgender phenomena.

The beginning of my research story coincided with Britain hosting 'The First National TV.TS [Transvestite.Transsexual] Conference' (1974) in Leeds, although I was unaware of it at the time. The conference was designed as a forum for those people self-identifying as transvestite or transsexual and for professionals working in the field. It included presentations from community activists who were the leading figures in both transvestite and transsexual organizations, personal stories from those who identified as transvestite or transsexual, and talks from social workers and psychologists. This meeting of minds of 'experts' and 'members' (transvestites and transsexuals) set the initial parameters for the growing stream of such conferences that took place during the 1970s and 1980s. A press report of the conference by Parkin informed general readers thus:

> The First National conference of transvestites, including radical drag queens and transsexuals is to be held at Leeds in March [1974]. Social workers, doctors and clergy have been invited to join them in discussing their problems of which the public largely knows nothing.
>
> Briefly, a transvestite is a person who gains psychological release through dressing in the clothing of the opposite sex. He (it is not often a she) is usually heterosexual. A radical drag queen is a transvestite who wears women's clothing in public, but does not try to hide the fact that he is a man.
>
> Mr. Martine O'Leary, a radical drag queen at Leeds, says that he buys old dresses from Oxfam shops, wears neither make-up nor substitute breasts, and tries to shake people out of their preconception of what a man is, a woman is, or more important, what he is.
>
> The other group, transsexuals, consider themselves to be women who have been trapped inside a man's body. They make their break for sexual freedom by proclaiming themselves to be women and living as women. Many seek the so-called 'sex change' operation and hormone treatment. (1974: 36)

In addition, the Conference Report (*The First National TV.TS Conference*, 1974) told tales of distinctions between 'radical' and 'conservative' wings in the debate on the future of transvestism. Radical feminist transvestites were said to identify with women's liberation; conservative transvestites were said to treat their wives 'like slaves' when dressed as men at home. There was talk that would take some 20 years to become widespread: of transsexuals seeking 'gender alignment'; of 'trans-gender' and 'trans.people' [*sic*] used as umbrella terms to include both TVs and TSs. On the other hand, there was much more talk of TV and TS being 'conditions', of being 'compulsive behaviour patterns', and of 'militant action' by TVs and TSs being inappropriate.

Della Aleksander, something of a celebrity at the time as a male to female (MTF) transsexual, had recently co-produced the BBC2 *Open Door* programme about 'transsexualism', which featured Member of Parliament Leo Abse, a well-known 'champion of minority causes' (*The First National TV.TS Conference*, 1974: 11). Aleksander had undergone 'sex change' surgery in 1970 in Casablanca, and the following year established GRAIL (Gender Research Association International Liaison), a group formed to campaign for equal rights for transsexuals. In her conference talk, she made the point that the conference unites all those 'crossing the sex border' and 'rejects petty differences between them as misplaced' before adding:

> Being a transvestite or a transsexual cannot, by its nature, be a social protest phenomenon, for it seeks to conform to accepted norms of the sexual division and the manner in which the sexes are distinguished by dress. In this it is very conformist and not to be confused with unisex of the David Bowie genre with which it is frequently confused. Unisex mirrors Man's sexual ambiguity. Transvestism and transsexualism does something about this ambiguity. (Aleksander, 1974: 11)

The organizers of the 1974 conference had sought to include main presentations on the law and psychiatry relating to TV and TS. However, the Chief Constable, Leeds City Police and Dr John Randell, Gender Identity Clinic, London were among those who sent their apologies for their non-attendance. This matter was rectified in the follow-up conference held at the University of Leicester in 1975 that did include legal and psychiatric contributions in the main presentations. It also included a contribution from the celebrated columnist Anna Raeburn, who gave a presentation entitled 'Male and Female Roles in Society with Reference to Transvestites and Transsexuals' (Beaumont Society, 1975). I was alerted to this conference by an advertisement in *New Society* and fortunately was able to attend.

These two conferences set the tone for my research. From the sociological point of view, what marked the two conferences were three major and related features. In the first place, it was evident that cross-dressing and sex-changing were non-normative (deviant) phenomena. In the second place, it was striking how knowledge in the area had been subjected to a pervasive medicalization. In the third place, it was notable how the conferences sought to garner what were thought to be the most favourable media representations.

I approached the area as a symbolic interactionist sociologist committed to labelling theory. In 1975, Ken Plummer had published his important text *Sexual Stigma*, which set forth a symbolic interactionist sociology of sexuality, with particular reference to male homosexuality. This book drew extensively upon labelling theory which studies how categories arise, and how they are disseminated and applied to self and others. I was fortunate enough to meet Plummer at a conference and in due course he became my PhD supervisor. As my research progressed, I began to separate out the main areas of focus, in particular those of identity, subculture, medicalization, and media representation. The empirical work was based on studies of the medical literature; a large number of media reports; fieldwork with transsexuals and transvestites; and, most importantly, interviews with surgeons, psychiatrists and psychologists, and others working in this field. Eventually, I produced a number of articles and my PhD thesis on this research (King, 1981; 1984; 1986; 1987).

4

Richard's story

As we have seen, Dave's transgender research story began, in a sense, with the work of British sociologist Carol Riddell on transvestism. Rather extraordinarily, my work as a serious student of sociology also began with the work of Carol Riddell. However, in my case, it was not Carol Riddell's work on transgender that influenced me. It was the work of Carol Riddell, in a different guise.

By 1971, I had become disillusioned at the prospect of continuing a career in law, and enrolled as a graduate student in the sociology of education at the University of London. In my first lecture, I was told that the best introduction to sociology was that by Margaret Coulson and David Riddell (1970) entitled *Approaching Sociology: A Critical Introduction.*

My principal teacher was Michael F.D. Young who at the London Institute of Education was spearheading, at the time, what became known as the 'new' sociology of education. It was a sociology of education that had, in the space of a few short years, jettisoned the 'old' sociology of education which was rooted in sociological positivism and structural functionalism.

In place of the 'old' sociology of education, Young and his colleagues were developing an entirely new approach to the area. They were re-formulating the discipline in terms of a sociology of knowledge which took its inspiration from humanist Marxisms and the 'new' interpretive sociologies of symbolic interactionism, phenomenological sociology and ethnomethodology (Young, 1971; Gorbutt, 1972).

At the time, there were no introductory books to sociology that combined all these theoretical approaches in one introductory text, but the great merit of Coulson and Riddell's (1970) introductory text, I was told, was that it did set forth the parameters for such an approach from a 'critical' Marxist standpoint. For this reason, it was the only recently written introduction to sociology that my teachers 'allowed' me to read.

I still have my original copy of this book sitting on my bookshelves. The book's publication date is marked as 1970 with a copyright © Margaret A. Coulson and David S. Riddell. Next to it is a 1972 reprint of the book but the authors are Margaret A. Coulson and Carol S. Riddell! Yes, Riddell had transitioned from MTF (male to female) in the period between the two print runs of her book. Unbeknown to Dave and myself, at the time, Dave's sociological transgender predecessor was my guide to introductory sociology: the former British MTF academic Carol Riddell.

While a schoolboy, one of my 'A' Level English teachers once remarked that I had a talent for writing about the relations between the individual and

5

society, and not much else. The teacher in question held a double first from Cambridge; he was eccentric to the point of craziness; and he seemed to hold in utter disdain the proprieties held so dear by his fellow teachers. I was fascinated by him and by everything he did and said. A man with such credentials must surely be right about me. In my sociology courses at the University of London, Institute of Education, I was introduced to the writings of philosopher-social psychologist George Herbert Mead (1863–1931). I soon learned that Mead had spent a lifetime developing and refining a brilliant and highly influential social theory of mind – a social theory of the emergence and development of self, with a corresponding pragmatist social ontology and social epistemology and a scientific social psychology. Inevitably, perhaps, I was hooked. Making sense of Mead's *Mind, Self, and Society* (1934), and then exploring its ramifications, became my academic and professional anchor and my inspiration. It has remained so ever since.

After the completion of my initial courses in sociology, philosophy, and education, I registered at the University of London for a doctorate entitled 'G.H. Mead: On the Contribution of George Herbert Mead to a Philosophy of Sociological Knowledge'. Following an extended period of study in the Department of Philosophy, University of Texas at Austin, with foremost Mead disciple David L. Miller and a period studying the 'G. H. Mead Archive' at the University of Chicago, I returned to England and submitted my doctorate in 1978. After these years of 'theorizing about theory', I decided to gain expertise in empirical sociology and turned my attention to an area that had intrigued me for many years: that of transgender.

Like Dave, I had been introduced in my early days as a student of sociology to Garfinkel's (1967) study of the MTF transsexual Agnes (originally, thought to be intersex). I had also read Michael Kosok's (1971) article 'The Phenomenology of Fucking' which had emboldened my desires to branch out as an 'outlaw' researcher. Later, I studied the developing work of Ken Plummer on the sociology of sexuality (Plummer, 1975). However, I was drawn principally to the research methodology of sociologist Herbert Blumer (1969), particularly when I learned that he had been a devoted student of Mead's at the University of Chicago. I also knew that it was Blumer who had developed Mead's philosophy and theoretical social psychology into the sociological and social psychological perspective he termed symbolic interactionism, to which my lecturers at the London Institute of Education had introduced me.

Last but not least, I should mention, perhaps, an extraordinary 'interview' I had with the great American interactionist sociologist Anselm Strauss. Shortly after finishing my PhD thesis, I received a postcard from Strauss asking me to meet him while he was on a visit to London. I went to the meeting feeling extremely flattered but with a degree of trepidation. In the course of a couple of hours, he seemed to 'milk' me dry of everything he was interested in, and, somehow, I never seemed to get the opportunity to put any of my questions to him. Strauss provided me with an object lesson in unstructured interviewing which I have never forgotten. I did determine, though, that I would attempt to be more 'reciprocal' in my own qualitative research, not wishing to leave my informants with the vaguely exploited feeling I experienced following my meeting with Strauss.

With this background, it was perhaps inevitable, therefore, that as I turned my attention to the study of an empirical domain, I did so from a symbolic interactionist perspective. My reading of Mead emphasized that he was a philosopher of process (Ekins, 1978) – specifically of social process – who saw all 'social objects' (minds, selves, meanings) as emergents within social process. The sociological corollary of Mead's philosophical position was that the principal task of the empirical social scientist wedded to this view was to plot the emergence and history of social objects in any given research arena, with reference to their origins, development and consequences. As a student of the sociology of knowledge, I approached the area in terms of the interrelations between the various 'knowledges' in the area, conceptualized in terms of three principal 'knowledges': those of 'science', those of 'members' (of transgendered people), and those of 'everyday life'.

As with Dave's work, this drew me to the detailed investigation of the interrelations between medical knowledge, subcultural knowledge, and the knowledge held by those people identifying as transvestite and transsexual, in terms of their origins, development and consequences.

As the only two UK sociologists working in the area at the time, it was only a matter of time before our paths crossed. I first met Dave at the 1982 British Sociological Conference on Gender in Manchester, UK, where I presented one of my first papers on transgender entitled 'Science, Sociological Analysis and the Problem of Tranvestism and Transsexuality' (Ekins, 1982). This paper drew upon Dave's pioneering sociological article on transsexuality and transvestism (King, 1981), included in Ken Plummer's *The Making of the Modern Homosexual* in 1981 (Plummer, 1981). Plummer's book was ground-breaking, establishing as it did a sociological reader for sexuality studies rooted in the social constructionism of symbolic interactionism and the 'archaeology of knowledge' approach of Michel Foucault (1970; 1972). Moreover, it was a reader that placed emphasis on both theoretical sophistication and empirical work so guided.

By 1982, I was making sense of my empirical work in terms of a 'basic social process' (Glaser, 1978) of 'femaling'. I had yet to write my paper 'On Femaling: Some Relations Between Sex, Sexuality and Gender', which I first presented in 1984 (Ekins, 1984), although it was not published for some ten years after that date (Ekins, 1993). My work was based upon observations of what later became several thousands of transgendered people, extended interviews with several hundred informants, and detailed life-long life history work with several dozen informants from a number of different continents. From the outset I took care to follow selected informants in the full range of their social settings. This often entailed detailed observational and interview work with medical and related professionals, with the families of my transgendered informants, and with the various service providers to trans people, such as beauticians and hair care specialists. At the same time, I immersed myself into the full range of transgender 'community' events such as private meetings, drag balls, erotic networks, and so on (Ekins, 1997).

It may be hard for present-day students to grasp the difficulties attached to developing a sociology of sex, sexuality and gender in the early and mid-1980s, let alone a sociology of cross-dressing and sex-changing which included sexuality in its remit. In the USA, Gagnon and Simon had paved the way for a sociology of sexuality, as they branched out from the US versions of positivist sexology (Gagnon and Simon, 1973). *Contra* their mentor and colleague Alfred Kinsey, they began to focus on the social meanings of sexuality, developing, in particular, their conceptualizations of sexual scripts. In the UK there was (and is) no university tradition of sexology, despite the significance of the Englishman Havelock Ellis in the history of sexology. Moreover, in both the UK and the USA, the influence of women's studies and the nascent sociology of gender led to a situation where almost all social scientists drew a sharp distinction between sex as biology and gender as social construction. They tended to leave 'sex' in the hands of biologists (Oakley, 1972). Sexual perversion or variation was left to psychiatrists and psychologists, apart from sporadic studies in the sociology of deviance (Sagarin, 1969). The few studies on the sociology of sexuality (Gagnon and Simon, 1970; Henslin and Sagarin, 1978) were swamped by the burgeoning literature in women's studies that focused on sociological constructions of gender, seen as largely separate from sex and sexuality. Such was the climate of the times, that at the very conference where I first met Dave we had been barred from attending a presentation on pornography. All men had been told to leave the room after a majority vote had declared the seminar room a 'women only' space.

In the early 1980s, I had all manner of obstacles placed in my way when I tried to develop a third year course in the sociology of sex, sexuality and gender as part of undergraduate BSc programmes in sociology and in social science at the University of Ulster, UK. My Faculty Dean bypassed the usual informal Course committee meetings and took the unprecedented step of setting up a Faculty committee to probe the sociological viability and validity of a course centred around an exploration of the interrelations between sex (the body), sexuality (eroticism) and gender. My Dean insisted upon external and internal letters of support from a number of sociologists and social scientists, before granting approval after a series of lengthy meetings. Likewise, the external examiner for sociology, a considerable name in social theory at the time, needed reassurance from me that it was possible for sociology under-graduates to consider sociologically what appeared to him, *prima facie*, to be matters of biology and psychology.

The exploration of the interrelations between sex, sexuality and gender came to form a major theme of my studies of cross-dressing and sex-changing. Unlike Dave, who situated his work primarily within the sociology of deviance, I, as a sociological theorist, was drawn to the research method-ology known as 'grounded theory' (Glaser and Strauss, 1967; Glaser, 1978) to conceptualize cross-dressing and sex-changing phenomena. This eventually led me to consider male cross-dressing and sex-changing in terms of the basic social process of 'male femaling'. I saw male femaling as taking place within diverse interrelations of body femaling, erotic femaling and gender femaling. I then identified an ideal-typical career path of male femaling developing within the interrelations of these modes over time through a phased career path considered in terms of beginning, fantasying, doing, constituting and consolidating male femaling (Ekins, 1984).

Particularly in evidence was the way those males who 'femaled' felt the need to 'explain' their untoward thoughts, feelings and behaviours; and in doing so – in interrelating with available conceptualizations of their thoughts, feelings and behaviours – constructed for themselves identities and courses of action.

Working together

On a number of occasions in the 1980s, Dave had tried to form a study group in Britain for those interested in transvestism and transsexualism from a soci-ological point of view. His attempts had always failed through lack of inter-est in the area. Instead, Dave and I maintained occasional contact, but for the most part worked independently and in relative isolation.

Nor were publishers very interested in what we were doing. Dave had written his PhD thesis in 1986 (King, 1986) but it was not to be published as a book until 1993 (King, 1993). Richard's paper 'On Femaling: Some Relations between Sex, Sexuality and Gender', that was eventually published as 'On Male Femaling: A Grounded Theory Approach to Cross-Dressing and Sex-Changing' (Ekins, 1993) had been rejected by the journal *Symbolic Interaction* on the grounds that it was 'better suited to a sexology journal'. It had then taken *The Sociological Review* over a year to find two reviewers.

In retrospect, it was no surprise that we had to wait until the early 1990s before we found a wider reception for our work. The 1990s ushered in an entirely new climate in transgender matters. In the space of a few short years, transgender became 'sexy'. Publishers in the arts and social sciences began to actively seek out writings on transgender with a view to publication. Within 48 hours of the publication of 'On Male Femaling' in *The Sociological Review*, Richard received a letter from Chris Rojek, then commissioning editor at Routledge, to write a book based on the article. Within a few more months, Routledge had accepted a proposal from both of us to edit what became *Blending Genders* (1996a), a text conceived by us as being the first sociological reader in a newly emerging field which we termed 'transgender studies'.

Routledge wanted both books quickly. We were left in the slightly uncomfortable position of being rooted in 'old-style' sociological symbolic interactionism at the very time new directions in cultural theory and cultural studies were expanding their sphere of influence in sociology as well as in what would become 'transgender studies'.[1]

Dave's 1993 book is substantially similar to his thesis of 1986. Richard's 1993 paper, setting out his sociological framework for the study of male cross-dressing and sex-changing was conceived in the early 1980s. Richard, after an initial period of fieldwork in the UK between 1979 and 1985, had established at the University of Ulster the first university-based 'Trans-Gender Archive' at the beginning of 1986. In his capacity as Director of the Archive, he had been receiving deposits from all over the world, particularly from the developing transgender communities in the USA, Australia, New Zealand and South Africa. He had, moreover, continued with his life history work with selected informants.

Our updating of our previous work took two principal forms. In the first place, we drew on our developing archive material to provide a less-UK-biased data base and one that took into account developments in the international transgender community since the mid-1980s. In the second place, Richard undertook another period of intensive fieldwork in the UK, between 1993 and 1995 as he was writing *Male Femaling*.

In part, both of these new directions demonstrated what anthropologist Anne Bolin had found in the USA (Bolin, 1988; 1994). In her first period of research, between 1979 and 1981, she reports on the three major categories available for transgendered people to identify with: (1) those of the transsexual; (2) the heterosexual transvestite; or (3) the homosexual drag queen. The TV/TS 'Berdache Society' which she researched was particularly preoccupied with 'the transvestite/transsexual dichotomy'. We, also, found most of our informants preoccupied with situating themselves with reference to this dichotomy in our first periods of fieldwork. In Bolin's later period of research in 1992, however, she discerned a movement from 'TV/TS dichotomy' to transgender 'continuity' and diversity. In broad terms, these findings were similar to our own in the UK when we compared our findings in the 1975 to 1985 period with those of the 1993 to 1995 period.

However, there was an important difference between our findings. Whereas Bolin was researching the transgender activists in the USA who were in the very process of bringing about a paradigm shift in the conceptualization of transgender, we were researching in domains where the impact of the new theorizations of diversity had yet to gain a grip.

With a research base primarily in the UK, what we did not appreciate fully, at the time, was that sometime between 1989 and 1991 something of a paradigm shift in the approach to cross-dressing and sex-changing was fermenting in the USA. In retrospect, we would date the first major publication announcing this shift as *Body Guards: The Cultural Politics of Gender Ambiguity*, which included the germinal paper 'The *Empire* Strikes Back: A Posttranssexual Manifesto' by Sandy Stone (1991). However, we were not to know the significance of this paper for what was just round the corner for trans-studies. When Marjorie Garber's landmark *Vested Interests* appeared in 1992, we read it primarily as affirming our sociological interest in the ubiquity of transgender, but were critical of its lack of attention to the 'lived experience' of transgender lives.

By the time Kate Bornstein's *Gender Outlaw* was published in 1994, *Male Femaling* was substantially completed. The focus of our work on 'gender outlaws' had been with the UK 'gender transient' Bruce Laker/Phaedra Kelly. Bruce/Phaedra had been living as a 'gender transient' since the early 1980s and, through the publication of his/her magazine *Chrysalis International* (Kelly, 1987–90), was advocating a conceptualization of transgender that in many ways anticipated those of Stone (1991), Feinberg (1992), Garber (1992) and Bornstein (1994). Indeed, Phaedra felt that her ideas had been stolen by the new wave of US 'gender outlaw' writers. However, Phaedra's temperament and her hostility to the conventions of either popular or academic writing meant that she found it impossible to get most of her voluminous writings published. Rather, she had to be content with the publication of short articles that had been carefully edited by editors of various sub-cultural trans magazines of the time (e.g., *Martine Rose's International TV Repartee*). Her main published outlet for her writing was self-publication in her magazine *Chrysalis* (Kelly, 1987–90) which had a tiny circulation. Certainly, she was unwilling (and, probably, unable) to frame her arguments in terms of the language of contemporary cultural theory which might have gained her a wider audience.

As it turned out, Bornstein's (1994) book marked the opening salvo in a steady stream of new books and other writings from transgender activists that, in the space of a few short years, would lay down the parameters for the paradigm shift in the conceptualization and study of transgender phenomena (see also Mackenzie, 1994). Such important texts as Feinberg (1996), Califia (1997) and Wilchins (1997), heralding the explosion of the 'new paradigm', had not been published at the time we were writing.

Male Femaling was a grounded theory study rooted in data collected in the UK. To that degree, Richard could be forgiven, perhaps, for not giving due weight to developments in the USA. The timing of the publication of our *Blending Genders*, however, was more unfortunate given its intended scope. Although imprinted with a 1996 publication date, the book was actually published towards the end of 1995, having been delivered towards the end of 1994. In that book, we had endeavoured to set forth the parameters for an emerging field of transgender studies from the standpoint of social science. In the widely cited penultimate chapter, Stephen Whittle considered the recent developments in cultural theory in some detail. Although the publishing schedule was such that Whittle did not have available to him any writings published later than 1994 when he wrote his chapter, the substance of his argument still stands today. Certainly, we would still stand by our conceptualization of the area of a sociologically informed transgender studies in terms of the five substantive parts of the book. Those parts were: experiencing gender blending; the social organization of gender blending; the medicalization of gender blending; gender blending and the media; and gender blending and gender politics.

As it turned out, it was in the very next year after the delivery of the manuscript for *Blending Genders* that US transgender activist Dallas Denny felt able to write of the paradigm shift that she saw as having taken place in the domain of transgender. In an article entitled 'The Paradigm Shift is Here!', she writes:

> With the new way of looking at things, suddenly all sorts of options have opened up for transgendered people: living full-time without genital surgery, recreating in one gender role while working in another, identifying as neither gender, or both, blending characteristics of both genders in new and creative ways, identifying as sexes and genders heretofore undreamed of – even designer genitals do not seem beyond reason. (Denny, 1995: 1)

After our manuscript had been delivered to Routledge, we began to appreciate just how much and how fast things were changing, particularly in the USA. Only then did we begin to approach transgender with greater emphasis upon the alleged paradigm shift. In our paper first presented at the September 1995 HBIGDA (Harry Benjamin International Gender Dysphoria Association) conference (Ekins and King, 1997; 1998), we made reference to Anne Bolin's percipient 1994 paper, and concluded our comments on 'gender blending and gender politics' with the following:

> In contrast, crossing the gender border is now seen by some as subversive, as transgressive ... Anne Bolin (1994: 485) argues that the transgenderist 'harbors great potential either to deactivate gender or to create in the future the possibility of "supernumerary" genders as categories no longer based on biology.' This is because of its 'decoupling of physiological sex, gender identity, and sexuality' (Bolin, 1994: 483).

We had to leave for later occasions, however, development of our thinking on this topic. In particular, we began to conceptualize the new approach to transgender in terms of 'transcending' and set ourselves the task of detailing the various senses of transgender that had emerged with reference to the paradigm shift that was now occurring. In particular, we found it necessary to distinguish three very different approaches to transgender that had emerged from within the transgender community, and to re-think our own approach with reference to them. We now turn to identifying these three different approaches and detailing our response to them.

What is transgender?

The terminology of transgender is less than 40 years old. 'Transgenderal' seems to have been first used in print by Virginia Prince in a paper published in her magazine *Transvestia*, in December 1969 (Prince, 1969a). Although the term 'transgenderal' is arguably the original lexical compound of the 'trans- + gend-' type, Prince did not stick with the term. Nor did it catch on. Rather, by 1978, Prince is using the term 'transgenderist', in place of it. In a paper entitled 'The "Transcendents" or "Trans" People' presented to the Western Regional Meeting of the Society for the Scientific Study of Sex, she describes 'three classes of such trans-people, generally called "transvestites, transgenderists and transsexuals."' She adds,

> The second class is a group of which I am a member and about which most of you haven't heard ... These are people who have adopted the exterior manifestations of the opposite sex but without any surgical interventions. Thus they are what may be rightly termed 'male women' (Prince 1978a: 86).

However, very shortly afterwards, a quite different sense of 'transgenderist' began to emerge. Prince's term presupposed a particular standpoint on the interrelations between sex (the body), sexuality (the erotic), and gender (social accompaniments of the division between the sexes). The alternative use of the term 'transgenderist' that emerged around the same time did not presuppose any such conceptual or theoretical sophistication. Rather, it acknowledged the existence of 'transvestites' and 'transsexuals' and used the term 'transgenderist' as an umbrella term to include both. The English agony aunt Clare Raynor interviewed on the radio one MTF 'transsexual', one FTM 'transsexual' and one male transvestite (a part-time cross-dresser) including them all under the term 'transgenderist'. As the UK *Radio Times* (6 June, 1979: 5) put it: 'It is estimated that about one person in 2,000 is a transgenderist; someone who feels an overwhelming need either to dress in the clothes of the opposite gender, or ... to "change sex" completely.'

It is important to distinguish 'trans' as transformation; 'trans' as crossing; and 'trans' as going beyond or through (Kessler and McKenna, 2000). In the initial formulations of the concept of the 'transgenderist', it was the first two meanings that were privileged. This remained generally the case until as late as the early 1990s, whatever lexical compound was used. Stuart, for instance, used the term 'transgender' in 1983 (Stuart, 1983: 25). She argued that 'gender conditions are quite different from sexual conditions or sexual preferences', before going on to state that 'The word transsexual is somewhat misleading, because the word sexual is incorporated into the term. Perhaps, the word "transgender" would have been a more suitable term.' The use of 'transgender' as another term for 'transsexual' came to be favoured by some once the term transgender became more widespread, as in 'I am transgender. And although I am still a man, as you can tell, I am in the process of becoming a woman. I am on the NHS waiting list to have the whole sex-change procedure' (*Daily Record*, 3 April, 2004: 5).

In the 1990s, however, the widespread use of 'transgender' in an overtly transgressive sense began to emerge. The 'trans', in this usage, refers to 'going beyond' or 'through'. In an early usage of 'transgenderist' in this sense of 'going beyond', the transgender activist Holly Boswell writes (1991: 31): 'But the transgenderist, whether crossing over part-time or full-time – even while masking their genital incongruity – gives honest expression to a reality that defies cultural norms.' As the 1990s progressed, this overtly transgressive sense of transgender came to be the preferred sense within much of the activist transgender community, particularly in the USA.[2]

Towards the end of 1985 when Richard had decided to establish a 'Trans-Gender Archive' at the University of Ulster – the first university-based archive of its type – the term transgender was not widely used. Somewhat arcanely, perhaps, he decided to use 'Trans-Gender' (with a hyphen and a capital 'G'). The use of the hyphen was in homage to 'psycho-analysis'. 'Psycho-analysis' as opposed to 'psychoanalysis' represented, until very recently, commitments to purity, integrity and authenticity in some quarters. Indeed, the British Psycho-Analytical Society still retains the hyphen. Richard rejected 'Transgenderal Archive' as too cumbersome. He used the term in the umbrella sense to include the widest possible range of 'transgender' phenomena. Unlike the orthodoxy of the time, it was apparent to him that transgender was not a rather minority and unimportant matter (Ekins, 1987). It was important to include transgender phenomena that had avoided the medical gaze. He took the view that 'transvestite' and 'transsexual' are medicalized categories of knowledge. They were relatively late additions to what Foucault refers to as the 'medicalization of the sexually peculiar' that began in the mid to late nineteenth century. The 1980s saw the phenomena dubbed by the media as 'gender bending' or 'gender blending'. The pop singer Boy George had featured as the front cover model of *Cosmopolitan* in full feminine make-up, jewellery, and hair styling in December 1984. His friend Marylyn had gained widespread publicity 'dressed as a girl'. Glam Rock and androgyny had long been a feature of pop music and youth style. Although such phenomena had not been 'medicalized', it seemed evident to Ekins that they were clearly transgender phenomena.

However, the term 'Trans-Gender' in Trans-Gender Archive was chosen not only to embrace the widest possible transgender phenomena. As a sociologist, Richard had been deeply impressed by Kessler and McKenna's *Gender: An Ethnomethodological Approach* (1978). Long before contemporary queer theory made the view fashionable, Kessler and McKenna had argued that aspects of sex, sexuality and gender ALL have socially constructed components. They argued that it is gender attribution in 'everyday life' that provided the bedrock upon which subsequent distinctions about sex, sexuality and gender are made.

Re-visiting their earlier book Kessler and McKenna (2000) write:

> By the mid-1970s most people, in and out of academia, were beginning to accept that roles, appearances, and characteristics (what they called 'gender') were socially defined and culturally varied. However, biological features (what they called 'sex') were considered to be given in nature. We argued that the biological is as much a construction as the social is. Although hormones, chromosomes, gonads, and genitals, are real parts of the body, seeing them as dichotomous and essential to being female or male is a social construction. That is why we believed (and continue to believe) that in discussions of this topic it is critical to only use 'gender' and never use sex (in the conventional meanings). If anything is primary, it is not some biological sign, but what we call 'gender attribution' – the decision one makes in every concrete case that someone is either a male or a female. Virtually all of the time, gender attribution is made with no direct knowledge of the genitals or any other biological 'sex marker'.

Kessler and McKenna (1978) in developing their arguments drew heavily upon the category of the transsexual but were writing at a time before conceptualizations of 'transgender' became more sophisticated. Only in retrospect did it become possible to return to this text and see it as germinal in the formation of sociological foundations for a coherent discipline of trans-gender studies, and germinal to a fourth conceptualization of transgender – a sociological approach to transgender – a conceptualization to which we sub-scribe. We will return to this point later in the chapter.

Aside from this fourth conceptualization, it is clear from the above discus-sion that there are, therefore, three rather different usages of the term 'trans-gender'. Arguably, Virginia Prince was the first to use the term transgenderist to refer to those people like herself who, though male, elected to live full-time as women while retaining their male genitalia. In parallel with this develop-ment, 'transgenderist' came to be used as an umbrella term to include both 'transvestites' and 'transsexuals' (*Radio Times*, 2 June 1979, p. 5) and, later, a much wider spectrum of transgender people that are seen as making up the 'transgender community'. Third, transgender came to be used in the overtly transgressive sense of 'going beyond' the binary divide (Boswell, 1991), and, in some uses, of 'going beyond' gender altogether. Many transgender activists in the transgender community adopted this usage as they developed their advo-cacy programmes during the 1990s and into the twenty-first century.

Although Virginia Prince probably coined the term transgender, her use of the term did not catch on beyond those individuals who specifically iden-tified with her position, and we will return to her ideas on the 'transgen-derist' in Chapter 2. In the following two sections, we map what came to be the dominant uses of transgender, namely, transgender as an umbrella term (approach 2) and transgender as transgression (approach 3).

Transgender as an umbrella term

It was during the 1980s that Prince's use of the term became sidelined as the umbrella usage came to the fore. When Ekins established *Archive News: The Bulletin of the Trans-Gender Archive* in 1989, he subtitled it 'A News and Information Bulletin for the International Trans-Gender Community'. Ironically, it was largely because of the work of Virginia Prince that the pos-sibility of a transgender community arose when it did.

Despite the innovations of Virginia Prince concerning her own chosen lifestyle as a transgenderist, it was actually Prince's work on behalf of trans-vestites (part-time cross-dressers) that had the much greater initial impact. It was she who popularized the abbreviations TS (transsexual) and TV (trans-vestite) and it was these categorizations that comprised the initial usage of transgenderist in its umbrella sense, as we have seen. It was this umbrella sense of 'transgender' (and sometimes 'transgendered') as an adjective, as in 'the transgender (transgendered) community' that became widespread in the late 1980s and early 1990s.

As we shall see in Chapter 3, it is Prince who is to be credited for establishing what became a world wide network of 'secret' groups for TVs to facilitate their occasional cross-dressing in an atmosphere of security and protected identity. Prince sought to exclude transsexuals, homosexuals and fetishists and attempted to ensure that her groups included only heterosexual and predominantly married transvestites (occasional cross-dressers). In point of fact, transsexuals (and others theoretically excluded) did join branches of Prince's organization and those based upon them. But with the model set of the 'secret' society with a newsletter, a contact system and occasional meetings, the template had been laid for similar styled organizations specifically for other groupings and it was 'transsexuals' who first began to form their own groups separate from the Prince-based organizations. These began springing up in the late 1970s and early 1980s. They tended not to have the same emphasis on social events. There was much more emphasis upon the exchange of medical knowledge and details of referral networks.

By the mid-1980s, there had emerged a network of separate groups for TVs and TSs, as were the favoured abbreviations at that time. These developments marked the beginnings of what came to be known as a transgender community, spanning, principally, the USA, the UK, Europe, Australia, New Zealand and South Africa.

Many of these groups were small and short-lived. Others, however, prospered. They began to organize meetings outside the privacy of a member's home – a monthly meeting at a local wine bar, for instance. The organization of 'high days and holidays' soon became a feature of many of the groups. The groups would organize an annual weekend event held at a hotel in a seaside resort. These might feature a special event, such as mock 'weddings' – providing the opportunity to dress as a bride.

Fantasia Fair, a particularly ambitious venture, pioneered a weeklong event in the mid-1970s in Provincetown, Cape Cod, USA, where participants could cross-dress for 24 hours a day for a full week. In 2004, *Fantasia Fair* claimed to be the longest-running continuous annual event in the transgender world:

Started in 1975, 'FanFair' has grown every year in its scope, character, and assistance to the gender explorer. FanFair continues to be the leading annual programme promoting an individual's ability to thrive in a real-life situation, and receive positive reinforcement and encouragement. This allows the cross dresser, MTF transsexual, FTM transsexual and all the gender diverse to experience life in an open and caring environment – something unique in a world that typically has difficulty understanding and accepting gender diversity. (http://fantasiafair.org/home/index.html).

Often the rooms or facilities used by gay and lesbian groups would be made available for TVs and TSs to hold separate regular meetings of their own. Drag balls had long provided a venue for TVs and TSs seeking to 'come out' in a congenial setting (Kirk and Heath, 1984).

Usage of the umbrella sense of the term 'transgender' gained prominence within the 'transgender community' quite quickly. To take just one example, if we look through the US transgender subcultural newsletter *Renaissance News*, we can trace the inception and consolidation of the use of 'transgendered' and 'transgender'. The August 1987 issue (Vol. 1, No. 1) refers to *Renaissance* as providing information about 'transgendered behavior' (p. 3). The December 1987 (Vol. 1, No 5) issue includes a reprint of an interview with Richard Ekins about the 'Transgender Archive' (pp. 4–5) throughout which the term is used extensively in the 'transgender community' sense. In the same issue, two articles are titled 'Conference on Transgender Issues' (p. 2), and 'Transgender Economics 101' (p. 3). 'A Brief History of *Renaissance*', in May 1990 (Vol. 4, No. 5) makes reference to the December 1988 'comprehensive anti-discrimination policy designed to keep *Renaissance* open to all transgendered people' (p. 4).

In this vein, individuals began to describe themselves as 'transgendered'. Some people who had previously identified as 'transsexuals' preferred the term 'transgendered'. Many 'transvestites' did likewise – although the term 'cross-dresser' for transvestite became especially favoured throughout the 1990s. Other 'transsexuals' took offence at being included within an umbrella classification and still do.

In the main, however, the umbrella term developed in two rather different directions. In the first place, it was used as convenient shorthand for a targeted population, membership, or audience as in the North American publication: *A Who's Who in the Transgendered Community and International Resource Guide* (Roberts, 1993). In the second place, use of the umbrella term could provide a focal point and rallying banner in the quest for anti-discrimination legislation and movements towards equal rights, more generally. Developments in this second direction were more controversial. Some self-identified transsexuals, for instance, felt that their rights and interests were best pursued outside the umbrella usage.

Significantly, the landmark 1993 publication *A Who's Who in the Transgendered Community and International Resource Guide* (Roberts, 1993) had in 1994 become *A Who's Who & Resource Guide to the International Transgender Community* (Roberts, 1994) (our emphasis). The 1994 publication included a 20-page listing of 'Support Groups In The Transgendered Community', four pages of 'Care Providers to the Transgendered Community', and 19 pages of 'Businesses in the Transgendered Community'. The publication was primarily concerned with the transgender community in the USA but entries did include those from Australia, Belgium, Canada, Finland, Germany, Ireland, New Zealand, Norway, Russia, South Africa, Switzerland and the UK.

Preceding these developments, there had occasionally been short-lived groups for transgendered people, including groups with more radical agendas. In retrospect, these radical groupings which included TAO (Transsexual Action Organisation), for instance, might be seen as prototypes for the explosion of such groupings in the 1990s. At least for part of their development, the philosophy and ideology of these groups were infused with various mixtures of Marxist and feminist politics. More closeted were the groupings of the sexually active whose activities continued, in the main, outside of the mainstream groups. Small networks, for instance, of fetishistic transvestites would meet and exchange enthusiasms and sexual favours. The more sexually adventurous might meet partners, other TVs/TSs or those who fancied them through the contact columns of such contact magazines as the UK-based *Relate* and *Accord* that were widely available in the 1980s (Ekins, 1997).

By around 1995, the new terminology of 'transgender', which had been pioneered by transgender activists and others, was beginning to be adopted by the medical profession. This was noticeable, for instance, at the 1995 meeting of the Harry Benjamin Gender Dysphoria Association (HBIGDA) in Kloster Irsee, Germany. Around this time, trans people themselves were increasingly making their presence felt at meetings organized by professionals principally for each other. At the 1997 meeting of HBIGDA in Vancouver, Canada, trans activists demonstrated against the exclusion of trans people from the Association. They were seen to be excluded both on the grounds of lack of academic and professional qualifications and because of their inability to pay the considerable conference fees and additional expenses of such events.

It was a significant marker of the interrelations between professional (scientific) and 'client' (member) conceptualizations of transgender 'knowledge' when Friedemann Pfäfflin who was President of HBIGDA in 1997 teamed up with Eli Coleman to found *The International Journal of Transgenderism (IJT)*. They adopted the term 'transgenderism' in the title of their fledgling journal to reflect its standpoint 'as more neutral on etiology', to encompass 'the vast complexity of gender manifestations and identities', and 'to stimulate new ways of thinking and understanding various aspects of transgenderism' (Pfäfflin and Coleman, 1997). Since its inception, *The International Journal of Transgenderism* has remained the only scholarly refereed journal exclusively concerned with 'transgenderism'. There had been one previous attempt (in the UK) to establish such a journal, which had adopted the more medicalized title: *The Journal of Gender Dysphoria*. The journal had foundered after two issues, one dated 1991 and the other dated 1991/1992. The *IJT*, on the other hand, which was established as an open access electronic internet journal by the German publishers Symposion Press, achieved a hit rate of some 30,000 per month, before eventually being taken over by Haworth Press, New York, in 2004. Fittingly, the opening paper in the first Symposion publication in 1997 was entitled 'Blending Genders: Contributions Towards the Emerging Field of Transgender Studies' (Ekins and King, 1997).

Also, by the mid-1990s, it was increasingly evident that a new theorization of transgender was becoming dominant within the activist transgender community. The transgender umbrella was now being deliberately construed with an openness to maximum transgender diversity and this increasingly came to be linked to an overtly transgressive conceptualization of transgender.

Transgender as transgression

Virginia Prince's approach to the term 'transgender' entails special pleading for a specific and limited 'transgenderist' position and one that takes a fixed stand on the interrelations between sex, sexuality and gender: gender is separate from sex and sexuality is underplayed. The transgender as umbrella term, on the other hand, adopts an encompassing approach in the interests of unity and community amongst a wide range of transgender people. Minorities should work together and not add to discrimination and ill will by what Freud referred to as the 'narcissism of minor differences' (Freud, 1918: 199; 1930: 114–15). Both of these approaches, in their different ways, have fostered the development of the term 'transgender' and contributed to the term's theoretical and practical impact.

However, with the third approach (transgender as transgression), 'transgender' is approached with a new political sophistication and a radical agenda. Under the new formulation, approach 1, whatever its radical potential, is seen to be too firmly rooted in an acceptance of the binary gender divide, and, in particular, often a very stereotypical and dated view of that divide. Approach 2 is thought to be too firmly rooted in an identity politics that in late-modern/postmodern political activism has fallen into disrepute. A major impetus to approach 3 was Sandy Stone's (1991) article 'The *Empire* Strikes Back' in which she conceptualized transsexuals as 'outside the boundaries of gender'.

Even as the new 'International Transgender Community' had arrived, there were misgivings about it. It was noticeable that for all its talk of transgender, it looked remarkably like the old TV and TS. It was also predominantly MTF. During the 1990s, the voice of the FTM transgendered person was increasingly in evidence. Many of the prominent early FTM activists of the 1980s had been conservative (with a small 'c') in their politics (Rees, 1996). However, most of the activist FTMs of the 1990s were politically radical. They were often steeped in feminist theory which they brought to bear on their transgender activism.

Whereas with previous conceptualizations of transgender the political had tended to take the form of working for equal rights, now transgender rights were linked to a critique of the binary gender divide, itself. Holly Boswell's work was notable here. Although, recognizing that in the interests of personal safety, trans people had to make efforts to 'pass', she questioned why this had to be so (Boswell, 1991). Moreover, with their openness to feminist and socialist theory, trans men began to link transgender to revolutionary socialism (Feinberg, 1992; 1996); to radical lesbianism (Nataf, 1996); and to the beginnings of a hitherto neglected transgender approach to class, race and masculinity (Volcano and Halberstam, 1999).

Of most significance, theoretically, in this third approach, however, was its links with developments in literary and cultural theory – postmodern and queer theory, in particular. Especially significant was Judith Butler's work on gender as performativity (Butler, 1990a). This alliance between literary theory, postmodernism and transgender politics exploded in the mid-to-late 1990s. In 1992, Marjorie Garber had set the trend by arguing that bipolar categories of gender create a 'category crisis'. She advocated a third category, a way of describing a space of possibilities (Garber, 1992). As Bullough et al. (1997a: 18) put it:

> They [bipolar categories] lead to a failure of definitional distinction and result in a border that becomes permeable and permits crossing. Border crossing itself threatens established class, race, and gender norms, and cross-dressing, she holds, is a disruptive element in our society that involves not just a category crisis of male and female, but also the crisis of the category itself.

In the space of a few short years, pioneering books by Leslie Feinberg (1992; 1996; 1998), Kate Bornstein (1994; 1998) and Riki Anne Wilchins (1997) established what was effectively a new paradigm for the conceptualization and study of transgender phenomena. While these writings were rooted in very different theoretical foundations – Feinberg in Marxism, Bornstein and Wilchins in postmodernism – they all presented a view of the transgendered person as a 'gender outlaw', above and beyond the bipolar system of gender which they were concerned to transcend.

Leslie Feinberg's pamphlet *Transgender Liberation: A Movement Whose Time Has Come*, first published in 1992, had a major impact in establishing the term 'transgender' as the term of choice for 'gender outlaws'. However, by 1996, Feinberg (1996: xi) was noting: 'As I write this book, the word *trans* is being used increasingly by the gender community as a term uniting the entire coalition.' Many within the transgender community had found the term 'transgender' a troubling one, but the term becomes particularly problematic for many of those who see themselves as transcending gender.

If the argument is for a position 'outside' or 'beyond' gender, why use the term 'transgender' at all? For many working within this tradition the term 'trans' or 'transperson' becomes the preferred term. Interestingly, it was, again, Virginia Prince who probably first featured the use of the term as part of a developed argument about transgender. She had referred to 'The "Transcendents" or "Trans" People' in her talk of June 1978, published in *Transvestia* (Prince, 1978a). However, for Prince, herself, as we have seen, the privileging of gender was crucial. It was, therefore, important for her to stay with the term transgender.

Those transgender activists with different agendas and different theoretical positions, however, had other concerns. In 1993/4, when UK transgender activist Stephen Whittle, along with Jason Cromwell, an activist from Seattle, and Susan Stryker, a San-Franciscan-based activist, set up a 'transgender' email list for academics studying transgender – many of whom were transgendered themselves – he used the term 'trans-academics'.

In the 1994 San Francisco Human Rights Commission's 'Report on Discrimination Against Transgendered People', 'a cornerstone document of the contemporary political movement for trans civil rights in the US' – activist Jamison Green used the term 'transperson' in his introductory essay (Zander, 2003: 63).

By early 1997, the leading UK transgender pressure group *Press for Change* was using the terms trans man and trans woman. Whittle (personal communication, 2004) describes the entry of the term 'trans' (and the dropping of the term 'gender') into trans politics thus:

> What actually happened was that at some point in a parliamentary forum meeting, around that time, we were using the term transgender and transsexual. Lynne Jones, MP, asked for a generic term – as writing the minutes was difficult and confusing. Transgender was used as an umbrella term, but also meant something different. Kate and I joked across the table that we could always use 'trannies' and we laughed a little about radios, and then Kate More suggested trans. And I think it was Christine Burns who suggested trans people, as we wouldn't call deaf people 'deafs' and so that was how it came to be used in the UK.

Once again, we can see how usages of the terms straddle the traditions. This account points, perhaps, to another variant of the umbrella usage. Yet, in other forums Kate More and Stephen Whittle were (and are) very much aligned with postmodernist positions on transgender. Our impression is that the omission of the 'gender' in transgender – the wholehearted embracing of the terminology of 'trans' and transpeople – became a feature of the discourse of approach 3 as it combined a maximally inclusive approach to transgender phenomena with radical politics of various sorts. This was especially evident at the Oxford Congress at the Third International Congress on Sex and Gender held at Oxford University in 1998, organized by Whittle.

A number of the conference papers were included in a co-edited book by Felicity Haynes and Tarquam McKenna (2001) which they called *Unseen Genders: Beyond the Binaries,* In her introduction to the book Haynes writes:

> There were people whose performativities were neither male nor female, or were, if you like, both male and female - gay people, lesbians, bisexuals, and transvestites. The categories of transsexual, intersex, or homosexual that labeled them were not exclusive, but fluid and complex ... Nearly all of these people saw themselves as queer, disenfranchised, or pathologized in some way by the prevailing male/female binary. They literally incorporated Judith Butler's (1993) point that what we think of as 'sex' is in fact embodied gender; the corporeal incarnation of a discursively constituted (performative) gender. (2001: 2)

To many of these people, therefore, there was no particular merit in retaining the 'gender' in transgender. They had 'gone beyond' even the use of the term. One informant at the conference, for instance, Del LaGrace Volcano, who we shall meet again in Chapter 5, identified then as primarily 'pansexual'. At that time, he considered himself a biological female with masculinized sexual characteristics both before and after taking testosterone. He identified with the male pronoun, but not with the category male or man. He described himself as a 'trans person into all forms of sexuality except "straight" sex'. Another informant, Christie Elan-Cane identified as 'ungendered'. Christie, who we shall meet again in Chapter 4, used the pronoun 'per' (derived from person). Per was a biological female who had undergone surgery to remove per breasts and per womb.

Beginnings revisited: Kessler and McKenna, Foucault and our sociological approach to transGender studies

The three approaches to the term 'transgender' that we have considered have been pioneered and developed, in the main, by transgendered people, themselves. Virginia Prince's was a competing 'member' story developed largely in opposition to the two major medical stories available to her: the medicalized 'transsexual' story (Harry Benjamin) and the medicalized 'transvestite' story (Magnus Hirschfeld). The second approach pioneered the flourishing of support groups, greater acceptance for transgendered people, and, to a degree, more equal rights. The third approach was part of a movement to redefine the binary gender divide itself and to radicalize transgender activism. Time will tell how successful it will be. All three approaches, however, have rather different aims and objectives. Indeed, each of the three approaches has tended to develop in opposition to each other, and often with the view that their view is the 'correct' view.

We, however, as academics and as non-trans identified people have a different approach, yet again. In retrospect, we can trace the origins of what would emerge as a social constructionist approach to the term transgender and to transgender studies to the paradigm shift that was taking place in the social sciences in the late 1960s. The starting point of this approach may be traced to Harold Garfinkel's paper 'Passing and the Managed Achievement of Sex Status in an Intersex Person, Part 1' in 1967. Garfinkel (1967) was principally concerned with what he called 'sex status'. He did not use the term 'gender' or 'transgender'. Yet, in our terms, he was concerned to study how we 'do gender'; how gender is accomplished (see also Kessler and McKenna, 1978; West and Zimmerman, 1987).

To this end, Garfinkel studied Agnes who was seeking sex-reassignment. In particular, he studied her interactions with her medical team, which included the celebrated Robert Stoller. Later, Agnes admitted to Stoller that she had been taking estrogens since she was 12 (Garfinkel, 1967: 287), but her very feminine appearance – taken with her denial of ingesting hormones – led to her medical team being fooled that she was intersex. She was diagnosed as suffering from 'a unique type of a most rare disorder: testicular feminization syndrome' (ibid.: 285). Garfinkel noted that what for most people is not problematic – passing as a man or woman on all occasions – was for Agnes. He studied Agnes's 'doing gender' – how she accomplished her femininity in various contexts.

Later, in 1978, Kessler and McKenna built upon Garfinkel's work, and spelled out very clearly how sex (the body), gender and sexuality *all* have socially constructed components, and privileged gender over sex and sexuality. This is because we are assigned as one sex *or* the other at birth, usually on the basis of a cursory look at our genitals. Gender attribution is the cornerstone of the arrangement between the sexes, they argue. The binary divide is, itself, a social construction.

We find this view persuasive. Once accepted, *all* particular viewpoints on the categorizations of sex, sexuality and gender (and their interrelations) become alternative – often competing – social constructions. In particular, all are seen as emergents within an ongoing shifting and changing process of social construction. There is no underlying 'truth' about sex, sexuality or gender, that 'scientists' and other sex, sexuality and gender 'experts' are seeking to unveil.

Bornstein (1994) drew upon the work of Garfinkel (1967) and Kessler and McKenna (1978) to support her conceptualizations of transgender theory and

24

practice. However, as a performance artist and gender activist, she has been concerned to use such writings as prefatory to expounding her own particular formulation of gender as performance. Wilchins (1997; 2002a; 2002b) draws on the postmodern writings of Michel Foucault and Judith Butler to argue for a position opposed to gender oppression in all its manifestations.

The writings of both Bornstein and Wilchins do not purport to be social science. Indeed, transactivist Wilchins (1997) is particularly hostile to a social science model of transgender studies which she argues 'tribifies'. The term is David Valentine's and refers to the 'propensity of social scientists to naturalize their own gender and genitals while treating mine as if they were the product of some quaint practice by an "exotic" or foreign tribe' (Wilchins, 1997: 26).

Garfinkel and Kessler and McKenna, on the other hand, are social scientists. In particular, they are social scientists for whom the categorizations of sex, sexuality and gender become a 'topic' of study as opposed to a 'resource' upon which to pursue positivistic knowledge-building claims (Zimmerman and Pollner, 1971: 81).

There is still a tendency for sexologists and social scientists committed to positivist philosophies of science to dismiss interpretive qualitative social science as non-scientific. From this standpoint, interpretive sociologies and social psychologies of the type pursued by Garfinkel and Kessler and McKenna might be seen as contributions to theory, to cultural studies or to preliminary enquiry in a research area, but not, in themselves, worthy of the name 'science'.

It is important to stress, therefore, that the interpretive tradition in sociology argues that it is a scientific *advance* on positivist approaches. As Zimmerman and Pollner put it with reference to the then contemporary sociology:

> Sociological enquiry is addressed to phenomena recognized and described in common-sense ways (by reliance on the unanalysed properties of natural language), while at the same time such common-sense recognitions and descriptions are pressed into service as fundamentally unquestioned resources for analyzing the phenomena that are made available for study. Thus contemporary sociology is characterized by a confounding of topic and resource ... Below we suggest how an analysis may proceed, respecting the distinction between the social world as topic of, and resource for, inquiry. (1971: 81)

A striking anecdote makes the point quite forcibly. Towards the end of the 1960s, a number of members of the University of London, Goldsmiths College Sociology Department had been impressed by the work of Harold Garfinkel and Aaron Cicourel and had (reputedly) travelled to California to study ethnomethodology. The story circulated that the Goldsmiths' sociologists had gone to California as positivist sociologists – committed to a view of the philosophy of science which entailed the slow incremental building up of knowledge about the social world – and returned home having to jettison all their previous work. They now saw 'positivist' science as pseudo-science insofar as its foundations were rooted in the unproblematized 'taken-for-granted' meaning frames of everyday life. They returned to the UK to put forward their 'new' sociology in the widely read and influential text of the 1970s – *New Directions in Sociological Theory* (Filmer et al., 1971).[3] As Filmer (ibid.: 216) summarizes: 'The task of professional sociologists in terms of ethnomethodology thus becomes a matter of *not* taking for granted what is typically taken-for-granted at the level of everyday actions.' Many of the contributors to this *New Directions* volume then went on to develop their careers, presenting empirical research programmes which put into effect their commitment to the 'new' view of social science.

Garfinkel (1967) acknowledged debts to a number of previous thinkers. From our point of view, however, his primary debt was to the social phenomenologist Alfred Schutz. Schutz argued that the 'provinces of meaning' of science emerged within the 'province of meaning' of everyday life, a world 'taken for granted' and returned to it (Schutz, 1953). Anthony Giddens draws on Schutz in his conceptualization of the 'double hermeneutic' (Giddens, 1976). The 'double hermeneutic' arises in social science because social science is concerned with pre-interpreted worlds, in which meaning frames are integral to their subject matter, i.e., the inter-subjectivity of practical social life. Thus the theories and provinces of meaning of social science (one hermeneutic) have to be linked with the pre-constituted world of its subject matter (another hermeneutic). We would add the point that when social scientists study 'science', the double hermeneutic becomes a triple hermeneutic. Their work emerges within the interrelations between the meaning frames of social science, the meaning frames of science and the meaning frames of everyday life.

If we combine these various insights of Garfinkel, Schutz and Giddens, we reach a position where it becomes evident that much of the 'science' of sex, sexuality and gender is rooted in what ethnomethodologists call the 'natural attitude': most fundamentally and pervasively, the binary gender divide viewed unproblematically. Thus, when scientists became confronted with 'exceptions' that don't 'fit' the binary, they typically seek to 'explain' the exceptional rather than problematize the 'natural attitude'.

Taking the insights of ethnomethodology seriously, it is no longer possible to argue that sex is nature and gender is socio-cultural. Both become seen as socio-cultural. The binary itself is a social construction. And if this is the case, the political and ethical nature of science in matters of sex, sexuality and gender becomes more apparent. 'Science' has consequences and the way is open for transgendered people categorized by 'science', to argue for alternative conceptualizations in the name of science, as well as in the name of ethics and politics.

It is at this point that the possibility of a fourth distinct usage of trans-gender appears that gives rise to our view of 'transgender studies' as an academic discipline. It becomes the task of a scientific 'transgender studies' to map the various constructions of transgender phenomena in terms of their origins, developments, interrelations and consequences. It also becomes nec-essary to be particularly sensitive to two of the major alternative uses of the term 'gender' in transgender. In the first place there is the usage (we might say, gender with a small 'g') that refers to 'the culturally established corre-lates of sex' (Goffman, 1979: 1). Here, we are referring to such social and cul-tural accompaniments as dress, posture, gesture and speech style. In the second place, there is the usage (we might say, Gender with a capital 'G') that privileges Gender over sex (the body) and sexuality (genital feelings and responses and bodily pleasures and desires more generally), in the light of the social construction of sex, sexuality, and gender.

However, we do not adopt Kessler and McKenna's proposal always to use the term 'gender' in place of 'sex' because we think that to do so is likely to lead to an insensitivity to researching the complex interrelations between sex, sexuality and gender. In the past, we have experimented with a written style that uses both 'Gender' and 'gender' (and transGender and transgender) depending on the meaning of the term being used. However, we have found this approach cumbersome and irritating to the reader. We prefer to sensitize the reader to the issue and suggest that the meaning will usually be evident from the context. In any event, we should be wary of overvaluing this twofold distinction because to do so is to run the risk both of essentializing meanings and to ride roughshod over other major uses of the term gender. Thus, to give just one important example, the use of the term 'gender iden-tity' has become widespread, since its construction in the early 1960s. In Stoller's (1964) original use of the term 'gender identity', 'gender' is being used neither in the capital 'G', nor the small 'g' sense that we have outlined. Rather, it refers to an identity that is seen to emerge from a particular set of interrelations between sex, sexuality and gender (with a small 'g').[4] The psy-choanalytical literature, in particular, with its focus on unconscious mental processes, has never argued for the simplistic separation of sex, sexuality and gender (Breen, 1993) that was a feature of so much of the early work in women's studies and the sociology of gender (Oakley, 1972).

We would situate our previous work within this scientific approach to transgender. Indeed, the Trans-Gender Archive, formally established in January 1986, was named and organized to reflect this view of the domain of transgender studies. A decade later, in 1996, we laid first claim for the emerging field of 'transgender studies' with *Blending Genders*. We had in mind that the book laid down parameters for what transgender studies might look like once the emphasis was made on problematizing previous conceptualizations and categories of 'transgender' knowledge, from the standpoint of the social construction of knowledge. Later, in *Male Femaling*, for instance, Richard Ekins (1997) argued that the 'reality' of transgendering is constituted within the interrelations between the various 'scientific', 'member' and 'lay' 'knowledges'.

In this book, however, we reframe our earlier work in terms of the 'narrative turn' in contemporary social science and cultural studies. In particular, drawing upon Plummer's work on sexual stories (1995), we consider the various conceptualizations and theorizations of transgender phenomena in terms of the various stories, or tales, that are told of transgendering.

Plummer situates his work as being a contemporary symbolic interactionist story. We do likewise. In particular, we situate our view of transgender studies within empirical social 'science', as opposed to a humanist cultural studies, cultural theory and/or political activism. We situate our theory, methodology and research techniques within the social interactionist (constructionist) view of science put forward by George Herbert Mead (1932; 1934; 1938) and Herbert Blumer (1969), a tradition which has been restated in more contemporary terms by Anselm Strauss (1993) and Robert Prus (1997).

Modes and processes of transgendering

In the previous section, we were concerned to map the diversity in usage of the term transgender. In doing so, we have hinted at the major issues and debates within the area. However, by focusing on the three major approaches to the term 'transgender' and detailing our own approach towards each of them, we have necessarily underplayed those views on transgender that do not easily fit with the major conceptualizations.

A major omission is what may be termed 'ungendering' which we deal with later in this section in terms of gender 'erasing' and gender 'negating'. Here, the emphasis is upon 'trans' as change rather than 'trans' as crossing in the sense of crossing the binary divide.

More fundamentally, it must be said that there is a strand of thinking within the so-called trangender community that takes exception to the term 'transgender' itself. We touched on the fact that many self-identified transsexuals feel their subjectivities are trivialized when they are included within the umbrella of transgender. However, this is to miss the more fundamental point that many 'transsexual' people see themselves not as trans-anything, but as misidentified. What they seek is gender confirmation. For these people, it is the social process that has misidentified and classified them. They merely seek what is, for them, the 'correct' identification.

It is the intention of this book to pay the proper respect to the full range of such diversity of thinking about 'transgender'. We turn, now, therefore, to the construction of a conceptual framework and theoretical approach that will enable sociological analyses of the full range of contemporary transgender diversity and the major formulations within which this range has been conceptualized. In particular, this last section of the chapter sets forth the framework to be developed in each subsequent chapter of the book.

When we began our study of cross-dressing and sex-changing in the mid-1970s, the terminology of transgender had not been invented. Transsexualism (transsexuality) and transvestism were the preferred terms. The abbreviations 'TS' and 'TV' were favoured by many in the fast-growing transvestite and transsexual community. Fisk had coined the term 'gender dysphoria' in 1973 and that term, together with 'gender identity disorder', became increasingly favoured by the medical community (Fisk, 1973). Right up into the mid-1980s the terminology of 'transgender' was rarely used except in the specialist sense of Virginia Prince's 'transgenderist': the full-time non-TS cross-dresser.

From one point of view, terminology is not particularly important. Different terms are seen by many to be describing the 'same' thing. Moreover, from the perspective of positivist approaches to science, good science is approaching the truth about the 'same' phenomena. From our point of view, however, attention to the nuances of terminology is important because changing terminology is almost always indicative of changing 'definitions of the situation'. It is indicative of changing meanings and changing social constructions of reality, indeed, changing realities. This is particularly evident when we study the shift from transsexual and transvestite to that of transgender.

Transvestite and transsexual are terms introduced by the medical profession and variously adopted by cross-dressers and sex-changers, themselves. Medical practitioners listened to the stories of those who cross-dressed or who wished to change sex and on this basis created medical and 'scientific' categories of knowledge. Having been coined, the terms enabled cross-dressers and sex-changers to identify with them and adopt the identity of 'transsexual' and 'transvestite'. They were coined in the context of the categorizing of people who were 'different', 'deviant', 'perverted', 'abnormal', 'in need of help', and so on.

The significance of the term 'transgender', however, is that it was coined by people who identified as transgendered and who, in the main, resisted their medicalization. Thus, Prince's 'transgenderist' is a male who is expressing his previously suppressed femininity. He is not a medicalized 'type'. The term 'transgender' community then helped to mobilize support for transgendered people and, in some cases, provided a fertile resource for activism – campaigning for civil rights and the like. With the work of the 'gender outlaws', many transpeople began to approach their gender expression and body modification in the light of postmodernism. Varied expressions of trans behaviour and identity and lifestyle were seen as lifestyle options; radical body modification could now be approached with a 'body as project' mindset similar to the body modification practices of those who underwent tattooing and piercings (Califia, 1997: 224). Finally, the discipline of transgender studies, as we have conceptualized it, opened up a whole new domain of enquiry – particularly in regard to studying the interrelations between sex, sexuality and gender and between 'scientific', member and lay conceptualizations of transgender phenomena.

Within each of these alternative conceptualizations what it means to be transgendered varies. Meanings are contested. Meanings shift and change. For some three decades up to the early 1990s, for instance, cross-dressers accepted the medical term 'transvestite' but tried to de-medicalize it, and also de-stigmatize it. However, by the mid-1990s, TV (transvestite) had become CD (cross-dresser) to many. CD for cross-dresser was preferred as being a less stigmatized non-medical term. In the late 1990s and into the twenty-first century, transgender activists were increasingly concerned with constructing a politically correct terminology. Indeed, FTM trans man and philosopher Jacob Hale, with a number of his colleagues, has produced an important document 'Suggested Rules for Non-Transsexuals Writing about Transsexuals, Transsexuality, Transsexualism, or Trans _____'. Significantly, the 'Suggested Rules' have the subtitle 'Still Under Construction. Dig We Must'. (http://sandystone.com/hale.rules.html)

If we are to deal with this diversity, as it shifts and changes over place and time, we need a framework that enables the plotting of this diversity – of its emergence, development and decline. In previous work, as we have indicated, we studied male cross-dressing and sex-changing in terms of the social process of 'male femaling' (Ekins, 1993; 1997). The gerund 'male femaling' placed the emphasis upon behaviour within which there arises categorizations of behaviour and classifications of identity and types of people that vary over time and place. The formulation took as its starting point the initial classification at birth as male and then examined the various manifestations of male 'femaling'. The work (1993; 1997) did not consider female maling. This earlier work was also framed within an exploration of the interrelations between 'scientific', 'member', and 'lay' conceptualizations of male cross-dressing and sex-changing. It studied how the various formulations of male cross-dressing and sex-changing emerged within the interrelations of these three 'knowledges'.

This book seeks to extend this work in three major directions. In the first place, it extends the study of male femaling to female maling. In the second place, it considers domains of transgender diversity that the male femaling/ female maling couple may omit from consideration. In particular, this male femaling/female maling couple tends to overlook the significance of 'ungendering', what might be termed demaling and defemaling without attendant femaling and maling, respectively. In the third place, this book develops our previous work in terms of the narrative turn in contemporary social science and cultural studies. To this end we particularly draw on the work of Plummer (1995) to consider our domain of study in terms of sex, sexuality and gender 'stories'. From this perspective, stories of medical, lay, and member 'knowledge' become transformed into varieties of stories or 'tales', each with their various origins, natures, forms, settings, and consequences. Within Plummer's 'sexual stories' approach our attention turns to scientific tales, medical tales, autobiographical tales, fictional tales, and so on. We are sensitized to such questions as What stories are told? What is their nature? What forms do they take? Who are they told to? Who takes the stories on board? Whose stories can be told? What is the relation of the stories to the storytellers? Like Plummer, we are not writing as literary theorists concerned principally with analysing the formal structure of stories or narratives. Rather, as social scientists – particularly, as sociologists – we are concerned with the multiple ways diverse stories link, as Plummer puts it: 'to the generic social processes and structures at work in social life' (1995: 24).

Plummer is concerned to develop a sociology of stories and focuses almost exclusively on 'the personal experience narratives of the intimate – a story that haunts us everywhere today in ways it did not in the recent past' (1995: 19). Tales of personal narrative are a central concern of ours, too. However, the feature of personal tales of transgender is the way they interrelate with other tales of transgender, most notably with medical and subcultural tales. We shall, therefore, be centrally concerned with medical and subcultural tales, as well as other 'expert' tales, such as those of psychologists, political theorists, and other social scientists.

More fundamentally, however, stories of transgender take their meaning and 'point' from 'every day', 'taken for granted' assumptions about sex, sexuality and gender rooted in the 'natural attitude'. In particular, they take their point from the binary thinking of the natural attitude. Trans stories are, in various ways, 'tales of the unexpected' in relation to the binary divide of the bipolar gender system: 'In the dressing room, I quickly tried the skirt on. It fit as though it were made for me. I turned around in front of the large mirror in the showroom. My aunt was enthusiastic. "We're buying it. Leave it on."'

Out of context there is nothing unusual about the incident reported here, In context, however, it becomes part of one of many 'tales of the unexpected', for the narrator is a boy and the aunt is cross-dressed as a man (von Mahlsdorf, 1995: 51–2). During, the Second World War, von Mahlsdorf murdered his father, called himself Charlotte (after his cross-dressing lesbian aunt), and has lived openly as a transvestite ever since. Charlotte, well past 60 when his auto-biography was first published, is a 'quietly passionate, steadfast and serene fig-ure' (according to the book-cover blurb) who shuns make-up, wears the most simple frocks and has become both 'his own woman' and 'his own wife'.

In order to provide a framework for the analysis of such tales of the unex-pected that pays the proper respect to contemporary transgender diversity, we find it instructive to consider such tales within the context of the generic social process of transgendering. Sociology as the study of generic social processes has its roots in the formal sociology of Georg Simmel. It has been developed by many of those working within the interactionist tradition, espe-cially in the formal sociology of Erving Goffman, and in the research method-ology of grounded theory set forth in a number of texts by Barney Glaser and Anselm Strauss (e.g., Glaser and Strauss, 1967; Glaser, 1978; 1992).

For Simmel, who conceived of society as interaction among individuals, 'the description of the forms of this interaction is the task of the science of society in its strictest and most essential sense' (Simmel, 1950: 21–2). Simmel argues that sociology does not have a distinctive subject matter; its distinc-tion rather lies in its concerns with forms of sociation as opposed to contents. For Simmel, 'societal forms' are 'conceived as constituting society (and soci-eties) out of the mere sum of living men' (ibid.: 22). Zerubavel (1980) applies the methodological principles of Simmel's formal sociology to fieldwork out-lining three main principles. These are, first, that the researcher should shift the emphasis from the 'actual facts' to the particular analytical perspectives from which they are viewed. Second, that the researcher should focus upon formal patterns that are abstracted from 'reality' rather than with its concrete contents. And, finally, that the researcher should study only selected aspects of concrete phenomena and make a commitment to particular analytical con-cerns and foci. Prus (1987) identifies a lineage of writers adopting this research methodology and argues that what unites the various approaches is the search for 'generic social processes'. For Prus (ibid.: 251), the phrase *generic social processes* refers to 'the transsituational elements of interaction, to the abstracted formulations of social behavior. Denoting parallel sequences of activity across diverse contexts, generic social processes highlight the emergent, interpretive features of association; they focus on the activities involved in the "doing" or accomplishment of group life.'

We find this search for generic social processes particularly apposite in any study of transgender that seeks to pay the proper respect to emergence, process and diversity. The basic social process researched becomes the gerund of transgender: that of transgendering. This strategy enables us to highlight the fact that transgendering is a generic social process within which the various and changing categorizations of transgender phenomena arise and within which they are contested. Similarly, it is within transgendering as a basic social process that transgender identities emerge, are contested, and ebb and flow.

Gendering and transgendering

Gender can be seen as a system of social differentiation and social placement. Societies have understandings about what constitutes gender, how many gender categories there are, who belongs to which category, what characterizes members of each category, and so on. This is what Ramet (1996) refers to as a 'gender culture'. Any particular society will express its understanding of gender in a complex, and largely unwritten, set of rules which tell us what to expect of other people's behaviour in both a predictive sense (what will happen) and in a normative sense (what should happen).

Gender is also, of course, an important part of individual identity. Following Garfinkel (1967) and Kessler and McKenna (1978), however, we find it useful to think of gender not as something which people have, but to see the production of a gendered social identity as an on-going accomplishment; something which is constantly being done. So we use the verb 'gendering', here, to refer to the processes whereby a person is constituted as gendered on an everyday basis. In a culture such as ours, which recognizes only two genders, gendering can be divided into two processes, those of 'maling' and 'femaling'. A basic rule of our gender culture is that only biological males are expected to male, and only biological females are expected to female. Where this rule is broken – where males 'female' (Ekins, 1993; 1997) and females 'male' (Ekins, 1984) – our favoured term is transgendering (Ekins and King, 1996b; see also Bolin, 1994). This is represented in Figure 1.1.

Gendering, transgendering and the modes of transgendering

The starting point of the social process of gendering is the initial classification of every person into one of two genders. Precisely how the boundaries

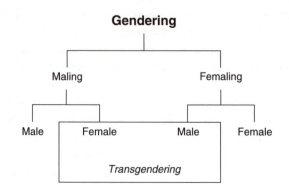

Figure 1.1   Gendering and transgendering

between the genders are to be established, the precise 'content' of each gender, and the mode of 'policing' and regulation of the boundaries between the
genders are all variously contested matters, in different times and different
places. However, whatever the substantive details of these matters, the starting point of transgendering is the wish for or enactment of processes that
entail the 'crossing' of the borders that the initial (and subsequent) classification into two has created. Given the classification – the binary gender
divide – there are four major modes of transgendering: (1) crossing the divide
permanently; (2) crossing it temporarily; (3) seeking to eliminate the divide;
and (4) seeking to 'go beyond it'. Our grounded theory work with informants
over the past three decades confirms that transgendering individuals variously transgender within and between these four major modes.

Each of the following four chapters is organized around each of these four
modes. We use the term 'migrating' to refer to the social processes entailed
in the crossing from one side of the border to the other on a permanent basis.
There are a number of variously dominant, competing, dissenting, and alternative migrating stories that we will consider in Chapter 2. The story told by
Harry Benjamin, the founding father of contemporary Euro-American transsexualism, is the dominant migrating story (Ekins, 2005). It traces the founding of a medical sub-specialty of gender dysphoria and gender identity
disorder justifying medical intervention to assist migration. It is a story that
must be told in interrelation with that of Christine Jorgensen whose personal
tale was the first widely publicized migrating tale syndicated in the press
world-wide. Public response from those people who identified with
Jorgensen's tale and wished to migrate across the gender border ensured the
maintenance of a complex relation between medical and personal stories
within which was fashioned the beginnings of the contemporary transsexual

story. It developed into a story of medical conditions, of gender identities being at odds with bodies (sex), and of medically assisted 'body migrating' alleviating suffering and enabling more productive lives.

In Chapter 3, we will consider the major variants of oscillating stories. 'Oscillating' entails a mode of transgendering that involves moving backward and forward across the gender border, only temporarily resting on one side or the other. Here the medicalizing of the oscillating story at the beginning of the twentieth century set the stage for many of the oscillating stories that followed. The dominant oscillating story became that of the male transvestite who wished to cross the gender border on a temporary basis from time to time. Unlike the dominant migrating story which thrives on an umbilical relation between medical and personal migrating stories, the dominant oscillating story that has emerged in the past 50 years has been that of Virginia Prince who conceptualized oscillating in terms of full personality expression. Stories are told of oscillating males expressing their 'inner woman'. Here are to be found tales of de-medicalization, subcultural tales and tales of identity quite different from those to be found in migrating tales. They are tales aptly viewed in terms of 'tourism' rather than of migrating.

Both migrating and oscillating tales are part of a broader category of 'modernist tales'. Plummer (1995: 49–50) outlines the main elements of one major type of modernist story as beginning with pain and suffering, usually in silence and secrecy. Then there is a crucial turning point, a new understanding and action, which leads to a transformation, a triumph, victory over suffering. Typical plots (forms) involve journeys or quests and the establishment of a home (finding oneself). Many of these elements feature in personal narratives of migrating. Some of these elements are clearly evident in the titles of some transsexual autobiographies: *April Ashley's Odyssey* (Fallowell and Ashley, 1982) and *What Took You So Long? A Girl's Journey to Manhood* (Thompson with Sewell, 1995).

Similarly, in oscillating stories there are elements of silent suffering, discovery, and coming to terms with 'being different', but these elements are less evident than in the migrating stories. In oscillating stories, we find less material on 'being' – on identity and relationships – and more detail about 'doing' – on excursions 'over the gender border'. As with the migrating stories, the border is accepted. Medical help is rarely enlisted, although other people may play a part in facilitating the excursions.

Variants of transsexual and transvestite stories are now so widely known that the fundamentals of our migrating and oscillating modes of transgendering are rather easily grasped, perhaps. This is not so with the mode of transgendering we consider in Chapter 4: that which we term 'negating'. 'Negating' denotes the 'ungendering' of those who seek to nullify maleness/masculinity or femaleness/femininity and deny for themselves the existence of a binary divide. Here we will find neglected, misunderstood and largely untold stories. They are stories that, for the most part, do not appear in medical tales. Here we will encounter two major and very different stories. There are the negating stories that thrive in fantasy fiction, on the internet and in private settings – stories often told in terms of transvestism or sadomasochism – those of the sissy maid. Very different are the stories told of unwanted gendered bodies; of story tellers who enlist medical help to remove unwanted body parts, of story tellers seeking a space within a bi-polar gender system to be 'ungendered'. Here we find 'raw' tales of experience and desire told to achieve a voice, as well as those told in justification. Elements of the modernist tale are sometimes evident. Emphases, as we shall see, are different, however.

Finally, in Chapter 5, tales are told of 'transcending', of being 'gender-full', of going 'beyond gender', entering a third space, and so on. Transcending stories are stories whose time has come. They are part of what Plummer (1995: 133) calls 'the rise of the late modernist sexual story'. These tales do not replace modernist ones but rather coexist with them. Plummer identified three main attributes of late modern stories: first, stories of authority give way to participant stories; second, stories of essence and truth give way to stories of difference; and, third, stories of the 'categorically clear' give way to stories of deconstruction. We can discern these elements in transcending stories as medical authority is questioned, diversity is celebrated, and the certainty of sex and gender categories is called into question.

The dominant transcending stories are not chronological personal narratives. The book-cover blurb for perhaps the best-known transcending story, Kate Bornstein's *Gender Outlaw* (1994), describes it as 'a manifesto, a memoir and a performance all rolled into one'. Similarly, in *Transgender Warriors* (1996), Leslie Feinberg uses his personal experiences to lead us through a transgender history to provide a tale of political philosophy. In *Read My Lips* (1997), Riki Wilchins mixes together personal tales with current gender theories and transgender politics. The linearity of the modern story is replaced by 'a little bit from here, a little bit from there. Sort of a cut-and-paste thing' (Bornstein, 1994: 3).

Gendering, transgendering and the processes of transgendering

What ethnomethodologists refer to as the 'natural attitude' towards gender (Garfinkel, 1967: 122–8; Kessler and McKenna, 1978: 133–41) assumes that all human beings will belong to one of two discrete categories permanently, determined on the basis of biologically ('naturally') given characteristics. This 'natural attitude' specifies that everybody must be either male or female.

A person cannot be both male and female, or neither. Not only are male and female held to be discrete categories, they are also held to be opposites.

Gendering is accomplished when a person is allocated to one of the two gender categories on the basis of certain signifiers which are taken to indicate the gender in question. Kessler and McKenna (1978) emphasize that persons are assigned to a gender category at birth, usually on the basis of their genitals, but thereafter, in everyday interaction, gender is attributed on the basis of other signifiers. Transgendering therefore is accomplished by altering the signifiers in some way.

Our data suggest five main sub-processes by which transgendering, in any of the four modes, is accomplished. The first sub-process involves 'erasing', which entails the eliminating of aspects of maleness or femaleness, masculinity or femininity. A genetic male may undergo castration. A genetic female may undergo a hysterectomy. Both males and females may wear unisex clothes and adopt ungendered mannerisms.

The second sub-process involves 'substituting'. The person who is transgendering (with or without outside help) replaces the body parts, identity, dress, posture, gesture, and speech style that are associated with one gender, with those associated with the other. In relation to the body, for example, a penis is replaced with a vagina; a flat chest is replaced with breasts; smooth skin replaces rough skin; no body hair replaces body hair; a short hair style is often replaced with a longer hair style, and so on. The degree of substitution will depend on a number of factors such as the particular personal project of the individual, the personal circumstances, the development of any technology and aids that may be used, and (where not covered by some healthcare scheme) the financial resources to afford them.

'Concealing', as the third sub-process, refers to the concealing or hiding of things that are seen to conflict with the intended gender display. It may involve hiding body parts – wrapping a scarf around the Adam's apple, tucking the penis, binding the breasts, and so on. But this will depend on the actual bodily features; a male femaler with a prominent Adam's apple and heavy dark beard growth will have more concealing to do than a male femaler without these recognizably male characteristics. However, even male femalers with ideal body characteristics for their projects, and who have undergone as much substitution as possible, will remain chromosomally male and in some settings (e.g., some sporting contests) this will require concealing. Concealing may also involve hiding the details of biography that are gender-specific – a marriage, a birth certificate, and so on.

For female maling, however, displaying male characteristics may be more important than concealing female ones if Kessler and McKenna are right when they argue:

In order for a female gender attribution to be made, there must be an absence of anything which can be construed as a 'male only' characteristic. In order for a male gender attribution to be made, the presence of at least one 'male' sign must be noticed, and one sign may be enough. This is because the basic categorising schema is 'see someone as female only when you cannot see them as male' (1978: 158-9).

In addition to concealing and displaying, transgendering may involve 'implying' certain body parts or gendered attributes. Because the body is usually apprehended in social interaction in its clothed form, it is possible to imply the gendered form of the body beneath. So, for example, males can wear breast forms inside a bra, or hip pads inside a panty girdle; females may place something in their underpants to imply the possession of a penis. Implying may be the only sub-process involved in the case of what Turkle (1997) calls 'virtual gender swapping' on internet discussion lists or, indeed, in any situation where interaction is not face to face such as that involving the telephone or written communication.

The fifth sub-process is 'redefining'. Whereas the meanings of substituting, concealing and implying are relatively easily grasped, particularly in relation to the acceptance of the binary divide, redefining is more subtle and multilayered. At one level, the nature of the body, body parts and gendered accompaniments may be redefined. The MTF transsexual may redefine her beard growth as facial hair. The penis may be redefined as a 'growth between the legs', as in 'I was a woman who had needed some corrective surgery. The growth was gone and my labia, clitoris and vagina were free' (Spry, 1997: 152). The male transvestite may redefine unisex clothes, such as jeans and T-shirts, as women's clothes because they were bought from a woman's boutique. Moreover, in the case of transcending – which seeks to subvert and/or move beyond the binary divide – the process of redefining the binary divide may entail selves, body parts, and gendered accoutrements taking on new meanings within the redefined system of classification.

As we shall see in subsequent chapters, the five major sub-processes are variously implicated in each mode of transgendering. The mode of transgendering may be decided by determining which sub-process is dominant. In migrating stories it is the substituting sub-process that is dominant. Migrating stories tell of erasing, concealing, implying and redefining, variously coopted in the service of substituting. In this sense migrating stories are tales of substitution. In oscillating stories it is the implying sub-process that is dominant. Here, erasing, substituting, concealing and redefining will be variously co-opted in the service of implying.

The negating mode of transgendering is often the most difficult to discern and differentiate from the other modes. The key in doing so is to focus on the sub-process of erasing. Where erasing features as the dominant sub-process and takes precedence over substituting, concealing, implying and redefining which will be variously co-opted in its service, we are observing the negating mode of transgendering.

The transcending mode of transgendering is identified by the dominance of the sub-process of redefining in relation to the binary gender divide. Erasing, substituting, concealing, and implying are all likely to be variously redefined and co-opted in terms of the variant of redefining adopted.

Finally, we may note that within each mode of transgendering, it will be the precise interrelations of the various sub-processes that will determine both the uniqueness of each experience of transgendering and provide the components out of which diverse behaviours, meanings and identities may be fashioned. Moreover, as we shall see in the following chapters, each sub-process will be variously sexed, sexualized, and gendered and the variations here will provide the components out of which the major alternative conceptualizations and theorizations of transgender phenomena will emerge.

Migrating, oscillating, negating, and transcending in the literature: a story of style and presentation

What we conceptualize as migrating and oscillating has now generated a large literature. When we began researching this area in the mid-1970s, the literature was comparatively small and we could be reasonably confident that we were at least aware of it all. The relevant sections in the bibliography by Bullough, Legg, Elcano, and Kepner (1976) contain about 450 references. More recent bibliographies demonstrate the growth of the literature since that time. Demeyere's (1992) bibliography, particularly strong on anthropological material, and Denny's (1994) bibliography, particularly strong on medical and psychological literature, each include more than 5,000 entries.

The growth in the literature since 1994 has been exponential. Not only has the literature increased in size, but it also now ranges across a large number of disciplines and fields of study. In the mid-1970s, the bulk of the literature came from medicine and psychology. Now, although these disciplines are still dominant, much can also be found in sociology, social anthropology, social history, law, lesbian and gay studies, women's studies, and cultural studies. Despite the shift in range of studies, however, it remains the case that the vast majority of the 'scientific', academic and professional literature deals with those modes of transgendering that we term migrating and oscillating, with the bulk of that majority being concerned with migrating. Only in recent years, particularly in cultural studies, has the focus on transcending become of real significance in the academic literature. Negating still remains a story largely unidentified in the scientific, academic and professional literature.

In addition, transgender topics appear regularly in the popular media, on television, in the cinema, in the press, and, of course, on the internet. There are transgender plays and novels, there is transgender photography, and there is transgender pornography.

Again, the vast majority of this non-technical literature is concerned with migrating and oscillating. A minority of it is concerned with transcending, and, outside of fantasy fiction and internet erotica, once again, what we term negating remains largely unidentified.

This imbalance in the present literature, in regards to our four modes of transgendering, inevitably affects our style of presentation in the chapters that follow. There is now a wide range of migrating and oscillating personal narratives widely and easily available in both technical and popular formats. For this reason, we have not felt it necessary to provide lengthy passages of personal narrative material in Chapters 2 and 3. Rather, we have emphasized the range of diverse and often competing stories from a range of medical, psychological, and social scientific sources. Where we do use personal narrative, we do so to illustrate the modes and processes of transgendering that we are considering.

Chapter 4 on negating, on the other hand, adopts a rather different approach. We have learned from our preliminary work in this area, that there is a strong tendency to read negating stories in terms of the other three modes of transgendering. Also, it must be said, that our own work in this area has considerably less material to draw upon than is the case with the other modes. We have chosen, therefore, to focus in Chapter 4 on two particular negating stories: both stories put forward by pioneers in the area. These pioneers are gender-identity innovators whose writings are largely unknown outside of their immediate circle and fan-base. The writings of these pioneers do, however, evidence a high degree of coherence and consistency. They deserve a mainstream publisher.

Again, the negating stories tend to be different in ways not just related to the particular mode. Migrating and oscillating stories, in the main, tend to be stories of justification. In the context of the emergence of such stories, the need was felt to legitimize (respectabilize) these stories, as we shall see. Note, for instance, Harry Benjamin's comments in his foreword to Christine Jorgensen's autobiography (Benjamin, 1967a: ix):

> But was this female gender role really new? The vivid description of her early life supplies a negative answer. This was a little girl, not a boy (in spite of the anatomy) who grew up in this remarkably sound and normal family. There was no broken home, no weak or absent father with whom the little boy could not identify.

Again, oscillating pioneer Virginia Prince argued that gender role socialization was so narrow and constraining in our Western society that it was incumbent upon her to advocate the development of the 'woman within' as 'necessary' for many males who felt constrained by their imprisonment (Prince, 1976).

The negating stories are sometimes tales of justification, but many are not. The story of the negating male sissy maid, for instance, has the quality of a tale of raw experience. It is a tale justified in the telling alone. It is a tale, moreover, that is most frequently told in a particular blend of fact and fiction designed to be read by enthusiasts of the genre. Furthermore, as there is no serious consideration of these tales in the scientific literature, and precious few of them, indeed, in the mass media, our emphasis, in the main, has been on the presentation of personal narrative material with minimal analytic comment. Our principal purpose is to use the narrative material to illustrate the relevant mode of transgendering and its attendant sub-processes and their interrelations.

We have, however, taken particular care to discuss our developing conceptualizations with our negating informants through a process of collaborative work with them. This is particularly evident in the final section of Chapter 4 ('a tale of refining') when we consider some of the comments on our work by our negating and erasing informants.

In regard to the mode of transcending, the literature in this area tends to be 'hot' and 'sexy'. It is, however, almost always 'hot' and 'sexy' in a theoretical sense. Despite its growth, there is still strikingly little material relating to the 'lived experience' of the transcending life. Cognisant of this, our approach is to leaven our treatment of the theoretical stories with apposite illustrations taken from our life history work with a number of transcending informants.

Again, following the pattern of the previous chapter, we have added a final 'Tale of caution' section that emphasizes the importance of continuing collaborative work with informants – in this case, to underline the different point that lives and categorizations are most typically in a state of emergent process.

We conclude this chapter with two more general points. In the first place, we are mindful that some of our readers will choose to focus on the particular mode or modes of transgendering that interest them, and largely ignore the other modes. For this reason, we have endeavoured to make the chapters on each of the four modes of transgendering relatively free standing – once the relevant conceptual introductions in Chapter 1 have been grasped. On occasion, this has led to us preferring to repeat fundamental points, particularly fundamental conceptual points, where relevant, rather than run the risk of unintelligibility to the selective reader.

Finally, we might add that, although our framework includes both MTF and FTM transgendering, our consideration of the major tales of transgendering devotes more time to MTF than FTM. The reality is that despite the increasing contribution of FTM in many tales of transcending, including the significant recent work on drag 'kinging', MTF tales of transgendering continue to be predominant. We have not taken our task to be rectifying this imbalance. Our main concern is to provide the conceptual framework which future work may utilize however and whenever it wishes.

TWO   Migrating Stories

A conceptual introduction to migrating

The idea of migrating in a geographical sense is well known. According to Castles and Miller (1998), we are now in the 'Age of Migration'. Over the past 50 or so years the rapid growth in geographical migration linked to processes of globalization has rendered problematic clear notions of citizenship, national identity and belonging (Castles and Davidson, 2000). We are also in the age of Gender Migration. In the last half of the twentieth century developments in medical technology were utilized in what is popularly called 'sex-changing'. Unknown numbers of people have left their assigned genders behind and migrated 'over the border', raising interesting questions about what it means to be a man or a woman.

The Concise Oxford Dictionary (1995) defines migrating as 'moving from one place of abode to another especially in a different country'. Moving to a different country involves the crossing of a boundary or border and signifies that there is a difference of some importance between what lies on either side: a different language maybe, different customs, a different way of life. Also, particularly in popular culture, gender relations are sometimes depicted in terms that suggest that men and women do indeed inhabit different countries, and different worlds or planets – the 'women are from Venus, men are from Mars' approach (Gray, 1992).

The dictionary reference to 'place of abode' draws our attention to the fact that migrating is not the same as going on holiday. Migrants buy a one-way ticket. While return may be possible, at its inception the journey is seen as one-way; it is not expected that there will be any turning back. Applicants for a gender recognition certificate available in the UK under the Gender Recognition Act, 2004, must sign a statutory declaration to the effect that they intend to live in their 'acquired gender until death' (http://www.grp.gov.uk/forms/guide_fast_track.pdf).

Migration therefore involves significant social or cultural changes for those involved, nothing less than a life shift of major proportions. So significant is the move involved in migration, in fact, that many migrants speak of starting a new life.

One result of migration is that someone is 'out of place', their right to be where they have arrived is, in some way and by someone, questionable. This raises two interesting areas to investigate: the first is the way in which migration is regulated; the second is the relationship of migrants to members of the 'host' society.

The MTF trans woman, McCloskey, highlights the essence of migrating in her autobiography:

> But people do after all cross various boundaries. I've been a foreigner a little, in England and Holland and on shorter visits elsewhere. If you've been a foreigner you can understand somewhat, because gender crossing is a good deal like foreign travel. Most people would like to go to Venice on vacation. Most people, if they could magically do it, would like to try out the other gender for a day or a week or a month ... But only a tiny fraction of the crossgendered are permanent gender crossers, wanting to become Venetians. Most people are content to stay mainly at home. A tiny minority are not. They want to cross and stay. (1999: xi-xii)

As we noted in Chapter 1, the theme of undergoing a perilous journey is a common one in transsexual autobiographies. As Stone, in her discussion of transsexual auto/biographies, writes:

> each of these writers constructs his or her account as a narrative of redemption. There is a strong element of drama, of the sense of struggle against huge odds, of overcoming perilous obstacles, and of mounting awe and mystery at the breathtaking approach and final apotheosis of the Forbidden Transformation. (1991: 288-9)

Della Aleksander, one of the speakers at the First National TV. TS Conference held in Leeds, England, in 1974, pointed out that:

> Transsexualism is not, by itself, a viable life style, for it is a journey, and as such must have a destination. Though it is a truism that it is better to travel than to arrive, what makes it so is the knowledge of the certainty of arriving. To be robbed of that certainty would be to consign the traveller to a permanent limbo. (1974: 11)

Often, of course, the right of the migrant to settle in the new country is questioned. Similarly, in gender migrating, the migrant may be treated as 'out of place', as somewhere he or she does not belong. Conversely, transgender migrants themselves may feel that they were 'out of place' before they migrated and that they have finally arrived 'home' where they belong. Countless transgender migrant autobiographies tell of exile in the 'wrong' gender role, of dreaming of being home in the 'right' one, of finally arriving home where one belongs. As Thompson (with Sewell) put it:

> The first time I was born, it was in a body which was other than male. By some cosmic mistake, as a budding human being I had somehow chosen the wrong body, or the wrong body had chosen me. I am a transsexual person, a man really. It took me more than thirty years to reach a stage where my body started to fit my identity as a man, but now there is no doubt about it. Here I am, well and truly the male that I have always known myself to be. (1995: 1)

In Chapter 1, we introduced the work of Garfinkel. In his germinal paper discussing the case of Agnes, Garfinkel outlines the 'rules' that create what he calls a 'morally dichotomised population' (1967: 122) that is the two sexes (Garfinkel doesn't use the term gender). In order to be able to make sense of the notion of migrating as a mode of transgendering, we first have to understand these 'rules'. We will highlight three sets of rules that are implicit within Garfinkel's analysis and consider each set separately in terms of gender.[1] The first set of rules are these:

- there are only two genders;
- everybody has to be one or the other;
- transfers from one to the other are not permitted.

The implication of this first set of rules is that transgender migrating must not occur but if it does, it has to be done in such a way as to disguise that fact. In the various migrating stories that we look at later in this chapter there are many examples of this set of rules in action.

A second set of rules relates to those things that are held to be 'appropriately' masculine or feminine. Most obviously men are expected to have male bodies, and women, female ones: since the 1960s this has been conventionally referred to as 'sex'. Then there are those things that Goffman refers to as 'the cultural correlates of sex' (1979: 1), conventionally referred to as 'gender'. Many aspects of our lives such as names, clothes, occupations, and physical spaces are gendered – they are either masculine or feminine. As Connell (2002: 3) says, 'As men or women we slip our feet into differently shaped shoes, button our shirts on opposite sides, get our heads clipped by different hairdressers, buy our pants in separate shops and take them off in separate toilets.' Then there is the area of 'sexuality' – the ways in which the erotic possibilities of the body are arranged by gender.

To write of men's and women's bodies, men's and women's clothes or men's and women's sexualities obscures the fact of variation in all of these areas, but nonetheless in contemporary Western cultures it 'makes sense' to dichotomize in this way. Moreover, such is the nature of our gender system, too, that not only are men and women held to be discrete categories in the above respects, they are also held to be opposite ones.

The implication of this second set of rules is that in the migrating mode, the prominent sub-process of transgendering is that of 'substituting' and again we can see this played out in the stories that we discuss later in the chapter. The transgender migrant is reconstituted by substituting one set of gendered characteristics for another. Complete substitution (transformation), however, is not possible, except in fantasy. The migrating mode of transgendering will, therefore, always involve transgendering sub-processes additional to substituting and its attendant erasing. To varying degrees, concealing, implying, and redefining will be implicated, depending on the individual's personal project, their biography, their physique and the particular setting.

A third set of rules may be seen as 'congruity' assumptions. They concern the relationship between sex, sexuality and gender. The assumption has been (and to a large extent still is) that men are biologically male and are sexually attracted to women and that women are biologically female and are sexually attracted to men (Marshall, 1981; Shively and De Cecco, 1977).

The implication of this third set of rules is that a substitution of one of the elements of sex, sexuality or gender will tend to create a pressure to bring the other two into line. In the 'classic' transsexual story where maximum substituting takes place, sexuality and gender substituting will variously precede, accompany, or follow the body substituting. The story of Gail Hill (see Ekins, 1997: 146–54) is illustrative. Gail identifies as a 'transsexual/new woman'. Post-surgically, she views herself as having a female body to match her female identity. Her presentation of self is as an attractive woman in her thirties (gender display). Prior to transitioning, she was married with a wife and child. Post-surgery, she soon began a relationship with a steady boyfriend with whom she has regular sexual intercourse (sexuality).

However, there is no necessary congruity between sex, sexuality and gender in migrating stories and the complexity of the relations between these components has been obscured in much of the literature. This is an important matter to which we will return.

Substituting sex (the body)

The medical arena differentiates body sex in regard to chromosomal sex, hormonal sex, gonadal sex, internal genital apparatus, external genital apparatus, and characteristics of body sex, such as facial, body and scalp hair, skeletal shape and musculature. As we have said, complete body substitution is not possible, except in fantasy. Modern medical interventions can accomplish a great deal, especially if administered early in the life of the body. Even so, chromosomal and gonadal substitutions are not possible and after puberty certain aspects of the body such as height or skeletal shape may be beyond substitution. As Rees put it: 'Practically and emotionally, becoming a man, physically, was the least difficult part of my role reassignment. It was, however, the most frustrating because it was only a compromise. I knew that, however good the treatment, I'd never be fully male, functionally, anatomically or chromosomally' (1996: 30).

Some aspects of the body that have gender significance may be altered in ways which can be reversed – a male can grow his hair long in a fashion culturally coded as feminine, for example – but in the migrating mode the focus is usually on more permanent substitutions. Since various hormonal and surgical interventions became available from the middle of the twentieth century, 'sex changes' have usually involved the permanent alteration of the genital and chest areas of the body. Many other body substitutions are possible with varying degrees of success. Recent developments in facial feminization surgery, for instance, make possible a degree of feminization of the face that might have been thought impossible a decade or so ago.

Most, but not all, permanent substitutions require some form of outside intervention and are usually, but not always, regulated by the medical profession. But males can undergo electrolysis without regulation and there are reports of self-surgery. Aleshia Brevard writes of her own self-castration, 'the messy deed done, and with my testicles flushed down the commode – I passed out' (Brevard: 2001: 11). An older FTM example comes from the memoirs of a surgeon who worked with Magnus Hirschfeld at the Institute of Sexology in Berlin in the 1920s and 1930s:

A sixteen year old transvestian (sic) girl came to us to have her well-developed breasts amputated ... We refused to operate because we considered that at the age of sixteen the girl's mental development was not complete. A few days later, the patient was brought to us having lost a great deal of blood; in order to necessitate amputation, she had inflicted upon herself deep and severe cuts with a razor. (Lenz, 1954: 463)

To what extent such desperate measures are still practised today is unclear, given the greater ease of access to surgical procedures, but there are reports of self-castration up until the 1970s (Haberman and Michael, 1979; Lowy and Kolivakis, 1971).

Aspects of body transgendering may be variously progressive, problematic, rapid and extensive, as is well illustrated by the following account from FTM trans man Mark Rees:

> The action of the hormones was almost immediate. A couple of weeks later I had my last period and within a month or so people began to notice a change in my voice ... Although the growth of my facial hair took much longer, I was surprised by the rapidity of the changes generally ... My superficial veins especially in the forearms became more obvious as the subcutaneous fat decreased. The decrease was most obvious around the breasts, hips and thighs. There was an increase in muscle development with a corresponding weight increase, redistribution and increase in body hair and clitoral enlargement. After six months I was able to live successfully as a man ... I had been living as a man for nearly three years before undergoing a bilateral mastectomy. This was straightforward and relatively painless ... The hysterectomy and oophorectomy (removal of the ovaries) a year later was less easy; I developed a massive haematoma which necessitated blood transfusions ... A phalloplasty (the construction of a penis) is probably what most female-to-male transsexuals yearn for more than anything else, yet it is a most difficult, risky and unsatisfactory procedure ... Other areas of the body have to be mutilated in order to acquire tissue for the construction. The involvement of the urethra increases the risk of infection and the ability to micturate in a male fashion cannot be guaranteed. (Rees, 1996: 30–2)

Before body migrating can take place, a number of conditions need to be met. On the 'supply' side, the techniques for substituting have to be developed and have to be made available to would-be migrators. On the 'demand side' the migrator needs to arrive at some idea of what bodily substitution is available and where it might be obtainable.

Although there were some earlier attempts, it is only since around the middle of the twentieth century that a number of technological developments have come together which made it possible, by altering the body in more or less limited ways, to grant the wishes of some people to 'change sex'. The term 'transsexual' (coined by Hirschfeld in 1923) began to make its appearance in medical and popular vocabularies around the mid-1950s and the question of whether (and, if so, on what grounds) 'sex change' should be allowed came to the fore, as we shall see.

In many countries that have accepted bodily substitutions, ethical and legal issues have generally restricted their availability to adults.[2] This means of course that the body has already fully developed the characteristics for which substitution is sought. In some parts of the world substituting techniques may be more readily available at a younger pre-pubertal age as the following two cases illustrate. These examples also illustrate some of the range of body substitution that is possible for the MTF trans woman.

Example 1: Thailand. At age 11, I began to take the Diane 35 anti-androgen [cyproterone acetate 2 mg & ethinylestradiol .035 mg oral tablet, Schering, Germany]. At 16, I began to take Premarin conjugated estrogens [conjugated estrogens, 1.25 mg oral tablet, Wyeth-Ayerst, Canada] and Progynon Depot + Prolution Depot [estradiol valerate USP, 10 mg + hydroxyprogesterone-Caproate USP, 250 mg combined injectable, Schering, Germany]. At 16, I had my sex-reassignment surgery (SRS). At 17, I had rhinoplasty; at 18, tracheal shaving; and at 25, breast augmentation (280cc silicone gel implants) with Dr. Suporn Watanyusakul [MD] in Chonburi, Thailand. (http://kim-lertsubin.com/nklomklao/) (Accessed 24 January 2005)

Example 2: Thailand. At age 13, I began to take the *Diane 35* anti-androgen [cyproterone acetate 2 mg & ethinylestradiol .035 mg oral tablet, Schering, Germany] and *Premarin* [conjugated estrogens, 1.25 mg oral tablet, Wyeth-Ayerst, Canada]. At 15, began to take *Progynon Depot + Prolution Depot* [estradiol valerate USP, 10 mg + hydroxyprogesterone-Caproate USP, 250 mg combined injectable, Schering, Germany]. At age 18, I had rhinoplasty, tracheal shaving, silicone injections to the chin and cheeks, and a chin implant. At 19, I had breast augmentation (February 2000) and at 20 – sex-reassignment surgery (SRS) (October 2000). In the future, I expect to have a world-class cosmetic reconstruction done by Dr. Suporn Watanyusakul [MD] in Chonburi, Thailand. (http://www.kim-lertsubin.com/nudomsak/) (Accessed 24 January 2005)

The 'demand' side has both an individual and a collective aspect. The individual's career path will vary in the extent to which he or she becomes aware of the possibilities of hormonal and surgical substitution and how these might be obtained. In the last 30 or so years of the twentieth century, subcultural networks have developed which are able to provide sophisticated information (much of it now on the internet) about the bodily substitutions that are available.

Body substitutions, particularly genital ones, may be taken as indicative that migration has taken place. Stone comments on the subjects of transsexual auto/biographies: 'each constructs a specific narrative moment when their personal sexual identification changes from male to female. This moment is the moment of neocolporraphy – that is, of gender reassignment or "sex change surgery"' (1991: 286). Similarly, Phillips (1993: 3), in *Raised by Wolves: A Transsexual Diary*, chronicles her '18-month journey from life as an apparently normal husband and father to that of an apparently normal woman'. In the penultimate entry of her chronicle, 'Saturday, January 18th, 1992', she is on the train leaving the clinic of her 'sex change' doctor, Doctor Biber. She writes:

So, here it is: the end of my journey – not just by train, but the entire train of events that describe my life for the last two and a half years. This diary began on August 1st 1989, the first day of my transition, and ends today on the last. For there is no more change; no more patterns of thought, no more biochemical balances, no more physical characteristics. When shortly I step from this train, my journey will truly be complete. (1993: 240)

In a final 'Backword' for August 29, 1994, she writes (1994: 241): 'so that's how the story ends. Yet, just as surgery was the final chapter in the story of my transition, transition itself is but a chapter in the story of my life.'

Not only does genital surgery often indicate for gender migrants that their journey is over, it may also be required before legal or other formal aspects of migration may be allowed, as in South Australia's Sexual Reassignment Act, 1988 (http://pfc.org.uk/legal/sa-act.htm). The Gender Recognition Act, 2004 in the UK, however, does not require any body substitution before a new legal status is conferred although the medical report which is needed to support the case for a change of status must state why body substitution has not taken place (http://www.grp.gov.uk/forms/guide_fast_track.pdf).

Given that total transformation is impossible, substituting will always be accompanied to some extent by concealing and implying. MTF trans women will never be able to menstruate, but many informants speak of buying tampons or sanitary towels and carrying them in their bags. Many FTM trans men will not be able to acquire a 'workable' penis but as Rees points out, a number of trans men 'have equipped themselves with very realistic looking prostheses, which enable them to urinate in a male fashion if desired' (Rees, 1996: 33).

Substituting gender

On a day-to-day basis, of course, the genitals are not the basis for gender attribution. As Cahill notes of Garfinkel's Agnes: '[her] male genitalia did not prevent her from being seen as a female nor did her pharmaceutically produced feminine form automatically make her a female in others' eyes. Rather, she secured her claim to a female identity by changing her clothing and hairstyle' (1989: 282). So, in some respects, the way in which the body is clothed and adorned may be more important than the body itself. The rules concerning the clothing and adornment of bodies according to gender are many and complex, as well as being historically and culturally variable. For Connell (2002: 10), gendered clothing is one of the ways in which similarities between male and female bodies are disguised and differences exaggerated. In some societies, occupation may be more important in transgendering than clothing and appearance (Whitehead, 1981), but in contemporary Western societies, transgendering will almost always involve 'transvesting'.

Not only is the way the body is clothed and adorned gendered, but so, too, is what is done with the body – the way in which the body is managed. Prince's handbook *How to Be a Woman Though Male* (1971) has a chapter devoted to this aspect of the body. It begins with the assertion that 'everybody knows that women handle themselves differently than men' (1971: 118). The chapter contains extensive and detailed advice on how to walk, sit, stand, run, eat, drink, and so on, 'like a woman'. One piece of general advice is 'try to be more gentle, less direct, less forceful, and more delicate and graceful in your movements' (ibid.: 119).

Migrating may therefore involve attempts to change this aspect of the body. Roberta Cowell, in one of the earliest transsexual autobiographies, gives us an example: 'One of the things most useful to me in my new social life proved to be the lessons I received on how to hold and move my hands. It was much easier to appear poised and relaxed when my hands were held and moved in the correct manner' (1954: 108).

Migrating will commonly involve many other substitutions. Among these, probably the most common are substitutions of names, pronouns, titles, and so on. Linked to this may be bureaucratic substitutions such as changes to driving licences, insurance documents, and so on. Here is Mark Rees again:

> A change of name brings about an appreciation of just how many documents bear it ... Names had to be changed on bank accounts, insurance policies, passport, driving licence, club membership, and on Department of Social Security, Department of Employment, Inland Revenue and medical records. The list seemed interminable. (1996: 34)

For many years trans people have sought the right to substitutions of their legal status and this is now possible in certain jurisdictions. Occupations, hobbies, interests, knowledge, skills and many other things are still divided by gender and in migrating many of these may be substituted.

Some of these substitutions involve learning new skills and establishing new routines. But, if others are not to know that migrating is in progress, this has to be done in such a way as to disguise the fact that learning is taking place. This is vividly illustrated in the detailed account that Garfinkel gives of Agnes's teenage migration when she is learning the rules of 'being a woman' at the same time as she is conveying the impression that no learning is taking place:

> Agnes was required to live up to the standards of conduct, appearance, skills, feelings, motives and aspirations while simultaneously learning what those standards were. To learn them was for her a continuous project of self-improvement. They had to be learned in situations in which she was treated by others as knowing them in the first place as a matter of course. (1967: 147)

Some transgender migrants tell of learning and practising such skills; others say or imply that they naturally possessed these skills and that no learning took place; others simply gloss over the topic. For a time, the Gender Identity Clinic at Charing Cross Hospital in London provided its transsexual patients with access to classes in gender-specific skills. A number of our MTF transsexual informants in the 1980s, who were patients at the Charing Cross Clinic at the time, took the view that 'real' transsexuals did not need these classes. In the next chapter we look in more detail at some of these skills.

Despite the separation of sex and gender in parts of the academic literature, the belief in their intimate entanglement and the primacy of the body is probably still pretty much 'common sense'. However, in the absence of a 'test' that will unequivocally demonstrate that a person is a transsexual, access to body substitution technologies (where that does not only depend on money) has been determined by the success or otherwise of gender substitution. Thus the Standards of Care (SOC) devised by the Harry Benjamin International Gender Dysphoria Association recommends the 'real-life experience' which is 'the act of fully adopting a new or evolving gender role or gender presentation in every-day life' (Meyer III et al., 2001). The SOC notes that 'when the patient is suc-cessful in the real-life experience, both the mental health professional and the patient gain confidence about undertaking further steps'.

The SOC recommends the real-life experience on pragmatic grounds (in other words, will the transition 'work'?) and cautions against viewing it as a test of the transsexual diagnosis. Nevertheless, it is noted that 'Professionals sometimes construe the real-life experience as the real-life test of the ultimate diagnosis. If patients prosper in the preferred gender, they are confirmed as "transsexual," but if they decide against continuing, they "must not have been."' This suggests that the 'professionals' referred to may be using 'gen-der' as a proxy for sex as, in fact, most of us do, most of the time.

As with the body, total gender transformation is not possible. When trans-gender migrating doesn't occur before adulthood, there will be a personal history spent in the assigned gender that cannot be substituted. In such cases migrating will involve other sub-processes and, to varying degrees – depend-ing on the individual's personal project, their biography, their physique and the particular setting – concealing, implying and redefining will be in play. A common example in our interviews relates to childhood school attendance particularly in the case of older informants who have been more likely to attend a sex-segregated school.

Substituting sexuality

This aspect of migrating is, perhaps, the hardest to get to grips with. After all, despite the fact that changes to the body and to gender presentation do not take place all at once, they do have a clear material reality; the day of the reassignment surgery or the day when you went 'full-time' can be pin-pointed. But definitions and meanings in matters relating to the sexual and sexuality are notoriously problematic (Plummer, 1982), let alone attributing 'a' sexuality to a social actor. Moreover, most sexual practices are expected to take place in private and are further complicated by the key role of fantasy in this area.

But of course, social actors – gender migrants or otherwise – do attribute a sexuality to themselves and others. The most usual component of this is the gender of those people to whom the actor feels attracted and/or the gender of real or fantasized sexual partners. Less so today than it once was, perhaps, the 'default' assumption is that the gender will be the 'opposite' one, i.e., that the actor's sexuality will be heterosexual.

Besides having the 'correct' gendered partner, there are other expectations about the sexuality of men and women. As with the body and gender presentation, to write of men's and women's sexualities obscures a great deal of variation, but nevertheless it is common to find in the mass media and in academic literatures, assumptions about how 'different' sexuality is for men and for women.

A distinction we need to make at the outset in discussing sexuality is between the sexual pleasure to be obtained from various parts of the body and the sexual object choice. Typically, but not exclusively, of course, the genitals are most usually associated with sexual pleasure and the normative sexual object has been a person of the 'opposite' sex. What aspects of sexuality, if any, are substituted in transgender migrating?

In point of fact, the issue of sexuality has been rather underplayed in the transgender migrating story. As we shall see below, those men and women who told their stories of wishing to cross the gender border to nineteenth-century psychiatrists were initially classed as 'inverts' or as fetishists. As the category of the transsexual emerged, it was differentiated from that of the homosexual/lesbian and from that of the transvestite. When techniques of body substitution became more widely employed in the early 1950s, the transsexual story became one that, if believed, 'qualified' the teller for such medical treatment. Thus sexuality was always a difficult topic. If an MTF transsexual admitted to having a sexual attraction to men, that implied homosexuality which ruled out surgery in some eyes. Similarly, to admit a sexual attraction to women somehow implied that the MTF trans person was not a 'real' woman who was thought to be attracted to men. The person who admitted to masturbating while cross-dressed risked being classified as a transvestite.

As most Western cultures have become more accepting of homosexuality and lesbianism, we have seen more transsexuals taking up a lesbian or a homosexual identity and at one time some writers wrote of a category of transhomosexuality (Tully, 1992). But as we shall see later, to discuss sexuality in relation to transgender migrating is still potentially controversial.

Of Agnes, first seen by Robert Stoller and Garfinkel in the late 1950s, Garfinkel remarks:

> the penis of Agnes' accounts had never been erect; she was never curious about it; it was never scrutinized by her or by others, it never entered into games with other children; it never moved 'voluntarily'; it was never a source of pleasurable feelings; it had always been an accidental appendage stuck on by a cruel trick of fate. (1967: 129)

This passage referred to a time before the publication of Benjamin's (1966) *Transsexual Phenomenon* which came to provide a blueprint for transsexuals who were seeking to qualify for sex-change surgery (Stone, 1991). Stone argues that applicants for sex reassignment surgery reproduced the case studies contained in Benjamin's book, and claims that:

> Benjamin's subjects did not talk about any erotic sense of their own bodies. Consequently nobody else who came to the clinics did either. By textual authority, physical men who lived as women and who identified themselves as transsexuals, as opposed to male transvestites for whom erotic penile sensation was permissible, could not experience penile pleasure. (1991: 291)

Stone claimed that 'Wringing the turkey's neck', the ritual of penile masturbation just before surgery, was the most secret of secret traditions. To acknowledge so natural a desire would be to risk disqualification.

Certainly, in 1966, Benjamin wrote that, 'many transsexuals have no overt sex life at all' (1966: 49) and his 'group three' transsexuals were described as having low libido or being asexual (ibid.: 22). However, despite the above quote, a close reading of the *Transsexual Phenomenon* suggests that Benjamin was probably less rigid in his thinking on the topic. A range of sexual practices and partners is actually discussed including masturbation, heterosexual intercourse, homosexual anal intercourse and fellatio (see Benjamin, 1966: 49–51, and the biographical profiles in Appendix D). Even Benjamin's 'true transsexual (high intensity)' allowed for the possibility of the transsexual having been married and fathered children (ibid.: 22). Arguably, Benjamin's writings on this matter became increasingly heteronormative into the late 1960s and beyond (Ekins, 2005).

The implications of using the pre-migration body for erotic pleasure are such that it may be used only minimally, or not at all, for these purposes. Stella (interview) says of her relationship with her wife before she began her migration: 'I was beginning to not want to have sex because I was ... I'd have to admit I was a man each time I done that'. Similarly, one of Devor's FTM respondents (1997: 265) says: 'I hated my body. Why would I want to masturbate? I didn't touch my body at all.'

Another possibility is that the sexual acts are accompanied by fantasies that redefine what is going on. As Devor (1997: 264) writes of the FTM transsexuals that she studied: 'most participants who recalled having masturbated as teenagers also recalled imagining themselves performing as heterosexual males in the fantasies which brought them to orgasm'. Or, as an MTF transsexual (Spry, 1997: 57) wrote of her pre-migration intercourse with her wife: 'the solution that I came up with that allowed me some degree of enjoyment from intercourse was to fantasize that I had female sex organs, that I was a lesbian'.

Homosexual (according to original sex assignment) encounters may likewise be avoided or redefined. Tula, for example, writes of one relationship: 'I didn't feel I was a man, yet I felt our relations were basically homosexual. I was only really happy when he lay on top of me, as in a heterosexual affair, but he wanted other things, like anal intercourse. We tried but I hated it and couldn't do it' (1982: 104).

Kane provides a similar example: 'With maybe one exception I never found any of the boys I had sexual relations with particularly attractive. What interested me primarily was the thrill of adopting a passive role, imagining myself as a pretty woman being ravished' (1998: 9).

More so in the past than today, same-sex encounters had to be carefully defined so as to avoid any implications of homosexuality. So we find Agnes and Coccinelle emphasizing the masculine (and by implication) heterosexual nature of their male partners. Coccinelle (Costa, 1962: 84) describes her 'first love', Robert, as 'far from being effeminate: he was built like an athlete and very muscular'. Coccinelle also wrote, 'he was unfaithful to me – and I suffered badly when I saw him preferring those I was struggling so hard to imitate' (1962: 86). Similarly, Garfinkel (1967: 129) notes that 'as a kind of dialectical counterpart to the 120 per cent female Agnes portrayed her boyfriend as a 120 per cent male'.

Some transgender migrators do, however, describe a process of substitution in terms of preferred sexual partner. Hewitt, an FTM transsexual, who had male sexual partners before migrating and female ones afterwards writes:

> Looking back, I'm surprised I had no idea at the time that men were not for me, but I really didn't. I just thought I had yet to find the right man. Despite my irrational sexual behaviour I had absolutely no feelings towards women at that point. The thought I might be attracted to females had never crossed my mind. (1995: 54)

One of our MTF informants detailed to us the effects of taking oestrogens on her sexual preference. She had been married and had fathered a child, although she said her interest in sexual relations was minimal. She reported that

> as the hormones began to act upon my body I noticed a distinct change in my choice of sexual partner, from very weakly heterosexual [based on her then still male genitalia], it passed through a period of asexuality and finally blossomed into a state of homosexuality [again based on her then still male genitalia] in that I go out with men and I fantasise myself with male partners.

As we shall see later, almost any claims made about aspects of sexuality are open to multiple definitions and may be contested. As Pfäfflin comments: 'Benjamin was open for sex [sexuality]. The Johns Hopkins Medical School (Baltimore, USA) when starting their Gender Identity Clinic (in 1965) was not. Benjamin accepted many patients who had lived and worked in the Red Light district' (personal communication, 2005).

Writing of his own work in Hamburg, Germany, Pfäfflin comments:

I re-explored the histories of those patients having been seen by my predecessors at the Department of Sex Research in Hamburg long after they had had sex reassignment surgery, and they reported quite different and much more active stories about their sexual histories than had been put down in the medical files. They knew what doctors of those times wanted to hear and what they did not want to hear. The same is true of homosexual activities. In many centres that believed in clear-cut differentiation between homosexuality and transsexuality, patients did not display homosexual history activities (e.g., Australia), but when the clinical staff had an open ear for such histories, they would tell them. The same applies for all kinds of sexual preference disorders (ICD) or paraphilias (DSM). (personal communication, 2005)[3]

Telling migrating stories

Migrating tales have been told for a long time in popular books, and biographies have been written of historical figures such as the Chevalier D'Eon and James Barry. At the end of the nineteenth century some men and women began to tell of their desire to migrate over the gender border to the newly emerging practitioners of sexology and gradually, as we discuss below, various medical tales were fashioned.

Initially these personal tales were told in private and then transformed into medical tales, told by medical men, in medical journals or books, and read by other medical men. Uneducated men may even have been explicitly excluded from gaining access to these stories by, for example, the use of Latin. Nevertheless, such books found their way into the hands of those who were seeking a means to explain some puzzling aspects of their lives. Some may also have used them for erotic purposes. In order to prevent this, only 'doctors of the medical and psychological professions' could write to the publishers of Benjamin's *Transsexual Phenomenon* for a supplement of illustrations (Benjamin, 1966: 287). Conversely, publications aimed more at the subjects of these stories were often disguised as professional texts. As Stryker puts it in her study *Queer Pulp*, 'many were compilations of spurious "case studies" supposedly collected for their scientific value but actually intended for more prurient uses' (2001: 81).

These stories have also been widespread for many years in the popular press, as sexologist Havelock Ellis noted as long ago as 1928 (Ellis, 1928: 29): 'although this psychic peculiarity is so difficult both to name and to define, it is, strange as that may seem, the commonest of all sexual anomalies to attain prominence in the public newspapers'. These early border crossings were, however, told in the popular press in terms of masquerade as in, for example, 'THE MASQUERADER: FAMILIAR FIGURE IN SKIRTS PROVES TO BE A MAN' – *Evening News*, 10 April 1915. When hormonal and surgical procedures began to be employed in the 1930s and 1940s, the press stories became medical ones of 'sex change'. Evidently such 'sex change' stories were common enough in the press in the late 1940s to prompt Norman Haire to write:

> From time to time one reads sensational reports in the newspapers of persons who are alleged to have had their sex-changed, usually by operation. And, whenever this occurs, well-known sexologists usually receive a spate of letters from persons who have read the newspaper reports and who write, asking for the operation to be carried out on themselves. (1950: 200)

It should be noted that this comment by Haire was published nearly three years before the case of Christine Jorgensen received world-wide press coverage. Since the cases of Christine Jorgensen and Roberta Cowell, many other sex change stories have been told. Most have probably been quickly forgotten but the subjects of some have achieved the status of national or international celebrities for a while, such as April Ashley, Jan Morris, Renée Richards, Julia Grant, Tula, Dana International and, most recently, Nadia, the winner of the UK's *Big Brother* television programme. The stories of women who have changed or who wish to change sex have also been told, although not so frequently. 'PAUL HEWITT HAS ONLY ONE WISH ... TO HAVE HIS BREASTS AND HIS WOMB REMOVED' was the rather wordy headline of one example (*The People,* 16 January 1994).

The press, in reporting these personal stories, turned to the medical profession for their 'expert' stories to help explain what was going on to their readers. *The Sunday Pictorial* seems to have first introduced 'transvestism' to English readers in its serialization of Christine Jorgensen's life story in 1953 when the term, and Hamburger's intersexual conception of it, were mentioned. A year later, however, the same paper was using the term 'transvestist' (*sic*) in a way which paralleled the later medical conception of the transsexual, in order to dispute the claim that Roberta Cowell had become a 'real' woman. At the same time, *The Guardian* (19 March 1954), picking up on a timely article in *The British Medical Journal*, also used the term 'transvestist' (*sic*).

Until the late 1960s, sex change stories were told mainly in the popular press but by the early 1970s transsexualism was seen as a legitimate topic to be covered by the more serious press with a corresponding increase in the display of expert terminology and opinion. A number of factors contributed to and constituted this change. First, there was the announcement in 1966 of the involvement of Johns Hopkins University Hospital in 'sex change' operations (Money and Schwartz, 1969). 1966 also saw the first appearance, as far as we are aware, of the topic of sex changes and transsexualism on British television in the BBC's documentary series *Horizon* (BBC 2, *Horizon*, 21/11/66). This was reviewed by *The Times* ('BBC TAKES A CANDID VIEW OF SEX-CHANGE', *The Times*, 22 November 1966) which, 12 years earlier, had ignored the Roberta Cowell story. In July 1969, the first International Symposium on Gender Identity was held in London and was widely reported in the press, including the serious broadsheets ('1,000 SEX-CHANGES IN 20 YEARS', *The Times*, 28 July 1969; '41 HAD CHANGE OF SEX', *The Guardian*, 28 July 1969). Then, the case of *Corbett v Corbett* (otherwise April Ashley) and the discussion of transsexual marriages in Parliament during the Nullity of Marriage Bill in 1971 were widely reported and raised an 'issue' on which the serious press could focus. In April 1974, Jan Morris's autobiography was published and a series of four extracts in *The Sunday Times*, together with many book reviews and background articles, brought the topic firmly within the purview of the 'serious' press.

The emergence in the 1960s and 1970s of the beginnings of what would later be termed the transgender community provided new opportunities for the telling of these stories both on a face-to-face basis and in countless subcultural newsletters and pamphlets. The early 1970s saw the growth of formalized associations among transvestites and transsexuals with national conferences organized in 1974 and 1975 (as we discussed in Chapter 1). Also, by the early 1970s, the identities of some of the doctors involved in sex changes had become known. The effect of this was that the media had easier access to experts, both doctors and patients, whom they could approach for material and who (less so in the case of the doctors) may even have been eager to 'educate' the general public.

During the 1970s and 1980s the transsexual story was increasingly told on television and became much more prevalent in this medium in the 1990s. The most significant change in the telling of transsexual stories, though, was the rise of the internet in the second half of the 1990s.

The 1950 quote from Haire that we considered previously is a clear indication that some readers found in these press stories a voice which enabled them to begin to make sense of their own lives. A little earlier, in the early 1940s, the involvement of London's Charing Cross Hospital with transsexual patients began when work with physically intersexed persons by the endocrinologist Broster was reported in the press in terms of sex-change, as in: 'WERE ONCE SISTERS', *News of the World*, 2 August 1943; 'TWO SISTERS TURN INTO BROTHERS', *The Star*, 25 August 1939).

In the early 1950s, the cases of Christine Jorgensen and Roberta Cowell received massive press coverage. Hamburger, the endocrinologist involved in the Christine Jorgensen case, wrote an article based on an analysis of the many letters he received from people around the world who learned of his existence through the press reports and who were seeking similar treatment to Jorgensen (Hamburger, 1953). One of them was an MTF trans woman from the UK who showed us a letter that she had written in 1954 saying:

> By 1951 I knew for certain that I wanted to be a woman ... Much as I tried I could find no one who would help me. I waited and hoped ... Two long years later, Christine Jorgensen achieved that which I had almost grown to accept as the impossible. She had changed sex. My pitiful little life became no longer liveable in the knowledge that it was possible. Dr. Hamburger, to whom I had immediately written, recommended that I should consult Dr . . .

Similarly, Mark Rees describes the impact that a newspaper article had on him: 'In 1969, four years after my WRNS discharge, I chanced to see an article in *The Times* of London which described the condition of transsexualism. It was a moment of enlightenment; at last it all fitted into place. I was transsexual' (1996: 30). These writers, then, credit such media stories with having a profound effect on their understanding of themselves. In the stories they found clarification of puzzling thoughts, feelings and behaviour; they found the suggestion of a possible solution to their problems.

We now turn to consider the major variants of transgender migrating stories that have been told. In the main, we follow a chronological approach. We start our exposition with the first tales told in a medical context at the end of the nineteenth century and into the first decades of the twentieth century. These are the tales associated with the rise of sexology as a discipline. We then discuss more modern stories beginning with the dominant 'body migrating story' that has accompanied the employment of medical technologies to substitute various body parts. This dominant story might be termed the 'traditional' migrating story. Within this story emerged the making of the contemporary Euro-American 'transsexual'.

Throughout this construction of the contemporary transsexual, there have always been tales of dissent. These tales that are critical of the medical subspecialty that emerged to assist migrating have taken three main forms: (1) those tales of dissent within the medical profession; (2) those tales emanating from religious belief; and (3) those tales that emerged within the women's movement of the 1970s.

In terms of the interrelations between sex (the body), sexuality and gender, the dominant body migrating story privileges body migration over that of erotic and gender migration. However, with the writings of Virginia Prince, an alternative 'gender-led' story emerged. Here is told the tale of gender migration with little or no permanent body substitution. Finally, in recent years, there has emerged the 'sexuality'-led migrating story, fashioned within the interrelations of psychologist Ray Blanchard's writings and the 'lived experience' and identity innovating of 'autogynephilic transsexual' Anne Lawrence and those who identify with her position. Indeed, there are now these three quite distinct formulations of transgender migration that may be grouped around their respective differential privileging of sex, gender and sexuality.

Medical tales of migrating: the first steps

We may suppose there have always been people who have wished to cross the gender divide but such people achieved a distinctive voice towards the end of the nineteenth century in the writings of the newly emerged discipline of sexology. This period marked the beginnings of what would later become known as transgendering. Moreover, the medical profession gradually fashioned a technology that has enabled some degree of body substitution to take place. Thus, while, in a sense, the initiators of transgendering tales have always been those who wished to cross the binary divide themselves (and did so, in varying respects), it was with the medicalization of their stories that a qualitatively different 'definition of the situation' emerged. We will begin, therefore, with an account of the development of the 'medical story' – or the development of 'medical stories', variously complementary and competing. As we shall see, for various periods of time medical definitions maintained their prominence, but, for the most part, there has always existed an umbilical cord between the definitions of the situation of members (the transgendered, themselves) and their medical consultants.

At the end of the nineteenth century, instances of crossing the gender border were often described in terms of 'masquerade', 'disguise' or 'impersonation'. The Victorian biographers of the Chevalier d'Eon (Telfer, 1885; Vizetelly, 1895) refer to his 'masquerade' as a woman. When, in 1895, *The Lancet* published a series of letters recounting stories and biographical details of James Barry, a woman who lived as a man and who worked as a doctor, an editorial response to one letter referred to 'the Chevalier d'Eon and others of the more notorious impersonators of sex' (12, 19, 26 October 1895; 16 November 1895). This conception clearly implies a mismatch between reality and appearances, that the Chevalier d'Eon, or whoever, was not a 'real' woman but only 'masquerading' as such, 'pretending'.

However, Havelock Ellis and other sexologists at that time began to tell the stories of men who said that they 'really' were, in some sense, women; and also stories of women who said that, in some sense, they were 'really' men. Some of the subjects of those early case histories were only able, or only wished, to cross the gender border on a temporary basis: but some of the men and women whom Ellis and Hirschfeld wrote about did manage to live for considerable periods of time as a member of the other gender – in our terms, they were able to migrate (see also, Farrer, 1987; 1996). While some of these migrants may have attempted some surgical alterations themselves, the majority of migrations would have been effected by means of the subprocesses of concealing and implying that we discuss in more detail in Chapter 3. Certainly, the extent of substituting possible today would have been beyond the wildest dreams of Ellis's 'eonists'.

These early manifestations of what later came to be seen as transsexualism and transvestism were first seen as variations of homosexuality. 'Real' men were masculine and heterosexual. Men who were homosexual were not 'real men', and were often conceptualized as feminine souls in male bodies. Two major figures in the history of sexology, Magnus Hirschfeld and Havelock Ellis, were responsible for establishing a new category that was separate and distinct from homosexuality. Both Hirschfeld and Ellis were broadly supportive of those who would later be distinguished as transvestites and transsexuals; they did not, for instance, employ the then fashionable language of degeneracy or perversion. Nevertheless, they did view such people as anomalies to be explained within a medical framework.

It was Hirschfeld ([1910] 1991) who coined the term 'transvestite' for those men who enjoyed behaving and dressing as women, or, indeed, wished to be women. In doing so, he argued that the transvestites' love of the feminine did not make them women. Rather, they were men who enjoyed expressing femininity. Hirschfeld redefined the link between being a man and masculinity. He argued that men (and women) are variously masculine and feminine, as in Hirschfeld:

> There are men with the gentle emotions of a Marie Baskiertschew, with feminine loyalty and modesty, with predominant reproductive gifts, with an almost unconquerable tendency to feminine preoccupations such as cleaning and cooking, also such ones who leave women behind in vanity, coquetry, love of gossip, and cowardice, and there are women who greatly outweigh the average man in energy and generosity, such as Christine of Sweden, in being abstract and having depth, such as Sonja Kowalewska, as many modern women in the women's movement in activity and ambition, who prefer men's games, such as gymnastics and hunting, and surpass the average man in toughness, crudeness, and rashness. There are women who are more suited to a public life; men more to a domestic life. There is not one specific characteristic of a woman that you would not also occasionally find in a man, no manly characteristic not also in a woman. (ibid.: 222-3)

By implication, male 'transvestites' are no less 'men'. In a similar way, Hirschfeld argued that renouncing masculinity did not necessarily involve homosexuality: 'one has to extend the sentence "not all homosexuals are effeminate" to include "and not all effeminate men are homosexual"' (ibid.: 148). Later he wrote that 'today we are in a position to say that transvestism is a condition that occurs independently and must be considered separately from any other sexual anomaly' (Hirschfeld, 1938: 188–9). According to Pfäfflin (1997), a major factor that lay behind Hirschfeld's creation of this new concept was the need to 'cleanse' the public image of homosexuality in 'an attempt to secure the success of the political action against a antihomo-sexual legislation'.

Havelock Ellis's non-judgemental approach to eonism was similar to that to be found throughout his sexology. As Crozier put it:

> He did not pass judgement on the moral nature of Eonism; he did not try to suggest it was a form of insanity (as Krafft-Ebing had suggested). Instead, Ellis lent his sympathetic ear to the study of the sexual impulse as it is manifest in Eonism and developed what he heard into a discourse which normalised a sexual aberration. (2000: 151)

Like Hirschfeld, Ellis (1928) also saw what he preferred to call eonism as separate from homosexuality, although he had a more conventional belief than Hirschfeld in the biologically given and fundamentally different (but complementary) natures of men and women (Ellis, 1914). Also like Hirschfeld, he was seeking to normalize homosexuality. 'Ellis was striving to emphasize that "inverts" were essentially ordinary people in all but their sexual behaviour' (Weeks, 1977: 63). In part, this involved a rejection of the view that a preference for sexual relations with members of the same sex is necessarily associated with the adoption of the dress, mannerisms, and so on of the opposite sex. Likewise, he wrote that it is possible for a person, 'to feel like a person of the opposite sex and to adopt, so far as possible, the tastes, habits and dress of the opposite sex while the direction of the sexual impulse remains normal' (Ellis, 1920: 1–2). Ellis originally used the term 'sexo-aesthetic inversion' (Ellis, 1913a; 1913b) to refer to this because he saw its essence as: 'The impulse to project themselves by sympathetic feeling into the object to which they are attracted or the impulse of inner imitation (which) is precisely the tendency which various recent philosophers of aesthetic feeling have regarded as the essence of all aesthetic feeling' (1928: 28). This term was later rejected because Ellis saw it as 'too apt to arouse suggestions of homosexuality', and he argued that just as 'a large proportion perhaps the majority of sexual inverts have no strongly pronounced feminine traits,' so, 'the majority of sexo-aesthetic inverts are not only without any tendency to sexual inversion but they feel a profound repugnance to that anomaly' (ibid.: 102–3). Crozier (2000: 127) points out that 'a reliance on patients' discourses in the form of a case history was an essential part of the burgeoning field of sexology'. Nowhere is this more evident than in the section on eonism in Volume 7 of Ellis's *Studies in the Psychology of Sex*. Here, Ellis uses autobiographical statements to support his arguments to a greater extent than in his other works.

According to Crozier (2000: 131): 'when Ellis was writing Eonism, he appealed to colleagues for "interesting cases"'. Crozier also quotes from a letter written by Ellis to Norman Haire in which Ellis wrote, 'I do not include homosexual cases and at all events only when the homosexual element is clearly a secondary feature. There are no women among the primary cases for in them the homosexuality always seems primary' (2000: 132).

Ellis preferred his term 'eonism' coined from the name of a famous transvestite, the Chevalier d'Eon and designed as a parallel to masochism (from Leopold von Masoch) and sadism (from the Marquis de Sade). This was the only alternative term to transvestism to enjoy any currency and survived in some writings at least until the early 1970s, being used to refer to the transsexual (Hamburger et al., 1953; Meyer and Hoopes, 1974). Ellis stated that there were two main types of eonist:

> One, the most common kind in which the inversion is mainly confined to the sphere of clothing and another less common but more complete in which cross-dressing is regarded with comparative indifference but the subject so identifies himself with those of his physical and psychic traits which recall the opposite sex that he feels really to belong to that sex although has no delusion regarding his anatomical conformation. (1928: 36)

Ellis seems, however, to regard this, 'less common but more complete' type as embodying the essence of eonism, and he objected to the term transvestism because it focused attention solely on the element of cross-dressing. He also objected to Hirschfeld's phrase 'impulse of disguise' because, 'the subject of this anomaly, far from seeking disguise by adopting the garments of the opposite sex, feels on the contrary that he has thereby become emancipated from a disguise and is at last really himself' (Ellis, 1920: 3).

Ellis was mainly attracted by a biological theory of the aetiology of eonism, although he was rather vague as to the specific mechanisms involved: 'Early environmental influences assist but can scarcely originate eonism. The normal child soon reacts powerfully against them. We must in the end seek a deeper organic foundation for eonism as for every other aberration of the sexual impulse' (1928: 110). He surmised that the 'real physical basis' of eonism was 'some unusual balance in the endocrine system' (ibid.: 10).

The stories told by Ellis and Hirschfeld became more important when, around the middle of the twentieth century, a number of technological developments came together which made it possible, by altering the body in more or less limited ways, to grant the wishes of some people to 'change sex'. Their ideas provided the basis for the work of Harry Benjamin that was to become central to the construction of the contemporary story of the 'transsexual', as we shall see in the next section. Benjamin wrote that 'many times in the 1920s, I visited Hirschfeld and his Institute' (Benjamin, 1966: 12) and he was also familiar with the work of Ellis, although whether they had ever met is uncertain. Of Ellis's two types of eonist that we discussed above, Benjamin remarked 'this concept is strikingly similar to my own: one group includes the transvestites, and the other the transsexuals' (ibid.: 33).

The 'traditional' or dominant body migrating story: the making of the modern transsexual

This story is essentially the story of the transsexual and the use of hormones and surgery to assist migrating by substituting relevant parts of the body. Underpinning this story (and most of the other stories that we consider later in this chapter) is a belief that the 'truth' of 'nature' will be revealed to us by scientific progress. This 'truth' can then be used to combat ignorance and non-scientific ways of thinking. It is a belief that is particularly prevalent within sexology whose practitioners have long seen themselves as battling against traditional moral views, not only in the wider society, but within medicine and science itself. As Steiner puts it, 'the medical world, in its traditional conservatism, has always been reluctant to explore the field of sexuality; today this reluctance is slowly being overcome' (1985: 419).

FTM trans man Reed Erickson, whose educational foundation sponsored Richard Green and John Money's *Transsexualism and Sex Reassignment* (1969; see also Devor, 2004) – one of the books which was influential in promoting the 'body migrating story' – wrote a Foreword to it in which he claims that the 'solution' to the problem faced by transsexuals (in our terms, the migrating 'solution') becomes possible thanks to the advancement of science and 'truth': Erickson states:

> only after years of effort by dedicated scientists who had to break through powerful barriers of superstition and prejudice ... [This] courageous and skillful group has ventured into the unknown area. Making their way through a confusing maze of mores, laying bare conflicting factless theories, they have disregarded the centuries of prejudice to blaze a trail for understanding and facts ... [So] where there was so much ignorance there is now some real, detailed knowledge. Where there was so much prejudice, now there is less of it, and we have some solid data to counter the prejudice that remains. (1969: xii–xiii)

It is significant that it was the pairing of a trans person and the medical and psychological professions that enabled the publication of the book *Transsexualism and Sex Reassignment* (Green and Money, 1969). Indeed, it is a feature of body migrating stories that they emerge principally within the interrelations of medical tales and the tales of those who wished to migrate. But how did it come about that particular 'definitions of the situation' – particular body migrating stories – became constructed? It is to this question that we now turn.

What may be termed the traditional migrating story (the story that became the dominant body migrating story) owes its inception primarily to two pioneers of transgendering, namely Christine Jorgensen and Harry Benjamin. Between them, they fashioned a categorization and identity that led to the making of the modern transsexual. Jorgensen was given oestrogen and underwent castration and penectomy in Denmark in 1951, later followed by the construction of a neo-vagina in the USA.

Jorgensen was not the first person to undergo the bodily substitutions made possible by the developments in endocrinology and plastic surgery that had occurred during the 1930s and 1940s (see King, 1993). Pauly (1965), for instance, reported on 16 cases published before 1953 of men who had obtained some form of surgery. All 16 had been castrated, seven had penectomies; in six cases neo-vaginas had been created (two in 1931, one in 1947, two in 1950, and one in 1952). However, what distinguished Jorgensen from her forbears was her orchestration of publicity – largely favourable – on her return home from Denmark to America.

The other major pioneer was the endocrinologist Harry Benjamin. It was essentially he who introduced the tale of the transgender migrant to the medical profession. Benjamin was referred his first 'transsexual' patient in 1948 by Alfred Kinsey. Benjamin was 63 years of age at the time, and had an outstanding track record as a sexologist – in particular, as an endocrinologist and a gerontotherapist – a sub-speciality to which he gave the name. In other ways, too, Benjamin was excellently equipped as potential founding father of transsexualism. He was in private practice and thus largely independent of institutional constraints. He had a large potential referral network. He was a persistent pioneer. His advanced years gave him a freedom denied to younger men and women mindful of their developing careers. Most important, perhaps, was his talent for listening to his patients and seeking to do what he thought was best for them.

In various assessments of his role, Benjamin is depicted as almost a lone fighter against social and medical convention, tradition and prejudice. As Ihlenfeld puts it:

His were the pioneering observations and efforts that called the attention of the medical community to the legitimacy of the transsexual's dilemma. It was he who listened while others scoffed. He showed compassion where others heaped abuse. He crowned his career by unlocking the door to an area of study that has the most profound implications for our understanding of human nature. (1978: 243)

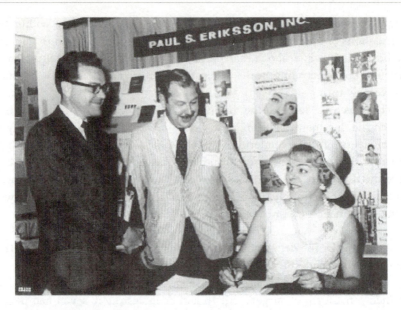

Figure 2.1   Christine Jorgensen at a book signing, 1967 (Reproduced with the kind permission of Linda Simpson)

Green, too, credits Benjamin's personal qualities with the creation of a new field of human knowledge: 'his compassion and courage in treatment of the transsexual patient opened a new frontier in the knowledge of human nature' (1985: x).

As has been mentioned previously, Benjamin did not coin the term 'transsexual', as is sometimes said. Magnus Hirschfeld had done that in 1923. Moreover, David Cauldwell had written quite extensively about transsexuals in the late 1940s and early 1950s (Ekins and King, 2001a). However, Hirschfeld had not developed a distinguishable clinical entity of transsexuality and Cauldwell was largely opposed to transsexual surgery which impeded the development of his thought on the topic.

Benjamin took the revolutionary step of seeking to secure hormonal and surgical 'sex change' for suitable applicants. He was making tentative steps in this direction before the publicity surrounding the case of Christine Jorgensen. But once he read of Jorgensen and wrote to her, it was only a matter of time before transsexuality became a distinguishable clinical entity – a diagnosis with a treatment programme. This did, of course, take some time. But with the opening of the first 'gender identity clinic' at Johns Hopkins University, Baltimore, USA, in the mid-1960s, the momentum became unstoppable. Slowly but surely, gender identity clinics began to span the globe. For every false start and backtracking step, expansions elsewhere took place. Throughout these developments, Benjamin's influence was paramount – particularly after the publication of his *Transsexual Phenomenon* in 1966, 'the first serious book on the topic', as Charles Ihlenfeld (1978: 243) was to describe it.

Leading up to the publication of *The Transsexual Phenomenon* in 1966, Benjamin published a number of articles in which he fashioned the nosography and nosology of the transsexual (Benjamin, 1953; 1954; 1961; 1964a; 1964b). Initially, Benjamin classified his transgender patients into transvestites Types 1, 2, and 3. Significantly, in 1953, when he published his first article on transsexualism, in which he distinguished transsexualism and transvestism, he began with a dedication to Christine Jorgensen: 'this article is the result of the wide publicity given to the case of Christine Jorgensen'. It is noteworthy, too, that the report by the Danish team involved in Jorgensen's castration and penectomy also resulted from the same publicity (Hamburger et al., 1953; Jorgensen, 1967: 209–10).

When Benjamin turns to aetiology, he is consistent in his view that some hidden biological phenomena would explain the phenomenon. He thought that environmental influences were important, but the genetic and endocrine constitution must provide a 'fertile soil' in order for them to have any effect. As he put it in Benjamin (1953: 13): 'if the soma is healthy and normal, no severe case of transsexualism, transvestism or homosexuality is likely to develop in spite of all provocations'. In 1967, Benjamin summarized thus:

> Most satisfying to me is a working hypothesis based on the experiments of brain physiologists and psychobiologists ... Their possible explanation for the transsexual phenomenon would be neuroendocrine in nature ... If something interferes, perhaps an abundance of the mother's estrogen or lack of response of the neural target organ, this particular center (a hypothalmic brain center) remains female, determining the later sexual behavior and possibly causing gender role disorientation. (1967b: 430)

In the case of FTM transsexuals, Benjamin suggests that the female hypothalamic centre may have been masculinized by an endocrine abnormality of the mother during pregnancy.

The sensational publicity surrounding the Jorgensen case and Benjamin's popularization of the term 'transsexual' certainly did not produce an outburst of research and publications on the subject. A few more cases were reported, usually still referred to as transvestites, but by the early 1960s the situation seemed little different from a decade earlier, except that some discussion had taken place concerning the desirability of the use of 'sex change' surgery. Benjamin described the period after the Jorgensen publicity thus:

> Few references to transsexualism could be found in the medical literature during the ensuing years. It seemed not only a *terra incognita* but also a *noli me tangere*. Undoubtedly, in the minds of many in the medical profession, the subject was barely on the fringe of medical science and therefore taboo. (1969: 5)

Notwithstanding the growth of gender identity clinics in the mid-late 1960s and into the 1970s, and the corresponding increase in sex reassignment surgery, it was to be considerably later before, as Green put it, 'Benjamin's child came of age' (1985: ix). This is marked for Green by the now widespread understanding of the term, by the dissipation of the controversy over the use of sex change surgery and by the inclusion of transsexualism in the American Psychiatric Association's *Diagnostic and Statistical Manual* (American Psychiatric Association, 1980).

The report of the Jorgensen case by Hamburger, Sturup, and Dahl-Iversen (1953) described 'transvestism' as a symptom that may appear in a number of conditions. However, the authors distinguished a category of transvestic men whom they thought justified the term 'genuine transvestism', 'psychic hermaphroditism' or 'eonism'. Believing the 'disease' to have a 'somatic' cause, and noting that attempts to cure it had proved futile, they argued that 'the object of the medical profession was to bring about ... by hormonal feminisation and operative demasculinisation ... conditions that may contribute towards the patient's mental balance and a certain sense of "purpose of life"' (1953: 393).

Such ideas gave primacy to biological factors in the determination of what would later be called gender differences and the strength of the transsexuals' demands seemed to make some kind of biological abnormality the only likely explanation. In 1958, in a presidential address to the Royal Society of Medicine's Section of Endocrinology, Armstrong wrote that he regarded transvestism, 'as being of a constitutional nature, doubtless on a genetic basis'. 'There is no sound evidence,' he wrote, 'for accepting the contention of psychiatrists that it is due to a castration complex or other environmental factors' (1958: 25).

These attempts to classify transsexualism (or transvestism as it was more usually called then) as an intersexual variant or to invoke biological explanations for the patient's identification with the opposite sex were clearly central to the task of justifying surgical and hormonal intervention, not only by members of the medical profession but also their patients (see Cowell, 1954). As Garfinkel remarked in respect of the case of Agnes (presumed to be a case of intersex), 'It is not that normals and Agnes insist upon the possession of a vagina by females ... They insist upon the possession of *either* a vagina that nature made or a vagina that should have been there all along, i.e. the *legitimate* possession' (1967: 127). At that time only some biological reason would have been accepted as grounds for the legitimate possession of a particular set of genitalia.

Apart from the intersex theory, surgery was also legitimated on pragmatic grounds. Walker and Fletcher, for example, argued that, 'conversion operations when performed on suitable cases ... would appear to produce better adjusted and reasonably contented "women"' (1955: 199). By contrast, they also argued that psychotherapy was ineffective: 'in over thirty years of practice the writer (K. Walker) has never seen a well marked case of trans-vestism cured or even materially helped by psychological means' (1955: 197). Similarly, Randell who, in 1959, was generally not in favour of the use of surgery nevertheless found two patients 'so manifestly lacking in masculine traits and so feminine in appearance, manner and speech that this step [surgery] is logical' (1959: 1449–50).

As stated in Chapter 1, Christine Jorgensen was originally categorized in terms of homosexuality by the medical team involved in her surgery. Sturup writes 'his medical history recorded what was medically identified as homo-sexual drives and he wanted to live as a woman' (1969: 455). Hamburger and Sprechler write: 'The patient was suffering from homosexual tendencies, and the oestrogens were given partly therapeutically, i.e. in order to suppress the sexual libido, and partly experimentally' (1951: 170) [Case number one in this article is Jorgensen's (see Hamburger et al., 1953)]. By 'experimentally', Hamburger and Sprechler are presumably referring to their general pro-gramme of investigating the endocrinological effects of administering various steroid substances (1951: 168). Sørensen and Hertoft, having examined the medical records and interviewed Sturup, the psychiatrist involved, concluded that the medical team dealing with Jorgensen 'were not aware of any inde-pendent nosological unity' (1980: 62). They 'regarded Chris Jorgensen as a homosexual man suffering from his homosexuality and since he himself asked for castration, they would not deny him this operation' (Hertoft and Sørensen, 1979: 168). In other words, castration and hormone treatment were originally employed not with a view to changing the patient's sex, but in order to treat homosexuality; the legal permission necessary for the castration was obtained with this argument. Hertoft and Sørensen make the significant point that: 'Not until afterwards, when the press published the case, did the team behind the procedure accept it as a sex change' (1979: 168). It might appear, then, that the media deserve more credit (or blame) than the medical profession for the 'invention' of transsexualism. However, once again, a new 'definition of the situation' emerged from within a complex set of interrelations between trans people, medical 'experts' and the popular press.[4]

Ironically, given his preference for a biological explanation, Benjamin's position with regard to hormonal and surgical 'sex change' was strengthened with the development during the late 1950s of the ideas of psychologist John Money (Money et al., 1957). Money and, later, Stoller, were developing a new terminology of gender, an important aspect of which was the conceptual dis-tinction between sex and gender. Stoller puts it this way: 'Gender is a term that has psychological or cultural rather than biological connotations. If the proper terms for sex are "male" and "female," the corresponding terms for gender are "masculine" and "feminine"; these latter may be quite independent of (biological) sex' (1968: 9).

Stoller (1964) and Greenson (1964) refined Money's conceptualizations with the term 'gender identity', a term which Money adopted. In particular, Money and Stoller stressed the immutability of gender when conceptualized as 'gender identity'. What became referred to as 'core gender identity' (Stoller, 1977) was regarded as unalterable after the age of two to three years, thus attaining a degree of 'reality' comparable to that of the body. On this conceptualization, therefore, it became possible to be both a male and a man in terms of the body and a female and a woman in terms of the psyche or, indeed, vice versa.

The importance of the new formulation is evident in the terminology of the 'Gender Identity Clinic' and the 'Gender Identity Disorder' that soon developed. The term 'gender identity', *per se*, is neutral in regard to both aetiology, and attributed pathology or psychopathology.[5] This, undoubtedly, facilitated the popularity of the term. The term also enabled the similar but more vague conceptualizations of previous writers to be firmed up around the new terminology. Benjamin, himself, the pivotal figure between Ellis's conceptualizations of the 'feeling' of being of one sex or the other and the new terminology of gender identity, began to drop his own preferred term 'psychological sex' in favour of the new language of gender identity.[6] There is no mention of 'gender identity' in his *Transsexual Phenomenon* of 1966. Here, for instance, Benjamin writes of the certificates he gives to his MTF transsexual patients, designed to help them in possible legal difficulties. The certificates contained the following sentences: 'Their anatomical sex, that is to say, the body, is male. Their psychological sex, that is to say, the mind, is female' (1966: 66). From 1967 onwards, however, the language of gender is increasingly superseding the language of sex and sexuality in Benjamin's writings. Benjamin and Ihlenfeld (1973: 457), for instance, start boldly with the sentence 'Transsexualism is a disorder of gender identity' (ibid.: 457).

Despite the separation of sex and gender that this new terminology highlights, there was still, however, an assumption that, as Stoller put it, 'masculinity fits well with maleness and femininity goes with femaleness' (1977: 173). According to this line of thought, it followed that if a 'fully differentiated gender identity' is immutable, it makes sense to achieve harmony by altering the body to the extent that technological developments allow'. In this vein, Money and Tucker write of the transsexual as:

> a person whose sex organs differentiated as male and whose gender identity differentiated as female. Medical science has found ways to reduce the incompatibility by modifying anatomy to help that person achieve unity as a member of a sex ... but medical science has not yet found a way to modify a fully differentiated gender identity. (1977: 69-70)

While gender identity has continued to take priority over morphological sex, the search is still on for what is assumed will be a biological determinant of the sexed brain. A document entitled 'Transsexualism: the Current Medical Viewpoint' written for Press for Change, the main UK campaigning organization, by a group of medical specialists claims that:

> The weight of current scientific evidence suggests a biologically-based, multifactoral aetiology for transsexualism. Most recently, for example, a study identified a region in the hypothalamus of the brain which is markedly smaller in women than in men. The brains of transsexual women examined in this study show a similar brain development to that of other women. (*Press for Change*, 1996)

Recalling Garfinkel's rule that no transfer between the sexes is possible, claims of a biological aetiology amount to a claim that no migrating is taking place since in some way the 'migrant' already belongs to the 'new' sex. In some quarters the terms 'sex-confirmation' or 'gender-confirmation' surgery are used in preference to sex reassignment or sex change to underline the point that no change has taken place. It is no coincidence that Milton Diamond, who for so long challenged John Money's position on the alleged social determinants of 'gender identity' (e.g., 1965; 2004), has more recently turned his attention to championing the contemporary variants of this tale of the biological determinants of the sexed brain as applied to transsexuals (GIRES, 2006a; 2006b).

Tales of dissent – migration as pathological

In 1976, Katz claimed that the medical treatment of homosexuals 'has almost invariably involved a negative value judgement concerning the inherent character of homosexuality. The treatment of lesbians and gay men by psychiatrists and psychologists constitutes one of the more lethal forms of homosexual oppression' (1976: 129). But he was also able to note the existence of a 'dissenting tradition', 'a form of treatment aimed at helping homosexuals feel good about – and give active, unsublimated expression to – their sexual-affectional attractions' (ibid.: 130). In the case of transsexualism, however, the dominant medical approach has long been a liberal one with the dissenters taking the negative stance.

In many contemporary societies the 'claims-making' activities (Conrad and Schneider, 1980) of some members of the medical profession have successfully established what we have called the 'traditional body migrating story' as the dominant lens through which to view the lives of those we have come to call transsexuals. As we saw, the traditional body migrating story amounts to a case for the substitution (so far as is possible) of gendered body parts. With the link between gender and biology still a strong one, many have argued that there must be, or have claimed to have found, the biological foundation for the transsexual's wish to migrate across the gender boundary. To many, that has seemed to be the only plausible explanation for something that is otherwise incomprehensible. The other main justification has been the belief in the immutability of gender identity after early childhood. Both aetiological stories accept in some way the legitimacy of the transsexual's migration and make a strong case for body substituting to assist it; but not everyone has 'bought' that story and in this section we look at some of the dissenting voices that have been heard coming from a number of different directions over the years.

There are three main dissenting stories which, despite their differences, share a refusal to accept that the transsexual's original gender assignment was in some way wrong and thus are unwilling to countenance any body substituting. For the transsexual, the problem is 'having the wrong body'. For the dissenters whom we consider here, the problem is that the transsexual believes he or she has the wrong body. For the former, the body is in need of correction; for the latter, it is the belief. In one story the dissent is based on a particular psychiatric theory, in another, on religious beliefs and in a third, on a particular feminist philosophy.

In telling stories and seeking to have them accepted, the language used to name and describe is of crucial importance; the label and its connotations shape our attitudes and actions: 'it is the definition of what the object "is" which allows action to occur with reference to what it is taken to be' (Strauss, 1977: 22). So, as Goode points out, 'naming has political implications. By devising a linguistic category with specific connotations, one is designing armaments for a battle; by having it accepted and used one has scored a major victory' (1969: 89). In these dissenting stories, their tellers avoid the language used by those in the previous section: the concept of gender identity is largely absent, as is that of gender dysphoria. 'Sex reassignment' becomes 'mutilation'; 'sex change' becomes a 'pathological fantasy'.

The first dissenting story is one of psychopathology and is based on a particular psychiatric or psychological position usually drawing on some strands of psychoanalysis.[7] Ellis thought that the main opposition to his belief (and that of Hirschfeld) in the constitutional origin of 'eonism' came from the psychoanalysts. He argued that they explained eonism as, 'largely or mainly a disturbance in the psycho-sexual mechanism, due to influences traceable in early life, and involving a persistence into later life of infantile traits', thus, 'the anomaly appears on a normal constitutional basis and is completely explained by psycho-sexual disturbance' (Ellis, 1928: 16).

In addition to challenging Ellis's and Hirschfeld's view that the explanation of transvestism lay in the 'constitutional' realm, some psychoanalysts also challenged their view that it was a phenomenon separate from homosexuality. Stekel, for instance, took issue with Hirschfeld. He wrote, 'I fail to understand the need of setting up beside the hetero and homosexuals, a third group, the so-called transvestites' (1934: 69), and 'it were [sic] nothing less than doing violence to facts to attempt to distinguish the transvestites from the homosexuals' (ibid.: 70–1).

Dissenting voices were heard again when the hormonal and surgical means to facilitate the transsexuals' migration developed around the middle of the twentieth century. Following the report by Hamburger et al. (1953) of the Jorgensen case (1953), there appeared two critical letters in *The Journal of the American Medical Association* (Ostow, 1953; Wiederman, 1953), but otherwise, there is little evidence of any opposition to the use of such procedures. In 1954, the case of Roberta Cowell in the UK was the subject of some debate in the popular press but it received little explicit discussion at that time in the medical press. Later, in the month in which Cowell's story was first reported in the press, however, *The British Medical Journal* (20/3/54) distinguished intersexuals from 'transvestists' and was somewhat less than enthusiastic about the use of surgery in the latter case.

In a later issue of *The British Medical Journal* a letter by the psychiatrist Clifford Allen (1/5/54) took a stronger line. Allen stated that 'transvestism [the term was then commonly used to refer to what would later be called transsexualism] is a psychical disease' and therefore, 'the abnormal minds should be treated in order to conform them with the normal body and not vice versa' (1954: 1040). Allen's view is still shared nearly fifty years later by some. Following a European Court of Human Rights' judgment which ruled in favour of a post-operative transsexual's 'right to marry' in her reassigned sex, eight psychotherapists at the Portman Clinic, London (variously psycho-analysts, psychiatrists and psychoanalytic psychotherapists) felt impelled to write to the UK newspaper *The Daily Telegraph* (15 July 2002) as follows:

The recent judgment in the European Court of Human Rights, in which a post-operative transsexual person was granted permission to marry in his adopted gender role, is a victory of fantasy over reality. The experience of many psychiatrists, psychoanalysts and psychotherapists working with transsexual patients is that they are individuals who, for complex reasons, need to escape from an intolerable psychological reality into a more comfortable fantasy. By attempting to live as a member of the opposite sex, they try to avoid internal conflict, which may otherwise prove to be too distressing. (Dermen et al., 2002)

And more recently, McHugh, a former head of psychiatry at Johns Hopkins Hospital, wrote:

As for the adults who came to us claiming to have discovered their 'true' sexual identity and to have heard about sex-change operations, we psychiatrists have been distracted from studying the causes and natures of their mental misdirections by preparing them for surgery and for a life in the other sex. We have wasted scientific and technical resources and damaged our professional credibility by collaborating with madness rather than trying to study, cure, and ultimately prevent it. (2004)

In these stories, gender and the body are not distinguished or, if they are, then gender is seen to be inextricably linked to, or caused by, biology, hence there can be no 'real' discrepancy. The transsexual's desire to cross over cannot, therefore, be attributed to the presence of an opposite gender identity. This argument is orthodox among those many psychoanalysts, for instance, who consider that 'healthy' development leads towards 'mature' heterosexual relationships that presuppose two members of the 'opposite' sex who each manifest 'healthy' degrees of 'masculinity' and 'femininity', respectively. Socarides, for instance, is a vociferous exponent of this view:

The fact that the transsexual cannot accept his sex as anatomically outlined ... is a sign of the intense emotional and mental disturbance which exists within him. It is the emotional disturbance which must be attacked through suitable means by psychotherapy which provides alleviation of anxiety and psychological retraining rather than amputation or surgery. (1969: 1424)

If this is so, then the gender identity and role that are seen to be at variance with biological sex must be a sham, an imitation of the 'real thing'. Socarides, therefore, writes of 'behavior imitative of that of the opposite sex' (1975: 131) and a 'caricature of femininity' (ibid.: 134). Usually, those who argue in this way employ traditional stereotypes of gender identity and roles. Ostow (1953: 1553) argued that in the case of Christine Jorgensen as described by Hamburger et al. (1953), 'there was no desire for sexual relations with men and no evidence of maternal interest.' Meyer and Hoopes have similarly argued that:

A true feminine identification, for instance, would result in warm and continued relationships with men, a sense of maternity, interest in caring for children, and the capacity to work productively and continuously in female occupations. Most often, if not inevitably, these attributes of a complete personality are absent. The adult 'transsexual' reaches accommodation with a simulated femininity or masculinity at a sacrifice in total personality. (1974: 447)

The second type of dissenting story is told from some religious perspectives. In many ways it is very similar to the psychopathology story, the only difference being the motivation behind it. What follows is a quote from a briefing document published by the Christian Institute:

medical and surgical possibilities now make people believe they can 'change sex' and created the idea of 'transsexuals' or people claiming to be 'trapped in the wrong body' ... The problem, however, is psychological: the evidence supports this view overwhelmingly. The transsexual's body is healthy. Traditionally invasive surgery has only been used to preserve the integrity of a body endangered by disease or injury, not to mutilate a healthy body. A painful operation cannot solve the mental disfunction [sic]. (Christian Institute, 2002)

In consulting widely, concerning its proposals for legal changes with regard to transsexualism, the UK government received a response from the Evangelical Alliance (Evangelical Alliance, 2004). The crucial points of that response are that the Alliance rejects the view that 'transsexualism is a determined condition rather than a matter of choice'. It rejects the view that 'transsexualism, rather than a disorder, is a normal variation of the human condition'. Finally, it rejects the view that 'transsexualism is a condition over which individuals have no power of choice or responsibility'. Arguing that 'it is not possible for a person to change their sex', the document argues that transsexualism has been 'reduced from its generally accepted understanding as a disorder to that of a social identity and lifestyle choice for which cosmetic surgery has become freely available'. It urges more research into the 'causes and treatment of the condition'.

Both the psychiatric/psychoanalytic and the religious variants of the dissenting story also dispute the claim of the traditional migrating story that sex reassignment 'works'. By contrast, it is claimed that sex reassignment fails to solve the transsexual's problems and may even make them worse, as evidenced in statements made to the press by Jon K. Meyer, the psychiatrist: 'these patients have severe psychological problems that don't go away following surgery', and 'surgical intervention has done nothing objective beyond what time and psychotherapy can do' (Meyer, cited in Fleming et al., 1980: 455)

The Daily Telegraph letter cited previously continues:

It is a measure of the urgency and desperation of their situation that they frequently seek surgery to make their fantasy real. By carrying out a 'sex change' operation on their bodies, they hope to eliminate the conflict in their minds. Unfortunately, what many patients find is that they are left with a mutilated body, but the internal conflicts remain. (Dermen et al., 2002)

Not only do the tellers of these dissenting stories advocate cure, but some also claim to be able to provide it. Or at least they claim that they could provide it, were not some of their professional opponents leading patients in the opposite direction. To quote again from *The Daily Telegraph* letter,

Through years of psychoanalytic psychotherapy, some patients begin to understand the origins of their painful conflicting feelings and can find new ways of dealing with them, other than by trying to alter their bodies. The recent legal victory risks reinforcing a false belief that it is possible to actually change a person's gender. It might also strengthen the view that the only solution to psychic pain is a legal or surgical one. (ibid.)

Following the publication of Benjamin's *The Transsexual Phenomenon* in 1966, the sociologist, Sagarin, castigated Benjamin for:

[going] to great lengths to create a favorable social atmosphere for these persons, by depicting them as constitutionally predisposed in their deviant direction, not changeable by psychotherapy, essentially well balanced and certainly non-psychotic individuals, who need only the right to cross-dress or undergo surgery in order to pursue the correct path in life. (1968: 87)

But, he went on, 'one need only read the case histories ... to note how disturbed are the patients' (ibid.: 88). Ten years later Sagarin denounced a situation in which, as he saw it, medicine had invented a disease which is then promoted by the mass media and eagerly grasped by 'impressionable and susceptible' people. He asserts that the diagnosis is eagerly embraced because it legitimizes homosexuality, transvestism and effeminacy (1978: 250).

A third dissenting story emerged from the radical feminism of the 1970s finding its most strident voice in Janice Raymond's *Transsexual Empire* (1980). The influence of Raymond's book may be gauged from Stone (1991: 283) who remarked that: 'here in 1991, on the twelfth anniversary of its publication, it is still the definitive statement on transsexualism by a genetic female academic'. Raymond argued that transsexualism is not an individual condition, a personal problem for which changing sex is merely a neutral, technical method of treatment, but instead is a social and political phenomenon. She argues that, not only does transsexualism reflect the nature of patriarchal society, but it is also ultimately caused by it:

The First Cause, that which sets other causes of transsexualism in motion ... is a patriarchal society, which generates norms of masculinity and femininity. Uniquely restricted by patriarchy's definitions of masculinity and femininity, the transsexual becomes body-bound by them and merely rejects one and gravitates toward the other. (1980: 70)

Raymond draws out the conventional assumptions concerning gender that are woven inextricably into the writings and practices of those psychiatrists, surgeons, psychologists and others who 'treat' transsexuals. She also examines the assumptions implicit in the behaviour and aspirations of transsexuals themselves.

Raymond is explicit concerning measures to deal with transsexualism. Apart from measures directed at the 'first cause' itself, she advocates restrictions on 'sex change' surgery, the presentation of other, less favourable, views of its consequences in the media, and non-sexist counselling and consciousness-raising groups for transsexuals themselves to enable them to realize their radical potential (Raymond, 1980, Appendix).

Raymond was not alone in arguing for such views. Eichler takes a similar position believing that 'individual transsexuals are casualties of an overly rigid sex role differentiation' (1980: 82). She writes:

some children who had yearnings to behave in a sex inappropriate manner may have simply found it impossible to overcome the feeling of inappropriateness and may have thereby been pushed to imagine themselves as members of the other sex who happen to be endowed with the wrong body ... What should be treated as a social pathology is treated as if it were normal and when it manifests its effect in individuals, it is treated as an individual pathology and is corrected, rather than any attempts made to combat the issue at its root: the oppressive (non-human) definition of sex roles. (ibid.: 79)

Also, like Raymond, Eichler notes that 'clinicians involved with transsexuals – at least those who perform sex reassignment surgery – must not only accept the present sex structure, but must passionately believe in its essential rightness' (ibid.: 80).

Within this view, transsexualism is not only caused by and a reflection of patriarchy, but it also supports patriarchy by maintaining notions of 'appropriate' gender roles, by deflecting attention away from the real cause, and by defusing the potential threat which transsexuals represent:

This group of people would – potentially – be the most potent group of people pressing for changes in the sex structure because their aversion to their 'sex appropriate' roles is apparently insurmountable. By declaring them, by surgical fiat as members of the other sex, this change potential is diverted and becomes as conservative as it could have been revolutionary. (ibid.: 88)

Transsexualism for Eichler, then, is a consequence of a 'pathological' society. Sex transformation is not a tenable possibility and, given the transformation of society, it will cease to exist. Eichler proposes no measures against transsexualism other than to suggest this possibility, although, like Raymond, she too argues that as well as reflecting patriarchal attitudes, the present approach to transsexualism also supports them. Thus, 'Patient and doctor jointly reinforce the idea that behaviour and character traits are legitimately determined by one's body' (ibid.: 87).

Commonly, the tellers of these dissenting stories also seek to undermine the truth claims of the Benjamin story by disputing the view that 'transsexualism' has always existed but has only recently been discovered. The medical conception of transsexualism is, it claims, an illusion, a fabrication whose explanation must therefore be sought in terms other than the putative 'thing' itself. Once conjured up, legitimated and disseminated, this illusion has real social consequences through the actions of members of the medical profession, 'transsexuals' themselves and other members of society, all of whom have been seduced into believing in it.

Thus, Raymond (1980) argues that by creating transsexualism and treating it by means of sex change, the political and social sources of the transsexuals' suffering are obscured. Instead it is conceptualized as an individual problem for which an individual solution is devised. By means of this illegitimate medicalization, then, the 'real' problem remains unaddressed. Medicalization also serves to 'domesticate the revolutionary potential of transsexuals', who are 'deprived of an alternative framework in which to view the problem' (ibid.: 124).

Raymond also sees other reasons for the creation of transsexualism and sex change surgery. She places these alongside 'other male interventionist technologies such as cloning, test-tube fertilisation, and sex selection', as an 'attempt to wrest from women, the power inherent in female biology (ibid.: xvi) or an attempt to replace biological women (ibid.: 140). She also sees 'gender identity clinics' where transsexuals are 'treated' as prototypical 'sex-role control centers' (ibid.: 136). Thus, transsexualism is not merely another example of the pervasive effects of patriarchal attitudes; it actually constitutes an attack on women: 'Transsexualism constitutes a sociopolitical program that is undercutting the movement to eradicate sex role stereotyping and oppression in this culture' (ibid.: 5).

All three dissenting stories have undoubtedly had some influence in some quarters. McHugh states:

> Until 1975, when I became psychiatrist-in-chief at Johns Hopkins Hospital, I could usually keep my own counsel on these matters. But once I was given authority over all the practices in the psychiatry department I realized that if I were passive I would be tacitly co-opted in encouraging sex-change surgery in the very department that had originally proposed and still defended it. I decided to challenge what I considered to be a misdirection of psychiatry and to demand more information both before and after their operations. (2004)

The eventual outcome of this, he says, was that it 'led us to stop prescribing sex-change operations for adults at Hopkins'.

Janice Raymond's book, or at any rate similar views to those contained therein, was for a while influential within some parts of the feminist community. In 1994, Carol Riddell wrote to us:

> a small but very active section of the feminist movement, the 'Revolutionary Feminists', were taking over some positions in the radical subcultures of extreme feminism. They owed a little intellectually to Mary Daly and her ex-student Janice Raymond, from whose doctoral thesis The Transsexual Empire was written. There were reports of threats to transsexuals in London, and I myself was threatened with violence when I attended a Bisexuality conference there.

The radical feminist story resulted in the exclusion of MTF transsexuals from some feminist spaces, most famously the Michigan Womyn's Music Festival in the United States. Califia (1997) argues that the transsexual response to this exclusion was one of the events which led to the more radical transgender politics of the 1990s which we discuss in Chapter 5.

These three dissenting stories – the psychopathology story, the religious story and the radical feminist story – alongside the traditional migrating story – have largely been told to different audiences. Since the late 1960s, the medical doctors who have facilitated body substituting have not, on the whole, had to contend with the psychopathology or the religious stories. The only serious exchange of hostilities within the medical world since the late 1960s occurred in the wake of the cessation of the sex change programme at Johns Hopkins Hospital mentioned before. However, that exchange did little to harm the traditional story in the long term. And it is doubtful if any medical members of Raymond's 'transsexual empire' lost any sleep over her claims.

However, as the earlier quote from Carol Riddell makes clear, transsexuals themselves have felt the impact of some of these dissenting stories in their everyday lives. Riddell ([1980] 1996), and later Stone (1991) and Wilchins (1997), as transgender activists, have all produced devastating critiques of Raymond's work. However, we suspect that for most non-activist transsexuals, the psychopathology and religious dissenting stories have had the most direct impact on their lives.

The gender migrating story

Benjamin's frequent emphasis on the 'normality' of his transsexual patients and their emergence as unremarkable members of their reassigned sex, typically heterosexual and conventional, led inevitably to a privileging of a certain sort of transsexual experience and outcome at the expense of others. In particular, his story was one in which transsexuals changed their bodies to accord with their mind. They gender migrated to accord with their bodies, and their sexuality was defined as heterosexual from the standpoint of their migration.

At certain points in the emergence of transgendering stories, however, members were not content either to accept medical definitions or to work symbiotically with 'experts'. The major 'member' migrating story to emerge – and the one that was developed in deliberate opposition to the medical story (an oppositional story) – was Prince's development of a 'transgenderist' position.

As we have seen, the traditional 'expert' medical migrating story came to be fashioned around the privileging of the body (sex). Sexuality was downplayed, and gender was viewed unproblematically. Very different are the migrating stories of those who place the primacy on gender, underplaying the erotic component to the point of extinction and only secondarily engaging in body migrating. The main proponent of the alternative gender migrating story is Virginia Prince. In a series of publications extending over some 40 years (e.g., Prince, 1967; 1979a; 1979b; 1997a; 1997b) she has argued for a position that she came to term 'transgenderist' (Prince, 1979a: 172). The 'transgenderist' male wishes to express the feminine side of his personality. To do so, maximally, he lives full time in the social role of a woman and dresses and comports himself, appropriately. Cross-dressing is not an erotic experience. Any body femaling he engages in is done in the service of gender femaling. Unsightly body hair may be removed; the ingestion of hormones may lead to body feminization; but there is no sex-reassignment surgery – that would be an irrelevancy. Becoming the 'other' gender on a permanent basis, and presenting as a woman socially (gender migrating) is the goal.

Prince was born male on 23 November 1912 in Los Angeles. She began cross-dressing at about the age of 12, at first using her mother's clothes. She writes that by the time she was in high school, she 'had progressed to the point of being a girl in public and passing as such' (1997a: 348). There is a familiar story of the pleasures and attractions of cross-dressing together with feelings of guilt and wondering what was wrong with her; of pursuing it as far as possible, and of giving up altogether (Prince, 1979a: 170). She visited six different psychiatrists 'seeking some answers without success' (Prince, 1967: 5).

In the mid-1940s, Prince worked as a research assistant and lecturer in pharmacology, and used the opportunity of access to the university medical library to become acquainted with the (then) small medical literature on transvestism. She also attended some psychiatric case conferences where she first knowingly saw another transvestite. Later, making contact with one of the people whose case had been presented, she took on the name of Charles Prince to hide her real identity. It was here that she also encountered Karl Bowman, a psychiatrist, who, as she puts it, 'gave me my first start toward self acceptance and understanding' (Prince, 1967: 5). Bowman was a psychiatrist, one-time president of the American Psychiatric Association, and Director of the Langley Porter Psychiatric Clinic and the California Sex Deviate Research Project (Freedman, 1987). On one occasion, Bowman said to Prince: 'Stop fighting it, it isn't so terrible. There are thousands of others like you and always have been. Medical science hasn't been able to do much for them, so the best thing to do is to relax and learn to accept yourself' (Prince, 1967: 5–6).

Prince took Bowman's advice and during the 1950s her 'feminine self' began to develop. As she put it: 'as time went on and I had more and more opportunities to dress, to go out, to learn more about fashion, grooming and feminine behaviour, I found that my feminine self was beginning to become a real personality in her own right' (Prince, 1969b: 444).

Prince's second marriage ended in divorce in 1968 after which, as she wrote in 1979: 'I was then free to live my life as I wanted having no domestic or business responsibilities. I therefore crossed the line completely and have lived as a woman full time ever since' (Prince, 1979a: 172).

Prince's gender substitution was accompanied by some body substitution, as she explains: 'I have had my beard removed by electrolysis and ... as a result of a course of hormone therapy I now possess a nice pair of 38B breasts' (Prince, 1979a: 172). Prince says she 'coined the words "transgenderism" and "transgenderist" as nouns describing people like myself who have breasts and live full time as a woman, but who have no intention of having genital surgery' (Prince, 1997b: 469). As far as we know, there has been no sexuality substitution.

For many years, Prince emphasized the distinction between male heterosexual transvestism (or femmiphile [FP] – 'lover of the feminine' – to use her preferred term), transsexuality and homosexuality. Living as a woman on a full-time basis she says, 'I am therefore to be classified as a "transgenderist" now and no longer as an FP' (Prince, 1979a: 172).

For Prince (ibid.: 173) a 'transgenderist' is:

one who has crossed the gender boundary on a full-time basis. That is, he dresses and lives as a woman twenty-four hours a day and works, travels and housekeeps like any other woman and is in fact a 'she'. She is not desirous of going through a sex change. She is content to be a male woman.

Precisely when Prince adopted the name of Virginia is not clear, but the earliest publication of Prince's that we have been able to find was published in 1957 and was credited to C.V. Prince. The article 'Homosexuality, Transvestism and Transsexualism: Reflections on their Etiology and Difference' was introduced by Harry Benjamin who wrote: 'Dr Prince is known to me personally. I have met him in his male as well as his female role. I have had lengthy and stimulating discussions with him. He is highly educated with a fine cultural background' (Benjamin, Preamble to Prince, 1957: 80).

Benjamin also described Prince as a 'lay student of psychology', adding that 'he' (sic) 'has studied his own case and many others of the same type'. How Prince met Benjamin is unclear but Benjamin had a summer practice in San Francisco (Person, 1999: 359) and, in *The Transvestite and His Wife* (Prince, 1967: 6), Prince acknowledges the help Benjamin was to her 'personally in my parental and marital problems', so presumably their first encounters were of a professional nature.

The distinction of three types of males who may share (in a beautifully out-dated phrase) 'the desire to wear feminine attire' (Prince, 1957: 82) is the main point of this first article. Pointing out that Havelock Ellis and Magnus Hirschfeld had distinguished transvestism from homosexuality almost 50 years earlier, she argued that there was still a tendency to confuse the two. The picture, she said, was further complicated by the 'discovery' of transsexualism and the possibility of sex reassignment surgery.

Prince went on to clearly distinguish the homosexual and the transsexual from what she calls the 'true transvestite' (ibid.: 84). She does this by distinguishing 'three different aspects of womanhood, the sexual, the psycho-emotional and the social' (ibid.: 85) and then argues that the homosexual, the transsexual and the transvestite are respectively identifying with these three different aspects.

In that early 1957 article, Prince makes no reference to the idea that transvestites may be sexually aroused by wearing women's clothes although this was an idea that she opposed in the transvestite story that she developed and which we discuss in the next chapter. Here, Prince was at odds with Benjamin, who wrote of Prince's views; 'to take sex out of transvestism is like taking music out of opera. It simply cannot be done' (1966: 37).

She admits to being attracted by the idea of sex reassignment for herself at the time of the publicity given to the case of Christine Jorgensen (Prince, 1978b: 271), but the development of her philosophy that the issues were to do with gender (psycho-social) and not sex (the body) led her to the view that it was 'perfectly possible to ... *be* a woman without having sex surgery' (ibid.: 268). As she said, 'I, at least, know the difference between sex and gender and have simply elected to change the latter and not the former. If a word is necessary, I should be termed a "transgenderal"' (1969a: 65).

Despite Prince's use of the term 'transgenderal' in 1969, she does not seem to have used any lexical compound of the 'trans- + gend-' type again in print until 1978. Interestingly, in 1977, in an important piece 'Woman by Choice or Woman by Default?' published in *Transvestia*, Prince is making similar points about the distinction between transsexuals, transgenderists and transvestites without using the term transgenderist at all. She writes of 'three classes': class one – the 'regular transvestite or femmiphile'; class two – those males who live as women openly and in society; and class three – those who undergo or who 'seriously plan' sex change surgery. There is no talk of 'transgenderal' or 'transgenderist'. Prince (1977: 82) comments:

> People in class two know the difference (between sexual and genderal identity) and consciously elect to change their gender identity without surgery ... Since class two people recognize the difference between sex and gender we can make a conscious decision to become a woman – a psycho-social gender creature.

When 'transgender*al*' became 'transgender*ist*' is not entirely clear. The earliest published use of the latter that we are aware of is in Prince (1978a). However, in an interview (with RE in Nashville, 2002), Prince recalled first publicly using the term 'transgenderist' at a conference as early as 1974 or 1975.

However, Prince not only described her own solution, she spoke out forcefully against sex reassignment surgery, again at odds with Benjamin, arguing that it is not appropriate for about 90 per cent of those requesting it, writing of 'so-called' or 'pseudo' transsexuals. 'Sex reassignment surgery is a communicable disease', she asserted (Prince, 1978b: 271), arguing that susceptible transvestites are seduced – by the publicity given to the topic – into thinking it is the solution to their problems.

When Fisk coined the term 'gender dysphoria syndrome' (Fisk, 1973), Prince argued that a distinction should be made between 'sexual dysphoria' and 'gender dysphoria'. In 'Sex vs. Gender', Prince writes:

> I was pleased to have Dr. Fisk use the term 'gender dysphoria syndrome,' but if it is truly a matter of gender dysphoria, why do you not offer a gender solution instead of a sexual one? What you really have is a 'sexual dysphoria syndrome.' We have sexual identity clinics in which people are examined, selected, screened, and finally have surgery performed on them which changes their sexual identity ... It seems a very sad thing to me that great many individuals have to go to the expense, pain, danger, and everything else when they could achieve a gender change without any of it. (1973: 28)

So Prince's transgenderist accepts the fact that people must be either male or female. Her transgenderist remains male. She also argues that they must be either masculine or feminine. The 'trans' in her transgenderist entails both change as transition and change as crossing in regards to gender only. Clearly, this position can only be maintained coherently by the strategy of separating sex and gender entirely and this is precisely what Prince does in constructing her category of transgenderist. Specifically, she renders the 'natural attitude' position problematic in a number of regards while accepting it in others. She constructs the idea of a 'male woman' as a person whose sex is one side of the binary divide and whose gender is the other side and whose sexuality *vis-à-vis* sex is heterosexual.

Prince's formulation pioneered the resistance of transgendered people to medical categories of knowledge. In particular, as we have seen, she was determined to distinguish her transgenderist from the transsexual and the transvestite. She took issue with many who considered themselves transsexual. She considered that the vast majority of 'transsexuals', through a confusion of sex with gender, embarked on an unnecessary and painful journey to 'sex re-assignment'. She took issue with medical formulations of the transvestite that emphasized the erotic motivation of cross-dressing. While recognizing an erotic component in cross-dressing at an early age, she argued that as 'the woman within' emerges, sexual aspects become less and less significant. In recognition of this fact, her preferred term for 'transvestite' became 'femmiphile': the lover of the feminine. She remarks how this point struck her when she was window-shopping one day outside a ladies' clothes shop. In the past, the clothes would have sexually aroused her. Now she felt she was looking at the clothes in exactly the same way as a woman might look at them (Prince, 1979b: 7–8).

It is notable that in her enthusiasm to privilege gender over sex and sexuality, little is said about the transgenderist's sex and sexuality. Others who have adopted a similar transgenderist position to that of Prince have been more forthcoming as regards sex. Particularly interesting in this regard is the position of a group of transgenderists who promulgated their position in the mid to late 1980s in South Africa. In a leaflet entitled 'What is Transgenderism?' by Joy and Marlene (nd), the authors adopt the same sharp division between sex and gender before going on to argue that the transgenderist 'generally speaking' seeks hormone therapy, beard removal, breast implants, removal of the testes, and job opportunities. For these writers, the transgenderist is a 'she-male'. Like Prince, they emphasize that the transgenderist remains heterosexual throughout the transition and the gender crossing, 'although some transgenderists will call themselves MALE LESBIANS' (nd: 12). Again, like Prince, Joy and Marlene are critical of the fact that the medical profession generally does not recognize them. Like Prince, they argue for a very stereotyped version of what is acceptable masculine and feminine behaviour and for the rigidity of the binary regard in these matters. Finally, like Prince, they consider many transsexuals to have taken the wrong route because they do not understand the distinction between sex and gender.

The erotic migrating story

Both the medical story and the alternative 'gender-led' Prince story are united in giving the erotic a minor role to play in the proceedings. In recent years, however, a number of self-identified transsexual migrants have claimed an erotic motivation and we explore their stories in this section. In a sense, these are also dissenting stories, but we consider them separately here because, although they dissent from the dominant migrating story in a number of ways, they do not reject the ideas of migrating or body substituting completely as did the dissenting stories that we considered earlier.

These erotic migrating stories have recently caused something of a stir in the transgender community but before we discuss that we must go back to the 1960s again. As we saw earlier, the publicity given to the use of 'sex change' procedures attracted large numbers of people who were eager to migrate. Some clinicians began to use the term 'true transsexuals'. As Meyer III et al. explain, this referred to:

> a person with a characteristic path of atypical gender identity development that predicted an improved life from a treatment sequence that culminated in genital surgery. True transsexuals were thought to have: 1) cross-gender identifications that were consistently expressed behaviorally in

childhood, adolescence, and adulthood; 2) minimal or no sexual arousal to cross-dressing; and 3) no heterosexual interest, relative to their anatomic sex. (2001)

True (sometimes 'primary' – Person and Oversey, 1974a; 1974b) transsexuals were contrasted with 'males who arrived at the desire to change sex and gender via a reasonably masculine behavioral developmental pathway' (Meyer III et al., 2001).

Of course, the opposite of 'true' being 'false', the implication was that only 'true' transsexuals are then deemed suitable candidates for surgery. The opinions of Stoller (1968; 1975) are perhaps the most well known of those writers who advocated this position:

> I think that only those males who are the most feminine, have been expressing this femininity since earliest childhood, have not had periods of living accepted as masculine males, have not enjoyed their penises and have not advertised themselves as males (for example female impersonation) should be operated on. (1968: 251)

However, according to Meyer III et al.: 'Belief in the true transsexual concept for males dissipated when it was realized that such patients were rarely encountered, and that some of the original true transsexuals had falsified their histories to make their stories match the earliest theories about the disorder' (2001).

Instead of attempting to diagnose the true transsexual on the basis of their case histories, the predominant approach to the question of whether or not to accede to the request for body substituting became a pragmatic one. Was a permanent change of gender and sex, as suggested by the patient's ability to pass successfully as a member of the desired gender/sex status for an extended period of time, a practicable one (Money and Walker, 1977; Randell, 1971)? The process now referred to as the 'real-life experience' was born.

In 1973, the term 'gender dysphoria' appeared in the literature (Laub and Gandy, 1973). 'Gender dysphoria' was introduced, according to its originator, Fisk (1973), to reflect the fact that applications for sex reassignment came from a variety of persons, by no means all of whom fitted the classic picture of the transsexual. What they all shared was the fact that they were 'intensely and abidingly uncomfortable in their anatomic and genetic sex and their assigned gender' (ibid.: 10).

So this new term named a 'disease', as Fisk termed it, rather than a type of person. The term legitimated the pragmatic approach to transgender migration which many had adopted. Sex reassignment could be considered as a treatment for 'gender dysphoria' without worrying about a more specific diagnosis. And it fitted in well alongside the gender terminology which by then had become commonplace.

'Gender dysphoria' did not, however, provide an identity, and the term 'transsexual' continued to be used by the groups that sprang up in the 1970s and 1980s to support transsexuals and to campaign on their behalf. The mass media also continued to use the term 'transsexual'. As the migrating story was told to the media, to health care providers, to politicians and others, the dominant story took shape. The diversity that the term 'gender dysphoria' sought to cover, however, was not apparent in a story that emphasized the need for medical treatment and legal recognition of a group of people with a particular medical condition.

Harking back to the diversity noted by Fisk in 1973, two recent alternative stories have sought to be heard and have been seen to pose something of a threat to the dominant story by stressing the erotic motivation for body substitution. These are stories about male transsexuals – female transsexuals are conspicuous by their absence. Again, in these stories, we see the interplay between expert and member stories and the struggles between different story tellers eager to claim the right to be heard and, indeed, to be believed. The first of these recent stories is that of the autogynephilic transsexual.

The term 'autogynephilia' ('love of oneself as a woman') was introduced into the transgendering literature by the clinical psychologist, Blanchard (1989a). Blanchard (1989b: 616) defines autogynephilia as 'a male's propensity to be sexually aroused by the thought of himself as a female'. The concept came to have a great importance to Blanchard in his attempts to refine diagnostic categories of 'gender disorder' and implement management strategies for his adult male gender patients (e.g., Blanchard, 1989a; 1989b; 1991; 1993a; 1993b, 2005).

Blanchard argued that bisexual, asexual, and heterosexual transsexuals were similar to each other, and dissimilar to homosexual transsexuals, with regard to, *inter alia*, degree of recalled childhood femininity, extent of interpersonal heterosexual experience, a history of transvestic fetishism, and a history of erotic arousal in association with the thought of being a woman. This led him to the view that there are only two fundamentally different types of transsexualism in males: homosexual and non-homosexual, and, moreover, that the common characteristic shared by members of the non-homosexual category is their tendency to be sexually aroused by the thought or image of themselves as women (Blanchard, 2000).

Blanchard's voice emphasizing the erotic component of migrating was a lone one and, for many years, his work was largely ignored, outside of his immediate coterie. This was to change with the popularization of his work by Anne Lawrence. Lawrence identifies as a post-operative transsexual woman and for some years has been popularizing Blanchard's concept (Lawrence, 1998; 1999a, 1999b; 1999c; 1999d; 1999e; 2000, 2004). She wrote that 'when I

Figure 2.2   Anne Lawrence and Ray Blanchard, at the 31st Annual Meeting of
the International Academy of Sex Research, Ottawa, 2005 (Reproduced with the
kind permission of Anne Lawrence)

first read it [Blanchard's work] in 1994, I experienced a kind of epiphany' and
went on to say 'I think this is one of the most brilliant and insightful analyses
in the entire clinical literature devoted to transsexuality. Certainly it spoke to
my own experience like nothing I had ever encountered before' (Lawrence,
1999a). Lawrence identifies fully with Blanchard's concept, describes herself
as an 'autogynephilic transsexual', conceptualizes autogynephilic feelings as
one of her principal motivations for seeking re-assignment surgery and maintains her autogynephilic identity post-operatively. Her account of how, after
periods of personal confusion, she 'found herself' with reference to
Blanchard's concept, echoes the many other stories we have heard of transgendered people 'finding themselves' when first becoming acquainted with
and adopting the terms 'transvestite' or 'transsexual'.

Had Lawrence been content to keep her story to herself, events would not
have taken the turn they have in the past few years. In the main, it is uncon-
troversial to consider 'transvestism' in terms of its erotic (autogynephilic)
components, but to do likewise with 'transsexualism' is controversial. So
when Lawrence began to tell her own story, and to solicit similar stories from
others who identify with Blanchard's concept, she created something of a
storm within sections of the transgender community. She wrote that she was
surprised to find that people thought that Blanchard's idea, 'was not so much
wrong, as heretical. The intensity of their reactions was astonishing. It was
as though thinking about transsexualism as a sexual problem involved such
a paradigm shift that it frightened people' (Lawrence, 1999a). Her critics have

been vocal and often personal, leaving her 'feeling defensive, perplexed, and deeply troubled' as she puts it (Lawrence, 2000). The storm has intensified recently with the publication of Bailey's popular account of Blanchard's work (Bailey, 2003) and a concerted campaign has been fought in an attempt to discredit this book alongside the work of Blanchard and Lawrence (see Conway, 2004; James, 2004).

The other story to emerge from Blanchard's research was that of the homosexual transsexual. This story is also an erotic story. Homosexual transsexuals are sexually attracted to men and typically have a history of femininity and cross-dressing from an early age. They have not been sexually aroused by their cross-dressing. They have usually been part of the gay subculture, often working (according to Blanchard) in stereotypical 'gay' occupations such as hairdressing or as female impersonators. They typically present for sex reassignment at an earlier age than the autogynephilic transsexuals. Such a pattern can be seen in the biographies of Ashley (Fallowell and Ashley, 1982), Brevard (2001) and Tula (1982).

Recently, there has appeared a website apparently produced by a small group of people who identify with Blanchard's concept of the homosexual transsexual. The website is called 'transkids (http://www.transkids.us/index.html), the title reflecting Blanchard's emphasis on childhood femininity:

> We want to offer an alternative to all of the agp [sic] [autogynephile] run websites on transsexuality and present our own perspective as hsts [homosexual transsexuals] which have been entirely absent from the recent debate ... Part of the problem with the AGP community's position is that it excludes us much in the same way that they were initially excluded, and it takes our experience and appropriates it into their community for their own purposes at our expense. This takes advantage of us while at the same time erasing our voices. (Transkids, 2004)

Nevertheless, the site's authors state that: 'We are not seeking to establish a social identity as "homosexual transsexuals 'identity'", we want to integrate into society as individuals in as normal a way as possible' (Transkids, 2004).

The website's authors are also keen to distance themselves from the autogynephilic transsexuals arguing that not all transsexuals are the same. Androphilic transsexuals have always behaved in a feminine way, are feminine in appearance and are sexually attracted to men. Autogynephilic transsexuals are masculine in behaviour and appearance and are attracted to women. According to 'Alex Parkinson' writing on the site, homosexual transsexuals do not transition because they have a 'female gender identity', they transition, 'because they are in fact, very female-like individuals in affect, appearance and behavior from an outsider's perspective and therefore find they have a great deal of outside incentive for becoming female and very little for remaining male'.

In the FAQ section of the website, the distinct nature of the two types of transsexual is again stressed:

These are etiologically unrelated, distinct conditions with entirely different and mutually exclusive symptomatological patterns. The only commonality between the two conditions that lead to gender dysphoria is that they both benefit from the same course of treatment, but like any other medical procedure that can be used to treat more then one condition, the fact that both groups benefit from sex reassignment does not imply that they are the same or even related disorders.

Homosexual Transsexuals (HSTS) are transsexuals who transition young principally for social reasons. As boys they are very feminine and have a difficult time socially, romantically, and sexually, so they transition to fit in better and have more normal lives in those three areas. They are etiologically similar to homosexual boys with commonalities in childhood and adolescence. HSTS sexuality is uncomplicated, typical, and unconfused, they are simply attracted to and desire relationships with men. They tend to view transition as a way to facilitate other life goals such as being regarded as normal by peers, having an easier time getting relationships with boys, etc.

Autogynephilic transsexuals (AGPs) on the other hand, transition to satisfy an intense internal urge to be the opposite gender. This urge is sometimes described as a paraphilia, a fetish, or an inverted heterosexual drive where they, attracted to women, want to become the objects of their desire ... Behaviorally as men, they tend to be averagely masculine, straight acting heterosexuals ... Unlike hsts who are never very successful socially as males, agps often marry as men, have biological children with their wives, and lead successful lives as men before they transition. Physically they are averagely male in appearance until transition, and rarely pass in a truly convincing way as women. (FAQ section)

There is another story within this story. This is a story about why the homosexual transsexual story has been a hidden one.

The 'Transkids' position argues that as the medical profession in the 1950s and 1960s saw sexual arousal to cross-dressing as an indication that surgery was not a suitable method of treatment, autogynephilic transsexuals lied about this aspect of their condition. Over time, the concept of gender identity was developed and eagerly grasped by the autogynephilic transsexuals as it legitimated their wish for surgery. The writers of the 'Transkids' site clearly do not see themselves as part of the 'transgender' community which they see as dominated by autogynephilic transsexuals to whom they (homosexual transsexuals) pose a threat:

Since their political and social identity is built around the notion that they were always really 'female' because they 'feel like women on the inside', that hsts who present far more cross gender attributes pre-transition, and are more convincing as women post-transition, do not share their unique psychology, would undermine the credibility of the way they think about their own disorder. (http://www.transkids.us/index.html)

The reaction to this website, as to Bailey (2003) and Anne Lawrence's work, has been a strong one. Some of the reaction can be seen at the website run by (http://www.calpernia.com/ubbthreads/showflat.php/Cat/0/Number/99671/page/0/fpart/1/vc/1). Many of the responses here are claiming that 'Transkids' website is bogus. Others claim that the website is an 'anti' trans people site, perhaps with links to groups on the 'religious right'.

There is much at stake in these story battles that are being fought. Although Bailey, Blanchard and Lawrence do not say that autogynephilic transsexuals should not undergo surgical and hormonal substitutions, their espousal of the 'theory' of autogynephilia is seen to undermine the 'gender identity' story which has brought about a modicum of respectability for sex changes. It is easy to see how the Blanchard story could be used to their advantage by those who would end completely, or greatly limit, gender migration.

There is no doubt that many of the critics of Blanchard's story attribute to Blanchard an explanatory intent greater than he claims for his 'theory' (Ray Blanchard, personal communication, 2000). In the main, Blanchard's less disciplined critics tend to conflate a number of rather different criticisms. These are the pathologizing and heteronormative trends in clinical psychology; the explanatory trends in Blanchard's work; the political (and, in some instances, personal) unacceptability of his 'findings'; and the 'lumping', indeed, reductionist, trends, in his work on autogynephilia. Bailey (2003: 162) places Blanchard's work within the diagnostic tradition of 'lumping', which occurs 'when two or more apparently different conditions are found to be different forms of the same, underlying pathology'. Many trans people who are critical of the work of Blanchard, Lawrence and Bailey take particular exception to this 'lumping' (interview material). They find it objectionable on personal, political and 'scientific' grounds to reduce MTF 'transsexuals' to two categories: homosexual and autogynephilic.

Our data over the years have always indicated the tendency to underplay the significance of the erotic in migrating (Ekins, 1993; 1997). As sociologists concerned to pay the proper respect to transgender diversity, we do think it an important area of enquiry to investigate the role of the erotic in migrating, and, indeed, in all modes of transgendering. In the spirit of this enquiry, after following the furore over Anne Lawrence's popularizing of Blanchard's theories, we returned to a number of our informants in order to address more closely the role of the erotic in their transgendering trajectories. In the final section of this chapter we will consider our work with three such informants: Rachael, Gail and Janice.

Male-to-female migrating and 'love of oneself as a woman'

Rachael, Gail and Janice all identify as 'transsexuals'. All three are postoperative and 'pass' in most settings as 'genetic women'. All three came to identify as transsexual and began their 'migrating' in their late thirties to early forties. However, each informant provides very different 'vocabularies of motive' (Mills, 1940; see also Ekins, 1983) for their migrating. 'Rachael' places the emphasis upon her envy of female bodies and a distaste and revulsion of her male body – her migrating might be seen as, principally, 'body-led'. 'Gail' reports an autogynephilic phase on the way to re-assignment. In different phases of her migrating trajectory the autogynephilic component varied. 'Janice' also describes her transition as being 'body-led', but she specifically identifies as autogynephilic, both pre- and post-operatively. We will outline their respective migrating trajectories with particular reference to the role of autogynephilia.

For some time, we had been carrying out life-history work with Rachael (15 years) and with Gail (6 years). Throughout this work, Rachael never spoke of being sexually aroused by the thought of herself as female, a girl or as a woman. Gail spoke of her 'erotic femaling' as being limited to a particular phase of her male femaling trajectory (Ekins, 1997: 146-54). Rachael and Gail were selected to provide examples of very different life-history material relating to the autogynephilic, in order to compare their trajectories with the self-identified 'autogynephilic transsexual', Janice. At the time of writing Janice had been an informant for some 18 months; we were introduced to her after we began to consider Blanchard's concept seriously. We then re-interviewed Rachael and Gail, after introducing them to Blanchard's concept. A series of open-ended questions were designed to elicit responses from them about their 'autogynephilic' responses over the course of their transgendering trajectories.

Rachael

Rachael's earliest recollections of what she now refers to as 'transsexual' feelings occurred when she was 6 or 7 years old. She was playing with a girl playmate, who lived next door to her and she remembers feeling she wanted her body to be like her playmate's. The playmate's clothes were of no particular interest to Rachael: both the children played in similar clothes – sandals and shorts. Rachael has no recollection of any erotic element to the wish. She simply wanted her playmate's body, instead of her own. Her first sexual encounter was when she was the victim of homosexual abuse when 9 years old. This left her confused and frightened. During adolescence she had a number of homosexual encounters, all of which she found unsatisfactory because, as she put it: 'I wanted to be making love to a man, but I wanted to be a woman making love to a man.' During this period, she had 'indecisive sorts of relationships' with a couple of older women. At no time during this period does she recall being sexually aroused by the thought or image of herself as a female. Rather, desperately wanting the physical body of a woman and being unable to face up to doing anything about it, she took flight into large quantities of drugs. At 19 years old, she married her first wife intending to embark on a heterosexual relationship as a man. Sexual relations were only possible when Rachael fantasized that she had her wife's body. The marriage fell apart when Rachael was 30 and she consulted a psychiatrist about her 'transsexual' feelings. She felt unable to proceed with re-assignment procedure although, for a while, did take oestrogen. Later, she married, again, with similar feelings and consequences to her first marriage. On occasions, Rachael would masturbate, but says she did not think about herself as a woman when she masturbated. Rather, as she puts it: 'I thought of a man making love to me as a woman.' She felt that to be 'transsexual', her psychiatrists expected her to naturally take the woman's role, to wear make-up, and so on. Because she felt no pressing need to do these things, she doubted her commitment to re-assignment; indeed, could not accept that she was transsexual. Rachael was a lorry driver by profession. Her 'Road to Damascus' experience came when she was sitting in her lorry as a man, and had the flash of insight that this is what she wanted – to be a woman doing this; to be a woman lorry driver. Henceforth, she pursued re-assignment surgery. Throughout, her priority was to 'remove any and every physical manifestation of maleness within my body'. Post-operatively, Rachael came to have sexual relations with men, feeling that she thinks, 'like any other woman ... I talk things over with women friends. There are difficulties having a relationship with a man ... but it just seems the right thing to do'.

Gail

Gail's first recollections relating to her later 'transsexual' identity are clearly autogynephilic. They began when she started masturbating in her early teens. She used to cut pictures of girls she found attractive out of magazines and 'masturbate to them', imagining that she was the girl in the picture. In particular, 'hair' was the big turn on at the start: 'long, wavy, shiny and very feminine hair gained my attention. The face and body next.' She was shy with girls but did have one steady girlfriend she was dating at the time of her 17th birthday: 'I certainly didn't have intercourse or anything like that. I was still relatively shy.' She continues: 'And then, on my 17th birthday, completely out of the blue ... I went downstairs ... and to this day, I'll never know why, I put on some of my mother's mascara and eye-shadow and lipstick.' There followed an episodic pattern of making-up and curling her hair and dressing in her mother's clothes. She was, she speculates 'becoming the woman that I used to masturbate to in the pictures'. Over the years, however, the sexual kick of her cross-dressing reduced and gave way to a feeling of inner peace and tranquillity. Meanwhile, the total confusion of not knowing who or what she was, in doing these 'strange' things, led her to the library and the discovery of 'transvestites' and 'transsexuals'. In due time she approached the Beaumont Society, met self-identified 'transvestites' and 'transsexuals', began to identify with the latter, and approached a psychiatrist about the possibility of her being transsexual. The psychiatrist put her on a course of oestrogen, the premise being, Gail reports, that when her sexual desire dropped – which it did fairly quickly – if she was getting a sexual kick from cross-dressing and wasn't transsexual, she would be horrified at the loss of her masculinity. In the event, she soon became unable to sustain an erection, went on to anti-androgen hormones, started electrolysis, and from this time onwards 'knew that [she] was transsexual'. A divorce followed. While preoperative, she had her first sexual relationship with a man. It was a revelation to her. For the first time she realized that this was where her sexual orientation was. She felt 'totally happy as a woman, with a man'. She enjoyed fellatio, whereas cunnilingus had disgusted her. Once post-operative, she soon met her present male partner, with whom she has been living for a number of years. She does not report autogynephilic arousal, rather the sexual pleasure of giving and receiving in a heterosexual sexual relationship.

Janice

Janice was 6 years old when she first recalls actively fantasizing about wearing girls' clothes and having visible breasts beneath her sweaters. The fantasies produced 'a pleasant state of excitement', which she later came to conceptualize as erotic. At 8 years old Janice was dressing in her mother's clothes whenever she had the privacy to do so.[8] Although she became sexually aroused with cross-dressing, she hated her erect penis, which reminded her of her maleness. Her fantasies quickly became more body-focused. By the time she was 14, she was fantasizing primarily about having a female body – having breasts, long hair, no penis, a vagina, and a hairless face. She affected an androgynous appearance and continued to cross-dress in private. These activities, like her fantasies, were highly erotic to Janice, which distressed her not only because this reminded her of her maleness, but because it seemed to preclude her (she thought) from being 'really' transsexual.

In her early twenties, Janice started experimenting with black market oestrogens. After taking oestrogen for a number of weeks her sex drive would disappear and with it most of her desire for a woman's body. The desire would return when she stopped taking the oestrogen. Eventually she found a dosage of oestrogen that she wanted to take continuously but, after a few years, stopped, concluding that she did not have the courage to transition. Instead, she focused on developing a career, later marrying and having a family. Sexual relations with her wife were accompanied and enabled by her fantasizing her body as female. Shortly after the birth of her children, she began taking oestrogen again, and during this period first encountered

Blanchard's concept of 'autogynephilia'. It was her 'Road to Damascus' experience. Her immediate reaction was 'This is me!' A year later, at the age of 39, she began living full-time as a woman, and aged 41, she underwent sex-reassignment surgery. She remains as sexually excited by her actual migrating as she was by her fantasying it:

> Nowadays my most common masturbatory fantasies usually involve little more than the sequential mental consideration of all the physical feminisation I've undergone. It's like going through a list: now I have breasts; now I have a vagina; now I have hair to my shoulders; now I have pierced ears, etc. Just the contemplation of all these physical changes is enough to get me reliably excited. (personal communication, 2000)

Something of the strength and power of the autogynephilic 'drive' is seen in the following. Janice, at 35 years of age, has just encountered the 'transvestite' and 'transsexual' fantasy fiction of Sandy Thomas in a New York bookstore:

> As soon as I entered for the first time and saw the vast array of erotica, I knew I had found something special. I must have browsed for two or three hours before purchasing about a dozen books. I promptly returned with them to my hotel room and read them and masturbated to the imagery long into the night. I think I had four orgasms that night, over about three hours' time – a more intense and concentrated burst of sexual activity than I had ever had before, or than I have ever had since. One of the books that especially excited me that night was *Just Like a Woman* (Thomas, [1989] 1997). In this book an investigative reporter is feminised and transformed at the "Chrissy Institute". The feminisation process at the fictional Institute involves hormones, electrolysis, and a diet and exercise regimen, as well as make-up, women's clothing, and training in feminine deportment [gender femaling co-opted in the service of erotic body femaling]. Some nine years later, and over three years after undergoing penectomy and vaginoplasty, I revisited *Just Like a Woman*. I re-read it, and found that the imagery still spoke to me erotically. I have continued to use *Just Like a Woman* as a stimulus during masturbation, although these days it serves mostly as a jumping off point for my own fantasies. (personal communication, 2000)

Rachael is insistent that she has never masturbated to the thought of herself as a woman. This might seem *prima facie* evidence that she has no autogynephilic response. However, she does speak of masturbating to the thought of herself having intercourse as a woman with a man. Blanchard would, presumably, see this as an example of what he calls an 'autogynephilic interpersonal fantasy' (Blanchard, 1989b). Anne Lawrence (personal communication, 2000) suggests that perhaps Rachael is primarily aroused by her feminized self, reflected not in a mirror, but in another (male) person. She remarks: 'I doubt that Rachael is truly aroused by men or by men's bodies.' Much the same might be said of the later phases of Gail's trajectory. But again, much the same might be said of many *prima facie* 'heterosexual' 'genetic women'.

This debate raises important issues concerning, *inter alia*, the relations of autogynephilic fantasies in the transgendered with what one informant referred to as 'the basic ingredients of heterosexuality'. Many of Blanchard's and Lawrence's transgendered critics argue that the autogynephilic fantasies they describe are no different from the fantasies of heterosexual genetic women. When this move is made, Blanchard's concept of autogynephilia as a male's love of himself as a woman is extended to a female's love of herself as a woman. There is no doubt, for instance, that many genetic women find erotic the thought of themselves as desirable and/or desired women. Relatedly, those who research 'heterosexual' spectator responses to 'heterosexual' pornographic film claim that the male spectator typically desires the females claimed by the (desiring) male protagonist, while the female spectator fantasizes about being the desirable and/or desired woman – the 'love of oneself as a woman' that this fantasizing may trigger may make the desiring person variously irrelevant. Put another way, the degree of narcissism in episodes of desire varies. From this standpoint the 'love of oneself as a woman' experienced by genetic women and MTF women might seem indistinguishable. Certainly, we have genetic women informants who identify with Blanchard's concept of autogynephilia once they have been introduced to it.

One transgendered MTF informant described how she would dress herself up as a provocative woman, attract the desire of a 'straight' man at a 'straight' disco, and on returning home, on her own, position a mirror in front of herself angled to reflect the image the man would have had of her when he found her sexually desirable. She would then masturbate to that image – of herself through the imagined eyes of the male admirer. It is evident that 'actual' others (and parts of others), memories of actual others, fantasy others, actual and fantasy interactions, actual and fantasy scripts, actual and fantasy props, and so on, may be variously implicated in erotic episodes, variously scripted and enacted. Others and props (both actual and fantasy) may be variously essential, optional, or irrelevant in particular episodes of arousal, arousal maintenance, and orgasm.

However, it is important to remember that on our sociological, processual and relational understanding of these issues, meanings of narratives and their constituents emerge within the frameworks they are placed. Within the migrating mode of transgendering, the sub-processes of erasing, concealing, implying, and redefining are variously co-opted and implicated in the service of the privileged sub-process of substituting. Once autogynephilia is considered in the light of the sub-processes and their interrelations, it becomes possible, *inter alia*, to detail the ways in which autogynephilic response in migrating differs from autogynephilic response in those not migrating, i.e., in other modes of transgendering and in genetic women. Many of our migrating informants, for instance, tell us of their erotic arousal to the thought of actual and fantasied erasing and substituting. The eroticizing of the respective sub-processes, the degree of the respective eroticizing, and the interrelations between the various eroticizations will vary between individuals and within individual trajectories. This is an exceedingly complex business. We will return to this issue in Chapter 4 when we compare the eroticization of the various sub-processes in the transgendering trajectories of migrating and negating informants. In our judgement, our framework provides the conceptual wherewithal to unpack such issues in a way denied to the taxonomic, typological and diagnostic approach followed by Blanchard.

THREE   Oscillating Stories

A conceptual introduction to oscillating

We use the term 'oscillating' to emphasize the movement to and fro between male and female polarities, across and between the binary divide. The essence of oscillating then is that stays on either side of the binary divide are temporary ones and not permanent as in migrating. *The Oxford English Dictionary* (1995) definition that comes closest to our usage here is 'to move or travel to and fro'. 'To and fro', 'back and forth' and similar phrases suggest the temporary nature of the stays in either place. There are a number of dimensions of oscillating that merit comment and exploration.

First, there is a temporal dimension. The frequency with which the oscillator ventures over the border and the length of stay will vary, depending on the oscillator's social circumstances and his/her personal project. Some oscillators may spend a few hours every week on the other side of the divide; others may only manage the journey every few months but they might be able to stay over the border for a week or more. There are oscillators who oscillate (in fantasy) minute to minute, indeed, second to second.

Second, oscillations vary in their amplitude – that is, in the distance travelled either side of the midpoint. Much variation is possible and there is no reason to suppose that the distance either side will be equal like the swing of a pendulum. So, in addition to the temporal dimensions of the border crossing, there is the question of how far over the border the oscillator is able or prepared to go. At one extreme is Kevin who occasionally slips on a pair of his wife's knickers in the bathroom; at the other is Mary who is able to cross-dress completely and convincingly and regularly goes out shopping or to a restaurant with her wife.

A third dimension relates to the extent to which fantasy is involved in oscillating, and the nature of the fantasy. Kevin's forays across the gender border are almost completely in fantasy and his opportunities to realize them are limited. Pauline ventures over the border quite substantially, but only in the privacy of her own apartment and fantasizes about 'going out' as a woman. Caroline is able to spend a considerable amount of time each week over the border. She 'passes' in most situations and is comfortable in public. Her fantasy is to meet and have a sexual relationship with a man although all her sexual experiences so far have been with women.

A fourth dimension is the extent to which, and the manner in which, others are involved in these oscillations. Crossing the gender border, whether in fantasy or in reality, can be a lonely experience; no one else needs to be involved or even aware of what is taking place. But other people can change the nature of the oscillating experience considerably; by removing the need for secrecy and facilitating temporal and spatial opportunities for it to take place; by providing needed material items such as clothing which enable the crossing or which perhaps make it more extensive; and by providing encouragement and support. The other people most likely to be involved are the oscillator's family members and friends, other oscillators and the commercial providers of various goods and services.

If migration is an appropriate way of conceptualizing permanent movements over the gender border, then when considering temporary border crossings we might usefully explore parallels with the phenomenon of tourism, which, like migration, is another feature of the contemporary global landscape (Graburn and Barthel-Bouchier, 2001; MacCannell, 1999; Rojek, 1993; Urry, 1990).

Both migration and tourism involve journeys but, in the case of the latter, 'periods of residence elsewhere are of a short-term and temporary nature' (Urry, 1990: 3). With day-trippers and holidaymakers, 'there is a clear intention to return "home" within a relatively short period of time' (ibid.: 3). So, importantly, thinking of tourism furnishes us with the concept of 'home'. The bald concept of oscillating privileges neither 'to' nor 'fro' – something more in common with the transcending stories that we consider later. And, if we think of an oscillating device such as a pendulum or metronome, then its 'home' or place of rest is its midpoint – 'neither one thing nor the other' – a possibility we explore in Chapter 5. In this chapter, however, oscillating for the most part, like touring, involves the idea of there being a 'home' and an 'away'. Nevertheless, like some tourists, some gender oscillators may come to spend more of their time 'away' than at 'home' and, in fact may come to feel that they are more 'at home' when they are 'away'.

If migration involves a total life-change, tourism, by contrast, involves a temporary departure from everyday life. As Urry (ibid.: 2) points out, tourism arose with the organization and regulation of work and the emergence of a realm of leisure. Some aspects of leisure remain within the sphere of the everyday, tourism takes us beyond it: 'tourist experiences involve some aspect or element which induces pleasurable experiences which are, by comparison with the everyday, out of the ordinary' (ibid.: 11).

Crossing the gender border does indeed take us away from the 'everyday' and 'out of the ordinary'. Urry's comments imply both geographical and temporal dimensions of this 'realm of leisure'; leisure occurs away from our place of work and out of working hours. Another essential ingredient in the nature of leisure in our society is a degree of wealth; enough wealth, first of all, to be able to set aside some time free from work. More importantly for our purposes here, however, is the fact that a certain degree of wealth is needed to enjoy this leisure time; leisure costs us money not just in the sense that it is time spent not earning it. This is true both of 'everyday' leisure activities (going to a gym, watching television or listening to music) and of 'out of the ordinary' leisure activities such as holidays.

Similarly, gender oscillating is primarily a leisure activity providing pleasurable experiences that are 'out of the ordinary'. As Hirschfeld wrote of his transvestite cases, 'the majority lead a peculiar double life, days at work and in society as men, at home and in the evening as women' ([1910] 1991: 126). When we speak of someone having a 'double life' we usually imply, of course, that one of them is a hidden one, and this is true of many of those who oscillate over the gender border.

In order to clarify some of our main points, we will begin with the (usually male) oscillator who, when he takes a gender 'holiday', has to keep that fact a secret. When he is away he wants to 'pass', as the jargon goes. As that term is used by male transvestites, it means to 'be taken for' a woman, to not be 'read' as a man and is usually used to refer to situations where the oscillator is in public spaces. This fits in well with Goffman's (1963) use of the term 'passing' to refer to a process of managing information, specifically to avoid the disclosure of stigmatizing information that might discredit the actor concerned. The stigmatizing information that we are concerned with here, of course, is that the person who appears to be a woman is 'actually' a man. Many oscillators aspire to pass in this sense for the pleasure it gives, even if there is no actual danger involved in disclosure.

But there are other aspects to this term 'passing'. One of *The Oxford English Dictionary* (1995) meanings is 'to be accepted as adequate' as in the phrase to 'pass muster'. What is adequate in this sense is very variable over time and in geographical and social settings. In the early stages of our 'ideal type' male oscillator's career, a single item of female clothing may suffice, or even a piece of cloth redefined as a skirt. After progressing to the point of being completely dressed in female clothing and wearing make-up, the earlier oscillations will often be acceptable no longer. Moreover, what 'passes muster' in front of the bedroom mirror will not be acceptable at the local transvestite group meeting and neither might be acceptable in more public spaces.

But when our oscillator returns, he has to keep secret the fact that he has been away. For most of the time he has to present as a man; not only as a man, but also as a masculine, non-transvestite and, usually, heterosexual man. So our male oscillator also has to 'pass' in the sense that the potentially stigmatizing information that he has been on a 'gender holiday' has to be kept a secret and he has to pass muster as a man. Unlike the returning holiday-maker who can proudly display their suntan, the oscillator will not, in many cases, want there to be any evidence of his excursions.

As we have seen, in the migrating mode the primary sub-process is that of substituting: as far as is possible, everything that denotes one gender is replaced by a substitute that denotes the other. Thus the need for concealing and imply-ing is minimal (although never absent). In the oscillating mode, except in fan-tasy, substitution is much less prominent and is mainly, but not entirely, restricted to reversible substitutions and to those which can be concealed, such as the removal of body hair. Where substituting is minimal, the need for imply-ing and concealing is at its greatest. Anything that indicates 'man' must be con-cealed and anything that indicates 'woman' must be implied.

Something of the complex interrelations between concealing and imply-ing can be seen in the following example. Gerry/Mandy had a set of false teeth made for him that he could wear over his front teeth. He told his den-tist he wanted them as part of his treatment to help with 'grinding' at night. He wore them whenever he oscillated. The false teeth were very white and very prominent in comparison to his natural teeth. They gave him a more feminine look, but they also played a major role in disguising his identity, concealing both his personal identity and, in some settings, his identity as a male. He felt that if he met someone he knew – at a Drag Ball, for instance, where we met him – they would not recognize him, even if they did know that he was male.

More obviously, clothing aids a particular gender presentation. At the same time, clothing conceals aspects of the body that would undermine that presentation and it implies the presence of body parts that cannot be seen. The FTM oscillator, in addition to binding the breasts, may need to wear loose fitting shirts and jackets to conceal the presence of the binding and imply a male chest, for instance.

Although concealing and implying are inextricably linked in oscillating, it is implying which may be seen as the major sub-process in oscillating. Oscillating demands the 'implying' of certain body parts, or gendered attributes. In Chapter 1, we gave the examples of breast forms and hip pads to illustrate the sub-process of MTF implying. Many oscillators follow mini-trajectories of implying in regard to particular body parts. Anne Marie, for instance, implied breasts, initially with her socks, then with stockings, and then with balloons filled with water. Finally, she purchased breast prostheses intended for women who had undergone mastectomy. Her implying trajectory took a reverse direction in regard to her hips. For a number of years, she wrapped towels around her hips and wore them under skirts, dresses and women's jeans. As she grew older, she came to feel more 'natural' with smaller hips and dispensed with the towels. By this time she was associating her larger hips with older women and she preferred the slimmer hips of younger women.

A very different example of implying comes from Virginia Prince who gives the following hint to male cross-dressers using the public 'ladies' toilet: 'If you are nervous about how adequate you look upon entering the inner room you can buy considerable authenticity by going over to the Kotex or Fems dispenser which is usually on the wall at one end and spend a dime for a pad and take it with you into the booth' (Prince, 1971: 141).

In oscillating, there is always the need to return 'home'. Altering the body creates particular problems in this regard and is likely to be limited to that which will not compromise the 'home' identity. The range can be considerable depending on the individual's personal circumstances. At one extreme there is Kevin who has a wife and two teenage children, none of whom know of his interest in crossing the gender border. His circumstances do not permit even the slightest degree of body femaling and his border crossings are almost wholly fantasy ones. Then there is Kathy, an MTF cross-dresser who, when we interviewed her, had undergone electrolysis to remove all facial hair, kept the rest of her body free of hair and had had some minor facial cosmetic surgery. These bodily modifications were possible because she had a settled conviction that oscillating would always constitute a significant part of her life; she did not have a close relationship with anyone who might query such modifications; and she had enough spare money to afford such procedures. These modifications serve a practical purpose in that they facilitate Kathy's frequent border crossings by enhancing her appearance as a woman but she is still able to appear unequivocally as a man. The modifications have a further function in that they added to her feeling of femininity – a feeling that is erotically highly charged.

'Gina Love', interviewed by Claudia Andrei, expresses the dilemma well:

I have had a few procedures done to my face to make it look more feminine, but I have to be careful not to cross the line. Or else I could run the risk of looking freaky in day-to-day life. On a couple of occasions I tried laser treatment on the face, but decided not to carry on with it because I like to look like a man during the week (stubble, etc.). (Andrei, 2002: 22)

101

However, where the oscillator is known to be a drag queen or drag king (Volcano and Halberstam, 1999), or is otherwise prominent in gay and trans-vestite settings, substituting can often be more extensive and visible. The American female impersonator Frank Marino has apparently 'had nine cos-metic surgery operations to look like Joan Rivers, from a nose job to cheek and chin implants' (http://www.frankmarino.com/news.html).

Since we began researching this area in the mid-1970s, body modifica-tions have become much more common. Cosmetic surgery has become more widely available, more affordable and (particularly for men) more acceptable. So whilst, as we have said, permanent substitution is not the principal sub-process in the oscillating mode, it may be that these develop-ments in body modification have made available some forms of permanent substitution that will facilitate oscillation for those who are able to make use of them. So, for example, according to figures produced by the American Society of Plastic Surgeons (2004), 28 per cent of the 623,297 patients undergoing laser hair removal in 2003 were male. Other body modifications of a more temporary nature, such as chest and leg waxing to remove body hair, have also become more common and more acceptable for men if a recent *Guardian* report is to be believed (T. Dowling, 'This may hurt a bit', *The Guardian*, 15 January 2003). Indeed, as we write, the British soccer icon David Beckham is receiving considerable publicity over his alleged practice of shaving his armpits.

Oscillating, like migrating, will always involve some clothing substitution, although in the oscillating mode that substitution will only be temporary. The gendered nature of clothing and its sale through gendered outlets means that access to it can be problematic for those wishing to oscillate. The male trans-vestite stories that follow often tell of using the clothes of female members of their household for their secretive childhood border crossings. As they move into adulthood they may acquire their own supply of women's cloth-ing, either bought in person or by mail order. These latter possibilities may seem straightforward at first glance but guilt and fear of disclosure may make them problematic. It may be embarrassing for many men to buy women's clothes in a shop, in any event, but the embarrassment is compounded when the clothes are being bought for themselves. As one of our cross-dressing informants put it:

> I am sure we've all been through this trial, looking around the shop, picking up the desired arti-cle, bursting into a sweat when you have to queue to pay and finally (though not always!) emerg-ing triumphant with the goods in your hot little hands. Some items were harder to tackle than others, personally I found shoes, bras and make-up the most difficult to buy, but it gets easier as you persist.

The use of mail order facilities solves such problems but requires the privacy to receive parcels and a bank or credit card account that will not be viewed by anyone else.

If circumstances and money permit, elaborate concealing and implying 'solutions' may be purchased. Indeed, many oscillators will make consider-able sacrifices in order to obtain something they really 'want' or feel 'com-pelled' to buy. Wigs, facial hairpieces, make-up that can conceal beard growth and many more items can be found. Thirty years or so ago this often entailed seeking out theatrical suppliers. Since that time, a number of spe-cialist retailers have emerged to cater exclusively to the transgender market. The size of this market can be gauged from the fact that one UK retailer has four stores nationwide. Not only have these commercial suppliers increased in numbers but the number and range of concealing and implying devices on offer have also increased. One UK supplier, for example, now offers an 'Authentic Vagina'. This device is:

> a complete replica of a female vagina with inner and outer vaginal lips, a sweetly protruding clitoris, perfectly authentic in every detail. Using our newly developed and improved soft smooth latex, they are hand made and individually crafted to transform you instantly from He to She, by encasing your male penis whilst displaying your new female genitalia. A must for every cross dresser who wants to be ultimately feminine! With or without pubic hair! (http://www.transformation.co.uk/cache 2.html)

Another supplier offers elaborate undergarments called 'Veronicas':

> Veronicas are custom fitted undergarments that give you the proper hip and derriere proportions of a curvaceous woman. Made of spandex and nylon, the garment has pockets on each side to hold spe-cial soft high density foam pads. These pads are individually shaped to give you the curvature that you desire. The Veronica 1 is our original hip-and-rear enhancing garment. It feminizes your propor-tions, by making your hips almost as wide as your shoulders. At the same time, it enhances your rear, allowing you to properly fill out feminine clothing. Each Veronica 1 is custom-padded to make you a better-looking girl! (http://www.ladylikeshop.com/v_intro.php)

The need to keep gender oscillations secret may mean that issues of time, place and cost are particularly problematic. Freedom is required both from work and from constraints resulting from close relationships and other com-mitments. Money is required for a second 'wardrobe' of clothes and for wigs, for instance, which may be necessary for the border crossing. Much inven-tiveness is often displayed to make the most of limited funds – such is the desperation to 'get away'. Early in Stella's oscillating trajectory, she would secretly borrow some of her sister's clothes. She would 'solve' the problem of acquiring a feminine hairstyle by using horsehair taken from an old sofa.

She tucked the horsehair under a borrowed headscarf and carefully styled the visible hair. Another informant, whilst a schoolboy at a boys' boarding school, was too frightened to acquire his own female clothes. He solved the problem by secretly borrowing the few female clothes that were stored in the school 'Drama Society' cupboard.

As well as problems connected with the storage of clothes, wigs and so on, safe times and places must also be found for border crossings and 'gender vacations'. Some oscillators are able to cross over in many public settings. Some oscillators use commercial facilities such as the 'tranny friendly' bars and clubs that have sprung up over the past 20 years in many metropolitan areas. Other oscillators restrict themselves to private meetings held by transgender groups in hotels or other meeting places hired for the occasion. Still others may never be able or willing to venture into any of these settings. Their oscillating may be done privately behind closed doors, either at home or in private public places such as the cubicles in public toilets.

Frequently, the oscillator shares his/her spaces and places with people who have some authority to invade his privacy on occasion. These people may have claims on his time or claims to know how his/her time is spent. If the oscillator wishes to keep secret his/her oscillating, he/she must hide both the secret and the traces that it may leave behind. Many informants speak of their attempts to engineer privacy and add that they are plagued with worries about discovery. 'What if my wife comes home early?', 'What if my wife has an accident and the police come to fetch me?', 'What if a neighbour has spotted me and called the police?', 'What if someone calls unexpectedly?', 'What if, despite all my precautions, some trace of my cross-dressing is found?', 'Can someone tell I've been wearing make-up, plucked my eyebrows, shaved my legs?'

At one time, Stella had an interest in photography and used a spare room in the family home as a dark room. This dark room provided a safe place in which to dress without fear of being disturbed by her family. Many oscillators give similar reports of such improvisations. They also report using hidden spaces for storage or for 'crossing over'. In the following quote, Rowe goes into considerable detail about the new room he had when he was aged 13 and his parents bought a new house:

> My new room had advantages other than privacy. Three of the walls had been outfitted with a folding desk, several sets of desk drawers, two sets of bookcases, a large cupboard and matching set of drawers, and a large closet with its own set of built-in shelves and four floor-level storage drawers underneath. Three of those storage drawers were housed in plywood frames, but the fourth – the one farthest from the entrance to the room itself, and the one easiest to conceal from view – was supported only by a pair of wooden runners. In other words, whoever designed and constructed all that built-in furniture accidentally left a foot or more of empty crawl space underneath the end of what was otherwise a rather elaborate clothes closet.

Probably no one else knew that space existed. In order even to examine it I had to get down on my hands and knees, pull the drawer entirely out of its frame, and use a flashlight to see anything at all.

As soon as I discovered that space, three or four months after moving into my new room, I realized I'd found something good. Upstairs in our old house I'd been able to dress up partially once or twice after my parents went to bed. After all, Mom had stored most of her blouses, skirts, and dresses in my bedroom! In our new house, though, I was able to dress up completely even in the daytime without much fear of discovery. The door to my room was equipped with two heavy locks. Even better, I could hide clothes in my 'secret place' (that was how I thought of it) and keep them safe and clean there for years at a time. All I had to do was to put whatever I wanted to hide into a paper bag, tape it shut, and push it back into the crawl space. (1997: 74)

One of our oscillating informants moved into a new house and devoted one bedroom to his 'male self' and another to his 'female self'. Each bedroom was suitably furnished with separate beds and wardrobes. Pride of place in the bedroom for his 'female self' was a very feminine dressing table suitably equipped with an array of women's hairbrushes, combs, and skin care products. He kept this bedroom locked when he was not using it. Yet, another oscillating informant owned a large house in which he maintained an 'oscillating' room in an upstairs attic which could only be reached via a staircase hidden behind what looked like a locked cupboard door.

Opportunities for cross-dressing, then, will be determined by the character of the oscillator's living arrangements, his/her relationship with the people he/she lives with, and the nature of the accommodation, the oscillator's and other people's jobs, and so on. All these factors can, of course, vary over the life span of the individual, with occupational changes, house moves and changes in the life style of others around him. The nature of the opportunity needed may change too. Putting on a few women's clothes, possibly masturbating and then returning to men's clothes, may need only an hour's privacy. If full dressing and make-up plus some time to just be 'dressed' is sought, then a whole evening or half a day at least may be required. A limited disclosure of the secret to sympathetic others may, of course, greatly increase the opportunities available by widening the range of times and settings in which border crossings are possible. Most often wives and girlfriends are the individuals confided in. At some point, contact may be made with other oscillators and then, if personal circumstances permit, the possibilities increase immensely.

Concealing and implying require certain skills if the temporary border crossings are to be successful. Depending on the direction of travel, facial hair needs to be hidden or suggested, breasts need to be concealed or implied, penises tucked away or hinted at. Efforts may be made to 'walk the walk' and 'talk the talk' of the other gender. All of these things require skills that may be acquired in various ways. Some are acquired without conscious efforts; others may be consciously sought and practised. The mass media may provide 'looks' to aim for and instructions on how to achieve them; 'guidebooks' specifically addressed to the gender tourist are available, as are web pages, videotapes/ DVDs, and magazines. Training workshops are also available, alongside more informal instruction from other more experienced gender tourists or knowing partners and friends. Sometimes, however, the skills are learned in an isolated and, perhaps, prolonged process of trial and error.

Tourism today is a large industry. In many parts of the literature (e.g., Urry, 1990) a contrast is drawn between the individual character of 'travel' and the mass nature of 'tourism'. The latter requires a degree of planning and organization – an industry – whereas the former does not. The differences in scale between travel and tourism, however, produce certain qualitative differences in the nature of the experience. The traveller sets off into the 'unknown'; a degree of danger and risk is involved. The tourist, by contrast, follows a well-marked route to a resort in the company of many others with virtually all risk and danger eliminated.

The historical research of Peter Farrer (1987; 1996), for instance, and the older case histories documented by writers such as Hirschfeld ([1910] 1991) and Ellis (1928), show that there have been individual 'gender travellers' for some time. It is only over the past 40 years, however, that 'transgender tourism' has developed. This has involved the growth of social networks and commercial ventures which have provided the 'resorts' and the means to enable large numbers of people to take 'gender holidays' on a regular basis. Virginia Prince, whom we discussed in the last chapter as an example of gender-led migrating, may be said to be the 'Thomas Cook' of the gender tourism industry.

Prince's book *How to Be a Woman Though Male* was first published in 1971. As the title suggests, this is a guidebook telling all 'about the whole process of changing one's gender from masculine to feminine' as the cover blurb puts it. It is, the cover blurb continues, 'a complete "how to" type book and presents a complete and detailed analysis of what it means and what it takes to be a woman in today's world' (Prince, 1971). The book includes a wealth of information about women's clothing, hairstyles and cosmetics of over 30 years ago. Some of this information is extremely detailed. There are, for example, five pages devoted to shoe styles, three to hosiery and one to gloves. There is also much information specific to the male oscillator on such things as men wearing women's wigs, how to deal with beard growth, and the wearing of false breasts. There is also instruction on how to behave appropriately as a woman. Here is Prince telling her readers how to walk:

> What you can do to help you achieve a more graceful feminine sort of a walk is to first stand next to a wall with your heels about 3-4 inches in front of it. Lean back onto the wall and tilt your pelvis

forward so that the small of your back is forced against the wall. Put your hand back there to see that it does. Force it back to the wall by forcefully tilting the pelvis. Now, without changing the pelvis angle at all let yourself come away from the wall, keeping the pelvis tucked under you and start to walk. (ibid.: 121)

We interviewed one oscillator who spent considerable time following this advice in the privacy of his bedroom and his office! And here is Prince, again, giving instructions on how to avoid detection when using a 'ladies' public toilet:

It is often overlooked or unknown to males that the female urinary stream not being focused as it were into a narrow stream by passing through a pipe (penis) before leaving the body tends to spray out and to hit the water in the bowl in a much bigger stream than a male urinary stream. For this reason it makes considerably more sound. A male sitting on the seat will have a thin stream falling only a few inches and will not therefore make a usual sound. While most of the time this might be of no importance, if you feel any qualms about your authenticity you might be well advised to make much the same sound as the other females. This can be accomplished by standing up, facing the door, and straddling the bowl with feet not too far back (this would seem strange to anyone in the neighboring booth). Aim the stream right into the pool of water and let go. The greater length of fall will allow the stream to spread out and make more noise. (ibid.: 142)

The older male transvestites whom we interviewed in the late 1970s and early 1980s told us about their oscillating in the 1950s and 1960s. Some of the more adventurous (and well-off) informants bought women's clothes openly for themselves, sometimes cultivating a relationship with the owner of a small dress-shop. They often obtained wigs and make-up from theatrical suppliers. Most of our informants, however, were too fearful to attempt to meet their needs openly and relied on secretly borrowing or stealing clothes from the women in their lives. In the 1950s and the early 1960s, there were no support groups available for cross-dressers; nor were there any suppliers who specialized in their needs. However, as the 1960s progressed, things began to change. First, many people were more affluent so that many of the men we spoke to had more money with which to meet their needs. Second, support groups developed around the transvestite label, and these provided both safe opportunities to venture across the gender border and links to sources of supply that would facilitate the crossing. Since the 1980s, facilities and services for oscillators have grown immensely, as a glance at *The Way Out Tranny Guide* (Lee, 2005) demonstrates. Since the 1990s, with the growth of the internet, much has become available online. We should emphasize, however, that not everyone who wishes to is able take advantage of this exponential growth in facilities and supplies. A young, single man with a reasonable income living on his own in London, for example, has almost limitless opportunities;

a married, middle-aged man living in a rural part of North Wales is little better off than his predecessors were 30 years ago.

Returning to the tourist theme, some of the risk, the hard work and the trial and error involved in earlier border crossings can now be avoided and it is possible for a man with the time, opportunity and money to cross the gender border in a safe and ordered fashion. He can visit a commercial 'dressing service' for professional make-up and hairstyling, stay in a 'tranny' friendly hotel, and go on escorted shopping trips or nights out to tranny clubs and restaurants. If desired, all this can be contained within a transvestite 'resort', as advertised on the webpage 'Luxury TV Hotel in Stately Home', from *Transformation* (http://www.tv-hotel.co.uk/tv_hotel.html).

> We have established a luxury hotel in a stately home set in 4,000 acres of the most beautiful North Wales rural countryside, to provide the ultimate experience of living full time as a woman in total comfort and privacy. Whether just for one day, a week or any time at all to suit your personal circumstances, you can now enjoy luxury hotel facilities in total security and be pampered as a woman for the full duration of your stay.
>
> After you have unpacked, it is time for your amazing Transformation into the woman of your dreams. If you haven't brought your own feminine outfits, don't worry because we can provide everything you will require from our huge selection.
>
> One of our staff will professionally apply your make-up and then give you a stunning hourglass figure with the help of our specialist foundation garments, next to the slinky, silky feminine underwear, then your chosen outfit and lastly a styled wig to complete the transformation.

Other facilities promise:

> You can also be escorted to lunch, dinner or afternoon tea, an Art Gallery or that long awaited trip you have always wanted to do. Let the girls know and they will do their very best to arrange it for you. The girls also arrange 'Girlie Nights' out to all the popular trannie venues. (http://www.adaman-deve121.co.uk/Welcome1.htm)
>
> We now offer a complete day of dressing and femininity, which includes full make-over, unlimited access to wardrobe, evening dinner, plus an overnight stay, commences 12 midday. 50 digital pictures on CD-ROM comes free with this package! We can also organise an afternoon shopping trip or an evening out on the town at an additional cost. (http://www.pandoradepledge.com/pages/dressing.htm)

Similarly, the American Diane Torr has for some years been providing 'Drag King workshops'.

> During the 10 hour workshop, either Diane or a make-up artist will give each person an individual make-over and will provide facial hair, 5 o'clock shadow, etc. Each person is responsible for the male clothes they will need for their male identity. Please also bring: hair gel, a wide elasticated bandage (5inches minimum) to bind breasts, and a fake penis – (condom stuffed with cotton wool for example). We will learn how to take up space, walk, eat, drink, pick up objects, smile, etc. as men. We will

interact with each other, in character, and develop our new identities. The workshop culminates in a visit to a public place such as bar, strip club, dance club, where we will test out our new identities. (http://www.dianetorr.com/drag%20king/frameset5.htm)

Oscillators do, of course, vary in the time they spend thinking about and taking advantage of such 'tourist' opportunities. Some oscillators regard such opportunities as inauthentic. A consequence of the mass nature of tourism is that the creation of tourist enclaves insulates the tourist from the culture of the visited country which is only experienced in carefully fashioned packages especially created for the tourist trade. A number of writers (e.g., Urry, 1990: 7–8) discuss the 'inauthenticity' of the tourist experience. Oscillators opposed to gender 'tourists', may prefer, for instance, to travel independently as 'women' in the 'real' world. Many prefer independent travel in women's worlds of clothes shops and hair and beauty salons. For many non-oscillators, of course, this is an extremely limited vision of the world of women. It is no surprise, perhaps, that the wives of the transvestites interviewed by Woodhouse 'felt that the kind of femininity portrayed by their husbands' cross-dressing was nothing to do with their own lives as women, wives and mothers' (1989b: 144).

However, whether the oscillator is principally a 'traveller' or principally a 'tourist', much time is likely to be spent in anticipation of his future trips across the border. Again, it is Urry who has emphasized the important role of anticipation in tourism:

> there is an anticipation, especially through daydreaming and fantasy, of intense pleasures, either on a different scale or involving different senses from those customarily encountered. Such anticipation is constructed and sustained through a variety of non-tourist practices, such as film, TV, literature, magazines, records and videos, which construct and reinforce that gaze. (1990: 3)

Today, as we have seen, there is a wealth of material available through magazines, books, videotapes, DVDs and, of course, the internet with which gender tourists can fortify their daydreams and fantasies in anticipation of their next, longed-for gender holiday.

Telling oscillating stories

Oscillating stories may, like migrating stories, be seen as modernist tales. There are elements of silent suffering, discovery and coming to terms with 'being different', but these elements are less evident than in the migrating stories. In oscillating stories, we find less material on 'being' – on identity and relationships; and more detail about 'doing' – on excursions 'over the gender border'. As with the migrating stories, the binary divide is accepted.

Like migrating stories, oscillating stories have been told to medical men who have then told and retold them, sometimes as case histories and sometimes reinterpreted as theoretical stories of one kind or another.

The transvestite stories told by Hirschfeld and Ellis that we introduced in the last chapter included both migrating and oscillating. As we saw, Ellis, in particular, began to separate his eonists out into two categories along the lines of the tranvestite/transsexual distinction that came later. This distinction became a more crucial one with the advent of technological means to 'change sex'. However, the term transvestite was sometimes used when sex changing was involved in both the medical literature up until the early 1960s and in the popular press into the 1980s (King, 1993). As the terms 'bedded in', however, separate transvestite stories began to be told alongside transsexual stories both in the medical literature and in the mass media.

Unlike migrating stories, it is rare to find oscillating stories in published autobiographies. Pepper (1982), Rowe (1997), and Novic (2005) are notable exceptions.[1] Often found in older medical case reports and occasionally in magazine feature articles, the most detailed oscillating stories are found in the newsletters of transvestite organisations such as the UK Beaumont Society. Typically this story begins in childhood or early adolescence with sporadic trips 'over the border' depending on the availability of suitable clothing and the opportunity to make use of them. Older informants, particularly, often tell of the guilt that initially accompanied their border crossings. These crossings were often experienced as the product of irresistible compulsions. Depending on individuals and individual circumstances, however, border crossings became more regular and less laden with guilt. We discuss the major interpretations of this story below.

Like the migrating stories, we find that oscillating stories told by medical and other professionals have been of two main types, one couched in the language of pathological conditions or perversions and the other told more in terms of acceptable orientation (see King, 1984). 'The traditional erotic oscillating story', as we term it, was told by sexologists Magnus Hirschfeld and Havelock Ellis early in the twentieth century. Other sexologists, most notably David Cauldwell and Harry Benjamin, have followed this story which tells a tale of oscillating as a 'peculiarity' rather than as a 'pathology' or 'perversion'. The second major oscillating story told, in the main, by medical and other professionals does tell a story of pathology and perversion. This 'sexual pathology story' is principally a psychiatric story.

In terms of the interrelations between sex, sexuality and gender, 'the traditional erotic oscillating story' and 'the sexual pathology story' both privilege sexuality (the erotic) over sex and gender. A third major oscillating story, however, takes issue with this privileging of sexuality. This third 'gender oscillating story' tells a very different tale that privileges gender. It is a tale principally associated with transgender pioneer Virginia Prince and has had a wide following among many MTF oscillators since the 1960s. Prince's story, although a gender oscillating story, is a story of heterosexual male gender oscillating. It is, moreover, a story that many contemporary oscillators find inappropriate for their oscillating lives today. We conclude the chapter, therefore, with two further stories: 'the contemporary oscillating story' and 'the oscillating drag story'. Both stories, in their different ways, may be seen as '"girls" just want to have fun' stories. First, we consider the traditional erotic oscillating story, the sexual pathology story, and the gender oscillating story.

The traditional erotic oscillating story

As we detailed in Chapter 2, the term 'transvestism' may be traced back to Magnus Hirschfeld ([1910] 1991). There he writes: 'We are clearly faced with the strong drive to live in the clothing of that sex that does not belong to the relative build of the body. For the sake of brevity we will label this drive as transvestism (from "trans" = over or opposite, and "vestis" = clothing).' Hirschfeld clearly regarded this drive as an erotic one writing that, 'the masculine part in the psyche of these people is sexually excited by their feminine side' (ibid.: 140). However, Hirschfeld also considered the manifestations of the drive to be related to 'inner personality'. He remarks, for instance, that 'the kind of costume is not the chosen expression of an arbitrary mood, but rather is a form of expression of the inner personality' (ibid.: 124).

Hirschfeld's analysis of the 17 cases he presented also included the observations that, 'in most of the cases we can trace the urge back into their early childhood' (ibid.: 125). The male cases (16 of the 17) 'take great pride in possessing, as much as possible, a complete and rich women's wardrobe with all that goes with it, when their means allow them' (ibid.: 127). They also 'played the role of the woman, too, for longer or shorter periods of time' (ibid.: 124). He continues: 'Also, above and beyond the clothing, these persons have the urge to live in women's surroundings. When feasible, they set up a boudoir for themselves much like a woman's, decorate their living and bedrooms with women's ornaments and toilet articles, and find great joy in doing women's handicrafts' (ibid.: 127), before adding: 'Most of them wish they had been born female' (ibid.: 129). Physically, Hirschfeld found that his cases did not display any characteristics of the other sex and were predominantly heterosexual (ibid.: 129–30). Some of the married men cross-dressed with the knowledge and even help of their wives (ibid.: 131). He also noted that the men were sexually aroused by their 'metamorphosis' (ibid.: 139–40). He described the men as 'intelligent, conscientious people who have diverse interests and a broad education ... in good financial standing and in good jobs' (ibid.: 141). He notes that none of the cases appeared on the stage as female impersonators and speculates that this may be

> 'because these persons, consciously or unconsciously, feel that the wearing of women's apparel is an erotic activity and, therefore, impulsively feel an understandable shyness and hesitation about opening themselves to the eye of the public. This inner resistance occurs less often in the case of homosexuals. (ibid.: 141).

He goes on to argue, however, that 'there are a whole lot of completely heterosexual transvestites among the female impersonators' (ibid.: 142).

Hirschfeld rejected the idea that transvestism was a form of homosexuality, writing: 'one has to extend the sentence "not all homosexuals are effeminate" to include "and not all effeminate men are homosexual"' (ibid.: 148). He thought that transvestites were sexual intermediaries although he said 'why the womanly admixture is produced in one case that a hermaphrodite arises ... in a second gynecomastia ... in a third case an urning ... in a fourth a transvestite we can up to the present not tell' (ibid.: 234).

Hirschfeld evidently didn't regard transvestism as a pathology but 'basically a harmless inclination by which no one is injured' so that 'nothing can be said against the actual putting on of the clothing of the opposite sex' (ibid.: 235). He was, however, doubtful about the wisdom of transvestites marrying because of the possible effects on the children (ibid.: 235).

Hirschfeld's magnum opus on transvestism was not published in English until the Lombardi-Nash translation (1910 [1991]), although snippets of his writings on the topic were available in translations of his other works (e.g., 1938). Much more accessible to English readers would have been the writings on the topic by Havelock Ellis (1913a; 1913b; 1920; 1928). Ellis objected to the term transvestism because it focused attention solely on the element of cross-dressing. He also objected to Hirschfeld's phrase 'impulse of disguise' because, he wrote, 'the subject of this anomaly, far from seeking disguise by adopting the garments of the opposite sex, feels on the contrary that he has thereby become emancipated from a disguise and is at last really himself' (Ellis, 1920: 3). Actually, a similar view can also be found in Hirschfeld:

> In the apparel of their own sex they feel confined, bound up, oppressed; they perceive them as something strange, something that does not fit them, does not belong to them; on the other hand, they cannot find enough words to describe the feeling of peace, security and exaltation, happiness and well-being that overcomes them when in clothing of the other sex. ([1910] 1991: 125)

Ellis preferred his own term, eonism, and outlined two main types:

> One, the most common kind, in which the inversion is mainly confined to the sphere of clothing, and another, less common *but more complete*, in which cross-dressing is regarded with comparative indifference but the subject so identifies himself with those of his physical and psychic traits which recall the opposite sex that he feels really to belong to that sex, although has no delusion regarding his anatomical conformation. (1928: 36, our emphasis)

Ellis regarded the 'less common but more complete' type as embodying the essence of eonism. Like Hirschfeld, Ellis distinguished eonism from homosexuality. He wrote that it is possible for a person, 'to feel like a person of the opposite sex and to adopt, so far as possible, the tastes, habits and dress of the opposite sex while the direction of the sexual impulse remains normal' (1920: 1–2).

Like Hirschfeld, Ellis was also attracted by a biological theory of the aetiology of eonism, although he was rather vague as to the specific mechanisms involved. He argued that 'Early environmental influences assist but can scarcely originate eonism. The normal child soon reacts powerfully against them. We must in the end seek a deeper organic foundation for eonism as for every other aberration of the sexual impulse' (1928: 10). He surmised that the 'real physical basis' of eonism was 'some unusual balance in the endocrine system' (ibid.: 10). Again, like Hirschfeld, Ellis seemed not to view the phenomenon as pathological, writing of eonism as an 'anomaly' or 'aberration'.

Hirschfeld's term 'transvestism' became the preferred term used by professionals and by the 1950s was used to refer to the whole spectrum of cross-dressing phenomena. As we saw in Chapter 2, following the publicity surrounding Christine Jorgensen's 'sex change', it became widely known that it was possible to 'change sex'. Doctors became inundated with requests from people who wanted to do just that. The medical profession began to adopt the term 'transsexual' to designate those for whom such intervention was justified and was faced with the job of devising diagnostic criteria. The profession was also faced with the problem of creating a respectable face for 'sex reassignment surgery' and this involved ridding it of the (then) unsavoury associations with homosexuality or sexual perversion. Sexual arousal by cross-dressing and same sex relations in the original gender came to be widely regarded as contra-indications for surgery. Transsexualism was purged of any taint of sexuality and was seen firmly as being about *gender*. Almost by default, transvestism then came to be more commonly seen as a '*sexual* disorder'.

In this vein, Benjamin (1966: 18–19) writes that for transvestites, 'the penis ... is an organ of pleasure' whereas for the transsexual, 'his sex organs are sources of disgust and hate'. Benjamin also claimed that 'no experienced clinician can doubt the sexual roots in the large majority of transvestites' (ibid.: 32). He discusses the alternative view of transvestism promoted by Virginia Prince that we discuss in the next section but seems unconvinced by it: 'it must also be remembered', Benjamin wrote, 'that the tendency exists with many TVs to minimize the sexual nature of their "caprice" because they like to conform to morality, that is to say, to the antisexual atmosphere of our culture' (ibid.: 32). More emphatically he claims that, 'to take sex out of transvestism is like taking music out of opera. It simply cannot be done' (ibid.: 37). However, he does distinguish two types of transvestite – the 'fetishistic' and the 'latent and basically transsexual' (ibid.: 34–5). He writes that in the latter type 'a low sex drive and gender dissatisfaction frequently predominated' (ibid.: 36). Earlier in the same book he refers in his 'Sex Orientation Scale' to this second type of transvestite – the 'latent and basically transsexual' type – as the 'true transvestite' (ibid.: 22), so perhaps he was more persuaded by Prince's arguments than he wished to admit. Rather confusingly, however, Benjamin then goes on to state that:

> A large group of male transvestites (TVs) can be called 'true' because cross-dressing is the principal if not the only symptom of their deviation. They dress out of a strong, sometimes overwhelming urge that – to say the least – contains unmistakeable sexual overtones. Some of them can resemble addicts, the need for 'dressing' increasing with increasing indulgences. (ibid.: 30-1)

Nevertheless, Benjamin's views on transvestism seem to resemble those of Ellis and Hirschfeld in not regarding it as pathological:

> The typical or true transvestite is a completely harmless member of society. He derives his sexual pleasure and his emotional satisfaction in a strictly solitary fashion. The absence of a partner for his particular sex expression differentiates him radically from all so-called sex offenders. (ibid.: 41)

Benjamin is aware, however, of the harm that a transvestite's behaviour may inflict on his wife and family stating that, 'no transvestite should ever marry a girl without telling her of his peculiarity beforehand' (ibid.: 44).

Another writer in the early 1950s to regard transvestism as a 'peculiarity' rather than a 'pathology' was David Cauldwell. Although Cauldwell was medically qualified, his writings hardly constituted a contribution to the medical literature. Cauldwell is best seen, perhaps, as a popular sexologist who re-told and popularized medical stories relating to sexual behaviour, especially 'deviant' sexual behaviour (Ekins and King, 2001b). He wrote about other sexual matters, such as reproductive issues, for example, but was something of a 'specialist' on transvestism, transsexuality and hermaphroditism (Cauldwell, 1947a; 1947b; 1949a; 1949b; 1950a; 1950b; 1951). He wrote widely in publications such as *Physical Culture* and the popular 'science' magazine *Sexology*. He also produced over 140 popular booklets that were 'written in plain and simple language for the average man to understand' (Cauldwell, 1947b: cover note). These booklets consisted mainly of what he calls 'confessions' – personal stories sent to him by his readers alongside historical and cross-cultural examples. The 'confessions' are interwoven with popular accounts of the scientific and medical knowledge of the day, and his own comments and advice.

Cauldwell stated: 'my work is to fight ignorance and intolerance' (1949b: 6) and, indeed, his approach is generally tolerant. Transvestism is often described as a 'personality quirk' (ibid.: 6). As such, it is not an illness or disorder. He argues that 'To attempt to medically treat transvestism would be as foolish as to try to treat some star to make it behave differently in its relation to the solar system.'

Cauldwell's major contribution, therefore, is as a popular writer disseminating information and helping to create a climate in which sex and sexuality could be discussed in a more open and liberal way. His writings on transgenderism, both in content and form, resemble writings in the later subcultural publications such as *Transvestia* in the USA and *The Beaumont Bulletin* in the UK. Arguably, therefore, they are best located in relation to the emergence of a transvestite/transsexual subculture rather than in relation to the scientific community.

In 1949, Cauldwell (1949b: 6) reported that several of his readers had asked him to form a society for transvestites. He died in 1959, just before his readers' wish was to be granted by Virginia Prince. Fittingly, the first copy of Virginia Prince's magazine *Transvestia* included an 'In Memoriam' to David O. Cauldwell, a 'longtime friend of the transvestite', presumably written by Virginia Prince herself (Prince: 1960: 45).

The post-Second World War period was one in which there was emerging a more liberal attitude towards sexual matters, as exemplified in the Kinsey Studies. Cauldwell's work fitted in well with this liberal approach, which can also be seen in the writings of Kenneth Walker (e.g., Walker and Fletcher, 1955). Such writers advocated understanding and public enlightenment, not condemnation; self-acceptance, not cure, was the goal. As Walker and Fletcher wrote:

> Instead of treating the patients themselves, we might treat with more profit the society which makes it so difficult for these unfortunate people to live. In time – but many years will be required for this – a society which at present regards these strange afflictions of their fellow men with loathing and horror may become sufficiently educated to look upon them with compassion. (ibid.: 209)

115

The sexual pathology story

From the very beginnings of the 'medicalisation of the sexually peculiar' (Foucault, 1979) in the mid-late ninteenth century, cross-dressing and sex-changing phenomena were variously interpreted as degenerate, abnormal, pathological or psychopathological by the medical doctors, alienists (psychiatrists), and students of sexual science (sexologists) of the period. Krafft-Ebing (1901) was the major pioneer in this regard. Writing in a period before 'transvestism' had been separated out from 'homosexuality', the following passage is illustrative:

> Effemination: In this group are fully developed cases in which males are females in feeling; and *vice versa* women, males. This abnormality of feeling and of development of the character is often apparent in childhood. The boy likes to spend his time with girls, play with dolls, and help his mother about the home; he likes to cook, sew, knit; he develops tastes in female *toilettes*, and even becomes the adviser of his sisters. As he grows older he eschews smoking, drinking and manly sports, and, on the contrary, finds pleasure in adornment of person, art, *belles-lettres*, etc., even to the extent of giving himself entirely to the cultivation of the beautiful. Since woman possesses parallel inclinations, he prefers to move in the society of women. (1901: 373-4)

This passage was translated from the 10th German Edition of *Psychopathia Sexualis with Especial Reference to Antipathetic Sexual Instinct: A Medico-Forensic Study*. The sale of the edition was 'rigidly restricted to members of the medical and legal professions' (Publishers' Preface).

As we have seen, in the previous section, Hirschfeld and Ellis were concerned both to separate out 'transvestism' from 'homosexuality' and to represent it as more in the nature of a 'peculiarity' than an 'abnormality'. The neurologist and founding father of psychoanalysis, Sigmund Freud, followed the sexologists in many regards in his theorizing of the sexual 'perversions', as he called them. However, unlike the sexologists, Freud's focus was upon *unconscious* mental processes. In a sense, we are all transgendered in our unconscious mental processes. As Freud (1899) put it: 'I am accustoming myself to regarding every sexual act as a process in which four individuals are involved.' However, Freud did regard the 'puzzling perversions of the sexual instinct' as 'inhibitions of development, fixations or lop-sided growths' (1913: 209).

Freud's follower Isidor Sadger was central in the move to focus psychoanalysis on the 'cure' of sexual perversions and with this came a special focus on 'transvestism'. Whereas Freud had nothing specific to say on 'transvestism', *per se*, Sadger described a number of cases and psychoanalytic 'cures' of transvestism (e.g., Sadger, 1921). Sadger set the trend towards the development of the 'sexual pathology' oscillating story establishing itself in psychoanalysis, with Felix Boehm following soon afterwards (e.g., Boehm, 1923).[2]

However, notwithstanding these early examples in the psychoanalytic literature, it is in the twentieth-century textbooks on psychiatry that we see the consolidation of the 'sexual pathology story' most clearly. In these countless textbooks on psychiatry or abnormal psychiatry, transvestism is almost always described using terms such as disorder, perversion, abnormality or deviation.

First published in 1940, Clifford Allen's *The Sexual Perversions and Abnormalities* began from the premise that 'to the normal adult person the mode of expression of the sexual instinct is genital copulation and the object is one of the opposite sex and about the same age (1940: 58). Classifying transvestism firmly as a perversion, Allen writes in the second edition of this book that 'we do not believe that transvestism is ever a manifestation of heterosexuality and are of the opinion that these cases should be regarded as apparent heterosexuals' (Allen, 1949: 146). Even though transvestism may be 'the only manifestation of homosexuality' (ibid.: 146), Allen claims that 'Transvests [*sic*] are usually to be found to be more or less homosexual' (ibid.: 148). In his later *Textbook of Psychosexual Disorders* (Allen, 1962; 1969), although 'perversion' has disappeared from the title of the book, Allen's views of transvestism are unchanged.

In 1957, in answer to a reader's question about a particular case of transvestism, an anonymous author in *The British Medical Journal* writes that:

> Transvestism is a complex behaviour pattern combining features of homosexuality, fetishism, and exhibitionism. In its typical form it occurs almost exclusively in men. The transvestite dresses himself and usually masturbates in female clothing, thus acting as a woman in possession of male genitals. (*BMJ*, 3 August 1957: 309)

The author warns that 'it seems that transvestites are nearer to psychosis than other perverts, and some are in fact schizophrenics'. He continues:

> this man ought to be treated with psychoanalysis or, if this should not be practicable, by psychoanalytically orientated psychotherapy. Such treatment should at least be a help to him in preventing his perversion from damaging him socially and threatening the precarious balance of his personality. (ibid.: 309)

Another exponent of the transvestism as homosexuality story was Sim who, in his *Guide to Psychiatry* in 1974, writes that: 'This is again basically a homosexual equivalent. Men and women do not dress up to resemble the opposite sex in order to attract the opposite sex. It is to attract their own sex, and this is homosexuality' (1974: 402).

In the late 1980s, the American psychoanalyst Socarides (1988) likewise classifies transvestism as a sexual perversion. In keeping with the psychoanalytic focus on unconscious mental processes he links the perversion to 'unconscious homosexuality'. Drawing, particularly, upon the psychoanalytic terminology developed by Margaret Mahler (Mahler et al., 1975), Socarides writes:

> transvestitism [*sic*] arises from the basic preoedipal nuclear conflict from which all sexual perverts suffer secondary to a failure to traverse the separation-individuation phases, with a resultant disturbance in gender-defined self identity. Transvestitism reassures against and lessens castration fears, and keeps in repression deeper anxieties of merging and fusion with the mother and fears of engulfment by her. (1988: 363)

He continues, 'beneath heterosexual transvestite sexual relations lies unconscious homosexual desire' (ibid.: 364), adding that 'it is never a manifestation of heterosexuality, even if the patient engages in sexual relations with an opposite-sex partner' (ibid.: 365).

From the early 1960s onwards, the influence of psychoanalysis in psychiatry became less pronounced. Behavioural methods of treatment for many psychiatric 'disorders' became popular. In psychiatric tales, transvestism is commonly depicted as compulsive behaviour and often linked to fetishism (e.g., Randell, 1959). All of these 'disorders' must have seemed ideally suited to behavioural treatment by those wedded to behavioural approaches in psychiatry and psychology. Indeed, almost all of the published reports of attempts to 'cure' transvestism by aversion therapy date from this period (Brierley, 1979: Chapter 8). The use of aversion therapy for transvestism certainly continued into the 1970s (interview data). One brave psychiatrist even gave a paper at *The Beaumont Society Conference in 1975* on 'The Use of Behaviour Therapy in the Treatment of Sexual Problems with Special Reference to Transvestism' (Bebbington, 1975). Although Bebbington states at the beginning of his paper that he does not regard transvestism as an illness, his paper is peppered with references to transvestism as a 'disorder' and an 'abnormality of gender role'.

Glynn and Harper give an indication of what was involved in aversion therapy intended to 'cure' transvestism:

> A man of 27 had been in the habit of dressing in female clothes since the age of 14. While his wife was away at work he dressed as usual in her clothes and went out shopping. He was apprehended by the police and referred for psychiatric examination.
>
> He was admitted to hospital ... Apomorphine hydrochloride (gr. 1/20-1/8) was injected intramuscularly 2-hourly for 4 days and nights. After injection he was asked to dress entirely in women's clothing, and he wore this throughout the period of nausea and vomiting. Apart from losing 1 lb. in weight he remained in good physical condition.

After 4 days' treatment the patient exhibited marked revulsion at the sight of female clothes and flatly refused to put them on. He no longer felt any desire to wear them, and this was still so when he was examined 7 months later. (1961: 619)

Today, the American Psychiatric Association's *Diagnostic and Statistical Manual of Mental Disorders* (DSM IV) uses the term 'Transvestic Fetishism' which is in the category of paraphilias. The diagnostic criteria follow:

A. Over a period of at least 6 months, in a heterosexual male, recurrent, intense sexually arousing fantasies, sexual urges, or behaviors involving cross-dressing.

B. The fantasies, sexual urges, or behaviors cause clinically significant distress or impairment in social, occupational, or other important areas of functioning. (American Psychiatric Association, 1994)

'Transvestic fetishism' continues to be discussed in contemporary textbooks on psychiatry in chapters on 'sexual disorders' (e.g., Sadock and Sadock, 2000; Bennett, 2003), but the tone of these discussions has become much more liberal in recent years. Kockott, for instance, states that 'paraphilias are not necessarily to be considered as diseases that always require treatment' (2001: 222). Similarly, Bennett writes that 'Transvestism is not a condition that requires treatment' (2003: 242). He does, however, go on to argue that 'nevertheless, people whose behaviour is affecting their relationships or who find their behaviour unacceptable may seek treatment' (ibid.: 242). Moreover, Bennett mentions aversion therapy and 'masturbatory retraining' as possibilities for treatment options.

Despite the distancing in these texts from the older and less liberal 'pathology' model, the newer versions of the 'pathology' tale continue to be told alongside other paraphilias such as pedophilia, sadomasochism and exhibitionism, typically included together in a chapter or chapters with 'disorder' in their title. These are the psychiatric stories that are told to today's students of psychiatry and clinical psychology.

We might add, too, that a religiously inspired story, expressing a similar sentiment, is also available for anyone who cares to read it. The following excerpt may be found on the Christian Apologetics & Research Ministry website (http://www.carm.org) under the heading 'Is being a transvestite okay?'

No, being a transvestite is not okay. A transvestite is someone who wears the clothes of the opposite sex. This is forbidden in the Bible. (Deut. 22:5): "A woman shall not wear man's clothing, nor shall a man put on a woman's clothing; for whoever does these things is an abomination to the Lord your God." The reason it is wrong is because it obscures the distinction between male and female, blurs the pattern of the created order of male and female (Gen. 1:27), and has the potential of promoting homosexuality. We are created as male and female and need to act according to the sex that God has ordained for us.

The gender oscillating story

In Chapter 2, we considered Virginia Prince as an identity innovator who has personally migrated over the gender border but without genital surgery. As we saw, Prince adopted the term 'transgenderist' for this type of gender migrating, in order to emphasize her gender motivation and to distinguish it from a sex (body) or sexual (erotic) motivation. Notwithstanding this conceptual and identity innovation, Prince is best known, however, for her work in establishing the transvestite subcultural publication *Transvestia* and a subcultural organization *The Foundation for Full Personality Expression* (FPE), both of which were important in the development of the contemporary transgender community. Here, too, she emphasized gender as the central motivating force, but in these activities her emphasis was upon gender oscillating as opposed to gender migration. On this formulation, as we shall see, the transvestite is a heterosexual male who enjoys dressing as a woman from time to time; that is to say, he oscillates across the binary divide.

Stories which tell of non-normative behaviours, especially sexually related ones, struggle to be heard: even if they can be articulated, a sympathetic audience is hard to find. In his influential theory of the emergence of new subcultural forms as the result of effective communication between people with similar problems, Cohen points out that:

> Where the problems themselves are of a peculiarly delicate, guilt-laden nature, like many problems arising in the area of sex, inhibitions on communication may be so powerful that persons with like problems may never reveal themselves to one another, although circumstances are otherwise favourable for mutual exploration. (1955: 71)

In consequence, it is no surprise to find Ellis (1913b: 249) remarking that the (transvestite) subject of one of his articles regarded himself as unique 'like so many persons affected by psychosexual anomalies'. Today, virtually every sexual variation imaginable is the subject of television programmes and webpages. However, as late as the 1980s we were talking to oscillators who had only recently discovered the concept of transvestism, and had only recently discovered that they were not alone in their desire to dress in women's clothes. In the early 1950s there was nothing like the level of information and support which is available to the transgender community today. A few people managed to make contact with others but, by and large, in the 1950s,

Figure 3.1 Virginia Prince at a Seminar at Fantasia Fair, Provincetown, 1992
(Photographer and © Mariette Pathy Allen)

transvestism and transsexualism (few would even have been aware of these terms then) were solitary affairs accompanied by guilt, ignorance and secrecy. Little information was available in print, even in the medical litera-ture, and most people's 'knowledge' would have been gleaned from sensa-tional reports of 'sex changes' in the popular press, or from the occasional tales of cross-dressing or masquerade reported in the popular press as part of criminal or divorce proceedings.

We have already seen that oscillating across the gender border requires a number of problems to be solved – women's clothes and other necessities such as wigs need to be acquired; opportunities and places to wear them need to be found; and feelings of guilt and self-loathing need to be overcome. Some of the cross-dressers that Ellis and Hirschfeld wrote about had devised their own individual solutions to these problems and there is evidence that some of these men managed to meet others with similar inclinations. One of Ellis's cases (D.S.) wrote: 'in 1920, through an advertisement, I got into cor-respondence with a young man in London who lived, as nearly as possible as a girl' (1928: 55). Similarly, the five cases presented by Talmey (1914) reveal a small network between 'transvestites' in Britain, America and Belgium who were exchanging, via correspondence, their case histories and speculating about the nature of their 'condition' in the medical language of the day. Today, however, as we have already indicated, solutions to these problems are provided by subcultural and commercial organizations for anyone who is able to make use of them. In large part, these organizations can be traced back to the pioneering efforts of Virginia Prince in the late 1950s and early 1960s.

In the mid-1960s, Prince was arrested and pleaded guilty (in a plea bargain) to the charge of sending obscene material through the post (Prince, 1997a: 353). She was placed on probation for five years and was, apparently, in danger of being imprisoned if she cross-dressed in public. Her lawyer persuaded the court to include educating the public about cross-dressing as part of the probation order so that she could cross-dress legitimately (ibid.: 354). This she did and in 1968 had her first television appearance (ibid.: 354). So, as she put it, her '"career" as friend, counsellor, philosopher and publicist for the CD [cross-dressing] community got under way' (ibid.: 355).

In actual fact, as we saw in Chapter 2, her 'career' in this respect had 'got under way' some years earlier. By 1957, she had worked out the basic format of her story distinguishing the homosexual and the transsexual from what she calls the 'true transvestite' (Prince, 1957: 84). The true transvestites are 'exclusively heterosexual ... frequently married and often fathers' (ibid.: 84). They value their male organs and enjoy using them and do not wish them to be removed (ibid.: 84). Prince's story (e.g., Prince, 1967; 1976; 1979a; 1979b; 1997a; 1997b) became more sophisticated over the years, reflecting the influence of psychological and sociological theories of gender, and of feminism, as they developed from the 1960s onwards. In its basics, however, it remained unchanged. Prince consistently argued that transvestism is concerned with gender, not with sex or sexuality, and that it is not a perversion or illness.

The interactions between member and expert stories is again illustrated by the fact that Prince gave a lecture to the Society for the Scientific Study of Sex in November 1963 which was published in the *Journal of Sex Research* in 1967 under the name of Virginia Bruce (Bruce, 1967). By that time, Prince was evidently familiar with the gender terminology and concepts that are taken for granted today. Sex, she points out in that article, is anatomical and physiological, and gender is psycho-social. Transvestism for Prince is very firmly about gender. She argues that sex, the division into male and female, is something we share with other animals. Gender, the division of masculine and feminine, is, on the other hand, 'a human invention' and 'not the inevitable result of biological necessity' (ibid.: 129). But in their socialization, children are pushed in one or the other gender direction and consequently anything associated with the other gender has to be suppressed, particularly in the case of males. Transvestism is the expression of this suppressed femininity. The article ends with the prediction that 'arbitrary distinctions of gender will ... disappear' and 'every individual will achieve full personality expression' (ibid.: 139).

By this time, in 1967, Prince thought that the term 'transvestite' had been corrupted and was used to apply to anyone who cross-dresses in the literal translation of the word and she devised new terms to reflect her own ideas. One alternative she proposed (under the pseudonym, Bruce) was the term 'FemmePersonator' – 'one who "personates", that is, makes a real person out of, and brings life to, his feminine self' (ibid.: 133). Also, from around the mid-1960s, Prince was advocating the use of the term 'femmiphile' which she defined as 'lover of the feminine'. The term was intended to draw attention to the motive for cross-dressing and thus underline the distinction between the heterosexual cross-dressers (whom she thinks Hirschfeld had in mind when he coined the term transvestite) and homosexuals or transsexuals who may also cross-dress (Prince, 1973: 22).

The term 'femmepersonator' and the idea of 'full personality expression' reflect Prince's image of the 'true transvestite' who, like Prince, herself, has a feminine – but initially hidden – part of their personality, which she refers to as 'the woman within'. Prince's magazine *Transvestia* that we discuss below included a message on the inside cover which stated: '*Transvestia* dedicated to the needs of those heterosexual persons who have become aware of their "other side" and seek to express it'.

Prince was not the first male to venture over the gender border, of course, but she was a true pioneer in the sense of being someone who ventures into strange territory and prepares the way for others to follow. Moreover, she was and is very clear about the road to be followed, and is intolerant of those who would take a different road. In *How to Be a Woman Though Male* (Prince, 1971), she tells us that society 'does have a right to protect itself from odd appearing and uncouth acting "pseudo women."' Therefore, the femmiphile who goes out in public as a woman should 'know how to look authentic, to behave properly and to just melt into the feminine world without notice' (ibid.: 135). Moreover, the femmiphile should not just try to be 'any' woman. No! Prince wags a finger at her readers and tells them: 'if you are going to appear in society as a woman, don't just be a woman, be a lady' (ibid.: 135). She continues:

> it is the best in womanhood that the FP seeks to emulate, not the common. Be the LADY in the crowd if you are going to be a woman at all, not the scrubwoman or a clerk. It is the beauty, delicacy, grace, loveliness, charm and freedom of expression of the feminine world that you are seeking to experience and enjoy, so 'live it up' – be as pretty, charming and graceful as you can. (1971: 137).

During the 1950s, when Prince's 'woman within' was emerging, she also began to develop her contacts with other transvestites. A particularly important contact was made through the clinic of psychiatrist Karl Bowman (Prince, 1997b: 350). According to Docter (2004: 45), this contact was Louise Lawrence who was 'the hub of an informal communications network of cross dressers spanning California'. Prince attended a case conference involving Lawrence, obtained her address and made contact with her. Other cross-dressers contacted Prince after her cross-dressing was publicized during the reporting of her first divorce case (Bullough and Bullough, 1993: 284). The informal and occasional meetings that came out of these contacts evolved into an organized national and, later international, movement largely as a result of Prince's leadership. As Docter put it: 'in her view, it was time to get organized' (2004: 50).

A key ingredient in the embryonic transgender community was the establishment in 1960 of the magazine *Transvestia*. Docter's account of the magazine's birth is as follows:

> The idea to begin a newsletter called *Transvestia* originated from discussions among the Long Beach cross dressers who had been meeting now and then, quite informally, at Johnny Thorn's house in Long Beach during the early 1950s. Selection of the name, *Transvestia*, should probably be credited to Thorn, who later claimed that Virginia 'stole it'; the facts of this remain unclear. (ibid.: 74)

Prince puts it this way: 'From various sources I managed to assemble a mailing list of twenty-five people, each of whom was willing to contribute four dollars, and so I started *Transvestia* magazine with a working capital of a hundred dollars' (1997a: 350). From its inception, *Transvestia* provided a point of contact from which Prince began to build her organization. As Docter puts it: 'this little magazine was an international stimulus for networking and social organization, much like we see on the internet today' (2004: 89). In 1961, Prince established her first club for transvestites, initially known as the Hose and Heels club. As Docter tells the story:

> She mailed invitations to all known cross dressers in southern California, most of them having been subscribers to *Transvestia* magazine, inviting them to attend a meeting, not cross dressed, and to bring along a pair of pantyhose and a pair of high heeled shoes ... the idea was that security would be enhanced when they all donned these items at the same time during the meeting. (ibid.: 50-1)

In 1962, this began to evolve into a national organization called The Foundation for Full Personality Expression (FPE or Phi Pi Epsilon) with a magazine for members called *Femme Mirror* (Prince, 1997b: 353). Membership of FPE could be applied for after having subscribed to and read five or more issues of *Transvestia*. Acceptance was then dependent on approval of the application form, payment of dues and personal interview with an area counsellor (*Transvestia*, 1972, Vol XII, No. 72). Prince encouraged the formation of local 'chapters' which then affiliated to FPE which Prince usually refers to as a sorority.

FPE was aimed at those oscillating cross-dressers who, like Prince, were heterosexual. Homosexuals and transsexuals, as she referred to them, were not admitted. According to Feinbloom (1976: 62), interviewers of new applicants for membership were cautioned against accepting 'bondage or masochistic people, amateur investigators, curiosity seekers, homosexuals, transsexuals or emotionally disturbed people'. In addition to the emphasis on keeping out those who were not seen as 'real' transvestites, great emphasis was placed on maintaining members' privacy and secrecy.

FPE continued until 1975/6 when it merged with a Southern Californian transvestite group, Mamselle, to become the Society for the Second Self or Tri-Sigma for short. Tri Sigma (later Tri-Ess) followed the pattern of FPE. It was, said Prince in 1976: 'an organization limited to heterosexual cross dressers and to those who are not involved in such behaviour patterns as bondage, punishment, fetishism for rubber, leather or other, or domination and humiliation' (Prince, 1976: 41).

Transsexuals were also discouraged from seeking to join FPE and the emphasis on security and the involvement of members' wives continued. But applications to join could be made after purchasing only three copies of *Transvestia* or Prince's book *Understanding Cross Dressing* and there is no mention of an interview (Prince, 1976: 42–3). Tri-Ess continues with about two dozen 'chapters' today (Docter, 2004: 93).

Transvestia gradually recruited subscribers from outside the United States particularly in England, Scandinavia and Australia, some of whom joined FPE. Some people bought *Transvestia* when working or holidaying in the United States and copies were sometimes to be found in 'adult' bookshops elsewhere in the world. According to Bullough and Bullough (1993: 285), Prince also made contact with European transvestites in the early 1960s when visiting her wife's family in England. In 1965, a European Region group of FPE was formed based in London and called the Beaumont Society. An independent Beaumont Society, affiliated to FPE, was formed in 1967 with a caucus of seven members. At about the same time, FPE (Northern Europe) was formed and is still in existence (as is the Beaumont Society). Eventually, organizations based on her principles developed around the world, most notably in Canada, Australia, New Zealand and South Africa.

Evidently Prince's dogmatic and autocratic style of leadership did not endear her to some (Docter, 2004: 85–6). Her insistence on the exclusion of homosexuals and transsexuals also became a source of conflict, with some chapters leaving FPE, to pursue a more open membership policy elsewhere ibid.: 90). Nevertheless, the impact of *Transvestia* and FPE has been considerable. In addition to providing a means of communication between part-time cross-dressers, *Transvestia* 'taught the cross dressers of the world how to organize and operate local support groups, and showed that this could be done without any harmful consequences' (ibid.: 89).

Gender oscillating, or being 'just a cross-dresser', as it is sometimes referred to within the contemporary transgender community, is still a highly stigmatized activity. Helen Boyd, the wife of a cross-dresser, recently authored a book on cross-dressing principally addressed to other wives or partners of cross-dressers. She points out that:

> very few of the crossdressers profiled here are completely 'out' and that even those who are exercise caution. I have changed some of their names at their request to conceal their identities. It may be obvious that my husband's name - Betty Crow - is his 'femme' name, but it's less obvious that mine - Helen Boyd - is a nom de plume. Unfortunately we learned the hard way why most cross dressers and their wives are still in the closet. My husband trusted his ex-girlfriend enough to share his secret with her, and when they broke up - and we began dating - she harassed us and blackmailed us for years on the basis of his being a crossdresser. We would love to be brave enough to throw caution to the wind, but it's not yet a realistic option. (2003: 15-16)

There can be little doubt that almost 50 years ago, when Prince began to pioneer the social organization of part-time cross-dressing, the need for secrecy was even greater. Prince's organizations and their offshoots provided a safe space within which a person could explore their gender oscillating. The system of vetting new entrants was one attempt to maintain security, as was her establishment of a medium of communication between members which ensured anonymity, thereby reducing one of the risks of entry.

In addition to providing security and support, Prince's creations provided social activities with opportunities to cross-dress, access to suppliers of clothing and other items, and access to skills in cross-dressing. Some instruction in the latter was provided in the pages of *Transvestia* and, as we saw earlier in this chapter, Prince produced the first guidebook for gender oscillators in her *How to Be a Woman Though Male* in 1971. She also wrote and published transvestite fiction and marketed various aids such as artificial breasts.

Prince's writings provided a positive philosophy of cross-dressing that aimed to encourage – as the inside cover of *Transvestia* puts it – 'understanding, self acceptance, peace of mind in place of loneliness, fear and self condemnation'. Prince's philosophy was not only a positive one, she promoted the acceptable face of transvestism; it was purged of anything that might offend, particularly anything sexual. Thus it could be accepted not only by transvestites themselves but also by their families and friends and the wider society.

To what extent Prince's story of the transvestite was consciously developed to legitimize and respectabilize cross-dressing is impossible to know. Benjamin seemed to think that it was and in 1966 wrote that 'the denial of sexual motives for transvestites is meant to make Tvism more respectable and therefore more acceptable to the public' (1966: 37). According to Docter, Prince kept the topic of sexuality out of *Transvestia* as much as possible in order to avoid conflict with the postal authorities (2004: 80). The exclusion of gay men and transsexuals from Prince's organizations fitted her tale of the 'true transvestite' but she also argued that it helped to gain the acceptance of members' wives and partners who were only too ready to associate cross-dressing with homosexuality and sex-changes (Docter, 2004: 90). Such a view is still a common one among partners of cross-dressers, as we are only too aware from our own interview material.

Although Prince's story was radical compared to the psychopathology story, her views of femininity and her attempt to distance transvestism from homosexuality were decidedly traditional. By the early 1970s, Prince's story was being criticized by sections of the gay and women's movements (e.g., Brake, 1976; Weeks, 1977: 224–5). In contrast to the assertive and confrontational approach of those movements, Prince had sought simply to carve out a safe space for cross-dressers (or a least a certain type of cross-dresser). She constructed a 'closet' for cross-dressers at the very time that many gay men and lesbians were seeking to escape from theirs. Prince's story was one that sought acceptance; she believed that acceptance of her story would follow when people realized 'the truth', as she saw it.

The contemporary oscillating story

When we began to research transgendering in the second half of the 1970s, the opportunities for telling transgendering stories outside a medical context were limited. The UK Beaumont Society had about 700 members then and the Prince-inspired gender oscillating story could be found in its monthly magazine, *The Beaumont Bulletin*, available only to members of the Society and to selected researchers. An unknown number of oscillators belonged to, or made use of, the other clubs or meetings that did not come under the auspices of the Beaumont Society. Outside of these subcultural settings, 'agony aunt' columns in magazines and newspapers regularly contained letters from cross-dressers and the replies often contained details of supportive organizations such as the Beaumont Society, rather than recommending medical treatment. The fact that two of the speakers at the Beaumont Society conference in 1975 were 'agony aunts' is an indication of their important role at that time. Later, telephone advice lines became another site at which stories could be told and refined. In the past few years, the oscillating story has been told fairly frequently in radio and television plays and documentaries, but today, of course, it is the internet that has emerged as the place where oscillating stories of all kinds can be written and read in the greatest proliferation.

What is the nature of the stories that we find on the internet? In some stories we see many similarities to those we heard 30 years ago – the subjects of the stories are still male, and they are still predominantly heterosexual. Cross-dressing is still a stigmatized activity and audiences for 'confessional' stories have to be chosen with care. People still tell stories of secretive cross-dressing, of living 'in the closet' before discovering others 'like them'. Years ago we were told by 'transvestites' that they discovered a name for themselves, and for what they did, in a magazine, in a newspaper article, or in a book; now they are more likely to make the discovery on the internet.

The established transvestite organizations now have a presence on the web and some of the features of the Prince-style organizations remain. Security issues are still important (the Seahorse Society of New South Wales still has an interview system before members can join). The idea of the 'woman within' is still common in one form or another in oscillating organizations. The basics of the Prince story appear to be intact, although the exclusion of gay men has been relaxed, and the exclusion of transsexuals has been abandoned. 'Transgender' has become the preferred inclusive term used on the Beaumont Society's webpage which now states: 'We are the largest and longest established transgendered support group in the UK, and have developed a support network which has been at the forefront of the transgender, transvestite, transsexual and cross dressing community since 1966!' (http://www.beaumontsociety.org.uk/). The emphasis of established organizations on public education is also still evident, as is illustrated in this further quote from the Beaumont Society site: 'the society keenly promotes the better understanding of the conditions of transgender, transvestism and gender dysphoria in society, thereby creating and improving tolerance and acceptance of these conditions by a wider public.' The established associations still tend to play down any erotic connotations, with the Beaumont Society site stating, 'The internet often displays transgendered people as sexual objects – the Beaumont Society aims to expel this myth and is not available for making sexual liaisons!'

It is certainly true that the erotic aspects of oscillating are very visible on the web. A 'Google' search using 'Transvestite' recently yielded 1,610,000 pages and in among the support and information pages are plenty of sites offering 'hard core pornography' for a fee, as well as many sites with amateur pornographic material produced by 'enthusiasts' and freely available to other 'enthusiasts'. In the 1970s, such material would only have been available in specialist pornographic publications purchased at a high price from specialist retailers.

So both 'respectable' and less 'respectable' stories can be found on the web. An extensive range of more minority oscillating stories can also be found there. Over the years, we have come across many oscillators who have felt that the gender oscillating story did not 'fit' them, and that the social and other activities created around that story did not cater for their needs. FPE, the Beaumont Society and most other 'transvestite' organizations expected members to attend meetings dressed as far as possible as 'ordinary' women. Many of our informants had an interest in cross-dressing in specific ways (dressing as nurses, schoolgirls and maids was common) that were not welcome at the monthly group meetings of most support groups for the transgendered. Some of these people did manage to meet others with similar interests but the openness of the internet has enabled the sharing of many of these more minority stories. One example is that of the 'Bow Belles':

> The Bow Belle Sorority ... is intended for those TV's and/or RGs (Real Girls) who appreciate and love to wear young female garments from any era to present day pretty clothes including bridesmaids. We wear from choice (as an example) Victorian style girls [sic] party clothes or 50's party wear. The two most sought after styles of Bow Belles clothes. Satin and Taffeta are everywhere.! [sic] Frilly lacy and/or satin as worn in the past to parties by girls from 6 or 7 through their early teens (but seldom today) is the Bow Belles dream. (http://www.tvoptions.co.uk)

According to the writer of the above, oscillators with these kinds of preferences are not made welcome at most 'TV' meetings, and with small numbers of such oscillators spread thinly across the UK the opportunities for face-to-face contact are limited.

In the late 1970s, those of our oscillating informants who went to Beaumont Society meetings or other TV/TS Support group meetings either arrived 'dressed' or they 'dressed' at the venue, which might have been a member's house or a church meeting room. Light refreshments would be available and people would sit around talking, most often about trans matters. The more adventurous might occasionally visit a welcoming gay bar. Some provision may have been made for the sale of clothes, wigs and make-up, but they were small scale and mostly run by the oscillators themselves.

Since the 1990s, however, a very different story has emerged. As we mentioned earlier in the chapter, alongside the success of the traditional 'transvestite' organizations with their supportive and educational roles has arisen a large commercial sector. Alongside the new proliferation of clubs, bars, hotels and events for the cross-dresser, we can discern a different oscillating story. The old style 'transvestite' is still there, but he is increasingly in a minority. The 'new' oscillators are more open and relaxed about their activities. They are less concerned with understanding and classifying themselves, although they may have done that in the past. Rather they are focused on enjoying the possibilities provided by the now widely available commercial and other facilities. They are more open about their oscillating with families and friends. They are likely to spend considerable time and money on the trans scene, particularly in the large metropolitan areas. They are less concerned with distinctions between gay and straight, transsexual and transvestite and so on, and are more likely to refer to themselves as trannies or cross-dressers or transgender than transvestites. Furthermore, they more likely to be part of an informal social network, perhaps via the internet, and less likely to join a traditional transvestite support group.

Parts of the new story are to be found in Charles Anders' book *The Lazy Crossdresser* (2002). There is a familiar story of secret cross-dressing but, as says Anders on *his* (note the pronoun) website, 'In the past year it's gone from being a scary secret to becoming a performance' (http://www.sfbg.com/SFLife/34/31/lead.html) (3 May 2000).

In some ways Anders' book belongs with the guidebooks for oscillators exemplified by Prince's *How to Be a Woman Though Male,* but the light-hearted and irreverent tone is at odds with Prince's approach. Anders (who has cross-dressed publicly for several years according to the book cover) states: 'The Lazy Crossdresser believes that it's OK for men to wear women's clothes. We're not even going to question that. Clothes have no gender, and anybody should be allowed to wear whatever clothes they want' (http://www.lazycrossdresser.tv/about.html):

He continues:

> a lot of crossdressers are overwhelmed by 'shoulds'. If you're going to wear women's clothes, you 'should' wear fake breasts. You can't wear a nice dress without five kinds of foundation garments. Women don't follow these rules — and I know tons of flat-chested women — so why should men wearing women's clothes? (http://www.lazycrossdresser.tv/about.html)

And adds:

> I don't try to look like a woman. Making people believe you were born female is the Holy Grail for many cross-dressers. But I don't worry about creating any kind of 'illusion,' either glamorous or womanly. I want to look good and have fun. To have fun, I have to feel comfortable and banish worries about getting away with deception. (2002: v)

Vicky Lee began to produce the *Transvestites Guide to London* in 1992, which later evolved into *The Way Out Tranny Guide* in 1995. She also co-founded *The Way Out Club* in London in 1993. In her many publications, videos and web-pages, we find many aspects of the contemporary oscillating story. While providing information and support is still an element of Lee's various activities, much more emphasis is put on enjoyment and simply 'having fun'. As she put it in the 11th edition of *The Way Out Tranny Guide*: 'increasing openness, better education and the internet are offering the latest generation wider options. Cross-dressing and transgenderism are less of a taboo now' (2003: 24). In the same guide, 'Kirsty' writes:

> you were born a tranny and you can't give it up any more than you can give up breathing ... So you may as well enjoy it. There is a name for people who do nothing out of the ordinary, BORING and trannies do not fall into this category. So be proud and loud and get out there and enjoy yourself. (ibid.: 28)

What is also very evident in the pages of *The Tranny Guide* is the diversity of the transgendering stories to be found there: in fact Vicky Lee advises her readers to 'embrace diversity. Realise there is no such thing as normal' (ibid.: 19). On occasion, this contemporary oscillating story begins to merge into the transcending stories that we examine in Chapter 5.

The oscillating drag story

The '"girls" just want to have fun' quality of the contemporary oscillating story is in many respects shared by the drag story to which we now turn. *The Oxford English Dictionary* provides a starting point for us with its definition, 'feminine attire worn by a man'. In that broad sense it has been used by the popular British press to refer to almost any instance of cross-dressing by men (King, 1993). *The Cambridge International Dictionary of English* gives us this definition: '(esp. of a man) the action of dressing in clothes of the opposite sex, often for humorous entertainment'.

Both of the above definitions suggest that 'drag' is more comfortably applied to male cross-dressing. Similarly, Baker (1994: 17) notes the theatrical origins of the term and writes that, 'the use of the word to refer exclusively to men suggests that a woman dressed as a man cannot correctly be described as being in drag, but lacking any other term it is used in that context'. As we shall see, the term has more recently enjoyed an association with female cross-dressing.

In general, drag stories are told in different places and in different ways to those of the other oscillating stories we have looked at. They appear more often in popular culture. More recently, drag has been at the core of a number of popular films such as *Priscilla, Queen of the Desert*, (1994), *To Wong Foo, Thanks for Everything, Julie Newmar* (1995), and *The Birdcage* (1996).

Although there have been a number of drag auto/biographies such as those by RuPaul (1995), Danny La Rue (Underwood, 1974), and Frank Marino (1997), these are by written (or 'ghost-written') by those who have become celebrities to some degree. On the whole, drag is about 'doing', not about writing about it. Most of the tellers of drag stories have not been the central characters themselves but those who have interviewed them. As Fleischer notes, the drag queens he interviewed were 'bored to death with talking about what they do and why they do it' (1996: 20).

Given the importance of the visual impact of drag, it is not surprising to find that pictures feature heavily in the telling of drag stories. For many years there have existed magazines devoted to drag, such as *Female Mimics International* or *Drag*, that consist mainly of photographs of drag performers, sometimes in the throes of their transformation from men to women. There have also been a number of popular books in which, again, photographs are prominent (Brubach, 1999; Chermayeff et al., 1995; Fleischer, 1996; Kirk and Heath, 1984; Montmorency, 1970).

The drag story is also told in more academic texts with a focus on the theatre such as Baker (1968; 1994), and Senelick (2000) and again photographs are much in evidence. It is also told in a number of ethnographies. Newton's *Mother Camp*, first published in 1972, is probably the best known of these ethnographies. More recently, the work of Tewksbury (1993; 1994; 1995); Tewksbury and Gagné (1996); Schacht (2000); and Schacht with Underwood (2004), have updated the story.

Terminology varies in different times and in different places. Schacht (2002: 158), who has been undertaking an ongoing ethnography of 'drag queens' in over a dozen different contexts in North America since 1993, notes that the participants in his studies use the terms 'female impersonators' and 'drag queens' interchangeably: 'quite simply, drag queens/female impersonators in this context are gay men who dress as women (typically donning glamorous female trappings) to play specific roles in this community' (Schacht, 2000: 265). On the other hand, the female impersonators interviewed by Tewksbury, also in the USA, rejected the term 'drag queen' as insulting and degrading; 'those who do accept the drag queen label are viewed by other performers as inferior, less serious about performing and less talented than other performers' (1993: 470–1). Schacht (2002: 162–3) provides an interesting typology which locates 'Female [MTF] drag within the matrices of gender and sexuality'. He finds 'four emergent traditions of doing female drag: high brow female impersonators, female illusionists, professional glamour queens, and professional camp queens'. This typology make for a useful starting point for any detailed analysis of the interrelations between sex, sexuality and gender in the lived experience of drag performers. As Schacht notes, 'an individual performer can actually undertake several forms – to me they have experientially felt like noticeably different types of doing female drag (ibid.: 163). Schacht's findings are similar to our own in the UK. Caroline was one of our key informants on the London drag scene for some 15 years. She identified principally as a female entertainer and dancer, second, as a 'sex change', and third, as a drag act. After her 'sex change', she preferred to work as a female showgirl and cabaret dancer in contexts where her 'sex change' status was unknown. When she fraternised with her TV and TS friends, she was content to be thought of as a very beautiful and feminine 'sex change'. She was a successful drag act before her 'sex-change', mainly in the London area. She preferred not to 'do drag' after her surgery, but frequently did so in order to earn a living. When 'doing drag' after her 'sex change', she would end her finale strip by 'revealing' an imitation penis where her original penis had been, in mock denial of her postoperative status. She rarely, if ever, referred to herself as transsexual.

Since the early 1990s, a number of writers have told the drag story from a postmodern perspective emphasizing its transgressive potential (Butler, 1990a; 1993; Garber, 1992). We shall consider this literature in Chapter 5, with particular reference to FTM drag 'kinging', as part of our consideration of transcending stories.

What, then, are the main elements of the oscillating drag story? First, is the crucial element of performance before an audience. As Newton says:

> *the* distinguishing characteristic of drag, as opposed to heterosexual transvestism, is its group character; *all* drag, whether formal, informal, or professional, has a theatrical structure and style. There is no drag without an actor and his audience, and there is no drag without drama (or theatricality). (1979: 37)

Judith Lorber (2004) in her preface to a recent collection of articles on drag makes a similar point: 'I have been puzzling over what distinguishes drag from other forms of occasional or long-term cross-dressing. Where does drag fit into the larger pantheon of transgendered behavior? What are its core elements?' And she continues:

> Drag's core elements are *performance* and *parody*. Drag exaggerates gendered dress and mannerisms with enough little incongruities to show the 'otherness' of the drag artist. In the exaggeration lies the parody. Drag is performance because it needs an audience to appreciate the underlying joke. (ibid.: xv)

The professional female impersonators studied by Tewksbury 'heavily value the public nature of their impersonations. The experience is not complete, or satisfying, unless it is presented publicly' (1994: 33–4). The idea of a 'closet' drag queen therefore makes no sense. As Newton argues, if there is no audience, then there is no point in wearing women's clothes. She refers to one of the drag queens she interviewed who, she said, 'has also tried to wear female attire around the house, but doesn't any more because he felt foolish. "Who am I performing to?" he asked himself' (1979: 52). And if the whole point of drag is the spectacle, then what cannot be seen has no importance; thus 'most drag queens do not wear women's underwear' (Kirk and Heath, 1984: 73).

As we have noted, previously, because of the linkages between sex, sexuality and gender, cross-dressing or cross-gender behaviour is often presumed to imply an 'inverted' (as it was once called) sexuality. Drag, in particular, carries this implication especially as in the term 'drag queen' defined by *The Oxford English Dictionary* as: 'a male homosexual transvestite' and by the *Cambridge International Dictionary of English* as 'a man, often a homosexual, dressed as a woman'. Certainly, another element in the drag story is that of the central character as gay. As Kirk and Heath put it: 'Drag queens are gay men who never forget that they are men, but who like to dress on occasion in clothes which society usually attributes to the opposite sex. They are never confused about their gender' (1984: 73).

In contrast again to the gender oscillating story, the drag queen or female impersonator is not seeking to 'pass' as a woman and typically has no erotic or other attachment to the clothes worn. As Schacht writes of the participants in his study,

> none aspires to surgically become a real woman or has any expressed erotic attachment to the apparel. Or, as more succinctly stated by one of the drag queens to me about professional pre-op female impersonators, 'That's taking it too far. When I go home after a show, I like to rip my breasts out and make love as a man.' (2000: 265)

So the identity of the drag queen then is just that – drag queen – and not female or woman. The drag queens that Schacht studied contend that 'drag queens typically refer to their feminine personas in the third person, or as "other"', this then, 'separates the male creators from the feminine identity they embody in such a manner that they seemingly can become very different individuals when in drag' (ibid.: 258). Put another way, the characters portrayed in drag remain just that – a character – there is no hint of the expression of a feminine self.

The photographs of transvestites that are to be found in the pages of transvestite support organization publications most frequently show their subjects in unremarkable women's clothes. The photographs in some of the soft pornographic magazines and websites show cross-dressed males showing their (female) underwear (occasionally with bulging genitalia prominently displayed). However, in the photographic images that fill the books on drag, the clothing worn is not simply 'women's' clothing but is glamorous, flamboyant, and 'over-the-top'. The drag is *exaggerated* gender display' (Lorber, 2004: xvi). The abiding impression left by these photographs is the playfulness of it all. So another crucial point that distinguishes the drag story from that of the transvestite is that, 'above all, drag is meant to be fun' (Fleischer, 1996: 6). That is not to say that transvestites do not enjoy their cross-dressing but that, as Kirk and Heath put it, 'transvestism is generally a more serious business for those concerned' (1984: 72).

In setting forth our material on the oscillating mode of transgendering, we have, on occasion, commented on the fact that 'at this point' oscillating merges into the transcending mode, for instance. Similarly, in the opening sections of the chapter, we made the point that once the oscillating metronome falls still, it rests upon a midpoint, which brings to mind the negating (neither male, nor female) mode we consider in the next chapter. More importantly, still, we repeat the point made at the end of the previous chapter that meanings of narratives and their constituents emerge within the frameworks in which they are placed. In that chapter, we were specifically contrasting our framework with that of Blanchard's. The point made there is a general one.

Recently, and particularly in the light of the deliberately transcending intent of much drag 'kinging' which we consider in Chapter 5, commentators have returned to the worlds of the drag queen, and male drag, in general, with a new vision which revisits it in the light of transcending. Taylor and Rupp (2004: 113), for instance, write: 'One of the burning questions about drag queens among both scholars and audiences is whether they are more gender-revolutionaries than gender-conservatives.'

Bode (2003), for instance, sets herself the task of answering the question: 'Is drag subversive of binary gender norms?' She adopts a measured approach that argues that male drag does not 'overthrow' 'socially embedded ideas of gender's binary nature', or 'consistently and universally' subverts gender, but it does, she argues, assist 'in the questioning, contesting and reformation of thinking in relation to gender' (ibid.: 19). She concludes: 'Drag is meaningful in questioning gender. While it may not be the ultimate answer to challenging current gender norms, drag can act as a legitimate subversion and contestation of gender's traditional dichotomous structure' (ibid.: 25).

It is instructive to contrast this sort of approach with ours. We assume from her writing that Bode is a feminist scholar who seeks to move towards 'the ultimate answer to challenging current gender norms'. From this perspective, male drag can at least be a 'help'. We, on the other hand, seek to pay the proper respect to transgender diversity, particularly from the standpoint of trans people, themselves.

In our sociological, relational and processual view, not only are there no 'ultimate' answers, but there are no 'ultimately' privileged positions. The same applies to our own framework. The range and diversity of oscillating are so great that this chapter can only make the claim to have considered the major oscillating stories we consider most appropriate for consideration in a sociological book on tales of transgendering. Consideration of these tales in terms of major modes and processes should not fool us into thinking that every incident of transgendering must 'ultimately' fit into one mode or another. Given our classification into four modes, however, we do find it useful to consider oscillating as the residual mode.

Where permanent 'substituting' is privileged over the other sub-processes, inclusion under the migrating mode is generally not problematic to us. Similarly, where re-defining of the binary divide is privileged over the other sub-processes, we generally have no difficulty making a classification in terms of transcending. Privileging erasing, over the other sub-processes, always sensitizes us to a classification of negating. However, oscillating is often much more opaque in its utilization of the sub-processes of transgendering. Take, for instance, the illustration of Barry in the following vignette.

Barry lives and works as a male. At home, he lives with his female partner who sees herself as heterosexual. Before Barry joins his partner in bed at night, he applies a toner and a hormone bust enlargement cream to his nipples (preparatory substituting). He is not sure that the cream is leading to breast development, but it is making his nipples more sensitive. Occasionally he supplements this regimen with a course of hormone pills that he has acquired from a prostitute he visits. These do lead to breast tissue enlargement and sensitivity (embryonic substituting). Naked, he joins his wife in bed. As he touches her body he feels heterosexually aroused and with his penis erect enters his wife. For this period he identifies as a man with a man's body. In due time his wife climaxes. To maintain his erection, he now oscillates into female mode. He disavows his male body and 'his' penis becomes his wife's. He now has his wife's vagina (fantasy substituting). When he climaxes, it is, he feels, a female orgasm. His pre-come is 'her' lubrication. His ejaculatory fluid is his wife's. With intercourse over, his male self slowly re-emerges.

There can be little doubt that in terms of our framework, this is a story of oscillating. However, where is the privileging of implying and concealing? To dwell on this issue is, we suggest, to misuse the intent of our framework. Better, rather, to use the framework as the sensitizing device it is intended to be. In this vein, we would code this incident in terms of 'fantasy rapid oscillating' and make the point that fantasy rapid oscillating transgendering provides particularly illuminating illustrative material on the complex interrelations between sex, sexuality and gender.

In the final section of this chapter, we consider Barry's story in more detail, with particular reference to his oscillating 'career path' or trajectory.

Barry's story: a tale of interrelations

The complexity of the interrelations between sex, sexuality and gender in Barry's 'fantasy rapid oscillating' considered above refers to a very short time frame: that between Barry's preparation for bed and the sexual intercourse that follows quite shortly and is over quite soon. However, were Barry to reflect on this incident he would be likely to invoke past experiences and conferred meanings in an array of complex interrelations. We will use further segments of Barry's story to illustrate something of the way the various oscillating stories we have considered in this chapter interrelate in the construction of meanings and identities, and to illuminate further something of the way the various sub-processes of transgendering may interrelate in diverse ways over a developing oscillating trajectory.

In *Male Femaling*, Ekins (1997: 19-20) considered Barry in the context of selected oscillating incidents from his first 'cross-dressing' incident at 5 years old to his time after leaving university when he is being increasingly drawn to the 'glamour and sleaze' of drag bars. Barry makes an excellent informant for a chapter on oscillating because his transgendering trajectory has always been within the oscillating mode. His non-transgendering commitments and attachments have always precluded migrating. He has never considered 'negating' as an option, indeed, has little or no knowledge of it, and he says he regards 'transcending' as unintelligible in its written form and 'weird' and 'not for him' in many of its practical guises. We will follow the framework developed in Ekins (1993; 1997) for the analysis of male femaling career paths, but here revisit that framework from the standpoint of the concerns of this chapter.

137

Phase 1: Beginning oscillating

Barry was brought up in a conventional middle-class family in Cambridge, England. He recalls his first 'cross-dressing incident' as taking place when he was 5 years old. He was playing 'schools' with his sister. They were the 'Browns' and he was Anna Brown. What was more natural than he should put on his sister's school skirt and blouse? Lost in the game, and attaching no particular significance to it, the children are called to lunch by their mother. They bound into the dining room, to be met by the stony gaze of their father seated at the head of the table. Barry becomes acutely aware of the tension in the air. He shuffles nervously feeling the cold of the seat on his bare thighs. He looks down 'his' skirt. Nothing is said. He knows he has done something dreadfully wrong. His parents disapprove. This is taboo. He will not do it again. Or will he?

Quite soon, however, he will, indeed, 'do it again'. But now he has learned that he must keep his oscillating secret. Up until the age of 13 it never crosses his mind that he might actually acquire his own female clothes, rather he occasionally borrows his mother's and his sister's clothes. At first, his preoccupations focus on the laundry basket in the bathroom in which he discovers a veritable treasure trove of items of clothing of his mother and sister. As a pre-adolescent boy his legs are hairless and as he admires himself in the bathroom mirror he takes care to arrange that mirror so that only his legs are visible to his observing eyes. He takes a pair of stockings from the laundry basket, carefully rolls up each stocking, places them over his feet and slides them up his legs. As he observes himself doing this he is, we may say, implying that he is a young woman. As his legs are hairless, he has no need to conceal any hair on his legs. He 'conceals' the rest of his body simply by not revealing it to his sightline in the mirror. We may say that the wearing of stockings has 'erased' any masculinity of his legs. Certainly, he has 'redefined' his legs as those of a young girl. Nevertheless, the major sub-process implicated in this incident of oscillating is that of implying. Quite soon, Barry feels that if he stays in the bathroom any longer he will arouse the suspicions of his mother and sister downstairs. He removes the stockings, replaces them and returns to his life outside the bathroom as a boy. This incident of oscillating is now over.

Phase 2: Fantasying oscillating

It is not until Barry is 13 years old that he will be left on his own in the house regularly and for extended periods of time. Up until this time, he finds himself increasingly 'fantasying' cross-dressing and, indeed, fantasying that he is a girl. His favourite fantasy for an extended period during his pre-teens is that it is Christmas time and he is out shopping with his mother. His mother chooses for him all manner of girls' clothes and accessories, and in great excitement and anticipation he waits for Christmas morning when he will be given them. Christmas morning comes and his happiness is consummated. It is during this period that Barry recalls masturbating with these fantasies in his mind. In these fantasies he has become a young girl, become, indeed, a daughter. The clothes and accessories conceal his masculinity entirely; they imply that he is, indeed, a girl.

Phase 3: Doing oscillating

In this phase we see the development of more 'serious' cross-dressing and acting out aspects of fantasy oscillating that build upon activities found in the 'beginning' and 'fantasying' phases. For Barry, doing oscillating in earnest is marked by the purchase of his first items of female clothing for himself. True, he may on occasions have placed his penis between his legs to 'erase' and 'conceal' his masculinity and to fantasy a girl's genital area but he attached no particular importance to that. It was done, he says, more in the spirit of idle curiosity. However, with the purchase of his own pair of girl's panties, he feels that while he is doing oscillating, he is, indeed, a girl. Soon he has his own stockings and he is making a pillowcase into an impromptu skirt. Now, several times a week he engages in 'doing oscillating'. The pleasure it gives him emboldens him. Soon he is secretly borrowing a dress of his mother's to complete his outfit. He takes photographs of himself in the mirror with his Polaroid camera while cross-dressed. But he is concerned. What is the meaning of what he is doing? Who and what is he that he should be doing such things?

Phase 4: Constituting oscillating

Constituting oscillating is the phase that marks the period where the oscillator begins to constitute the meaning of his activities in a sustained and more serious way. It is to be Barry's fifteenth birthday when his move to constituting oscillating becomes marked. He is in the public library working on a school project when he chances upon a book entitled *Sexual Deviation* (Storr, 1964). He is drawn to the chapter on transvestism. It is by a psychiatrist who tells a variant of the 'sexual pathology story' that we have detailed previously in this chapter. Barry's reading of the chapter provides him with the only detailed story he knows about both what he is and what he does. He is a transvestite. Transvestism is a 'sexual deviation' considered perverse or deviant. He is a sexual deviant. He wrestles with this definition of the situation for many years and begins to seek out reading on this 'perversion'. Later he comes across the story told by Hirschfeld and Ellis (our 'traditional erotic oscillating story') in more detail than the brief mention in the chapter in *Sexual Deviation*. But by then Barry reads the story in the light of the 'sexual pathology' story and conflates what we have distinguished as two separate stories. He is a sexual pervert and that is that. He continues to 'purge' – to throw away his clothes – only to buy another set within an increasingly short time. Things are getting serious. What is he to do?

Barry is now 17. He has his first 'serious' girlfriend. He feels close to her; he enjoys petting with her and he feels constantly sexually aroused in her presence. Maybe he is not a pervert? He is not sure. What he does notice in his more reflective moments is that now he has a girlfriend of his own he seems to have lost interest in his fantasying and 'doing' oscillating. Alas, the initial excitement of his new relationship begins to wear off and he is back to his old ways. Away from his girlfriend at Christmas he finds himself returning to his old 'Christmas fantasy'. Only, now that he is older, he can play out both parts. He buys for himself some of the items his mother used to buy for him in his fantasies. Yes, he is, indeed 'suffering' from a sexual perversion. It is an affliction. He cannot cure himself. What is he to do?

Barry's reading of himself in terms of the 'sexual pathology' story fluctuates in its grip over him. Frequently, he finds it impossible to accept it. After all, in all other regards he is surely so 'normal'. And then one day as he is furtively reading his mother's *Woman's Weekly*, he chances upon a letter on the 'Problem Page' concerning a boy just like himself – a transvestite. Now, for the first time, he has come across what will lead him to our 'gender oscillating story'. He learns there is a group for people like him, indeed, a 'Society': the Beaumont Society. However, it is to be several years before he plucks up the courage to write to the PO Box number and address listed in the magazine. His heart is beating fast as he reads his first communication from the Beaumont Society. In it he learns that he is not alone, that there are many like him and that there is no point 'fighting it'. Indeed, some of what he reads seems to suggest he is 'blessed'. He is in touch with his 'woman within'. He does not feel very blessed but on the other hand he does not feel as much of a 'pervert' as his reading of psychiatry books suggested that he is. Which story is he to believe? Which story is 'true'? He wrestles with this dilemma for many years.

Phase 5: Consolidating oscillating

Consolidating oscillating marks the period where a more full-blown constitution of oscillating self and world is established. It is to be years before his consolidating begins. Barry is now 30. His marriage is in tatters. His wife has left him. He has a new girlfriend. She seems to be sympathetic to his 'feminine' side. Finally, he tells her of his oscillating. He underplays its erotic significance for him, but in no time she is assisting his oscillating. She shaves his body hair; he wears her clothes. Soon he has his own female wardrobe. Soon the couple are regulars at the local Beaumont Society meetings. Now, finally, the 'gender oscillating story' is making sense to him. He reads the story's views on 'wives and partners' with a newfound relevance. He learns that his partner is a 'Grade A – Excellent' accepting partner in Virginia Prince's 'Wives – A To F' listing of 'TV Wives' (Prince, 1967: 68–77). He notes Prince's observations on the 'completely accepting wife' (1967: 140): 'It has been my observation that there are few marriages happier than those in which the wife of a transvestite completely understands and accepts her husband's other self'. Can this really be true? He wonders. He seems to be in clover. His concealing and implying progress in leaps and bounds with the help of his partner. Soon he is beginning to feel that he is more of a woman than many 'born' women or 'real girls' as they are termed at the Society meeting. He believes this because he seems to have more interest in make-up, fashion and jewellery than many 'real girls'. In no time he seems to have consolidated his oscillating in terms of the 'gender oscillating story'.

Fast-forward three years. Sexual relations with his partner are less frequent and less intense than they used to be. He finds himself drawn to prostitute calling cards in telephone booths. Soon he is visiting a prostitute most weeks. He finds he does not want sexual relations with them. Rather, he wants to talk 'girl to girl' with them. He would not dare suggest to his partner (now his wife) that he might ingest female hormones. She has been becoming increasingly less enamoured with his inability to maintain erections during their lovemaking. Talk of his taking her contraceptive pill might weaken their relationship still further. Rather, Barry procures them from Bethany his prostitute 'friend' who seems so understanding about such things. Now when Barry joins his wife in bed, he finds that if he swallows his contraceptive pill it seems to 'put him in the mood' for sexual relations.

It is at this point that the incident we closed the previous section with occurred. Now we are able to see the context from which the reported tale of 'fantasy rapid oscillating' emerged. As Barry lies awake reflecting upon his situation he consoles himself with the fact that his visits to his prostitute 'friend' in some way sustain his marriage. He seems to be more sexually active with his wife after his visits to Bethany. His wife seems to like this. And yet, there are nagging doubts. He is concerned about his disloyalty to his wife. What if she finds out? Where will this ingestion of hormones lead? He knows he does not want a 'sex change'. Is he, perhaps, a sexual pervert after all? He turns on to his side and cuddles into his sleeping wife. Thank goodness his wife is still so accepting of his oscillating. He loves her even more because of this. There is no way he can be 'suffering' from a perversion. The Beaumont Society story is good enough for him and he intends to stick with it. Besides, his implying and concealing are so good that he is able 'pass' in many settings now. Life is good! Thus does Barry's oscillating life continue to oscillate.

FOUR   Negating Stories

A conceptual introduction to negating

When we first introduced our conceptualization of transgendering in terms of migrating and oscillating, their use and application were instantly appreciated by many of our informants. One such MTF 'migrating' informant sought us out after we had presented our first conference paper on migrating and told us how helpful she found our presentation. She said that she had taken her female (migrant) name from that of the name of a ship in her hometown port. The ship had been a famous migrant vessel that had taken migrants from Europe to North America. She had chosen the name of the ship, for herself, quite self-consciously in recognition of the journey on which she was embarking 'to a new land'. In a similar vein, many 'oscillators' have picked up on our term 'oscillating' and used it in their conversations with us, to make the point that they are occasional cross-dressers, not 'transsexuals'. In the language of grounded theory, the conceptualizations of migrating and oscillating easily 'fit and work' (Glaser, 1978).

We experience more difficulty with the concept of negating. Stories of negating are stories which privilege 'ungendering'. Processes of 'ungendering' are implicated in both migrating and oscillating trajectories. Take, for example, the trajectory of the migrating MTF transsexual. In the course of this trajectory, aspects of her maleness/masculinity will be permanently erased (penectomy, for example), and aspects of femaleness/femininity will be permanently substituted (vaginoplasty, for example). In this instance, we might say that 'ungendering' of maleness/masculinity has preceded a new 'gendering' across the binary gender divide. Re-gendering (of the body) is probably the most apt word for what is taking place. 'Ungendering', in this instance, is a transient, liminal phase in this process of migrating. In the language of our sub-processes, erasing has been co-opted in the service of substituting.

On the other hand, there are transgendering trajectories within which erasing becomes the major sub-process, and other sub-processes are co-opted in its service. In these cases, the mode of transgendering becomes what we term 'negating'. Negating privileges ungendering, as opposed to co-opting it in the service of migrating, oscillating or transcending. The binary gender divide, itself, is not redefined in negating as is the case in transcending. Redefining is not the major sub-process, as it is in transcending. Rather, negating individuals seek to 'ungender' themselves in the sense of halting, eliminating, or reversing their previous genderings.

The acknowledgement of 'negating', as a conceptually distinct mode of transgendering, is in its infancy. However, in recent years it has begun to emerge within certain sections of the contemporary transgender community as an identifiably different story with its own attendant identity.

According to *The Concise Oxford Dictionary* (1995), negating has two principal meanings: to nullify, make ineffective, invalidate, expunge, wipe out, cancel; and to deny, deny the existence of. Those negating negate in both senses. Those with male bodies seek to nullify their maleness/masculinity and eliminate in themselves the existence of a binary divide. Similarly, but conversely, this occurs with female-bodied negators.

Migrating and oscillating stories are in abundance, and are widely and easily available to anyone who takes the trouble to look for them. This is not the case with negating stories. They do not feature as identifiably different stories in medical, legal, or other 'expert' tales. They have only recently begun to appear sporadically in transgender community tales of diversity (O'Keefe and Fox, 2003). Yet, once the trouble is taken to search them out, they can be found, and it is a major purpose of this chapter to initiate investigation into this hitherto neglected story.

The most widespread negating tale is that to be found in fantasy fiction. Indeed, so little known are some of the tales that we tell in this chapter, that many readers might be inclined to dismiss many of them as fantasies. The reality, rather, is that though many negating stories are more in evidence in fantasy, almost all the 'fantasies' are being enacted somewhere by someone. We would do well to recall from Chapter 2 that a contemporary variant of the medical tale of migrating still considers transsexuals to be fantasists, and their surgeons and psychiatrists to be 'colluding with delusion'.

Whereas migrating and oscillating stories are clearly evident in the most cursory examination of the literature of cross-dressing and sex-changing, negating stories are not. On our initial visits to this literature, we were inclined to consider many of what we now identify as examples of the conceptually distinct negating story as belonging to the migrating or oscillating categories. However, when revisiting the literature and our field notes from the standpoint of deliberately mapping the detail of transgender diversity, it became clear to us that many of the stories we had previously considered as variants of migrating or oscillating were more sensitively considered in terms of negating.

Redefining in the service of erasing is a major feature of the negating mode. It is easy to miss this aspect in a cursory examination of the experiences of those stories that we differentiate as negating stories. Only detailed examination of the precise interrelations between the various sub-processes of transgendering, in each case, enables the researcher to identify the story as a negating story.

The magazine *F.M.I. Female Mimics International* (1988), unusually for a primarily 'drag' magazine of the period, reprinted a number of sections excerpted from the first issue of *The Sissy Times*. One such section, from 'Dominant Lines from Miss Helen Highboots' is entitled 'Fifteen General Rules for Sissies to Observe' (Highboots, 1988). When considered in terms of the framework developed in Ekins (1997), it might seem to be paying the proper respect to transgender diversity to consider the rules in terms of the eroticization of body and gender femaling, or of erotic oscillating in terms of the framework of this book.

Most of the rules seem to entail various combinations of body and gender male femaling. There are rules for male sissies about the removal of body hair; wearing clear nail polish on the finger nails; wearing 'two coats of clear base and two coats of lacquer (any shade)' on toenails; wearing only female undergarments; and sleeping in a feminine nightgown. There are rules about using only feminine deodorants, shampoos, conditioners, skincare products and fragrances; plucking eyebrows, and so on. An aspect of Rule 8 is 'You will never make sexual overtures or attempt to play an aggressive role in social relationships'. An aspect of Rule 15 is 'You are encouraged to masturbate as often as possible unless I instruct you to abstain'. It might seem evident, therefore, that we are dealing with an aspect of erotic cross-dressing or transvestism.

Again, bearing in mind that the sissies featured in this article are under the instructions of a Mistress – Miss Helen Highboots – it might seem that we are dealing with a sadomasochistic facet of oscillating transvestism.

However, when the rules are examined more closely in conjunction with life history work with sissies who draw on these rules, it becomes clear that for many it is not the erotic oscillating or the allegedly sadomasochistic components that are privileged. Rather, the apparent body and gender femaling is co-opted in the service of the erasing of masculinity, as opposed to the crossing of the binary divide. In terms of the sub-processes of transgendering, it is the erasing of masculinity that is privileged. Moreover, those following the rules do not see themselves as oscillating to and fro across the gender border. Rather they permanently identify as sissies and follow the rules as an aspect of their sissiness.

Rule 10, for instance, features the mimicking of the female menstrual cycle. This often features in oscillating stories. Part of crossing the gender border is seen to entail this aspect of crossing. The sissy, however, defines the mimicking as an aspect of his sissiness: 'Once a month you will mimic the female menstrual cycle. In a future lesson you will be given explicit instructions on how to carry out this assignment. In the meantime, you may begin by wearing any brand of post-menstrual panti-liners in your panties daily' (Highboots, 1988: 42).

Sissy Michael, who identifies permanently as a male sissy, always wears panti-liners following his period, which he simulates by inserting a tampon in his rectum. Dressed in unisex jeans and t-shirt at the time of the following incident, he reports that on one occasion he was buying panti-liners for himself from his local supermarket when he was confronted by two boys who had watched him place the panti-liners in his shopping basket. He reports: 'Two young boys were playing near the check out desk and they asked me if I was a girl. I am not a girl, at all, of course, and they knew that, but it was obvious that these young boys knew I was not a man either.' For this self-identified sissy, the incident confirmed that he was neither a man, nor a woman. Buying and wearing panti-liners was simply what a sissy like him did as part of being a sissy (re-defining). It did not in any way imply that he was a woman. He supposed that his sissy manner and the way he bought the panti-liners confirmed to the boys that he was not a 'man'.

There is, of course, a literature on the eunuch (Ayalon, 1999; Ringrose, 2003) and the castrati (Barbier, 1996). Stories of the eunuch may be considered in terms of negating. norrie mAy-welby, for instance, tells the story of how zie came to wear harem pants for a period in norrie's 'Journey to Androgyny' (O'Keefe and Fox, 2003: 40–1):

> I acted on a strong, long-lasting urge to shave my hair off, only realizing in retrospect why I did it. I was shaving off the identities other people had given me. I was shaving off the perm my mother had suggested for me. I was shaving off the back-combed bouffant I used to attract boys. I was shaving off the biggest gender signifier I presented to the world. And my head was so smooth, so beautiful, so free to be itself without possibly being measured up against other hairstyles.
>
> The shaved head made my gender appear neutral, allowing me to explore the identity of neuter. I started wearing harem pants, for the only image I knew of eunuchs was harem guards. Then I did some research and found that eunuchs had been the power behind the thrones of many empires. In imperial China, for example, castration was the key to a great career in public service. I devoured Mary Renault's *The Persian Boy*, about the eunuch who became a lover to Alexander the Great.

Richard Wassersug has recently begun a project studying various aspects of androgen deprivation in genetic males to better understand the psychological impact of chemical and surgical castration. This project includes reviewing the sexuality of eunuchs in history, examining the language of emasculation as it influences one's expectations of the effects of castration, and surveying voluntary eunuchs and eunuch 'wannabes' about their sexual history and sexuality (Wassersug, 2004; Wassersug et al., 2004). There are, also, the ungendering stories told in the women's movement of those women who argue for androgyny as a means to overthrow androcentrism (Bem, 1993). However, in this chapter we are concerned either with variants of the negating story that have emerged within the contemporary transgendering community like that of norrie mAy-welby's above, or those variants within which aspects of transgendering are clearly implicated, as in many of the male sissy stories which we consider.

There are two principal variants of negating tales in relation to the binary gender divide. In one variant, negating self-consciously buttresses the traditional version of the binary male/female divide for all males and females that are not negating/being negated. Many of the sissy stories that we consider, for instance, evidence a preoccupation and fascination with the minutiae of binary divide stereotypes. In the other variant, those negating consider the binary divide a source of personal oppression and seek a modification of the binary system that will provide a space for them to live their lives without gender.

There are, also, two principal variants of negating tales in relation to the interrelations between sex, sexuality and gender. In the first variant, body (sex) and gender negating are co-opted in the service of the negating of sexuality, which is primary. In the second variant, it is body negating which is primary, and erotic (sexuality) and gender negating are then co-opted in the service of primary body negating.

In our search for data to illuminate the social process of negating, we have focused upon contemporary Western negating; in particular, on contemporary male femaling 'sissies'. There is now a growing literature on males who identify as neither men nor women and who seek to eliminate their masculinity in the service of an increasing 'sissification'. There is also now a small literature on biological women who seek to become genderless and define themselves in terms of 'ungendering', and in the service of this ungendering undergo surgical procedures to remove unwanted aspects of their female anatomy.

'Sissies' may be defined in different ways, and sissy stories that entail the erasing of maleness and masculinity may be variously classified. *The Sissy Times* is a publication for sissies and their 'female companions and friends'. The editorial of the first *Sissy Times* begins: 'Noah Webster says in his New Universal Unabridged Dictionary (second edition) that "a sissy is a boy or man whose behavior, tastes, interests, etc. seem more feminine than masculine."' It continues: 'Well Noah, we at *The Sissy Times* think that your definition is a bit simplistic and wimpy to say the least. In our estimation a sissy not only "seems" to have more feminine tastes, interests, behavior – a sissy is more feminine in all those respects' (*Sissy Times,* Editorial, 1988: 41). The editorial then lists the new magazine's areas of interest including such trans-gendering activities as cross-dressing, petticoat punishment, corset discipline, male submission and humiliation, female superiority and dominance. It is orthodox in both the psychosexual and relevant subcultural literature to con-sider such interests in terms of transvestism and sado-masochism. Regarding sissiness in this light, however, risks masking the significance of erasing and negating in the trajectories and life stories of many sissies.

There are, of course, many self-identified transvestite sissies who use the props of such feminization deliberately to enable or to intensify sexual arousal centred on their genitals – erection, ejaculation, and so on. In erotic fantasy fiction such as Christine Shelly's *Silken Slavery* (Shelly, 2002), for instance, each of the transvestite sissy's episodes of cross-dressing and humil-iation is described with an emphasis upon the sissy's erect 'bursting' penis.

However, there are also many other sissies who find such an overtly erotic emphasis irrelevant to them, and, indeed, distasteful. In these cases the props of sissification feature as part of an increasing sissification process that entails a move to the asexual: to the negating of their sexuality, as well as to the emasculation of their male sex (their bodies) and masculine gender. It is these sissies that this chapter considers under the rubric of the social process of negating.

Prior to the distinguishing of transvestism and transsexuality from homo-sexuality, 'sissies' were most usually associated with effeminate homosexu-ality. Effeminate 'sissies' were featured in many Hollywood movies in the 'sissy's heyday' of the 1930s, for instance, most usually taking on the role of an asexual helper to a master or mistress (Morris, 2005). They often took a special interest in clothes and soft furnishings and in the love affairs of their masters or mistresses. A number of Hollywood actors such as Franklin Pangborn specialized in the 'sissy' role. In a sense they lived vicariously through their employers and had no evident independent life – including sex-ual life – of their own.

This aspect of asexuality is fundamental to many contemporary articula-tions of sissy male sexuality. Although sissies are drawn to women and women's worlds, there is an important sense in which the asexual sissy is neither heterosexual nor homosexual. We might say that they are not 'man enough' to be either. The sissy is an asexual wimp.

This aspect is well brought out, for instance, in a series of advertisements run by Guinness which feature the 'GuinnLess Man of the Month'. Although the framed prints we have of these advertisements are undated, internal evi-dence suggests that they were used in bars and public houses as advertising paraphernalia in the 1980s.

The message of these advertisements is clear: the man with Guinness is virile; the man without Guinness is not a 'man'. One such 'GuinnLess Man of the Month' features a picture of a nubile young woman, stripped down to her revealing camisole and briefs, ringing out her wet camisole with the end rolled up into a phallic-like object. As she squeezes her camisole, water spurts from the end of the tightly rolled-up material. She turns round to make eye contact with a boyish 'nerdy' looking boy scout who is approaching her with a bunch of twigs resting across his arms. The caption reads: 'Thank goodness I've found you! If I don't get out of these wet things and find some-where warm to snuggle up, I'll catch my death of cold.' The boy scout replies: 'Here, you slip into my tent. I can make myself a shelter from these fourteen pliable birch twigs.' The tent is seen behind the young woman with a vaginal-like orifice at its opening. It is the young woman that is to enter the tent, while the boy scout is left with his 'fourteen pliable birch twigs'! Despite his posturing as more grown-up than he is – he sports a tiny thin moustache – the moustache only makes him look more ridiculous. He presents as an immature four-TEEN year-old boy – dressed in shorts with a plaster across his scratched kneecap. The bottom line reads: 'Moral: Always be Prepared: Scout Around for a Large Guinness Four-Pack'.

A second 'GuinnLess Man of the Month' features a predatory curvaceous young woman wearing high heels and a tight dress, with an ample slit up its side, dragging a terrified-looking young boy-like man into a fairground Tunnel of Love. The caption reads 'You're not taking me on that ride Godfrey, are you? You know I can't control my primeval lust in the dark.' The young man – wearing an 'I love mum' t-shirt, and clenching a small thin phallic-like torch from which rays spray out onto his own face – replies: 'Fear not, Fiona. I never go anywhere without my quartz long-life pocket torch.' The bottom line reads: 'Moral: With a Guinness There's Dark at the End of the Tunnel.'

Significantly, in this Guinness series the wimps are represented as under-developed males in every way. They look like pre-adolescent boys as opposed to men. They hold tiny and ineffectual looking phallic objects in their hands.

This pre-adolescent aspect of the sissy provides the particular focus of that sub-genre within the sissy literature that concerns itself with 'sissy boys'. 'Sissy boys' include men dressed in juvenile, effeminate clothes, and gener-ally treated as effeminate little children by their mothers, aunts and their female friends. Their stories are told, for instance, in *The Sissy Boy Digest* pub-lished by Empathy Press, Seattle, Washington.

In a different vein, within the history of cross-dressing there has long been a specialty interest which focuses on the erotic interest in dressing up as a maid or carrying out aspects of maid service: the French Maid, for instance. The aspect of being humiliated in the role of servant often features prominently in these stories.

More generally, 'Sissy maids' are men who serve their mistresses in various capacities as housemaids, as personal maids, and so on. Some sissies make fine-tuned distinctions according to the type of clothing worn, or activities performed, by the sissy. As Millie, a self-defined Nancy Maid, puts it (personal communication, 1997):

> I always make a sort of distinction between Cissy Maids [sic] who like to dress up in Frilly French Maid uniforms and prance around in front of a mirror and Nancy Maids who wear proper domestic uniforms and are put to work as domestic maid servants. I shall be interested to see what your own research produces.

Rather than develop further arguments concerning the multiple varieties of sissy, we focus on two systematic ideologies that have been put forward in the past two decades that may be seen as illustrations of the major variants of negating stories we have introduced.

Debra Rose's male sissy maids are illustrative of that mode of negating which buttresses the binary gender divide for all those that are not sissies, and in which erotic (sexuality) negating is primary. Rose was a prolific advocate of the sissy maid lifestyle throughout the 1990s, and her work has continued into the present decade. Her novel, originally entitled *Domestic Bliss: Life as a Fashion Model's Maid* (1990), was published in revised form by Sandy Thomas under the title *Maid in Form – 'A', 'B', 'C'* (1993a). It has recently been revised and re-published as *Domestic Bliss: My Life as a Supermodel's Maid*, Books 1–3 (2003).[1] Other publications detailing Rose's sissy maid lifestyle include *Where the Sissies Come from* (Rose, 1995c) and *The Sissy Maid Academy*, Vols 1 and 2 (Rose, 1993b). A number of Rose's writings have been published under a nom de plume, as is the case with 'Masturbation and the Male Maid – Practical Solutions' (Smythe, 1993). In 1994 she launched the journal *Sissy Maid Quarterly* (SMQ), a Sandy Thomas Publication, produced in conjunction with Rose Productions, which lays down the foundations of her particular version of the Sissy maid lifestyle (SMQ, 1994–96).

Rose's writings are a blend of fact and fiction. They do, however, provide a particularly systematic account of one major sissy maid lifestyle that has a considerable following. In the light of this, we consider Rose to be a major 'gender-negating identity innovator'. Many of our sissy informants, indeed, tell us that her journal *Sissy Maid Quarterly* (SMQ: 1994–96) 'plugs into' their innermost thoughts, fantasies and wishes with astonishing insight and accuracy.

Debra Rose-style sissy maids may ingest female hormones to reduce sexual desire and erectile function. They do not, however, undergo surgery to emasculate themselves. The second major variant of negating story does focus on body negating, however. In particular, it concerns those biological females who undergo surgery to remove unwanted female body parts, such as breasts, wombs and ovaries in order to become 'ungendered'. Here the 'ungendering' activist Christie Elan-Cane has advanced the most systematic argument in favour of such ungendering. Christie began publicizing an ungendering position in the early 1990s (Elan-Cane, 1992). Christie was also featured in a number of television documentaries and spoke at a series of transgender conferences throughout the 1990s. More recent publications include Elan-Cane (1998; 1999a; 1999b; 2000–1).

Conceptualizing the Debra Rose-style sissies and Christie Elan-Cane in terms of the social types of which they are characteristic, we may say that they are both variously outsiders to the social worlds of men and women. In the sissies' case, it is because they are neither men nor women. In an important sense they are males who have not developed into 'real' men. They may be seen as in various regards like children or juveniles. In Elan-Cane's case, it is because Christie's position is so unfamiliar to members of society who take the binary divide for granted, that Christie's persona, to many, takes on the quality of an alien.

Simmel (1908) makes a number of points about the 'stranger' that are highly pertinent to the negator. For Simmel, each particular social type – of which the 'stranger' is one – is shaped by the reactions and expectations of other people. As Coser (1977: 182), puts it: 'The type becomes what he is through his relations with others who assign him a particular position and expect him to behave in specific ways.' The sissy maid's position is marked by the fact that he acts as servant and help mate to his Mistress. In a sense, he participates in the world of women, in the way that 'men' do not. He is privy to women's 'secrets' – their preoccupations with their appearance, with the intimacies of their body rhythms: their menstrual cycles, and so on – but as a male sissy, he is unable to participate fully as a member of the social world of women. He is neither female nor a woman. His sex (body), sexuality and gender preclude it. On the other hand, he is not able to approach women's worlds as a man. Although male, he has not 'developed' into a man. He is seen as juvenile and sexless. Rather, he is both inside and outside the world of woman. He is a 'stranger' to their world, as Simmel (1908) puts it: '"an element of the group itself" while not being fully part of it' (Coser, 1977: 182). He can learn of the intimacies of his Mistress's relationships with her boyfriends. He can help her prepare for her dates, and so on.

Simmel makes the point that being distant and near at the same time, the stranger will often be called on as a confidant. Confidences that must be withheld from more closely related persons will be given to him just because with him they are not likely to have consequences. As we shall see, this is an important feature of the male sissy maid's 'special' relationship with his Mistress. Moreover, in his capacity as a maid, he is never taken as an adult person in his own right. Here Goffman's concept of the 'non person' is particularly apposite.

For Goffman (1971), 'non-persons' are persons without an individual identity. They 'are present during the interaction but in some repects do not take the role either of performer or of audience, nor do they (as do informers, shills, and spotters) pretend to be what they are not' (1971: 150). Goffman illustrates the concept with reference to children, servants and slaves, as well as to patients when they are treated 'only' as objects of medical procedures.

The Debra Rose-style sissy is a non-person in the sense that he does not participate as an equal in 'adult' interaction. Like a child, however, he may be 'played with', or be disciplined. His major role is to serve as a helper to his Mistress. His relationship with the worlds within which he interacts is voyeuristic from his subjective point of view. He observes but does not fully participate.

The Elan-Cane type negator, on the other hand, is outside the gendered worlds of men and women. Although, on certain formulations, such negators may be viewed as juvenile, that is not the way these negators conceptualize themselves. They seek the right to exist as 'ungendered' people. They seek a space for their 'kind'.

Telling negating stories

Debra Rose and the Male Sissy Maid

Becoming a sissy maid entails taking on the duties of housemaid and personal maid for a mistress, either permanently or temporarily, and living for longer or shorter periods of time as a 'neither male, nor female' sissy servant. This will entail systematic 'sissification', either by the mistress that employs the maid, or by a 'training' mistress, prior to service. In particular, the sissy maid's male sex, sexuality and gender are systematically erased. He comes to accept a sissy self-concept and identity, along with the fact that he and sissies like him are best suited to a life in service, making the lives of their mistresses 'easier and more luxurious' (Sissy Bobbi, 1996: 35).

In Rose's world, being male involves being masculine, active, virile and – by virtue of maleness – attracted to females; being female involves being feminine, being attractive to males and finding males attractive because of their virility and masculinity. In short, it is a world where the congruity between sex, heterosexuality and presentation of gender is taken for granted. There is no space for homosexuality, feminine men or masculine women. In

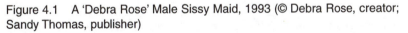

Figure 4.1   A 'Debra Rose' Male Sissy Maid, 1993 (© Debra Rose, creator; Sandy Thomas, publisher)

particular, heterosexuality and success in dating are necessary conditions of manhood and womanhood. And herein lies the problem for the sissy. Quite unable to compete for a female's affections in the conventional way, he must come to accept that he is neither male nor female but a 'third gender' (Rose, 1995a: 2). To secure this outcome, his already weak maleness must be systematically expunged (negated).

In this way, it is evident that Rose's vision of sissy maids buttresses the essence of the traditional version of the binary male/female divide for all males and females who are not sissies. However, this view of the binary divide is given the modern twist that recognizes that women are increasingly

153

successful in the world of work and, in consequence are ill suited – and, in any event, have no time – for housework and the traditional role of the housewife. It is here that the sissy maid comes into his own. Unable to compete for a female's affections in the conventional way, he is best fitted to take on the role of the housemaid and do the work previously done by the traditional housewife, and, before that, by the various maids in service. To be best fitted for this role, his already weak maleness must be systematically expunged (erased). To effect this the maid must be 'trained' – most usually, by a training mistress, prior to service; or, less frequently, the training will occur in service. Alternatively, the trainee may be sent to a Training Academy, or follow a course of instruction elsewhere. Internet sissy training programmes are now widespread, as is sissy training by email.

While the details of the trainings vary, the *sine qua non* of all of them is systematic erasing. There is much concealing (of attributes of masculinity). There is much redefining (sissies dress in effeminate and feminine attire NOT in order to cross the binary divide, but to further their emasculation). Such substituting and implying as there is, is co-opted in the service of erasing.

It is often said that gender identity and sexual object choice are quite separate aspects of our being (Gooren, 1998). This is not the case with sissy maids. Their emerging identities as sissies are pursuant upon their ineffective heterosexuality. The precondition for sissification is their ineffective heterosexuality. Body (sex) negating then follows. The sissy's body will be stripped of its body hair, including pubic hair, giving the sissy a pre-pubescent look, making him even more sexually unattractive to women, and even more unmanly to himself. The removal of body hair features prominently in many guides to sissification. The role of hair is well summarized, for instance, in rule '1' of 'Fifteen General Rules for Sissies to Observe' (Highboots, 1988: 41) which states:

All body hair should be removed by shaving or the use of commercial depilatories at least once a week. Facial hair, i.e. beards and mustaches are strictly forbidden. Hair on top of the heads should be grown out to a longer length but sideburns must be trimmed short. Hair may be dyed or tinted. Hair should be shampooed and conditioned daily and kept neatly arranged and combed.

A special feature of the Rose-style sissy, however, is that the shaving is followed by permanent 'gaffing', a practice which receives much attention in Rose's writings. A gaff is 'a small, tight, panty-like item whose sole purpose is to firmly pin a sissy's genitals back between his legs under his bottom, where they belong' (Rose, 1994a: 36). As Rose puts it: 'Being gaffed is a very basic condition for a sissy male, with psychological as well as physiological benefits. By firmly pinning his small, sissyish appendage, a gaff allows a sissy's appearance to more closely match his personality and inner (ineffectual) sexuality' (ibid.: 37). And again, 'Their gaff basically becomes almost part of their body – and the way it smooths their frontal appearance certainly becomes part of their body *image*' (ibid.: 37). Here we can see the intimate link between the concealing of male sex (the body), the erasing of male sexuality (genital feelings) and the emerging of a sissy identity. Gaffing will make erections impossible, a necessary condition for the construction of an alternative sissy sexuality, designed to further reinforce the sissy identity.

With the body appropriately sissified, attention now turns to the clothes appropriate to the sissy (gender negating). His male attire is replaced, initially by gender-neutral clothes and later by clothes appropriate to his servant status. To erase masculinity, these clothes will be variously effeminate or feminine. In particular, his now hairless body will be introduced to feminine and sensual fabrics designed to give him sensual pleasure (re-direction of sexuality to himself – solitary narcissism). The clothes are designed to erase his masculinity, NOT to create a sense of himself as a woman, as in oscillation. Any woman's clothing worn will be redefined as male sissy maid clothing, either because they highlight his sissified body or his subservient station, as in: 'But perhaps the benefits of proper gaffing are most useful when a sissy maid is in lycra tights or "bike" shorts. The smooth, sleek way these tight garments hug a gaffed sissy's front is actually quite cute, and is a visual reminder of a male maid's innate sissiness' (ibid.: 37).

Debra Rose would like to see shopping outlets available exclusively for the sissy male, stocked with clothing and servants' uniforms similar to those she has designed in her *Sissy Maid Quarterly* (personal communication, 1999).

Suitably depilated, gaffed and attired, the sissy maid is now prepared for service, to take the role of housemaid. Not only is he being increasingly neutered, but his passivity and subservience are reinforced. The will of his mistress is all-important. His training in maid-service will have two major aspects: (1) initiation into the tasks of keeping house – cleaning and cooking; and (2) care of his mistress's personal wardrobe and boudoir. The latter will entail initiation into the intimacies of a woman's world.

As one sissy devotee of Debra Rose put it: 'The mistress/maid relationship is quite special and quite unique . . . A real bond grows up between you which I don't think you could establish in any other way' (Millie, personal communication, 1997). Within this relationship, what might be termed the paradox of sissy sexuality is played out. He is close to his mistress and privy to the intimacies of her boudoir and personal relationships which gives most sissy maids particular pleasure. It is, however, a pleasure that has to come to terms with the fact that his mistress will only choose a 'real' man to have 'real' intimacies with. The sissy's unsatisfied and unsatisfiable heterosexual yearnings for his mistress will be displaced from being genitally focused toward her (in yearning and in fantasy), to a variety of peculiarly 'sissy' pleasures. Sensual pleasure will be obtained from the fit and texture of his effeminate clothing; from the subservience of working for her; and from vicariously participating in her life generally. In particular, the diffuse pleasure he obtains from the subservience of housework, is, in effect, a sexualization of housework.

With all semblance of masculinity fast evaporating, the sissy now gains pleasure from being the 'perfect little helper'. He takes pleasure in doing what he does do so well. As Sissy Jennie (1994: 21) puts it:

> My world is now a gentle, soft, and scented one in which my duties are perfectly and strictly defined. And I am proud of my growing abilities as a cook, seamstress, housekeeper, and personal maid-servant. The approval of my mistress means much to me now, and I bask in any small compliment or favor she bestows upon me.

With his sexuality re-directed and his initiation into worlds of female sex, sexuality and gender maximized by his intimate relationship with his mistress, the sissy is now prepared for a life which is lived vicariously through his mistress. He becomes privy to the intimacies of her sexual relationships and will eventually act as a maid to her boyfriends, and later, perhaps, her husband. Furthermore, his sexuality (eroticism) will be increasingly vicariously genderized as he takes increasing pleasure in the paraphernalia of his mistress's femininity, as in 'Jeanette takes care of *everything* for me. The sissy takes wonderful care of my clothes, too. He really seems to enjoy making sure everything in my closet and dresser is perfect for me all the time' (Stephanie, 1994: 5).

Some mistresses put their sissies on a light dose of female hormones. Some sissies ingest breast enlargement preparations widely available from health food shops. These latter will do no more than make the sissy's nipple area slightly sore and his 'breasts' slightly swollen, which one informant described as 'suitable for a sissy like me'. With constant gaffing, the re-direction of sexuality, and reduced libido, the sissy's sexuality becomes increasingly diffused over his entire body. The pleasure he obtains from serving his mistress, living vicariously through her and feeling the fit and texture of his feminine clothing come to compensate, and, indeed, be preferred, to any lingering regrets at his lost masculinity. He comes to accept his sissiness. Debra Rose reports a fantasy interview with 'Stephie' (Rose, 1996: 7) who when asked about his

> personal life blushed deeply and hesitated. But he eventually opened up a little. 'Well, it's not like it was before,' he said slowly. I still . . . ahhh . . . play with myself at night. But I can only do it maybe once or twice a month now. I'm used to it. Besides, I'd rather look good and feel good in my clothes anyway'.

Moreover, although permitted to masturbate, the elimination of his masculine sexuality will be enhanced by a particular form of masturbation deemed appropriate for sissies in the Debra Rose vision of sissy maid sexuality. Rose makes much of the pink rubber 'sissy sheets' fitted to the sissy maid's single bed (e.g., Rose, 1994b). They are easy to clean, a constant reminder of his sissiness, and are fitted with the intended outcome that eventually the sissy will, in effect, be having a sexual relationship with his sheets, as in (Rose, 1993b: 1: 42):

> when I get excited, a little dribbles out. This makes my sheet feel incredibly smooth and slippery. It's such a great feeling that I always get 'in the mood' by rubbing myself against my rubber bottom sheet. Although I sometimes think of my cute gym instructor when I do it, more and more I don't really think of anyone at all. Rather than think about a girl, I like to concentrate on how great the slick, wet rubber sheet feels!

Thus in time, many sissies will simply rub themselves 'off' against their rubber sheets, focused on the pleasurable sensation, with no heterosexual fantasy, a semi-flaccid penis, and a weak dribble of an ejaculation (ibid.: 42). In due course, many sissies cease to masturbate entirely. The sissy maid becomes an increasingly asexual 'neither male, nor female', maid in service.

The fictional element in Rose's writings should not lead us to dismiss them as pure fantasy. The celebrated Mrs Silk, a UK-based Mistress who has had many sissy maids working for her over many years, compares the 'reality' of her sissy maids with what she considers to be the 'completely fictitious' *Sissy Maid Quarterly* published by Debra Rose (personal communication, 1997).

Debra Rose, however, claims that each component of her blend of fact and fiction has been enacted by sissies of her acquaintance. In 1998 (personal communication) she makes the point that:

> SMQ is not about a 'game' where someone's boyfriend acts submissive for a laugh. Rather, the sissies who are employed as maids are just that – maids and servants. There is no man/woman relationship between employers and their sissy servants. This is for two obvious reasons: the fact that 'he' is a sissy and is therefore not interesting to women in a physical way (and indeed may be impotent with them anyway), and the fact that he is a servant and is therefore not on the same social level as his employer. In large cities here in the States (New York, Los Angeles, San Francisco, etc.) sissies already work on a full or part-time basis as women's effeminate houseboys or sissy maids. This is NOT to say this arrangement is common – it is not. But it DOES exist in relatively rare cases. However, there is a slowly growing trend toward this unique solution to the problem of who does the housework now that women work as professionals.

We did not need convincing. As we began to make contact with a number of self-identified sissies, we found that Rose's particular emphasis upon

Figure 4.2   Christie Elan-Cane with per partner, David, at the 3rd International Transgender Film and Video Festival, London, 1998 (Photograph by Phaedra Kelly; reproduced with the kind permission of Christie Elan-Cane)

'negating' featured prominently with many sissies. In particular, a number of key informants emerged that identified specifically with the Debra Rose-style sissy and sought to enact the Debra Rose lifestyle. We will return to them shortly.

Christie Elan-Cane's story

In marked contrast to Rose's vision of erasing is that of writer and activist Christie Elan-Cane. Debra Rose-style sissies may occasionally be referred to as 'she' as an aspect of their sissiness. More usually, however, they are referred to as 'he', for they identify as *male* sissies. Christie, on the other hand, rejects both 'he' and 'she' and 'his' and 'her' for those who negate, preferring the term 'per' derived from person. To our knowledge, Christie is the first person to pioneer publicly a consistent and coherent 'ungendering' position and form of address for those who negate within the transgender community. Christie argues that 'To gain validity and social legitimacy, it is imperative that the Third Gender has a proper title that is non-gender specific and a correct form of address' (Elan-Cane, 1998: 3–4).

Per chosen terminology for per gender identity has shifted over the years from androgyne, through 'third gender' (Elan-Cane, 1999a) and 'gender free', to the now preferred 'ungendered' or 'non-gendered' (Elan-Cane, 1999b). Christie, a biological female, felt 'in the wrong body' from per earliest days. With the onset of puberty, per development of breasts and per menstruation was particularly distressing. As Christie (Elan-Cane 1997: 1) puts it: 'I was never able to come to terms with "womanhood". I had the body of a woman and therefore I was considered by everyone to be a woman and I was repelled.' Per elaborates in Elan-Cane:

> When I reached my twenties I began to fantasise about changing my body. I wanted to get rid of both tits. I wanted my chest to be flat like a man's, although I did not consider myself to be a man. I wanted the womb to be removed. I wanted the periods to stop forever. I hated what was going on inside my body and its bloody physical manifestation. I hated my body but it went much further and deeper. I hated the idea that I was perceived as a woman. (1999a: 119)

It is important to note that at this time, Christie had formulated no sense of a gender identity other than as a woman. She (as 'she' referred to herself, then) did not think she was a man. Nor did she think she was transsexual. It did not occur to her to seek help from a gender identity clinic. As Christie, tellingly states it: 'I did not know there was an alternative to identifying as a woman' (research interview, 1999).

Rather, per priority and preoccupation were to remove the offending female parts of her body (body erasing). For this, medical intervention was necessary. After considerable effort, Christie eventually found a plastic surgeon who was prepared to remove per breasts ('The best purchase I ever made'). Some two years later Christie had a hysterectomy through the British National Health Service. At no time were psychiatric services involved.

Now at ease with per body, Christie began to identify as 'neither male, nor female': 'a third gender person'. Christie's shifting preferred terminology for per self-identification – from androgyne, through third gender and gender free to ungendered – in one sense represents a refining of that self-identification. Mostly, however, it reflects per attempts to avoid misrepresentation by others.

Particularly in the worlds of fashion and youth style, androgyny is represented by gendered males and females taking on the attributes of both genders.

From Christie's point of view such representations are hyper-gendered. Critics of per position, with some justification, perhaps, found the identification as 'third gendered' to be inconsistent with per advocacy of 'ungendering', a term which Christie has now adopted, especially in the public domain.

Although open to the possibility of further body erasing – having per ovaries removed, for instance – for Christie, 'everything fell into place' once surgery was completed. Most important to Christie is the separation of gender from sex and sexuality. Christie regards per sexuality as a private matter and irrelevant to per gender identity. It is important to note, however, that it was following per body erasing that the possibility for per present male object-choice (sexuality) emerged. Prior to surgery, Christie found both men and women as potential object-choices, provided they were not 'fluffy' feminine women or 'macho' masculine men. Christie was attracted to androgynous feminine men and masculine women. However, during this time per said 'there was no way I would show my body to a man'. Whereas Christie had flirted with a lesbian identity prior to surgery, following surgery Christie found perself able to pursue per attraction to men, provided they related to per as a non-gendered person. Per sexual partner is now a male who relates to per as ungendered – neither male nor female.

Per gender (social accompaniments) negating follows from the non-gendered identification. Christie wears androgynous 'gender-free' clothes – mostly black 'neither male, nor female' 'shirts'; black trouser-suits – a sort of contemporary Chairman Mao suit, and keeps per head meticulously shaven – all appropriate to per 'ungendered' identification, following per body negating. Having erased all undesired vestiges of per femaleness and femininity, Christie has no need of further concealing, redefining, substituting or implying.

Secure in per personal negating, Christie increasingly turned per attention to publicizing per position, with the intention of enabling a space to be provided within a bi-polarized gender system, for 'ungendered' people like perself. Initial steps include campaigning for the use of a non-gender specific form of address (Pr as a title to replace Mr or Mrs), and the inclusion of the gender-free in equal rights legislation (Elan-Cane, 1997; 1998). In Christie's view: 'there is no reason why there should be two diametrically opposed genders, nor is there any reason why gender should exist at all' (Elan-Cane, 1998: 7) and, in these senses, per position might be seen as a subversive and transcending one. However, it is not per present intention to seek to undermine the binary divide, an approach which Christie regards as both unrealistic and impracticable. Rather, Christie seeks social legitimacy for perself and others like per (personal communication, 1998).

Christie has largely withdrawn from high profile public transgender activism since 2000. Per last presentation at a professional or academic conference was Elan-Cane (2000–2001). Christie comments:

I have not done any presentations since Gendys 2000 because I really did feel that I had made my point, and that I was not achieving very much or enhancing my life in any way through attending such events. I do not feel at all inclined to do any more presentations unless there is a fundamental change to my marginalized situation, and I actually have something extra to add. I also felt there was a lot of wilful ignorance projected towards me by people from whom I had the right to expect better, and I do not intend to set myself up for more until I decide the time is ripe. (Elan-Cane, personal communication, 2005)

Per private attempts to get per ungendered status recognized is making steady, if slow, progress, however (personal communication, 2005):

I am still trying to get my title addressed correctly. I have had some success – most correspondents including my local GPs (general medical practitioner's) surgery have amended their records and use Pr to address me. I successfully got an educational body to remove gender categorization from their website registration process so that I could complete the online registration.

On a recent visit to see their local MP (Member of Parliament) Simon Hughes, Christie accompanied per partner, David, who needed to raise an issue with Hughes. Christie took the opportunity to raise per objection to per exclusion from any of the 'rights' accorded under the UK Gender Recognition Act, 2004. Per intends to continue these private efforts until accorded the right to co-exist and have per non-gendered identity recorded on official documentation.

Christie feels particularly let down and betrayed by Press for Change who campaigned so successfully for the passing of The UK Gender Recognition Act, 2004. Per comments:

You wanted to know more about my thoughts about Press for Change and the Gender Recognition Act. I actually feel pretty disgusted that I was being asked to support a piece of legislation that awarded privileges to 'respectable' transsexuals, i.e., those who are able to assimilate into mainstream gendered society whilst ignoring the far greater plight of those who cannot. I was not entirely surprised at this outcome as I never really felt Press for Change was terribly interested in diversity. I feel, however, that the complete exclusion of my identity from this piece of legislation has marginalized my position further and that Press for Change has betrayed everyone left behind by this discriminatory piece of legislation. (personal communication, 2005)

Such is the contemporary predicament of those who negate, a predicament only rarely treated with the proper respect in the professional or academic literature (O'Keefe, 2004).

Sissy Diana's story

Debra Rose and Christie Elan-Cane are both gender-identity innovators who in their writings and activism promulgate an innovative position that then becomes available for others to identify with. Self-identifications are variously influenced by available 'definitions of the situation'. The impact of Debra Rose's formulation became the guiding motif for Sissy Diana's development of a distinctly sissy lifestyle. Interestingly, here is a lifestyle and identity that have developed completely outside the pervasive medicalization of sex, sexuality and gender that has taken place in the case of 'transsexualism' and 'transvestism', the major migrating and oscillating stories, respectively. It is not surprising, therefore, that such stories have been ignored in the professional literature. Sissy Diana's story, like that of Debra Rose's story, is what might be termed a tale of 'raw experience'. Here, there are no tales of 'explanation' or 'justification'.

Sissy Diana dates his journey into sissification (becoming a sissy) to when he came across the article 'She-Male Maid: Masturbation and the Male Maid – Practical Solutions', in the transgender publication *Transformation* (Smythe, 1993: 46, 47, 50). Prior to this redefining of himself as a sissy, Diana, throughout a number of periods of his life, had experimented with occasional cross-dressing, but did not identify as a transvestite. He felt that as he could never pass as a woman, transvestism for him was a 'dead end'. He had no wish to dress in secret or to undergo hormonal or surgical intervention that might enable him to 'pass' as a woman more successfully in the long term. Now in his mid-40s, he had become aware that it was important for him to have the company and friendship of women – particularly, one 'special' woman – but was never able to sustain a satisfactory long-term sexual relationship with a woman. When, on occasions, a platonic friendship turned into a sexual relationship, Diana was unable to maintain an erection to enable sexual intercourse, and the ensuing frustration on the part of his friend led the relationship either to end, or become non-sexual, with Diana's friend finding a sexual relationship elsewhere. This had been the pattern since Diana's late teens.

The article 'She-Male Maid' was ostensibly written by 'Susan Smythe', but was actually written by Debra Rose. It purports to be a letter written by a woman who has a male 'sissy' maid in the household. It deals with the 'male maid's tendency towards frequent masturbation', and offers tips to women who have sissies working for them at home. 'Susan Smythe' purports to be a long-time employer of a male maid.

As Diana came to accept that he seemed unable to be able to have a sexual relationship with a woman, his sexual life had revolved more and more around masturbation. In consequence, he was fascinated immediately by the article which introduces the idea that as more and more women are employing male maids, they need to know how to deal with their maid's sexuality, in particular their frequent masturbation. As he read the article, it dawned on him that the article was laying the basis for a type of 'sissy' sexuality that seemed to fit his situation and with which he could identify.

The article argued that as women have no sexual attraction towards sissy males, such males are perpetually without the possibility of a sexual partner. Furthermore, the article made clear that in the unlikely event of a woman being willing to sleep with a sissy, the sissy would be unable to perform sexually. This insight resonated powerfully with Sissy Diana's own experiences.

The article then outlines the merits of masturbation for sissies. Sissies enjoy it – indeed, are usually quite addicted to it. The sissy need not worry about pleasing a woman, which was something they would be unable to do, anyway. Moreover, they need not worry about getting (or staying) hard, or how small their penis is. Susan Smythe's strategy is to make it clear to her sissy or potentially sissy reader that because of his ineffectual sexuality it is almost inevitable and perfectly appropriate that a sissy's sexual life should consist of solitary masturbation. From a theoretical point of view, it is the ineffectual sexuality of the sissy that is the bedrock from which the increasing sissification will develop.

The sissy's sexual status is depicted as that of both an 'outsider' and a juvenile. Much play is made of the fact that men enjoy women, and women enjoy men, but a sissy is just a sissy and masturbation is simply what sissies do: 'You can explain that you have feelings towards your boyfriend, and that you enjoy making love with him. And you can tell your maid that your lover enjoys sharing your bed and having sex with you' (1993: 47).

In addition, a sissy's sexuality is depicted as juvenile, and permanently 'stuck', as in: 'Free from pressure to "perform," sissies enjoy their solitary little interludes. In fact, in many ways sissies have all the sexual sophistication of a ten-year-old boy – except sissies retain this childish perspective FOREVER!' (ibid.: 47).

The article then goes on to detail a particular feature of the sissy's world that was quite new to Diana, namely, rubber sheets – specifically pink rubber sheets. The use of rubber sheets on the sissy's 'little single bed' emphasizes his difference from adult men and women. His frequent masturbation runs the risk of soiling ordinary bed linen. Rubber sheets, on the contrary, can be quickly and easily cleaned. Again, there is the resonance with the juvenile masturbation and the fear of stained sheets. However, whereas the juvenile may fear that his masturbation will be revealed, the rubber sheets are designed to be a public indication of the sissy's 'entirely appropriate' sexual life. Moreover, the suggestion is made of a specifically sissy way of masturbation which incorporates the rubber sheets, as in:

> Some sissies report that, in time, they begin to simply rub themselves 'off' against the rubber sheets themselves, so they can masturbate with a minimum of fuss and bother. They report that the slick feeling of the sheets becomes most addictive. In a sense, many sissies basically end up 'making love' to their rubber bottom sheet – an adorable and harmless focus to their childish sexuality. (ibid.: 50)

The article's conclusion made a big impact on Diana: 'Think of it this way – there are THREE sexes – male, female and sissy. Males make love to females – females make love to males – and sissies masturbate in their little beds at night!' (ibid.: 50).

Having become sensitized to the existence of such sissies, Diana found himself thinking of his favourite themes from this article when he masturbated. He found particularly exciting the notion that he was somehow neither a man nor a woman, and that masturbation was 'simply what sissies DO'. Furthermore, as his method of masturbation was to rub his 'little weenie' against his bottom sheet without touching his penis, he became increasingly intrigued about the possibility of acquiring rubber sheets for his own bed, to increase his sissiness.

The next stage in Diana's journey into sissification began with his acquisition of his first copy of *Sissy Maid Quarterly* (SMQ). Since he had come across the sissy masturbation article, he had become sensitized to the term 'sissy maid', so when in listings of transvestite material he came across material on sissy maids he sought it out. The significance of his acquisition of his first *Sissy Maid Quarterly* could not be overestimated. Here were the outlines of a lifestyle option with its own world, its own props, its own relationships, and so on, all distinctly sissy, which he slowly began to adopt for himself.

The lifestyle option presented in *Sissy Maid Quarterly* includes articles on four main topics. These topics are the sissy's relationship with his Mistress; details of suitable clothing and accoutrements for sissies; details of where the sissy fits into the Mistress's life generally, particularly in regard to her boyfriends; and details of appropriate sissy skills such as household chores – cooking, washing, cleaning, and so on. The first SMQ read by Sissy Diana (*SMQ 2*) that had such an impact upon him included articles on all these four main topics. 'Summer Fashion' is a 'a full, illustrated preview of the best looks for sissy maids for Summer'. 'Sissy Servants and Boyfriends' gives advice to Mistresses on 'How best to mix the two "males" in your life'. A special edition of a regular column 'The Maid's Room' features the testing of rubber sheets for the sissy's 'little single bed'. 'Reports from the Lingerie Room' provides details on 'How to properly care for your employer's delicate, and expensive, "hand wash" lingerie'. 'In the Kitchen' gives advice on 'How to wash dishes and scrub pots and pans, the right way.'

Diana was particularly drawn to three features of the SMQ sissy lifestyle that were quite new to him and that seemed to him to be unique to a sissy lifestyle. The first was a special relationship with a woman that enabled him to be close to a woman without having to have a sexual relationship with her; the second was the particular voyeur role in relation to his Mistress's relationship with 'real' men – her boyfriends and lovers. The third was the opportunity it provided him to develop a uniquely sissy role – of living his life free of the pressures of expected masculinity, in the service of 'acceptance' of what he 'really' was – a sissy.

He determined to seek out a Mistress with whom he could enact these features. But first he decided to do what he could on his own to enact the life style. Initially, this entailed removing his body hair, and building up a collection of feminine deodorants, shampoos, conditioners, skin care products and fragrances. He then bought rubber sheets for his bed and converted his bedroom into a 'maid's room', drawing upon his reading of SMQ for inspiration on how to furnish it. As regard to the effect of his reading on his sexual response, at first, he found that his reading of the Debra Rose publications gave him stronger erections than he had been used to for some years. Gradually, however, as he learned that it was appropriate for a sissy to have weak erections, he found that he was drawn to masturbation in the 'sissy' way we have described above. He would lubricate his rubber sheet with baby oil, and fantasize the tip of his penis as his tiny 'sissy weenie'. Then he would turn on his stomach, move up and down on the sheet creating friction between his sissy weenie and his rubber sheet. The softer his erection and the weaker his ejaculation, the more of a sissy he felt. It was soon important to him to masturbate with thoughts of what an ineffectual sissy he was to be masturbating in this way. In effect, he was 'getting off' on his emasculation, but 'getting off' in a manner that his mentor Debra Rose deemed appropriate for sissies like him. Put another way, his pleasure at identifying as a sissy (and his erasing) took precedence over any lingering concerns he occasionally felt at the way he was cutting himself off from future possibilities of a more 'manly' sexual life.

His sissification to this point, in effect, entailed following the model of a favoured gender identity innovator – Debra Rose. As he did so, he began to notice changes in himself going beyond what he was reading about. Now when he saw women he found attractive at work or elsewhere, he would fantasize that they were his Mistresses and he was their maid. This gave him a pleasure denied to him when, as previously, he would have thought of them as fantasy partners totally out of reach to him. He chose as a particular fantasy Mistress a model in a men's magazine and would imagine giving her manicures and pedicures, brushing her hair, preparing her clothes for her, listening to her talking about her boyfriends, and so on.

He now felt increasingly drawn to seek a Mistress of his own in 'reality' with whom to live out his 'chosen' role. His attempts to secure a Mistress took many months. His first attempts in responding to prostitutes' calling cards were unsuccessful. These produced short and expensive encounters with 'Mistresses' who he felt had little understanding of his desires and little willingness to learn them. However, eventually he found a Mistress with whom he was able to explore his innermost desires and develop a fully-fledged sissy lifestyle. In particular, this Mistress gave him a copy of a book that was new to Diana, entitled *A Charm School for Sissy Maids* by Lorelei (1995).

The purpose of the book is to 'give fresh insight into the psychology of the sissy maid fantasy and the best way to make the fantasy real' (ibid.: 5). It provides a 30-day course that 'teach(es) the willing submissive the basic skills of sissydom' (ibid.: 5). Sissy Diana was highly selective in the use of this book, much of which he found distasteful – 'too sadomasochist', and too overtly sexual in intent. Rather, he adapted those parts of it to which he was drawn, to fit in with the Debra Rose-style sissy with which he identified.

In the introduction to the book, the novitiate sissy is instructed to make a sissy vow to follow the sissy way and instructed to make a sissy pledge of allegiance to his Mistress. In a subsequent early lesson he is then told to carry out a number of written assignments with titles such as 'Why I Am a Sissy'; 'What Does Being a Sissy Mean to Me?' 'Three Ways I Can be More Sissyish'; and 'Three Specific Attitudes I Must Change to Become More Like A Proper Sissy'.

The sissy vow that Sissy Diana adopted and carefully wrote in his 'Sissy Book' read as follows:

> I swear to follow the sissy way. I will serve Mistress B. I will practice my sissy skills, and I will maintain a sissy attitude at all times. I will do all these things because I long to be an acceptable sissy maid and serve Mistress B without question. Each morning when I awake, and each night when I go to bed, I will recite the sissy pledge.

Two additional entries in Sissy Diana's notebook well express both the negating and 'outsider' aspects of the Sissy lifestyle. They are those headed 'Why I am a Sissy' and 'Three Specific Attitudes I Must Change to Become More Like a Proper Sissy'.

The first read as follows:

1. My Name is Sissy Diana

2. I depilate my body hair.

3. Every morning when I put on my cotton panties, I repeat to myself: 'My name is Diana and I am a sissy.'

The second read:

1. When I see a man and a woman together, I must always remember that men like women and that women like men, but that a sissy is just a sissy and must sleep in his little single bed alone every night.

2. When I am away from Mistress and I see a woman, I must be more grateful to Mistress that the only woman in my life is her.

3. If I play with myself at night I must only think of what a total sissy I am.

Initially his Mistress had crossed this out and had written in its place: 'I must never ever play with myself unless Mistress gives me permission to do so.' Eventually these instructions were changed to: 'You may play with yourself whenever you feel lonely. When you play with yourself try to keep your wee-nie as small and as soft as possible.'

We have given prominence to the reorientation of Sissy Diana's sexuality in the context of his body and gender negating, because in theoretical terms it is Sissy Diana's perceived lack of virility that provides the foundation upon which he constructs his identity. As his sissy trajectory proceeds, however, he co-opts ever new worlds, objects and procedures into his sissy body erasing and gender erasing.

The world of the domestic servant was a world that Sissy Diana had given little thought to before his encounter with the world of the sissy maid. Following Mistress B's instructions, however, he was instructed to visit a 'Hospitality, Workwear and Healthcare Clothing' shop and select a 'polyester/cotton pleated dress' suitable for domestic service which he wears while cleaning his Mistress's flat.

In the main, however, his increasing sissification followed the pattern of initiation into women's worlds with a two-pronged strategy. In the first place, he had to learn more about the gendered accoutrements of femininity in the service of helping his Mistress. In the second place, he had to co-opt women's worlds and its objects into his own 'sissy' world. For a period, his Mistress would give him detailed instructions on how to occupy himself until his next visit.

In one such instruction, for example, his Mistress wrote: 'For magazines keep your eyes open for new or any magazine of interest for clothing hints and cosmetic hints. One monthly magazine called *Clothes* (sometimes is good), *Vogue* (America or English), *Allure*. Many others you'll see. Please keep abreast of any new ideas for me.'

He was instructed to 'devote one night a week – at least – to research your position'; to 'practise your sissy posture and walk, etc.', 'to improve your massage technique'; 'to talk with me about your progress, and feelings', and so on.

Currently, Sissy Diana is working for his Mistress one day a month, telephones her twice a week to talk about his 'progress and feelings', and is contemplating early retirement from his job in order to live full-time as a Mistress's maid. He identifies permanently as a sissy, a feeling continually reinforced as he feels the pressure of his gaff restraining his genitals throughout his waking hours. He follows the lives of the men and women in his place of work, as an outsider. In particular, he seeks to adhere to Rule 8 as listed in 'Fifteen General Rules for Sissies to Observe' (Highboots, 1988: 41): 'In the presence of a woman or a group of women you will always be in a passive and subordinate role. Always smile and present a cheerful outlook. Don't argue with a woman or presume to correct her. Always be obedient, cooperative and courteous.'

Throughout the writings of Debra Rose there is a tension in regard to the source of the sissies' sissiness. On the one hand, the reader is told a sissy IS just a sissy. He is just born like that. No one made him that way. He should accept that fact that he was born this way. On the other hand the process of sissification is often written about as though it is an initiation process. He 'becomes' a sissy. Rose's 'solution' to the tension is to suggest that only a 'true' sissy would 'allow' the sissification process to be so effective. She does not offer any explanation as to the 'cause' of his sissiness. The sissy just IS a sissy, and happiness for the sissy lies in accepting that fact. Rose's writings, therefore, are in marked contrast to those that feature, for instance, the masculine man who is punished and forced into femininity; or those in which the masculine man is castrated and 'negated' of all sexuality forcefully, and becomes the very thing he despises. Fittingly, one such fantasy story (with no date and no publication details) is entitled *Non-Man*. It tells the story of a former 'man' 'being driven ... toward the world of being a nothing, a purposeless, in-between creature, neither feminine nor masculine, attractive to neither, repulsive to both' (Anonymous, n.d.: 15).

The Debra Rose sissy maid story is principally, then, a story of acceptance. It is, as we suggested, a bare tale of experience. It is a tale that provides intimate details of an acceptance of a sissy identity, of thoughts and feelings about a revered Mistress, and of refinement in developing a sissy lifestyle, and there the matter rests.

Millie's story

Debra Rose and Sissy Diana notwithstanding, many sissies do feel the need to construct a story that is seen to 'explain' the fact that they are, or have become, sissies. In terms of the sociology of motivation, the 'untoward' nature of their identity, feelings, sexual response, and life-style calls forth a 'vocabulary of motive' (Mills, 1940; Ekins, 1983).

One of us had written briefly about maid 'Millie' in *Male Femaling* (Ekins, 1997: 99–101). After *Male Femaling* was published, we determined to undertake further research on male maids and wrote to Millie asking if she would share her experiences with us. The request led Millie 'to sit down and search carefully down through (her) memories of the past for any events which might explain the male maid phenomenon' (personal communication, 1997). She introduces her story *Millie: The Story of a Male Maid* (Millie, 1997) with the comment: 'The realization that I am not alone, that others have experiences and desires and that the whole area can be the subject of serious academic research has been the catalyst which has led me to write the following pages' (ibid.: 4). She adds:

> It is also important to insist that in concealing my real identity nothing has been falsified. This is a true and genuine account of the past as I remember it today. It is also a true account of how I live out my life as a maid at the present time. Nothing is a fantasy. (ibid.: 5)

In a 'Foreword' (ibid.: 3), Mrs Silk who employs Millie writes: 'Millie has only got her own personal experience to draw on, but as a Mistress who comes into contact with a wide range of cross-dressers and especially male maids, I know that her experience is not uncommon.' Following this celebrated UK Mistress, we will continue to refer to Millie as 'she'.

Her story provides an excellent illustration of what (following Plummer, 1995) we have referred to as a 'modernist' sex, sexuality and gender story. Her story involves the reconstruction of her past experience from the standpoint of the present. It is a reconstruction to 'explain' an untoward event, in particular to explain what Millie refers to as 'a strange, some would say perverted aspect of my life' (1997: 4). Past incidents are selected to provide a coherent beginning, middle and end point. The past events are seen to explain existing presents and likely futures. For Millie, her desire to be a male maid IS, indeed, strange:

> Being a maid servant is hardly the most pleasurable of experiences. Having to obey orders, be respectful and work hard scrubbing floors, cleaning up dirt etc. [*sic*] is not an enjoyable experience for most people. Yet I seek out such a situation and even spent the Christmas season working as a maid in a household. There is no doubt that I derive a great experience of relaxation and escape from everyday pressures from it. Nonetheless, a little voice inside me often asks the question 'why?'. (1997: 4)

Here is Millie's story that we have divided into its key phases or stages.

Phase 1: Mother's little helper: intimacy, pleasure and housework
Millie's story starts with the death of her father when she was 18 months old and her growing up with her mother as her daily companion. She tells us how 'houseproud' her mother was; how she would observe her putting on her housecoat and tying up her hair in preparation for housework. Soon her mother was enlisting the help of her son, dressing her in a blue smock over her shirt and short trousers and giving her a coverall cap to keep the dust out

of her hair. This continued, until at 8 years of age Millie was sent to board at school. From then on her mother employed maids, and Millie's helpmate role was over. However, the die was cast according to Millie (1997: 7). 'I never talk about these memories with my mother, and I am sure she would attach no importance to this early formation, but for me they are still vivid and I suspect sowed the seeds of something strong and powerful in my psyche.'

Phase 2: Public school: sexual fantasy and maid service
With the onset of puberty, Millie came to have two erotic preoccupations. The first was a plastic apron she had found hanging behind the bathroom door in an aunt's bathroom.

> I experienced an irresistible urge to put that plastic apron on. I don't think I had started to mastur-bate yet but wearing the apron brought on strong genital feelings and I think feelings of submissive-ness. These were new and alarming feelings, but pleasurable. I spent a lot of time in that bathroom wearing that plastic apron. (1997: 7)

Millie's second preoccupation was the maids who worked at her boarding school:

> I would fantasize that I had been rude to several of the maids and that they had captured me, stripped me naked and put me into one of their uniforms. I had to wear the dress, the cap and the pinny, and they put me to work as their maid. Often I would have to wear their blue denim working apron and scrub floors for them. I was their maid and they were in control of me. Sometimes I was put into one of their little pink dresses with a frilly cap and pinny, and made to serve their evening meal. These adolescent masturbatory fantasies were immensely strong and deep. (ibid.: 9–10)

Phase 3: The fantasies subside
At university, and in the years that followed, the erotic charge of her sissy maid fantasies subsided. She did, however, have a preference for tea shops where the waitresses 'were properly uniformed in caps and pinnies'. She liked to stay in hotels where the female domestic staff wore traditional uni-forms. She also enjoyed watching *Upstairs, Downstairs* (a television series that featured life 'Downstairs' in the servants' quarters in Victorian London) and period films which contained scenes with Victorian maidservants.

Life at university included girl friends, but Millie was not looking for a wife 'or even a partner for my bed'. In no time, it seemed to her, she was 30 and a confirmed bachelor. In no time, 30 became 40. Now 'through the 40 year barrier things started to change gradually but relentlessly'.

Phase 4: Enacting the adolescent fantasy
Now into her forties, Millie became irresistibly drawn to enacting her ado-lescent fantasies. She theorized that if she could turn the fantasies into some

sort of reality, they would go away. For ten years she tentatively explored her fantasies, hoping that they would abate. This exploration centred round unsatisfactory attempts to find a Mistress with whom she could enact the Mistress/Maid relationship, and an ever-increasing preoccupation with the clothing and paraphernalia of being a maid.

Millie's first attempts with a series of prostitutes were unsatisfying to her. The prostitutes could offer her little more than dirty and tatty maid's clothing, and the prostitutes had no 'idea how the Mistress of a maid servant behaved' (1997: 13). Here, her experiences echo those of Sissy Diana, considered previously.

She decided to buy her own maid's uniform, which she did from a shop specializing in uniforms for employees:

> My excitement was intense when I returned to my flat and tried on my first maid's dress. It fitted well and looked good except that I had no wig and no make up. I acquired a wig but never got around to make up. However, for some six months or so I often put on my pretty maid's outfit. (ibid.: 14)

Gradually, over the next number of years, she acquired more knowledge of suppliers of maid's clothing and catalogues, and began to fine-tune her own preferences. These latter always led to the favoured clothing of her adolescent Maid's fantasies. She was becoming the object of her old desires. Once equipped, she felt ready to find her own Mistress. She had *discovered that being a Maid without a Mistress was no fun* (ibid.: 17, emphasis in the original).

Phase 5: The first training – becoming a lady's maid

The meeting with Millie's first Mistress, Mistress Alexander, was crucial to her. She did not know what to expect, but unexpectedly began to take pleasure in her required duties. There was no attempt by the Mistress to confide or to talk about each other's private lives. Rather, Millie was expected simply to carry out the required household duties, which Millie found she enjoyed very much.

> I soon made two discoveries. *The first was that I really enjoyed the housework.* The opportunity to spring clean a room without any interruption, working methodically to make sure nothing was missed proved to be very enjoyable ... It was as if I had returned to that happy childhood experience of housework with my mother. I can remember reflecting that she would have been pleased with the efforts of her little housemaid.
> *The second discovery was delight I experienced when I thought how pleased the Mistress would be when she returned home to find another room all clean and bright.* (ibid.: 19–20, emphasis in the original)

Again, unexpectedly and without design on Millie's part, Mistress Alexander introduced Millie to the arts of becoming a lady's maid as well as a domestic.

> When the meal was over ... she made me sit and watch the late news with her and then sent me upstairs to run her bath. This I dutifully did. When it was ready she came upstairs and undressed and got into the bath while I got her bedroom ready for her. To my utter surprise she then summoned me into the bathroom to wash her back and then dry her when she got out of the bath. She stood there in the bathroom while I towelled her down until she was dry. She sent me into the bedroom to lay out a fresh dry towel over the bed. Lying naked on the towel she ordered me to use her lady shave to shave her legs, her armpits and trim her bikini line. Then it was time to cut her toenails. She taught me how to massage her shoulders and back. Once everything had been done to her satisfaction she would get off to bed and I would turn back the bedclothes and tuck her in.
>
> I had become a lady's maid as well as a domestic. It had never been part of my adolescent fantasies. Nothing had been said, Mistress Alexander had casually issued her instructions as if nothing could have been more natural. With my genitals tightly gripped by the panty girdle and wearing my black and white housemaid's uniform I felt deeply submissive and merely carried out her orders anxious to please and perform my duties efficiently. There was nothing erotic about it, it all seemed very natural. (ibid.: 21)

Millie concludes her description of this episode with the comment:

> I was very surprised by the turn of events . . . I had found that instead of being filled with lascivious thoughts I was very anxious to do her bidding and be of real service to her. It really was a strange feeling which I can only describe as a sense of devotion. (ibid.: 22)

Phase 6: Consolidating: intimacy, asexuality and not being a man

Millie entered into service with Mistress Alexander in 1990. Now confident in the 'reality' of her fantasies, Millie embarked on a period of working for other Mistresses. She soon learned 'the obvious': that 'no two Mistresses are the same and so every experience of service was different' (ibid.: 22). Millie used her experiences as a Maid under her various Mistresses to explain the role they played in her development as a servant and to her understanding of why she wanted to be a maidservant.

She outlines a number of 'important elements' associated with dressing as a maid. Several elements concern aspects of the dress: the cap and apron as a badge of servitude; the uniform as an indication that others in the same role wear it; the way the uniform brings out the dominant side of some Mistresses. Other elements refer to the psychological change: 'I was not prepared for the sort of personality change I underwent once I am dressed as a maid. Deep feelings of submissiveness and respect for the Mistress come over me' (ibid.: 28). She concludes:

> **Emasculation.** As an adolescent my masturbation fantasies involved wearing a maid's uniform. However, as an adult when I am wearing a panty girdle and a maid's uniform I do not feel genitally aroused in the normal way. Instead of an erection I have these deep feelings of submissiveness and a desire to serve. It is almost as if I have been emasculated by my maid's underwear and uniform. (ibid.: 29)

Millie reiterates the point in a personal communication (1997):

> There is NO sexual activity with any of the Mistresses I have served. It is important to me that that there should not be any at all. I seek to become entirely asexual when in the company of my Mistress. This is not a fantasy but a reality. Two of the Mistresses I serve are quite happy to walk about their bedroom totally naked while I am making their bed. One Mistress has me assist her in her bath. I wash her back and dry her when she gets out. There is nothing sexual about this. The Mistress's total lack of concern and total disregard for the masculine side of my nature effectively switches off any sexual feelings. I hasten to add that I did not seek ways of being present while the Mistress was dressing and undressing etc. I was usually summoned in and told what to do. I must confess it came as a surprise at first, but the initiative came from the Mistresses. It only serves to accentuate the asexual nature of the sissy maid, at least in the eyes of the Mistress ... As for me there is nothing really sexual with my Mistresses. I can also add that this asexuality is one of the real attractions of the sissy side of my nature.

It is evident in these passages both how Millie privileges her maid's uniform, and how what was erotic to her in her youth is now implicated in her emasculation and asexuality.

Ungendering processes as components of transgender masturbatory scripts

In this section of the chapter, we detail the manner in which modes of transgendering and their sub-processes are variously eroticized. In particular, we will compare selected favourite masturbatory scripts of 'Sissy Diana', considered previously in this chapter, with those favoured by 'Janice', the autogynephilic transsexual person introduced in Chapter 2. The purpose of the comparison is to highlight how Sissy Diana's scripts and Janice's scripts variously eroticize the transgendering sub-processes of 'erasing', 'implying', 'concealing', 'substituting', and 'redefining'. In particular, the scripts demonstrate the various ways in which 'ungendering' can manifest as either a central or a subsidiary sub-process within a transgendering trajectory. The autogynephilic transsexual's scripts eroticize erasing in the service of erotic 'substituting', while erasing within the male sissy maid's script nominally diffuses the erotic in the service of a developing asexuality.

Janice

Janice, you will recall from Chapter 2, encountered the transgender fantasy novels of Sandy Thomas prior to her transition, and used favourite scripts from these novels during masturbation. After undergoing sex reassignment surgery, she revisited these erotic novels, and found them still stimulating.

She considers herself to be an autogynephilic transsexual. That is, she sought sex reassignment in part because living as a woman and having a woman's body were the most sexually exciting things she could imagine.

Janice has chosen her favourite masturbatory script from the transgender fantasy novel *Just Like a Woman*, by Sandy Thomas ([1989] 1997). *Just Like a Woman* tells the story of a young investigative reporter sent undercover to investigate the fictional 'Chrissy Institute of Beverley Hills' – a clinic 'where they turn boys to girls'. It might be expected that a self-identified autogynephilic transsexual would focus on those 'substituting' aspects of migrating stories. However, Janice also eroticizes the ungendering (erasing) aspects that are part of transgender substituting.

This first script features the 'half-hour visit to the *control salon*'. The following erasing excerpts (ibid.: 33–4) Janice finds particularly erotic:

> I had wondered how the boy in the bikini eliminated the tell-tale bulge. It didn't take long for me to find out. It looked like a g-string. I was shown how to position my maleness and given a lotion to apply. It was cold and seemed to tingle. When the g-string was applied and tightened it took my breath away. Dr. Holt laughed: 'This should curl your toes.' He gave it another good tug.
>
> 'It's not only good for your appearance, it eliminates unwanted behavior patterns and aids in a sense of well-being.'
>
> 'The Institute has designed the french style elastic g-string so that even in a bikini masculinity cannot be detected. Once fitted, you are taught to sit to urinate and to never remove the garment. While these garments are in place erection is impossible, there is however no lessening of the voluptuous thrills you will find in your new identity.'

Janice has chosen her second favourite masturbatory script from *That' A Girl*, also by Sandy Thomas (1991). It relates the tale of a young boy who spends the summer in Malibu as a girl. His father hopes that this will cure the boy of his unusual 'hobby' of cross-dressing. The story is given the added twist that his father's new wife (Laura, the protagonist's step-mother) is a young woman of 24 who encourages her stepson's cross-dressing and initiates him into the arts of womanhood. Here are some excerpts (ibid.: 26–8) that Janice finds particularly stimulating:

> [Laura] held up a thong type g-string that was made of a stretch material . . . 'It's a special material that actually interacts with the heat of your body, moulding that boyish projection into a femininely smooth curve. It's going to be tight, darling, but it will do the trick. Put it on.'
>
> 'Oh my,' I said seeing my absolutely girlish front. My belly curved down between my legs without any boyish flaw. Visually, I was no longer a member of the male sex. Smiling, she handed me my panties. I truly fit unquestionably into my white high-cut panties now.

After dressing in tight shorts and a halter-top, the boy walks into the living room where his Dad is reading the paper: '"Oh my gawd," he moaned. He looked me up and down and focused on the obvious shorts that showed a bit

of my fanny. Showing between my bare naked thighs was only femininity.'
When Dad objects, Laura argues for her stepson's feminization:

> It was Laura and I against my father ... Laura took my side and told my father of her plans for femi-
> nizing me; that is, making sure no one would know. As she told him of how pretty I was going to be, I
> felt a lurch of excitement surge through me. They discussed my figure and Laura proclaimed to my
> father, 'His new flatness is perfect. Wait until you see him wearing a bikini on the beach.'

In these scripts, for Janice, erasing occurs as a subsidiary sub-process, which
is both eroticized and functions in the service of transgender substituting. For
example, the protagonist's male characteristics (e.g., visible protrusion of the
male genitalia) are erased primarily so that female characteristics (e.g., the
ability to wear revealing feminine clothing, like a bikini) can be substituted.
Note that in both scripts the protagonists are quite young. Age regression relative to the age of most readers is also a gender erasing mechanism, situating the protagonist in a less gender-differentiated developmental stage, which
permits alternative re-gendering.

These two scripts, especially the second, also demonstrate three recurring
themes in many transgender masturbatory scripts that focus on erasing. We will
term these themes the 'scopophilic,' the 'intimate', and the 'oedipal'. 'Scopophilic'
(following Freud, 1905) refers to pleasure in looking. Great emphasis in these
scripts is placed on the sight of the protagonist's emasculated/feminized genital area. 'Intimacy' refers to closeness to females: in the second script, intimate
interaction with the stepmother is part of the protagonist's initiation into femininity. 'Oedipal' (following Freud) refers to simultaneous relationships with
desirable female characters and conventionally masculine characters: In both
scripts, the presence of male figures provides a contrast to the protagonist's situation, emphasizing his inability to compete for females with other males. This
is particularly erotic for Janice.

Sissy Diana

Sissy Diana's favourite masturbatory script is taken from Debra Rose's *Sissy
Maid Academy, Volume 1* (Rose, 1993b: 61–2), which features the diary entries
of a sissy at a fictional training academy. Diana has copied into his own 'Sissy
Notebook' his favoured selections from Rose's writings. Occasionally, he (he
almost always refers to himself as 'he') has personalized his selections from
Rose. For example, whereas Rose refers in her text to 'Miss', Diana has replaced
the 'Miss' with Mistress. On other occasions, which we indicate below with
words in brackets, Sissy Diana has slightly altered Rose's wording. Sissy
Diana has also incorporated himself into the script in order to further the

fantasy that Mistress is giving her instructions to him. Similarly, we have indicated this substitution in brackets in the text.

The Rose script has Mistress 'coming down the hall, dressed only in bra and panties'. Mistress instructs (Diana) to follow her down the hall – giving her full view of 'her beautiful bottom swinging back and forth in her skimpy lacy panties'. (Diana) is then instructed to help Mistress on with her dress – an 'elaborate cocktail affair in a flimsy black fabric', in preparation for Mistress's date, 'who will be here any second'. (Diana) is needed to tie up the elaborate back lacing, which Mistress would be unable to secure for herself. After interchanges about what a 'lovely' dress it is, Mistress adds: 'I hope my boyfriend likes it. You help me get into it, and hopefully, *he'll* help me get out of it later!' After further assisting Mistress with her hair, perfume and shoes, the script ends with Mistress saying 'thanks' as she leaves (Diana) to meet her date. (Diana) is left in good spirits. He feels 'proud and needed and important' because Mistress has thanked him.

Jenny's second favourite masturbatory script consists of sections from Debra Rose's *Maid in Form 'B'* and *'C'* (Rose, 1993a) which chronicle the life of a sissy maid with his Mistress.

In the first section, Mistress ('Cindy' in Rose's original text) gets (Diana) to stand in the corner of her bedroom to watch how Mistress and her lover Frank engage in sex. After Mistress removes her panties, there is a more or less conventional scene of heterosexual lovemaking. Interspersed throughout, however, are descriptions of the (Diana's) feelings about what he is observing (Rose, 1993a, 'B': 17):

> Frank went on to the bed as beautiful (Mistress) raised her knees and spread her gorgeous legs in preparation. As her lover slowly slid into her, (Mistress) glanced at me with one of her superior looks. A smile of pleasure appeared on her face unlike any I had ever seen before. It was the special smile a woman has when she is being made love to.
>
> In spite of myself, I was fascinated by the sight in front of me. The jealousy inherent in the situation was beyond description, however, and made me burn inside with intense frustration and (confusion).

After the first episode of sexual intercourse, Mistress tells (Diana) to go to his room, where he hears Mistress being made love to 'yet again', and (Diana's) sexual activity is described (Rose, 1993a, 'B': 52):

> I slowly dressed in my frothy baby-doll nightie with the prissy, ruffled-rear panties. Sighing, I slipped between the pink rubber sheets of my little bed ... With frustrated (confusion), I reached into my pink panties and (began to touch my soft and useless weenie). Moments later, my panties wet and sticky from my childish actions, I rolled on to my tummy and squirmed in my bed.

As (Diana) tries to sleep, he hears his Mistress being made love to 'yet again', and begins to 'weep (himself) to sleep'.

The above passages are all taken from two stories that Diana uses as masturbatory fantasy scripts. Here, we detail a masturbatory episode in which Diana incorporates the first script into his masturbatory fantasies. As he reports to us:

> When I play with myself, I always slip between my rubber sissy sheets on my little single bed and think what a total sissy I am. I slide my gaff down my legs and look at my smooth body with its tiny little weenie. I think how useless I am as a man. I then read through my sissy story. I imagine looking at Mistress's bottom in her skimpy lace panties. I think of her sexy dress. I feel warm all over. I think about Mistress taking off her dress in front of her lover. I turn over on my stomach and rub my little weenie on my rubber sheet. I think about my Mistress's instructions: that when I play with myself I must stay as soft and as small as possible. I think what a total sissy I am as my sissy leak dribbles out on to my rubber sheet.

What enables Sissy Diana's 'ejaculation' (his 'sissy leak') is his eroticization of his own 'erasing', the thought of his own sissiness. In short, while looking at his Mistress in her 'sexy' clothes feature as foreplay, it is his own 'ungendering' that enables his 'sissy' orgasm. His ungendered body underscores his sissy personality and his lack of 'masculine' response to his 'sexy' Mistress. These components of his negating enable his orgasm. As he orgasms, he is not thinking of his 'sexy' Mistress; rather, he is thinking of what a 'total sissy' he is to be behaving in such a way.

Note that in both of Sissy Diana's scripts, the erasing of the sissy protagonist's male characteristics (e.g., by depilation, genital restraint) is not accompanied by substitution of feminine gender signifiers. The presence of a virile male character within his chosen masturbatory scripts underscores the incapacity of the sissy protagonist to be sexually active with women; but the protagonist does not take on female gender role behaviours in relation to the male character. The sexuality of the protagonist becomes diffused, and is expressed either vicariously through identification with the Mistress and her lifestyle, or in solitary masturbation in a manner that is distinctively 'sissy'.

Diana's scripts are also structured around the three major tendencies we described earlier: the scopophilic, the intimate and the oedipal. Much time is spent 'looking' at Mistress: sometimes at her body, but most usually at her clothes, particularly her undergarments. What for a 'real' man might lead to thoughts of sexual conquest, for the sissy leads to 'intimacy' with his Mistress. Like girls together, Mistress and Sissy can take shared pleasure in 'lovely' clothes, for instance. Finally, thoughts of the boyfriend or his actual presence are never far away: Sissy is participating as part of a threesome.

The comparison of Janice's and Diana's scripts demonstrates how ungendering, in the form of gender erasing, can function either as a subsidiary or a central sub-process within a transgender script. In the case of a transsexual like

Janice, erasing functions as a *subsidiary* sub-process, ultimately in the service of transgender substituting. By contrast, in the case of a male sissy maid like Sissy Diana, erasing functions as the *major* sub-process, thus giving rise to the distinctive mode of transgendering as negating. An exploration of these scripts using our conceptual framework sensitizes us to the significance of 'ungendering' in transgendering scripts, where ungendering is often overlooked.

Interestingly, another informant of ours who once took anti-androgens and identified as transsexual, but who has now decided not to transition, wrote to us as follows:

> [Over] the last 2 or 3 years as I left the transsexual lifestyle and was slowly re-acclimatizing as a male, another fantasy entered the picture. It would be me as a male who was locked into a chastity belt by a dominant woman. She would make me do things (chores, sexual favours, etc.) for her in order to win release from the chastity belt. ('Gretchen', personal communication, 2002)

In Gretchen's case there was a transition from migrating fantasies of being a woman to fantasies of being a negated man. Here is a realm of human experience – the complex interrelations between migrating and negating – that warrants further investigation.

Janice, Sissy Diana, and paradoxes of erotic erasing: a tale of refining

We sent an earlier draft of the previous section to the journal *Sexualities* for possible publication. One reviewer, *inter alia*, felt that there needed to be a more specific linkage made between text, script and reader. We have sought to address this problem as we revised the section for this book. However, from preliminary comment on our developing ideas about 'erotic erasing', we are only too aware how paradoxes of erotic erasing make this a difficult area to grasp for those unfamiliar or unsympathetic to it.

It will be recalled that Janice identifies as an autogynephilic transsexual who has based her identification on the writings of Ray Blanchard and Anne Lawrence. This literature and identification highlights the complex interrelations between 'masculine' and 'feminine' transgendered sexuality, insofar as many self-identified MTF transsexuals are committed to erasing many elements of their masculinity, though paradoxically this desire derives from a sexuality that is in important respects stereotypically masculine.

Janice's 'getting off' on her identification with the erasing sub-processes detailed in her favourite masturbatory scripts was an aspect of her eventual enactment of the fantasy: her subsequent 'actual' penectomy and castration. Moreover, her voyeuristic pleasures accompanying her gazing both at attractive women, and at men who had been negated and feminized and who now present as women, remained substantially similar both pre and post reassignment. The 'reality', as well as the fantasy, of losing her own male genitalia paradoxically maintained what to many would be seen as a stereotypically 'masculine' sexual response to feminine beauty. In another interesting 'fantasy' variant of negating males, web sites are now emerging which feature the 'virtual identity' of the 'real' woman (a celebrated supermodel) fantasied as being a negated male whose genitalia are permanently gaffed.[2] Both Janice and Gretchen find these sites highly erotic (Ekins, 2002; 2003).

Arguably, the paradox of sissy sexuality is harder to grasp. Why would a sissy who is purporting to be moving towards an increasing asexuality use sissification material for masturbatory purposes? Why, indeed, does he find the need to masturbate at all?

Here, the distinction many clinicians make between masturbation to relieve a consciously felt sexual drive or 'tension', and masturbation for 'comfort', is helpful. For instance, Sissy Diana follows her Mistress's instructions in regard to masturbation, namely: 'You may play with yourself whenever you feel lonely', and 'Keep your weenie as small and as soft as possible'. He feels no particular 'drive' to masturbate; rather it gives him relief from loneliness.

Certainly, our data suggest that as the negating sissy's trajectory develops, it is the 'comfort' aspects of masturbation and masturbatory fantasy that become increasingly dominant. While the 'comfort' may be tinged with discomfort as the sissy reflects upon his sissiness after an incident of masturbation, or even during it, eventually, acceptance of a sissy identity tends to dissipate any residual discomfort, as in the following sissy 'rule' set forth in a sissy's diary:

> Remember that men have sexual relationships with women, and women have sexual relationships with men, but a sissy can only have a sexual relationship with himself, his bedding, or his cum pad. This is quite natural for sissies and there is no need to feel ashamed or guilty about this.

Debra Rose's comments on what we term the paradox of sissy sexuality are significant. She writes:

> Yes, it is a 'paradox' in that the sissy is usually quite ineffectual sexually with women (though is often attracted to women). It is somewhat (but NOT only!) 'sexual' fantasy where the sissy's non-performance in bed is somehow 'sexualised' a bit. How can something like impotence or a very small penis be seen as 'sexy'? Well it isn't, *per se*. It is, rather, the mild humiliation and overt sissiness that his ineffectuality (impotence, etc.) denote to others that is (perhaps) eroticized somewhat.

In the main, however, Debra Rose is concerned to stress that our focus on sissy sexuality and masturbation gives it an importance it simply does not have in her writings of sissy theory and practice. In particular, it tends to obfuscate what the 'boss' or 'employer' of the sissy gets out of the relationship, as well as the importance of the unique relationship that often develops between employer and sissy. Rose prefers the term boss or employer to 'Mistress' because Mistress conjures up black leather and boots 'which is not what this is about', she says. She emphasizes that the sissies in her stories are paid employees.

In particular, she stresses the importance of including material on the sissy lifestyle within which sissy sexuality and masturbation play the most minor of parts. Here the experiences of Sissy Bobbie, another sissy informant who identifies with Debra Rose's writings, are most pertinent.

Typical of Sissy Bobbie's activities, detailing what the sissy's employers get out of it, are the following:

> Just last Saturday evening I served as the 'waitress' for eight women at a very nice and formal catered (five course!) dinner at the Club I work at. First, I helped the caterer in the kitchen – then dressed in a nice taffeta and petticoated uniform before serving the women both before and during the dinner. They just enjoyed themselves and did NOTHING. After they were done, the women just got up from the table, and the hostess of the event called to me 'Bobbie, you may clear the table now'. Unfortunately, this started a clean-up process that took me almost three hours (!) – all the while the women relaxed and went about their leisurely evening. This part is not 'fun' in any sense and I do not get 'turned on' by it at all. But it is a part of the 'sissy maid lifestyle'. I DO get paid, so it is really 'just my job' in a way.
>
> Anyway, while I guess it was (is) 'my fantasy' – it was the women's as well. They got to spend an evening spoiled by a devoted, obedient and nicely uniformed maid – not a bad thing for them at all.

Sissy Bobbie has been working for three years at this Club on the East Coast of the USA as their staff waitress/maid. Through contacts made at the Club, he has procured work as a maid in a number of women's houses, especially for parties.

Sissy Bobbie experiments with different styles of clothing. 'I dressed pretty somewhat conservatively at first, but now pretty much anything I think is right goes'. He continues:

> I sometimes wear very tight brief short-shorts, there now. But – as always with me (very tightly gaffed, well groomed and shaved, etc.) I am never 'X' rated: a lot of leg shows; and sometimes later in the evening maybe even a bit of the bottom curve of my rear, due to wearing very brief 'booty' shorts. But all this 'sexiness' is really kinda sexless in a 'Ken Doll' kind of way. I have no problem there – people just like my service. I have become the 'official' Club 'sissy waitress' or whatever – and now regularly work there ... I do not get 'hit on' by women (or men, for that matter) and am simply treated as what I am – a cute, 'waitress' and 'server' – simply there to do mostly menial things.

FIVE   Transcending Stories

A conceptual introduction to transcending

Since the early 1990s there have emerged a number of transgendering stories which we focus upon in this chapter under the general title of 'transcending' stories. We have chosen the term because of the suggestion of 'going beyond'. While transcending may take place by means of erasing, substituting, concealing, and implying, as in the other modes, the meaning of the transgendering and its attendant sub-processes is fundamentally redefined in the transcending mode. Redefining is the major sub-process. Self, body and gender redefining in the particular transcending story seeks to subvert and/or move beyond the binary divide. In the process of this redefining, selves, bodies, body parts, sexualities, and gender, within the redefined system of classification, will take on new meanings.

One of the best-known and widely quoted publications concerned with the transcending of gender is Kate Bornstein's *Gender Outlaw* (1994). The transcending gender stories considered in this chapter are 'outlaw' stories in many ways. They are stories of lives lived 'outside' the 'laws' of gender but they are also stories of going beyond merely living 'outside' those laws to subverting those laws and substituting alternative ways of conceptualizing gender.

The term 'gender outlaw', together with others chosen by those who wish to 'transcend' gender, such as 'gender warriors' and 'gender terrorists', give something of the flavour of the social role of those who transcend *vis-à-vis* the binary gender divide. These are stories that tell of a future society 'beyond the binary' and of the development of new means to achieve the new goals. They are stories in which the 'gender outlaw' is a harbinger of a new gender order to come. From the standpoint of the sociological literature it is instructive to draw upon a number of conceptual distinctions made to differentiate various types of 'outsider'. One conceptual distinction that we have found useful is that made by Robert Merton who wrote that: 'Two major varieties of deviant behavior can be usefully distinguished on the basis of their structure and their consequences for social systems. The first can be called "nonconforming behavior"; the second "aberrant behavior"' (1971: 829).

Elaboration of Merton's distinction between the two types of behaviour provides an excellent way of distinguishing transcending stories from those of migrating and oscillating, and, more subtly, of negating. Although Merton's typology makes no mention of gender deviance, far less is he concerned with the binary gender divide, his twofold typology proves instructive, if applied with care, to diverse positions on the binary gender divide.

Merton distinguishes nonconforming and aberrant behaviour on five major grounds. In the first place, 'the nonconformer announces his dissent publicly; unlike the aberrant, he does not try to hide his departure from the social norms' (ibid.: 830). Merton cites the political or religious dissenter, who makes his departure from the norms known to as many people as possible who will look at him and listen to him. 'Contrast the pacifist who burns his draft card in public with the draft dodger who tries to escape into obscurity' (ibid.: 830). The transcending 'gender dissenter' does likewise. Whereas migrating and oscillating stories place the emphasis on 'passing' and assimilation (an escape into the 'obscurity' of the 'opposite' gender), transcending stories are most usually linked with a degree of political activism. This political activism almost invariably presupposes being 'out' as transgendered; personally, the personal and the political become intertwined. It is a story of what Merton refers to as 'patterned visibility'. It is no coincidence, therefore, that Jamison Green, one of the world's most prominent transactivist transmen, titles his recent autobiography *Becoming A Visible Man* (Green, 2004).

Merton links this 'patterned attitude towards visibility' with a second basic difference between the nonconformer and the aberrant. Whereas the aberrant acknowledges the legitimacy of the social norms he violates, the nonconformist challenges the legitimacy of those social norms. Such is the case with the norms of gender and the binary divide. The gender 'aberrant' migrator and oscillator both find it necessary to violate the norms of the 'natural attitude', but both acknowledge the legitimacy of the binary itself. The negator variously accepts the legitimacy of the binary for others, but not for him/her/perself. The gender nonconformer, on the other hand, challenges the legitimacy of the binary, itself.

Third, and relatedly, the nonconformer seeks to change the norms he/she is denying in practice. The aberrant seeks to avoid the sanctions of his/her aberrance from the 'natural attitude', but he/she does not propose substitutes for the binary within which he/she migrates or oscillates. The transcender, on the other hand, seeks precisely for a personal and political transcending of the 'laws' of the binary, itself.

The application of Merton's fourth point to the transcending story is, perhaps, more contentious. Merton argues that whereas the aberrant is generally thought to be deviating from the norms to serve his own interests, the nonconformer is generally thought to be deviating from the norms for 'disinterested purposes'. Merton distinguishes the aberrant highwayman Dick Turpin from the nonconformer Oliver Cromwell. In the present era of greater cynicism, we find it less easy, perhaps, to attribute 'disinterested purposes'. Moreover, given the suspicion of gender nonconformers within the 'natural attitude', many people find it particularly difficult to accept claims of 'disinterested purpose' in their case. Nevertheless, it is an important argument in the armoury of most gender transcenders that the rigidities of the binary divide constrain us all, and not just those who particularly feel its oppression.

Finally, for Merton, it is an important function of the nonconformer to draw to our attention the discrepancy between the ultimate values of a society and its particular norms. As Merton puts it: 'He is trying to make justice a social reality rather than an institutionalised fiction' (1971: 831). This point is particularly evident in the case of those transcending stories that argue for the 'reality' of human rights in the sphere of gender. For many gender transcenders, a commitment to human rights presupposes a move beyond the binary for all those that so wish it. The 1995 *International Bill of Gender Rights* (reprinted in Feinberg, 1996: 171–5), for instance, claims that 'all human beings have the right to define their own gender identity'. They also have the right to 'free expression of their self-defined gender identity,' and to change 'their bodies cosmetically, chemically, or surgically, so as to express a self-defined gender identity' (ibid.: 172–3).

In the migrating and oscillating modes, it is possible to question the content of particular gender roles. Indeed, those migrating and oscillating are often particularly sensitive to variations in gender roles. Consider Ginger for example:

> I really get into feminine role playing. I like to choose a typical feminine role and then dress and make-up for a stereotype of that kind of girl. I try to also suit my actions, manner, and personality to the role. In the past I've experimented with these various female stereotypes: hooker; chic fashion model; dominatrix; French maid: little girl; slut. (1980: 5)

However, whatever the variation in gender role, migrating and oscillating presuppose acceptance of the basic binary structure. This acceptance of the binary by migrators and oscillators raises a paradox concerning 'essentialist' notions of sex and gender. We saw, in Chapter 2, for instance, how certain opponents of migrating argued, in effect, that 'males were male' and 'females were female' and that male or female 'essence' could not be changed. A number of commentators used these arguments to oppose 'sex change' surgery on the grounds that it entailed 'collusion with delusion'.

Paradoxically, however, many of the arguments in support of migrating and oscillating mirrored the same essentialist arguments. In the case of migrating, many commentators claimed that transsexuals 'really' belonged to the other sex or gender, in some biological and/or psychological sense. In the case of oscillating, the (male) transvestite was said to be expressing 'the woman within'.

Transcending stories, however, in their different ways, all render problematic the binary structure of gender and the socially prescribed interrelations of the body, gender and sexuality. As we shall see, many of those who transcend do make use of the same erasing, substituting, implying, and concealing procedures as those that migrate or oscillate. However, the meaning of the procedures and objects used within the various sub-processes are variously redefined in the light of the transcending.

Telling transcending stories

As we outlined in Chapter 1, the dominant transcending stories are not primarily personal narratives. They tend to be tales of personal experience, performance, politics, theory, manifesto and, occasionally, 'science', 'all rolled into one' as Bornstein (1994) puts it. This fact is reflected in our organization of the various stories we consider in this chapter, to which we take a broadly chronological approach.

Migrating, oscillating, and negating stories, as we have seen, are often preoccupied with personal identity, with 'finding oneself'. Transcending stories, however, very often problematize this notion of personal identity. Again, as transcending stories came to predominate in sections of the transgender community, the transgender community came to view itself differently, and to focus on different concerns. The focus shifted from 'what are we?' to 'what do we do?' and 'what will we do?' Time and energy spent on debating the similarities and dissimilarities between, say, 'transsexuals' and 'crossdressers', and issues of personal identification, could be spent, instead, on planning shared strategies to combat 'gender oppression'.

An aspect of this transition was a move from identity politics to transactivism against 'gender oppression' in general. Contemporaneously, postmodern cultural theory was making its impact felt in transcending stories. In particular, many transcending stories began to draw upon Judith Butler's critique of 'identity' and her emphasis upon gender performativity. In due time, a potent mix of personal 'gender fluidity', postmodern gender politics, and transactivism began to form the core of many, though by no means all, transcending stories whose principal intent was to undermine the privileging of the binary divide and its oppressive ramifications.

In elaboration of these various points, we might say that migrating stories are not in themselves critical of the binary divide, and where they have been prominent in political discourse, they have been told in terms of people with a particular identity who have rights that need to be fought for. By contrast, the political message of transcending stories serves to undermine the binary divide. Thus, Garber argues that: 'One of the most important aspects of cross-dressing is the way in which it offers a challenge to easy notions of binarity, putting into question the categories of male and female (1992: 10). Similarly, Straub and Epstein claim that 'gender ambiguity has become the focus of some of the most serious political debates in recent critical theory' (1991: 9). Their reference to 'recent' critical theory (in 1991) refers to the rise of post-modernism in the 1980s. Postmodernism as a theoretical perspective pro-vided much of the fuel that has powered what came to be known as 'queer theory' during the 1990s. Postmodern theory has also provided the starting point for much transcending transgender theorising. Some transcending stories have been critical of aspects of both postmodern and queer theory (Namaste, 2000). Other transcending stories, like Feinberg (1996), have ignored them. However, most of the influential transcending stories, like those of Riki Anne Wilchins (2002a; 2002b) and Susan Stryker (Stryker, 1994; 1998), have enthusiastically embraced a mix of postmodern and queer theory in their trans theory and practice.

Contemporaneous with the emergence of the influence of transcending stories has been the increasing influence of the internet. The internet, of course, was and is used to further facilitate migrating, oscillating and negating stories, but it became particularly important in the emergence of transcend-ing stories and their development and influence.

Stephen Whittle makes the fundamental point thus:

> Cyberspace had allowed networking on an unprecedented scale. Despite the redrawing of the mar-gins of community identification, there are still only a few transgendered people in any one geo-graphical location at best ... Cyberspace provides a neighbourhood in which many people, otherwise separated by great distances can interact at a local level. (1996b: 65–6)

It is important to draw attention to two other aspects of the impact of the inter-net which Whittle discusses in his account. In the first place, the new avenue of communication facilitated the development of new community-based per-spectives which were not constrained by the medical paradigm. In the second place, as a result of the 'disembodied' nature of cyber communication, some of the divisions within the transgender community (Whittle specifically mentions the division between those who can 'pass' and those who cannot) became irrelevant, at least in cyberspace, leading to greater inclusion within the trans community. Whittle comments that cyberspace 'presents a safe area where body image and presentation are not amongst the initial aspects of personal judgement and social hierarchy within the transgender community, so extending the range of potential community members and voices' (ibid.: 63).

One of the divisions within the trans community (or at least in respect of trans women) that Whittle refers to is the hierarchy based on the extent to which the trans woman passes as non-trans. Another consequence of the development of the internet is that it has provided 'a locale in which transsexual women have been able to discuss over whether "looks" are important without "looks" getting in the way' (ibid.: 62). Thus the issue (heretical from the migrating mode) of whether passing was necessarily desirable could be aired.

Being able to pass meant, of course, that after sex reassignment surgery, the MTF trans woman became invisible as trans. As Whittle points out, however, even the most passable of trans women can never entirely be sure that their trans status has been left behind. This is evident in the instance of the British model Tula whose trans status was exposed by the *News of the World*. But on a day-to-day basis, as Whittle says, trans men do not have an issue with passing as 'any transsexual man can take testosterone, grow a beard, have his voice break, and pass anywhere, anytime, with great success' (ibid.: 63). The main issue for transsexual men concerned the penis, or rather the fact that surgical techniques cannot create male genitalia as successfully as they have been able to create female ones. So trans men have been forced to face the fact that the body and gender presentation/position do not have to align in the culturally preferred fashion. The redefining of this 'misalignment' in a positive way is now one of the notable facets of the transcending story whether told by trans men or trans women. As Cromwell says, 'Through networking and the sharing of discourses many transpeople are resisting the imposed order that dictates the necessity of being either a man or a woman. Those who choose not to give into that order find that their self-definition does not have to include society's "ultimate insignias"' [the genitals] (1999: 117).

We turn now to our chronological account of the major transcending stories.

The prehis/herstory of transgendering as transcending: Dr Charlotte Bach and the Cockettes

Transgendering as transcending emerged as an alternative 'paradigm' for understanding cross-dressing and sex-changing in the 1990s (Denny, 1995). It was during this period that transgendered people specifically linked their personal and political lives with the terminology of transgender and began to speak of moving 'beyond the binary'. It must be said, however, that with hindsight, we can see precursors of the 'transcending' approach in a number of other confluences that emerged much earlier.

The general tenor of the early migrating and oscillating stories, as we have seen, were about 'passing' on the 'other' side of the binary. Transgendering identities were mostly forged in relation to the medical categorizations of the transsexual and transvestite. Less often, transgendered people, most notably Virginia Prince, forged identities which were opposed in fundamental regards to the medical categorizations. Nevertheless they were forged very much in relation to them.

Transcending stories, however, took their inspiration, in the main, from outside medical categorizations. Some drew on the literature of androgyny and made links with evolutionary theory. Some took their inspiration variously from revolutionary politics, from socialist and Marxist ideology and from anarchism. Still others drew upon the language of performance and the theatrical.

To illustrate the precursors, it is instructive to go back to the late 1960s and early 1970s and distinguish the case of Dr Charlotte Bach who wrote as a psychologist putting forward a new theory of evolution, from that of *The Cockettes*, a radical drag street-theatre group. Dr Charlotte Bach appeared on the London academic scene in 1971 and after placing an advertisement in the court and social page of *The Times* embarked on a career to publicize her 'emergent theory of evolution' (Wheen, 2002: 7–8).[1] Bach purported to have lectured at Budapest University before being driven out by the communists in 1948. After the shock of the loss of her husband and son within two weeks of each other in 1965, she absorbed herself in the project of compiling a dictionary of psychology. As she researched the section on sexual perversions, she built up data from her interviews with those that practised variant sexualities and theorized about their sexual preferences. In due time, she had a Eureka experience: 'perversion was the engine of human evolution'. Once she had developed this insight in the context of her study of evolutionary theory, she felt able to advertise her theory, thus:

Having investigated thoroughly and objectively all the phenomena at present haphazardly, incompletely subsumed under the blanket term sexual deviations and in particular the phenomenon at present misleadingly termed 'transsexuality', I was able to establish the laws governing the phenomenon at present known in ethology as the 'ritualisation of displacement activities'.

My findings (a) conclusively prove that the evolution of all aspects of the behaviour of all living organisms has occurred in accordance with these laws; (b) which in turn conclusively proves that the evolution of all living organisms has occurred with identical and in essence the same laws; (c) which in turn leaves no reasonable doubt that the evolution of all inorganic matter must have occurred in an essentially homologous fashion.

These findings further (a) largely disprove Darwinian theory; (b) largely prove Lamarckian theory; (c) altogether prove beyond reasonable doubt all the main contentions of the theory at present known as 'emergent evolution'. (cited in Wheen, 2002: 7-8)

Her 521-page typescript '*Homo Mutans, Homo Luminens*' sent to the celebrated writer Colin Wilson soon after the advertisement was, she explained, 'merely the "prolegomenon" to a projected work of about 3,000 pages which would demonstrate beyond doubt that sexual deviation was the mainspring of evolution' (Wheen, 2002: 9). In April 1973, Wilson felt able to write in the London magazine *Time Out*:

Charlotte Bach has developed a theory about sex and evolution ... If she is correct, or even half correct, then the implications of her theory are so tremendous that it is one of the greatest intellectual advances of the twentieth century, and she should be classified with Einstein and Freud as a revolutionary thinker. (Wilson, 1973)

Wheen continues:

Five years later, in his book *Mysteries*, Wilson wrote at greater length about Dr Bach's theory of evolution as inner conflict, 'all stemming from that fundamental "platonic" pull, the desire of each sex to become its opposite, or rather to blend into unity ... It is this inner stress, Charlotte Bach believes, which has transformed our instincts into intellect, and which accounts for the extraordinary development of the human brain in the past half million years. The whole notion could be compared to Newton's theory of gravitation.' (2002: 14)

In the spring of 1972, Bach began a weekly seminar in which she promulgated her ideas. One of us attended several of those seminars, intrigued by the heady mix of 'mathematical knowledge', 'Shamanistic Ecstasies', 'Jung, Freud and Alchemy', 'Husserl, Bertrand Russell and the Book of the Dead'. Bach's use and abuse of all the figures she introduced, however, was always in the context of her starting point that the conflict between the masculine and feminine provided the mainspring of evolution. Richard Ekins recalls that:

Her most favoured visual aid in the classes of hers that I attended was the 'quaternion'. In each class, she would draw upon a blackboard a vertical line. The top of the line indicated the future; the bottom of the line indicated the past. She would then divide the vertical line in half with a horizontal line that indicated the male principle at one end and the female principle at the other end. Each and every thinker and idea that she brought up in her classes could then be placed on the quarternion in terms of the way they had variously glimpsed or, more usually, failed to glimpse, aspects of her theory.

However, intrigued as I was by the 'quaternion' which she returned to, time and time again, to illustrate various aspects of the opposition of the male and female principles as the driving force of evolution – I was equally intrigued by her and her style of presentation. Despite my attempts to wade through her mimeod texts bought for 50p a time at each meeting, I recall that most of the talk with my friends after the meetings concerned her appearance and manner of presentation. She seemed to be suffering from a runny cold at all the meetings I attended, and would punctuate her 'profundities' with pauses, filled in by the most extraordinary 'delicate' dabbing of her nostrils with the pointed end of a tiny hankie. Mimicking this gesture provided a number of us with endless fun. It seemed to encapsulate all that was odd and eccentric about Charlotte. Here was a broad-shouldered, thick set, heavily made-up lady with heavily coiffured hair delicately punctuating her heavily Central European accent with the sort of gesture more appropriate to an Oscar Wilde stage play.

Little did we realize that on her death in 1981, when she was undressed at the mortuary 'the ample breasts proved to be foam rubber, and the removal of her knickers exposed a penis' (Wheen, 2002: 17). It became clear to many of her erstwhile followers just how far Bach's theories were the projections of her own 'oppositions'. Here was a tale of justification of monumental proportions.

The great significance of Bach's tale in the context of this book is that, in putting forward a theory of emergent evolution which 'redefined' cross-dressing and sex-changing from that of a pathology to the engine of evolution, she constructed a theory of transgendering as transcending, *par excellence*. Yet she felt it necessary to personally migrate, rather than personally transcend. As Wheen concludes:

> The dreams of fame and Nobel prizes may have been absurd, but by carrying her secret almost to the grave she did 'make the grade' ... It would be ungenerous, after witnessing such heroism, to say that she was 'really a man'. Which man? In her final identity she achieved an authenticity that gave her far more pleasure and fulfilment than any of the feckless personae she inhabited previously. (ibid.: 140–1)

The tales we now turn to are by those whose fusion of the personal and the political make it impossible for them to migrate or oscillate. These are doubly tales of transcending. With hindsight, it is instructive to trace the roots of the different facets of contemporary personal and political transcending to the insurrectionist and revolutionary politics of the late 1960s. However, it was to be a considerable time before the facets became organized into aspects of the transgender community and transgender activism that we are familiar with today.

Particularly instructive is the mix of hippie 'free love', revolutionary politics, street theatre and gay drag that coalesced in the 'gay hippie' theatre of *The Cockettes* in San Francisco, between 1969 and 1971. In the space of two short years they moved from being one of many communes with a penchant for drag and street theatre in San Francisco to a stage act performing in New York to the celebrities and glitterati of the day.

Fleischer (1996: 37–8) provides an illuminating account of their opening night and of 'how the mirror cracked when the curtain went up'. They could proudly boast the presence of no less than Andy Warhol, Anthony Perkins, Gore Vidal, Allen Ginsberg, Angela Lansbury, and Anthony Quinn as the curtain went up:

'At the height of New York's "radical chic" period, anyone who was anyone was fighting for the chance to get a bunch of cross-dressed, tripping hippies up for tea, and for a fleeting couple of days the *Cockettes* were literally the toast of New York high society' (ibid.: 37). The opening night was generally considered to be fiasco: they were considered to be a bunch of unskilled San Francisco amateurs by their sophisticated New York audience. Nevertheless, John Lennon and a host of other rock stars and celebrities attended subsequent performances, and their influence on transgendering in rock music, youth style, and radical drag was to be germinal.

The leader of *The Cockettes* was a gay man on a spiritual journey who renamed himself 'Hibiscus' once he had set up base in San Francisco. Hibiscus developed what might be seen as 'hippie drag', a forerunner to what became more widely known in the 1980s as 'gender fuck'. He wore his long hair and beard very much in the style of the stylized portraits of Jesus Christ. However, to the 'Jesus Christ' look he added elaborate 'over the top' drag queen-style make-up and exotic women's costume in the style of such camp icons as Isadora Duncan and the glamorous movie stars of the 1930s and 1940s.

As his erstwhile followers were to report later in the movie *The Cockettes* (2002) directed by Bill Weber and David Weissman: 'He looked like Jesus Christ with lipstick.' 'He was outrageous. At the time his appearance was just so outlandish: with the skirts and the robes, and stuff woven in his hair, and stuff woven in his beard.'

Within *The Cockettes* were those that identified variously as spiritual and mystical adventurers, androgynes, political revolutionaries, and explorers of free love. What bound this disparate group together, apart from their charismatic leader, was their quest to move – in the language of later years – 'beyond the binaries'. These were people 'living at the end of their imagination'. As one group member puts it: 'We really did think there would be a revolution any moment, and we wanted to come down on the right side.' 'This was the dream ... we were on a spiritual quest. This is what we were born to do. We were born to change everything', says another (*The Cockettes*, 2002).

It was drag, above all, however, that brought the group together. 'We completely communicated through drag. That's how you met other people' says one follower. 'It wasn't just a drag show, it was a hippie side show' (*The Cockettes*, 2002).

Film director John Waters, a great fan of *The Cockettes*, summarizes:

They were the first kind of like bearded drag queens, they were like hippy acid freak drag queens which was really new at the time, really new. It still would be new ... You couldn't tell if it was men, or women. It was straight people, too. It was complete sexual anarchy which is always a wonderful thing. (*The Cockettes*, 2002)

Such comments as these, selected from the soundtrack of the 2002 film *The Cockettes*, make the point that, in essence, the group presaged the full range of 'transcending' gender stories that came to fruition in the mid-late 1990s. Here are transgendering tales of anarchy, of liberation, of revolution, and of performance.

Transcending and the social organization
of transgendering

As we saw in Chapter 4, the social organization of transgendering developed in the mid-1960s initially along the lines dictated by Virginia Prince. On the whole, self-identified transvestites and transsexuals were largely concerned to conform to gender stereotypes and 'pass'. They did not see themselves as performing gender but, rather, as being 'true to themselves'. Within the gay cross-dressing community, however, the element of performance had long been a feature. *Men in Frocks* (Kirk and Heath, 1984), for instance, traces the history of drag from theatrical reviews of the British armed forces, through to the British drag balls of the 1960s into the mid-1980s.

Nevertheless, as Walter (1980: 22) puts it, 'in the community of gay men, queens have always occupied the lowest rung'. That was because they 'confirmed straight society's worst prejudices' (ibid.: 22; see also Brake, 1976). For a while, however, drag came to the forefront of the gay movement in the early 1970s, as some attempted to tackle sexism as well as heterosexism:

> From a certain reading of radical feminism, many gays felt that in order to struggle against male privilege, they must do everything possible to show that they were prepared to give up this privilege themselves. One way of doing so was to give up clothes which they termed as masculine, such as jeans and trousers, shirts and jackets, in favour of frocks, heels and make-up. (Walter, 1980: 23)

Traces of ideas which seem similar to the more recent ones we examine below can be found in this extract from an anonymous article in the early 1970s gay liberation magazine *Come Together:*

> Some of us are opposed to roles because they can limit self-discovery. We don't want to discard the male role just to take on the female role. Others think that transvestites can show people that roles can be fun, if you're free to take the ones you want and discard them when you don't want them any more. The important thing is, no one should tell you, as a man or a woman, this is the role you have to play, and you have to play it all the time. (ibid.: 165)

191

However, later in the article, the anonymous author writes in a less radical vein that 'when we talk about our hopes and fantasies, it becomes apparent that what we want above all is to be accepted as women, primarily by other women' (ibid.: 166).

As the 1970s continued, drag became again less welcome within the gay community. However, 'radical' groupings of transgendered people who were dissatisfied with the political conservativism of the dominant transvestite and transsexual voice began to emerge by the mid-1970s. In retrospect these early radical and rather short-lived groupings might be seen as continuing those aspects of *The Cockettes* concerned with radical politics:

> In the early 1970s, some transsexual groupings began to align with radical politics. One such group was the US-based Transsexual Action Organisation (TAO) whose president was Angela Keyes Douglas. In 1976, for instance, this grouping had asked the American Civil Liberties Union to file a suit against the City of Miami because the Police department had violated the civil rights of several transsexuals by raping them in custody. (*Gay News*, 15–28 June 1976)

The American TAO had offshoots elsewhere. The British TAO group broke away from its American sister in 1975. Its activities indicated something of the tensions in these earliest transsexual organizations with radical tendencies. UK transgender activist Stephen Whittle, reflecting on his involvement with TAO (UK) in an email discussion (kindly revised by Whittle for this chapter in 2005), writes:

> I was involved with TAO in the UK, for a short time in around 1974/75. TAO/GB [I'll distinguish it by calling it TAO/GB] at that time was a very small and short-lived organisation – though organisation seems a somewhat over-blown description.
>
> I was to ring up the London gay switchboard in 1975 when I thought I was not going to be successful in getting GRS [gender reassignment surgery]. I was told of TAO/GB and I travelled to Birmingham to meet Brooklyn (FTM) and Leyla (MTF) who appeared to be running it. They lived together (they were having a relationship at that time) in a bedsit and I went to stay a couple of times along with other TSs. The fact that a MTF with a penis could have a sexual relationship with an FTM with a vagina amazed me. Brooklyn and Leyla greatly influenced my 'trans' politics (and have done so to this day). I eventually lost touch with them around 1976, but discovered shortly after that Brooklyn had changed his name to Lou. In 1990 I was to meet Leyla again, when I took my Master's course at Edgehill College. Leyla was by then again living as a man, and working in Liverpool. He married one of the other students and dropped out of the course fairly soon after. He told me that Lou was still living as a man but had had a very hard time adjusting to his life as a trans man.
>
> When I originally met Brooklyn and Leyla, TAO/GB consisted of some headed paper designed by Brooklyn and a clear anarcho-transformative, transsexual-separatist agenda – for example we (the three of us) went to protest at the National Front March that was taking place one weekend through Birmingham. I also met some other trans people at their place including the 2 Alans from London: Alan and Alan the Finn, and eventually through them met other FTMs.

At around the same time as all this was happening, I was leaving the radical-separatist lesbian collective I had been involved with in Manchester, and was involved with setting up the Manchester TV/TS group which met in Stan's bedsit in Camp Street in Salford. It was mixed TV/TS.

Sometime in late 1975 (and I'm not sure how this came about, at all) there was a meeting/party held in Leeds in Carol's bedsit. Carol had become involved with the Leeds TV/TS group which was run by John/June Willmot – a TV who died in the late 1980s, who lived with his partner Audrey – a TS.

Carol (and company), who had already produced a couple of magazines wanted to do something more radical than was happening in the TV/TS groups – and so TAO became the obvious vehicle. Both myself and Pat who ran the London TAO group went to the party (though at the time we did not know we both knew Brooklyn and Leyla). Brooklyn and Leyla's influence was strong during that evening even though they did not attend. It was a night when many intimate partnerships were formed, between trans women and trans men, transvestite men and trans women and men, and between trans women and trans women. Suddenly we gave ourselves permission to drop all of the rules and to get on with being sexual people who could see beyond what was between somebody's legs. It didn't however really last – Brooklyn and Leyla never came up from Birmingham and eventually they simply disappeared.

As for TAO/GB – well we had one night of glorious partying and radical sexual relationships in Leeds in autumn 1975. And well – that was probably it! But TAO/GB's influence has, in my opinion, lived on at the core of trans politics in the UK.

One aspect of the 'separatist agenda' was the separation of transsexual groups from transvestites. Stephen makes the point:

However, it is worth noting that transsexual separatism started with TAO/GB – really to distinguish our issues and our needs – and through the 1970s those were about getting access to hormones and surgery, and avoiding aversion therapy and the locked ward. But it was NOT about condemning TVs at all – in fact there was real close co-operation for some time but it was about separate issues.

A leaflet produced by Birmingham TAO in the mid-1970s focused primarily on hormones, surgery, helpful books, and so on:

The T.A.O. is a national organization which is open to all transsexuals (whether they are presently undergoing sex change treatment or not) irrespective of their race, religion, politics or sexual orientation. The T.A.O. has no official membership at present and is not structured. All decisions as to the running of the organization are taken collectively. The T.A.O. seeks to do the following:

- Give advice and information to transsexuals and their friends and relatives.

- Befriend lonely transsexuals and organize meetings so that transsexuals can meet others like themselves and discuss their experiences and feelings.

- Encourage co-operation between transsexuals, doctors and social workers.

- Campaign for equal rights under law so that f-ms can have full legal rights as men and m-fs have full legal rights as women.

- Try to improve that attitude of society towards transsexuals so that we need no longer live in fear of exposure and ridicule.

- Support campaigns for the rights of women, gays and transvestites.

- Encourage the formation of transsexual organizations in other countries.

Gradually, the 'radical' aspects of the agenda were jettisoned. For instance, the London branch membership was less radical and much more centred on social support activities. In a letter one of us (DK) received from the London TAO, the information and advice-giving role was again stressed. DK was informed: 'we are strictly non-political and non-religious ... we are a law-abiding group and are trying to demonstrate that the T.S. is a normal decent member of society so we do not approve of exhibitionism or anything which might get us a bad name'.

Theorizing transcending

Transcending stories may be seen as constituting a paradigm shift in the conceptualization of transgendering. Virginia Prince and Anne Lawrence notwithstanding, the voices of transgendered people themselves were largely missing from the conceptualizations we have considered under migrating and oscillating. They appeared largely as cases in the medical literature or as dupes of the medical profession in the dominant feminist discourses (Raymond, 1980).

In negating, it is very much the case that we as transgender theorists have sought to give a more prominent voice to a story that has been relegated to something of a peripheral side-show in the transgendering literature. This neglect of the voices of the transgendered, themselves, was to change radically in the 1990s as a new discourse emerged constituting a major paradigm shift. A key work in this new approach was Sandy Stone's 'The *Empire* Strikes Back' in which she argued that 'the people who have no voice in this theorizing are the transsexuals themselves. As with males theorizing about women from the beginning of time, theorists of gender have seen transsexuals as possessing something less than agency' (1991: 294). Stone was writing as a male-to-female transsexual who had been the victim of discrimination at the hands of 'womyn only womyn' groups in the USA.

Stone pointed out that transsexuals had failed to develop a counter-discourse. It is easy to see why, because the main 'traditional' transgender identities have 'worked' only to the extent that they have been covert and temporary. The male transvestite who oscillates for varying amounts of time most usually does not want to be 'read' as such. Except within a small subcultural setting, he wishes to be seen as a 'normal' man or (to the extent that he is able to 'pass' in public) as a 'normal' woman. Similarly, the male transsexual who is renouncing his masculinity permanently, like the female transsexual who is seeking to embrace it, are also seeking to be read as a woman and a man, respectively. Both identities are also temporary ones; the transvestite oscillates between masculinity and femininity; the transsexual passes through a trans phase on the way to a permanent masculine or feminine identity.

Where these identities have become open and/or permanent, they have been seen as pathological and/or problematic. In other words, no permanent 'in-between' identity was allowed for. To the extent that the transvestite or transsexual passes as a person of the other gender, and to the extent that the transgendering remains hidden, the 'fact' of two invariant genders remains unquestioned. As Stone (1991: 295) put it, 'authentic experience is replaced by a particular kind of story, one that supports the old constructed positions'. In consequence, Stone argued that transsexuals can develop their own discourse only by recognizing their unique gender position:

> For a transsexual, as a transsexual, to generate a true, effective and representational counterdiscourse is to speak from outside the boundaries of gender, beyond the constructed oppositional nodes which have been predefined as the only positions from which discourse is possible. (ibid.: 295)

Stone contended that the dominant binary model of gender and its employment in the category of transsexuality has obscured the diversity of the transsexual experience. It 'foreclosed the possibility of analyzing desire and motivational complexity in a manner which adequately describes the multiple contradictions of individual lived experience' (ibid.: 297). What began to happen, in fact, during the 1990s, was the recognition of the vast diversity of transgender experiences. Some people did begin questioning 'the necessity of passing for typically gendered people' and began to develop new gender identities. For some people, 'the experience of crossed or transposed gender is a strong part of their gender identity; being out of the closet is part of that expression' (Nataf, 1996: 16).

Stone had articulated, forcefully, a viewpoint that was emerging within certain sections of the transgender community. She articulated it in terms of transsexualism, but contemporaneously, others were beginning to articulate the new formulations specifically in terms of transcending and transgender. Notable here was the work of the US transgender activist Holly Boswell.

Holly Boswell's story

Holly Boswell was one of a group of US transgendered people active at the end of the 1980s and into the 1990s who began to fashion the hitherto rather

Figure 5.1 Holly Boswell, the creator of 'Kindred Spirits', at the Southern Comfort Convention, Atlanta, 1999 (Photographer and © Mariette Pathy Allen)

disparate groups of transsexuals and transvestites and other 'gender variants' into a transgender community that favoured diversity in transactivism. Initially, and for some years thereafter, the terms transsexual and transvestite (or cross-dresser) remained the favourite ones. The International Foundation for Gender Education, for instance, was formed in 1986, as a separate educational branch of the Tiffany Club. Its first major project was to organize the first international convention – held in Chicago 4–9 March 1987, for 'the community'. The convention, aptly named 'Coming Together – Working Together', had the express purpose of providing an 'actual and effective service to the Transvestite/Transsexual Community, and those affected by the Community' (*The TV-TS Tapestry*, 48: 82; *The TV-TS Tapestry*, 49: 129). 1986 saw the establishment of an IFGE account and the co-operation of over 25 different transvestite and transsexual organizations.

From these beginnings, it was only a matter of time, perhaps, before an umbrella term was adopted for this new 'community'. As we saw in Chapter 1, the umbrella term of 'transgender' was adopted in the UK by Richard Ekins when he founded the Trans-Gender Archive in 1986, and was in use in the USA – in *Renaissance News* – certainly by 1987. Each country has a rather different story to tell.

There were those like Holly Boswell, in the USA, who were beginning to formulate alternative conceptualizations to give voice to the newly emerging developments. Although, not 'out' in the national transgender community until late into the 1980s, she nevertheless identified very much as a child of the 1960s in regard to the sorts of cultural changes groups such as *The Cockettes* were anticipating.

We had been engaged in face-to-face and email interviews with Holly Boswell for some time, when we chanced upon the 2002 release of the film *The Cockettes*. We asked Holly if she had seen it. She commented:

> Yes, I have watched that video of *The Cockettes* twice. The second time, it made me cry, because I realized just how closely related I am to those people and that phenomenon. I love that movie. It is a snapshot of my queer youth, even though I was still closeted at the time. If I had been in the Bay Area [San Francisco], I probably would have succumbed to AIDS just like them. I am grateful I grew up in an area [Washington, DC] that, while culturally conservative, at least allowed me to feel my way into a subculture that gave me some freedom of expression. (personal communication, 2004)

An important Boswell publication linking the 'transgender alternative' with transcending was published in the second issue of *Chrysalis Quarterly* (vol. 1, no. 2, 1991). This journal was a major innovation and emergent within the transgender community. It was the brainchild of Dallas Denny, who remained its chief editor throughout. Boswell became its Associate Editor and remained in that position for all the issues except its last, Issue vol. 2, no. 4 of 1996–97. Dallas Denny had come from a background in psychological behaviourism, whereas Boswell came from an arts background with an expertise in English literature and the performing arts. Between them, they fashioned a journal which, apart from leading the field in its visual presentation, began to set forth a politically correct terminology of transgender. Denny fashioned it in the direction of an academic journal insofar as it had an impressive editorial board of transgender scholars. However, in presentation and style it bore the mark of a literary magazine. *Chrysalis Quarterly* soon began to attract articles from the leading transgender activists and writers, and professionals and academics that identified in various ways with the voices of transgendered people themselves.

One such article was Holly Boswell's 'The Transgender Alternative' (1991).[2] Boswell recognized the umbrella usage of 'transgender' that included both 'transvestites' and 'transsexuals' but argued for a 'transgender alternative' that was a middle ground between the two. However, unlike Virginia Prince's middle-ground 'migrating' position, Boswell argued for a middle ground having its roots in androgyny. She writes 'I shall attempt to define transgender as a viable option between crossdresser and transsexual person, which also happens to have a firm foundation in the ancient tradition of androgyny' (Boswell, 1991: 29).

In a particularly crucial passage that makes the clear link between transgender and transcending, as well as linking the term 'trans' to positions she wants to 'go beyond' Boswell writes:

Transgenderism serves as a bridge of consciousness between crossdressers and transsexual people, who feel unnecessarily estranged within our own subculture. And in the vast majority of instances, we are not so much 'gender conflicted' as we are at odds – even at war – with our culture. It is our culture that imposes the polarization of gender according to biology. It is our culture that has brainwashed us, and our families and friends, who might otherwise be able to love us and embrace our diversity as desirable and natural – something to be celebrated. Crossdressers are instead made to feel they must still be 'men', but men who are deviant, or even perverted fetishists. Transsexual people must often deny their maleness altogether and become stereotypical second class females (a sad fact) in order to assimilate into society. Occasionally, these options may be appropriate, but most often I doubt how conducive these forms of socialization are to personal growth and happiness. (ibid.: 30)

The link with 'transcending' is made explicit in the following passage:

I believe the truth of a solution to our dilemma is all-encompassing – not polarized. We know, deep down in our hearts, that we are more than our culture dictates. We can reject those limitations, in all their manifestations, if we have a vision that transcends – if we believe we must go beyond. We need to recognize that each of us, in our own small way, are makers of our own culture. We can express that function by expressing our true selves – not by simply fulfilling our culture's expectations. We are all in transition, in that broad evolutionary sense. (ibid.: 30)

From these beginnings, Boswell began to sketch out a transcending gender-identity, rooted in formulations variously drawn from Sandra Bem, Carl Jung and social anthropological work on 'third gender' peoples. With hindsight, she regrets that she was 'merely addressing the MTF perspective' in her early writings and feels she should have addressed 'the issue more fully many years ago'.

Up until the age of 30, Holly had been closeted, dressing up whenever she could. She was trying to figure out a way to 'both become her and be with her'. She felt 'rather insecure and sometimes clueless' in her male role and wanted to 'transcend' her male role on many levels – those of personal identity, social interactions, and spiritual awareness.

Between the ages of 30 and 34, she was unpartnered and free to 'come out'. Holly used her interests and involvement in theatre to come out in what she describes as 'a joyous, ecstatic period'. We see the mixture of 'orthodox' body femaling and gender femaling mixed with her particular interest in the stage, in the following:

> My primary venue to express myself as Holly was at the big gay bar in Asheville [North Carolina], which happened to be three blocks away from my apartment. I went there every Thursday, Friday and Saturday night for about three years. I even wound up performing a few times in their monthly talent show, just lip-sync. But mostly, I would indulge in a ritual of transformation before heading out around 10.30. Bubble bath, shaving body parts, dressing in different outfits, different make up - accompanied with evocative music, a little dancing and a cocktail - quite delightful! Once I got to the club, I'd have a drink and schmooze awhile with friends, or meet new people for maybe an hour. The rest of the evening (until 2 or 3.00) I danced - with anyone and everyone. During this period, I also started going out around town in the daytime, doing average things, and had a pretty active social life.

The next ten years - between the ages of 34 and 44 - saw Holly meet the mother of her child. There followed a period of 'compartmentalizing' - hiding Holly from family, friends and co-workers - in order to preserve the relationship. Unbeknown to her partner Holly began to take hormones. Within a year her partner and her parents found out and the relationship began to unravel few years later. 'Around age 40, I changed my name to Holly, legally. This was the biggest step in my transition, because it gave me license to insist that everyone re-identify me.' She continues: 'By age 42, I could no longer contain myself, so I went full-time.' After a 'rebound relationship' for almost two years, Holly then 'consummated with a lesbian-feminist-activist visionary who had been her friend for five years'. She concludes:

> Here is where I am at: I love gender; I hate gender. Gender used to enslave me, and now it liberates me. My pendulum has swung from the dictates of maleness, to the forbidden fruits of femininity. And now, just as I predicted, I am returning to my center - which cannot help but transgress and transcend the entire paradigm of gender. Of course, I don't live in a perfect world where the ideal will be able to manifest itself fully in my lifetime - unless perhaps I pull out the stops, and exercise my 'artistic license'. But my angst is still alive, and my transition will never be over. My aim is not simply to transit gender, but to transit what it means to be fully human. As a Trans person - and as a bridge - that is my intended gift to humanity.

Now it is important to stress that sex reassignment surgery has always been irrelevant for Holly. In terms of her presentation of self in everyday life, her position on the transgender spectrum might not seem that different from that of the 'gender migrant' who lives full-time as a woman without genital reassignment. However, the 'meaning' she gives her body and her transition could not be more different than is the case with the gender migrant.

To delve deeper into these meanings is to grasp the distinctive point of view of Holly's version of transcending. Holly presents as an attractive woman who appears very much younger than her years. The gender transcender and activist Riki Anne Wilchins' account of Holly could not make the point better:

> But what of Holly Boswell? Holly is a delicate Southern belle of long acquaintance. I may occasionally feel like an extra from *Gone with the Wind*, but Holly actually is one. S/he has tender features, long, wavy blonde hair, a soft Carolina accent, a delicate feminine bosom, and no interest in surgery. Holly lives as an openly transgendered mother of two [actually one] in Asheville, North Carolina. Her comforting advice to confused citizens struggling with whether to use *Sir* or *Madam* is, 'Don't give it a second thought. You don't have a pronoun for me yet.' This goes over famously in the Deep South. (Wilchins, 1997: 118)

Wilchins' use of the S/he alerts us to the fact that there is no gender migration. Holly is not concerned to 'pass' on the other side of the binary divide. At a personal level, she is concerned to transcend that divide. The various subprocesses of transgendering are all coloured by this redefining. But what of Holly Boswell's sexuality? How does her body 'fit' that sexuality? Riki Anne Wilchins relates how Boswell had described to her an intersexed adult video 'of two people, both with penises and cunts, penetrating and being penetrated by each other simultaneously' (1997: 119). Boswell had referred to this video as the 'most complete moving, and beautiful merging of two human bodies she had ever witnessed' (ibid.: 119).

For Wilchins, being confronted with such bodies as Boswell's necessitates negotiating new meanings. In a sense, this might be considered as the case in all new sexual encounters. However, there are no widely available social scripts to draw upon in the case of encounters with these non-binary bodies. As we saw previously, the tendency in migrating and oscillating is to read the variant bodies in terms of the binary. Thus for the oscillating Barry, considered in Chapter 3, his penis became his partner's; her vagina became his. In transcending, however, new 'transcending' meanings are being inscribed.

Thus when asked for her view on transcending sexuality, Boswell replied (personal communication, 2004):

> I certainly can't speak for all 'transcendent' trans people, yet I would suspect that my experiences are somewhat in line with most of them. Basically, the boundaries fall away, leaving only two spiritual essences interacting in a loving, sexual way: two swirling balls of light, dancing within a magnetic field ... That is the essence of my view – as well as my experience – in terms of sexual relationships. I don't care at all who has what genitals, nor do I reinscribe (à la Riki), because for me it is all about spiritual/energetic essence and unconditional love. I'm probably 'off the scale' with that attitude, but that's just who I am.

When it comes to the interrelations between the body, gender display and eroticism, Boswell is specific: 'I like authentic femme (and in my fantasies, ultra-femme), yet I also like soft males, like Johnny Depp or James Spader, i.e., the pretty boys with gentle energy.' In regards to the intersex intercourse we referred to above, Boswell writes:

> As for that film about the two hermaphrodites: for a person like myself, what could be more appealing than coupling with another person – both of us having BOTH male and female genitalia. But maybe that's because I've always sought parity and equality in all my relationships. I don't want either one of us to dominate or submit. I want us to share equally, in a give-and-take that allows for some dynamics of imbalance while we play, yet it is underscored by a mutual respect that isn't founded on that old paradigm of BDSM [bondage-domination and sado-masochism] – which is all too binary for me. That's one way that the paradigm of transcendence really kicks in.

The holy trinity of transcending story telling

There are three writers, above all, who have laid down the parameters for the paradigm shift towards transgender as transcending. These authors are Leslie Feinberg, Kate Bornstein, and Riki Anne Wilchins.

Leslie Feinberg's best-known work is his *Gender Warriors*. However, Feinberg first set forth the fundamentals of his Marxist approach to transgender history in a 22-page pamphlet first published in 1992, entitled *Transgender Liberation: A Movement Whose Time Has Come* (Feinberg, 1992). Unlike most transcending tales this is a modernist story setting transgender history within the grand narrative of Marxism. It is a story of the origins and history of the oppression of gender self-expression, on the one hand, and a tale of transcending on the other: 'we are talking about people who defy the "man"-made boundaries of gender' (ibid.: 5). It is also a tale of social constructionism. 'Simplistic and rigid gender codes are neither eternal nor natural. They are changing social concepts' (ibid.: 5). For Feinberg, transgender is an ancient form of human expression that predates oppression. It is 'passing' (migrating) that is new. Passing is redefined as 'hiding' (ibid.: 7).

Feinberg's principal strategy is twofold. On the one hand, he locates various historical sources of oppression of transgender people and details their origins and influences. In the second place, he details example after example of trans people, sometimes revered and sometimes not, reclaiming the previously erased or oppressed to provide a contemporary lineage of transcending 'gender warriors'.

Feinberg is a long-time member of the Marxian Workers World Party and his pamphlet reflects an appropriate view of Marxist knowledge and of history. Particularly significant in locating the source of oppression is Frederick Engels' *The Origin of the Family, Private Property and the State*, first published in 1884. Feinberg's story harks back to a golden age of ancient communal societies in which goddesses, not gods, were worshipped, and in which deities and many of their shamans were transgendered. Male domination, private property and the oppression of the transgendered then become linked via Feinberg's utilization of Engels' arguments.

Drawing on various studies by Bachofen and Lewis Henry Morgan, in particular, Engels argued that early societies were based on collective labour, communal property, and cooperation. Engels roots the oppression of modern-day women in the class system based upon the private ownership of property. Feinberg's contribution is to locate the oppression of transgendered people in precisely the same cleavage of society. Patriarchy, for Feinberg, led, sooner or later, to the oppression of women and the transgendered. Feinberg writes (1992: 12): 'Transgender in all its forms became a target. In reality it was the rise of private property, the male-dominated family and class divisions led to narrowing what was considered acceptable expression. What had been natural was declared its opposite.'

Of all the acclaimed transgender warriors mentioned by Feinberg, Joan of Arc is highlighted for the most extensive treatment. Feinberg reminds us that it was Joan of Arc's refusal to stop dressing as a man that led to her being burned at the stake following the Inquisition of the Catholic Church.

However, despite the oppression that Feinberg documents, it could not be eradicated. Rather, in the Western world, it increasingly took the form of 'passing'. At this point, Feinberg links transgendering with capitalism. As he puts it (ibid.: 19): 'While, as we have seen, transgendered expression has always existed in the Western Hemisphere, the need to "pass" washed up on these shores with the arrival of capitalism. Many women and men have been forced to pass.'

Again, various 'invisible' lives of those who passed and were later 'outed', or 'outed' themselves are recorded by Feinberg. This is a tale of ancestry. Finally, in the spirit of revolutionary literature, there is a call to arms, not merely to understand the world, but, more importantly, to change it. Again, the story is reiterated of a golden age of non-oppression that can be regained once the oppressed who have been 'divided' and 'conquered' forge bonds of solidarity and rise up against their oppressors. 'The institutionalized bigotry and oppression we face today have not always existed', Feinberg informs his reader, 'They arose with the division of society into exploiter and exploited. Divide-and-conquer tactics have allowed the slave-owners, feudal landlords and corporate ruling classes to keep for themselves the lion's share of wealth created by the laboring class' (ibid.: 22).

Feinberg concludes:

> Like racism and all forms of prejudice, bigotry towards transgendered people is a deadly carcinogenic. We are pitted against each other in order to keep us from seeing each other as allies ... the

militant role of transgendered women, men and youths in today's fight-back movement is already helping to shape the future. (ibid.: 22)

Here, then, is a story told to all the oppressed transgendered peoples of the world. It is a story of revolution and hope to unite. The call is made to unite with all the oppressed of the world, to overthrow those with a vested interest in existing class divisions. To do so will lead to a new order within which all diversity, including transgender diversity will receive the respect it deserves: like so many variants of Marxist stories, a utopian tale, perhaps, presented as scientific socialism?

The style of Kate Bornstein's story could hardly be more different. Feinberg turns to the 'scientific socialism' of Marx and Engels to construct his tale of gender transcending modelled along the lines of a classic tale of revolution founded upon 'science'. Bornstein's starting point, on the other hand, is her identity which like fashion, she says (1994: 3), is 'based on collage. You know – a little bit from here, a little bit from there? Sort of a cut-and-paste thing.'

Nevertheless, Bornstein, too, draws upon social science: in her case, her analysis of Garfinkel's natural attitude and where she stands herself in regard to it and the work of Kessler and McKenna on the primacy of gender attribution. However, rather than remaining committed to social science, she moves to the celebration of gender fluidity in order to move into a third space beyond the binary gender system. The move is now being made to a postmodern position wherein she sets gender fluidity within a particular conceptualization of gender as performance. Moreover, it is a fluid identity that identifies as neither male nor female. However, Bornstein's 'neither male nor female' celebrates going beyond the binary gender divide into a 'third space'. It is not a gender negating identity, as the following passage makes clear:

> And then I found out that gender can have fluidity, which is quite different from ambiguity. If ambiguity is refusal to fall within a prescribed gender code, then fluidity is the refusal to remain one gender or another. Gender fluidity is the ability to freely and knowingly become one or many of a limitless number of genders, for any length of time, at any rate of change. Gender fluidity recognizes no borders of rules of gender. (ibid.: 51-2)

Bornstein's playful approach to gender fluidity leads her to celebrate paradox. In consequence, it is not difficult to find inconsistencies in her work. It is possible to pick out in her work passages that seem to be arguing for a society without gender, and other passages (more frequent) that celebrate a multiplicity of genders. Others have commented that her entire work is predicated on incoherence. For Ailles (2003: 77), for instance, 'Since pomosexual ["pomo" for postmodern] play depends on "the existing gender" to subvert, gender, for any pomosexual activist, is necessarily a "cornerstone of their view of the world"'. In similar vein, Ailles (ibid.: 77) argues that 'one cannot be an "outlaw" without maintaining the law – without maintaining the three distinct categories of "man, woman, and the rest of us"' (ibid.: 77). How then, asks Ailles, are we to 'totally change the binaristic gender system'? Ailles' 'solution' is to look to intersex people. She argues that:

> with the existence of the intersex, the male/female female/male transgendered/transsexual becomes more of a logical impossibility since the individual requires a unitary fence that necessarily has two sides to cross-over and trans. With the realization of the multiplicity of intersex, the fences can no longer exist in binary form of either/or. Arguably, the new configuration of material habitats could create an endless chain of fences with each fence representing another Normative intersex space for individuals to cross-over and play with. (ibid.: 82-3)

It might be objected that we are on strange ground here: most of us are not intersex, after all, we might think. Ailles (ibid.: 82) provided an interesting 'solution' to this objection, arguing that 'It is quite possible that those who have felt internally at odds with the gender that they have been ascribed may actually be intersex individuals who have never been allowed their own systemic legitimacy in the first place'; an intriguing redefinition and a coherent means, suggests Ailles, to transcend the binary. She concludes that political activism designed to encourage pomosexual play will unlock our intersexualities which will lead to the collapse of the binary divide.

But how are we to best make moves from the personal to the more overtly political in that direction? It is here that the work of Riki Anne Wilchins is so germinal. Arguably, Wilchins draws upon both of the major influences that have inspired Feinberg and Bornstein, respectively: those of revolutionary socialism and theatrical metaphors of 'performance'. However, in the hands of Wilchins, these lines of thought are co-opted in the service of what might be termed 'libertarian anarchist' transcending. For us, the distinctive feature of Wilchins' thought, writings and activism is the way it opposes 'authorities' generally. 'To change the master is not to be free' and 'Where there is authority, there is no freedom' are the two anarchist maxims that best encapsulate, perhaps, the sentiments that have led Wilchins to reject much of what many within the transgender community hold dear. Although Wilchins is an MTF who has undergone sex reassignment procedure she rejects the categorizations 'transsexual' or 'transgender', for herself. Although her writings are pivotal for any so-called 'transgender studies', she opposes the very idea of a 'transgender studies'. Most recently, she has incurred the wrath of many within the transgender community for what they take to be her rejection of their very community, itself. She now opposes all arguments for 'transgender rights' and argues instead for 'human rights' and an end to 'gender oppression'. In short, while the anarchist tradition in political theory and practice may not be Wilchins' acknowledged inspiration, it is, we feel, her spiritual home, in a way that it is not the spiritual home of Feinberg or Bornstein.

Wilchins became prominent in the trans activist movement in the early 1990s. The Michigan Womyn's Music Festival had a 'womyn-born womyn only' policy and in 1991 a transsexual woman was forcibly ejected from the Festival. This ejection inspired Wilchins to become active in 'Camp Trans' that sprang up to contest that policy. As her activism developed, she went on to play major roles as co-founder of 'Transexual Menace'[3] in 1994 and as founder and Executive Director of Gender PAC (Public Advocacy Coalition) in 1995. 'Transexual Menace' was notably anarchist and insurrectionary in its theory and practice (Wilchins, 1997). Note, for instance, the following entry for 'Transexual Menace Confronts Janice Raymond':

> [New York, NY: November 94] Janice Raymond speaks at Judith's Room, NYC's feminist bookstore. Her book, *The Transsexual Empire: The Making of a She-Male*, alleges that transpeople are designed expressly by deranged surgeons to invade women's space. She is met by two dozen pissed-off she-males, designed expressly by deranged Menace surgeons to invade women's bookstores. (1997: 203)

Like Feinberg and Bornstein, a main focus of Wilchins' theoretical approach to sex, sexuality and gender is to question the whole system of binary gender. Like Bornstein, she follows Butler in arguing that 'gender refers not to something we *are* but to something we *do*' (2002a: 24). More specifically, gender for Wilchins is a 'system of symbols and meanings' (ibid.: 25) involving 'rules, privileges, and punishments' (2002b: 14). She sounds very similar to Garfinkel (1967) when she outlines the 'rules' of gender – rules that we only become aware of when they fail (1997: 160). She considers the five basic rules to be: '(1) there are only two cages; (2) everyone must be in a cage; (3) there is no mid-ground; (4) no one can change; and (5) no one chooses their cage' (ibid.: 156).

However, unlike Garfinkel, Wilchins includes sexual orientation and sex in her consideration of gender and makes the additional point that:

> [it is] self-evident that the mainspring of homophobia is gender: The notion that gay men are insufficiently masculine or lesbian women are somehow inadequately feminine. And I include sex, because I take it as obvious that what animates sexism and misogyny is gender, and our astonishing fear and loathing of vulnerability or femininity. (2002b: 11)

Indeed, she questions the categories that have formed the basis of the gay and the women's movements. Drawing on the work of Butler, she writes, 'feminist politics begins with the rather common sense notion that there exists a group of people understood as women whose needs can be politically represented and whose objectives sought through unified action'. She goes on to ask, 'what if this ostensibly simple assumption isn't true?' (1997: 81). Her analysis of the tension between the women's movement and transgenderism and 'gender-queerness' more generally, is profound and fundamental. She states: 'Gender-queerness would seem to be a natural avenue for feminism to contest Woman's equation with nurturance, femininity, reproduction: in short to trouble the project of Man.' She concludes that feminists have not taken this 'natural avenue', however, 'in no small part, because queering Woman threatens the very category on which feminism depends' (2002a: 57).

Moreover, she extends her arguments to the categories of 'transexual' and 'transgender'. She says she is 'not a transexual', nor is she 'interested in a transgender rights movement', because 'unable to interrogate its own existence, [it] will merely end up cementing the idea of a binary sex which I am presumed to somehow transgress or merely traverse' (1997: 67).

In a particularly significant passage, Wilchins states:

While I recognize how important it is to produce histories and sociologies of transpeople, I am wary of anything that might cement the category more firmly in place. I'd also like us to investigate the means by which categories like *transgender* are produced, maintained, and inflicted on people like me. It's not so much that there have always been transgendered people; it's that there have always been cultures which imposed regimes of gender. It is only within a system of gender oppression that transgender exists in the first place. It would be impossible to transgress gender rules without the prior imposition of those rules. Studying transgender (or for that matter, homosexuality) by itself risks essentializing the category and, at the same time, naturalizing the gender regimes that install it and the 'normal' gender displays that go unregulated. (ibid.: 67–8)

Wilchins, like Bornstein, regards identities as 'temporary and fluid, rather than fixed' (ibid.: 86). For Wilchins, moreover, an approach to transgender activism based upon 'an identity organized around transgression' is suspect. She observes that debate has arisen about who is 'most transgressive' and as a result 'a voice that originated from the margins [has] begun to produce its own marginalized voices' (2002a: 59).

She concludes, therefore, that no political movement should be based on an identity. It should be based, rather, on an issue. Moreover, that issue must go further than 'gender rights' to extend to 'human rights':

So that it's never just about gender, and always about gender and sexual orientation or gender and race or gender and age or gender and class. So that whenever there's a wall, we should be with those outside of it. And whenever there's a vote on inclusion, you and I should be standing among those voted on. (2002c: 296)

New feminist stories, female masculinities and the drag king

Wilchins' first book, *Read My Lips: Sexual Subversion and the End of Gender*, was published in 1997 by Firebrand Books, a feminist and lesbian publishing house: an indication of the changes that have taken place with regard to feminist positions on transgender, particularly from the late 1990s onwards. Feinberg, Bornstein and Wilchins were theorists and activists who held no university affiliations even though their work came to form an important core to many of the university courses that included 'transgender studies' in the late 1990s and into the twenty-first century. Inevitably, perhaps, a new story would soon emerge amongst these university students and their teachers who were studying the new 'transcending' approaches to transgendering.

An important new transcending story to emerge from the writings of our 'Holy Trinity' of transcending is that put forward by a number of contemporary feminist writers who, while broadly committed to transcending, provide a critical commentary on certain aspects of it. The most notable proponents of this story are Surya Monro and Katrina Roen.

Like Bornstein who drew on the writings of Butler, and like Wilchins (2002a, 2002b, 2002c) who drew more obviously on both Foucault and Butler, this new generation of writers are heavily influenced by postmodernism. However, before we consider the directions taken by these new feminist writings it is necessary to set the context for their work within the historical development of feminist approaches to transgender.

In Chapter 2, we discussed the radical feminist position of Janice Raymond as one of three main 'dissenting stories' that have been critical of the dominant migrating story. From an essentialist view of men and women, Raymond allowed no possibility of 'changing sex'. The root of the desire to 'change sex' was dissatisfaction with existing sex roles and she argued that transsexualism was a fabricated condition created to diffuse the potential threat that this posed. Dismissing FTM transsexuals as tokens to maintain the illusion of a human problem rather than a gendered one, she also saw the creation of MTF transsexuals as part of an attack on feminism and particularly lesbian feminism.

At the time of its first publication, Raymond's (1980) book fitted in with the dominant feminist perspective at the time and there was little dissent or even comment from other feminists. When Woodhouse (1989a; 1989b) reported on her research into transvestism at the end of the 1980s she discussed the relationship of transvestism and transsexualism to sexual politics but could cite only Raymond's book and a derivative piece by McNeill (1982). While clearly not impressed by the arguments that transvestism or transsexualism might be a positive way of tackling gender inequalities, Woodhouse was critical of Raymond's 'cultural feminism' with its essentialist view of masculinity and femininity. She argued that Raymond's position led to the conclusion, 'what is the point of engaging in struggle against gender divisions at all. If it all boils down to some innate, essential quality, any attempt to change this state of affairs would be futile' (1989b: 81).

However, by the time of the republication of *The Transsexual Empire* in 1994 things had changed both in the field of transgender and in the field of feminism. The essentialism of Mary Daly had been largely replaced by the postmodern approach of Judith Butler with its querying of the category woman. These ideas were used by the new breed of transcending transgender 'terrorists' and were also much in evidence in the writings of a new wave of feminist writers. Feminism and feminist theory initially drew its strength from the basic notion that it made sense to speak of 'women' as a category of persons who were in a subordinate position in a gender hierarchy in relation to another category of persons – 'men'. As Butler put it: 'Inasmuch as the construct of women presupposes a specificity and coherence that differentiates it from that of men, the categories of gender appear as an unproblematic point of departure for feminist politics' (1990b: 338).

During the 1980s this position began to be questioned, partly as a result of arguments that other forms of inequality such as those of race, ethnicity or class could fragment the supposed unity of gender categories. At the same time, the influence of postmodern ideas in academia favoured a deconstructive approach towards identities and categories such as 'woman' and 'women'. This led Butler, among others, to pose the question, 'does feminist theory need to rely on a notion of what it is fundamentally or distinctively to be a "woman"?' (1990b: 324).

The developing influence of postmodern ideas particularly within what came to be known as 'queer theory' led to a radically different view of the political role of transgender phenomena. Despite a few dissenting views such as an early article by Brake (1976) which we considered in Chapter 1, and despite the 'radical drag' which we discussed earlier in this chapter in the context of both *The Cockettes* and the early history of the gay movement, the prevailing view came to be that transvestism and transsexualism – and perhaps most other cross-dressing phenomena – were conservative, reinforcing traditional gender roles and (in the case of transsexualism) reinforcing the link between gender and biology.

With the widespread influence of postmodern ideas and the advent of 'queer theory' in the early 1990s a different story began to be told. With the central task to demystify, to deconstruct, queer theory, as Segal put it, 'seeks to transcend and erode the central binary divisions of male/female, heterosexual/homosexual in the construction of modern sexualities' (1994: 188). From this perspective, crossing the gender border is seen as subversive and transgressive. In the preface to the second edition of *The Transsexual Empire*, Raymond (1994) noted that 'The issue of transsexualism has been largely superseded by debates over transgenderism or what has been called "sexuality's newest cutting edge"'.

In the same vein, Straub and Epstein (1991: 21) refer to the 'tyranny of binary sex oppositions' and go on to argue that:

> Since gender definitions offer one of the primary differentiating principles by which binary structures are socially initiated and maintained as hierarchical relations, ambiguous gender identities and erotic practices such as those manifested in transvestism, transsexualism and intersexuality offer a point at which social pressure might be applied to effect a revaluation of binary thinking. (ibid.: 4)

One of the features of the radical feminist perspective of Raymond (1980) and Jeffreys (1996; 2003) has been a refusal to try to get to grips with the experiences of transsexuals themselves. Transsexuals are dismissed as either duped pawns in a patriarchal attempt to undermine feminism if they are MTF, or misguided lesbians if they are FTM. In large part this is a reflection of Raymond's and Jeffreys' commitment to a binary view of gender which allows no space outside or between the categories of man and woman. By contrast, the new feminist stories that are now emerging have both taken on the postmodern/queer conceptions of gender fluidity and diversity and are at pains to give credence and respect to transgender experiences. Monro and Warren, for instance, take the point head on when they write:

> Transgender poses a serious theoretical challenge to feminism. Feminisms, particularly radical feminism, are based on the notion of an unequal gender-binaried system. Transgender scrambles gender binaries and opens up the space beyond or between simple male-female categorization. It also highlights the flaws in some types of feminist theory, for example the simplistic equation of masculinity with oppression. (2004: 354-5)

Monro (2005a; 2005b) and Roen (2001a; 2001b) are influenced by postmodern and queer theories and the transgender theories that have developed in relation to them, but are not uncritical of them. In particular, they explore the issues raised by transgender with a respect for and sensitivity to trans people which is noticeably absent in the writings of Raymond and Jeffreys. They also bring a welcome injection of empirical research into an area marked by its abstract theorising.

Monro and Roen are also sensitive to the diversity within the transgender field and avoid the prescriptive approach of many transgender activists. Roen (2001a), for example, notes the tension in the transgender community between what she calls the 'either/or' and the 'both/neither' discourses on gender. The latter is akin to the transcending story and is critical of the binary view of gender and promotes 'subversive crossing' (ibid.: 502). The former is more akin to the migrating story in accepting the binary view of gender and valuing passing. She notes the emergence of a hierarchy in transgender politics and theory in which subversive crossing is viewed as superior to passing. Her empirical research with transpeople in New Zealand shows that the polarization of 'subversive crossing' versus 'passing' is too simplistic and she is critical of those theorists and activists who 'fail to take into account the diversity of context and experience of transpeople' (ibid.: 521).

Monro's criticisms of what she prefers to call 'poststructuralist transgender theory' are likewise grounded in her research with transpeople – in her case, in the UK (2005a; 2005b). She notes the value of poststructuralist accounts in providing a way of 'beginning to theorise the areas beyond the structures of "male" and "female" via the notion of the freeing of gender and sex signifiers from the body' (2005a: 13). She goes on to argue that 'only poststructuralist and postmodernist approaches enable the inclusion and representation of the full range of gender diversity' (ibid.: 14). Nevertheless, she is critical of poststructuralist theories, both for neglecting the lived experiences of transpeople, specifically the sense that some have of an 'essential self', and for ignoring the limitations imposed by the body and biology. She argues for the development of a pluralist theory of gender (which she characterizes as 'post-postmodernist') that builds on the poststructuralist acknowledgement of gender diversity but takes on board her criticisms and those of others. Gender pluralist theory would then 'develop notions of sex and gender as a spectrum, with standpoints which would include female and male as well as a range of (probably) less common, but socially viable, other-gendered positions' (ibid.: 19).

What seem to be emerging within these new feminist tales, then, are stories of respect for 'lived experience' and transgender diversity and in many regards these writers echo our own sentiments.[4] However, these writings take much of their point from their critique of previous feminist positions on transgender which still persist. Raymond's position, for instance, has continued to be argued by Sheila Jeffreys (1996; 2003), who most recently has argued that there has been 'an epidemic of female-to-male (FTM) transsexualism' which she views as a way to 'get rid of lesbians' (2003: 122). Jeffreys is particularly scathing about postmodernism, queer theory and transgender activism which she claims is mostly professed by men 'who have had radical surgery in their obsession with gender' (1996: 84).[5] This statement very soon lost any validity it might have had when she made it because, as the 1990s continued, it was the FTM writers, academics and activists who were increasingly in the forefront of the most outstanding contributions to the transcending literature (Nataf, 1996; Halberstam, 1998; Cromwell, 1999; Volcano and Halberstam, 1999). The work of Judith 'Jack'

Halberstam on female masculinity and the drag king is particularly significant in this regard.

Under the influence of Butler's *Gender Trouble* which became 'yoked together' (Sullivan, 2003: 95) with the film *Paris is Burning* (1991) and Garber's *Vested Interests* (1992) 'drag came all too often to be unquestionably associated with subversion' (Sullivan, 2003: 87). In our terms, drag became redefined in terms of transcending as opposed to oscillating. However, whereas Butler and Garber's emphasis was on MTF drag, this began to change as the 1990s progressed.

It was not surprising that both Butler and Garber tended to focus on MTF because when they were writing, neither FTM transsexuals, nor cross-dressing females, were very much in evidence in either the literature or in the transgender movement. A small number of FTM autobiographies were available (Martino, 1977; Johnson and Brown, 1982) and these told a story which was almost a mirror-image of that told by their MTF counterparts (Johnson and Brown, 1982). Stories of female cross-dressing outside the transsexual context were usually framed as lesbianism (Faderman, 1981), or as a response to the limited employment or other opportunities available to women (Bullough, 1974; 1975). With the rare exception, oscillating stories of females who cross-dressed were only to be found in histories of drag (Baker, 1968; 1994; Stoller, 1982), which usually included some material on male impersonators on the music hall stage in the late Victorian and Edwardian period. However, as Halberstam remarks, these performances were often 'used to emphasize femininity rather than to mimic maleness' (1998: 233).

However, by the time Butler's and Garber's books were published, the situation was changing. As Rubin pointed out at that time, 'transsexual demographics are changing. FTMs [female-to-males] still comprise a fraction of the transsexual population, but their numbers are growing and awareness of their presence is increasing' (1992: 475). Since then, FTMs or, more accurately, 'female-bodied transpeople' to use Cromwell's (1999) term, have become a more visible feature of the transgender community and in fact have come to play key roles within that community and within transgender politics. It is also during this period that the phenomenon of the 'drag king' emerged. Beginning in the late 1980s and becoming more widespread through the 1990s, writers began to talk of an 'explosion' of drag kinging in the mid-to-late 1990s in various cities across the world (Crowley, 2002; Willox, 2002).

Drag kings entered the academic literature with the work of Judith 'Jack' Halberstam (1994; 1998). Halberstam has turned the spotlight onto 'female masculinity' or 'masculinity' without men thus avoiding what she sees as the limitations of using masculinity as 'a synonym for men and maleness' (1998: 13). Halberstam discusses a range of female masculinities in a range of different settings and eras arguing that they have been largely ignored because of their subversive potential. In appearing to be a natural adjunct to maleness, the detail of masculinity is obscured. Eager to prise apart masculinity and maleness, Halberstam argues that 'masculinity ... becomes legible as masculinity where and when it leaves the white male middle-class body' (ibid.: 2). In consequence, 'the shapes and forms of modern masculinity are best showcased within female masculinity' (ibid.: 3).

Halberstam defines a drag king as 'a female (usually) who dresses up in recognizably male costume and performs theatrically in that costume' (ibid.: 232). She then goes on to distinguish the drag king from the female impersonator and the drag butch:

> Whereas the male impersonator attempts to produce a plausible performance of maleness as the whole of her act, the drag king performs masculinity (often parodically) and makes the exposure of the theatricality of masculinity into the mainstay of her act. Both the male impersonator and the drag king are different from the drag butch, a masculine woman who wears male attire as part of her quotidian gender expression. Furthermore, whereas the male impersonator and the drag king are not necessarily lesbian roles, the drag butch most definitely is. (ibid.: 232)

According to Halberstam, 'mainstream definitions of masculinity' depict it as 'nonperformative'. As she puts it: 'current representations of masculinity ... depend on a relatively stable notion of the realness and the naturalness of both the male body and its signifying effects' (ibid.: 234). The assumption she argues is that, 'masculinity "just is," whereas femininity reeks of the artificial' (ibid.: 234). Thus, drag kings are not simply the female counterparts of drag queens; they are a much more subversive phenomenon because of the mainstream view of masculinity as nonperformative.

A number of other writers on the drag king make substantially the same point. Willox, for instance, argues that the drag king is 'infinitely more subversive than the drag queen'. This is because:

> drag queens simply parody the masquerade of femininity through their performances, yet femininity as masquerade is always already parodic as it is only ever a performance. Drag kings, on the other hand, question the distinctions between masculinity and femininity, camp and masculinity, performance and masquerade, by parodying that which society presumes to be a pre-given: masculinity. (2002: 280)

Again, Crowley suggests that the drag king promises 'a re-gendered and multi-gendered world in which the binary of male/masculinity and female/femininity loses its vice like grip on the body' (2002: 287).

Unsurprisingly, Sheila Jeffreys is not impressed. Jeffreys considers such arguments as an attempt to make the 'project of adopting masculinity seem politically and academically respectable' (2003: 135). She opines that 'masculinity cannot exist without femininity. On its own, masculinity has no meaning, because it is but one half of a set of power relations' (ibid.: 136). Yet, 'in the queer, postmodern theory which informs Halberstam, masculinity has slipped its moorings from any connection with the power relations of male supremacy, and has floated off on its own as a sort of fashion accessory' (ibid.: 136).

A return to lived experience: the case of Del LaGrace Volcano

Since the mid-1990s, as is evident from this chapter, writings on transcending have proliferated and have dominated much of the theoretical and cultural debate about transgendering, particularly within the transgendered community, itself. Notwithstanding the recent turn to 'lived experience' in some of the 'new feminist stories', it still remains the case that transcending writings, in the main, eschew intimate detail of the sort necessary to enable detailed explorations of the interrelations between sex, sexuality and gender; and between self, identity and social world. Indeed, insofar as these writings emphazise performance as opposed to identity, they might be seen as ending the need for a concept of identity. In particular, the material on transgendered subjectivity, so prominent in accounts of migrating, oscillating and negating, gives way in these texts to a different emphasis, namely, the theorizing of gender performance in terms of the deconstructions of postmodernity. Similarly, feminist writings that are hostile to postmodernist transcending theory and practice, like those of Jeffreys (1996), tend to ignore the detail of 'lived experience'.

With these issues in mind, we approach the life and work of the prominent transgendered photographer Del LaGrace Volcano who (at the time of our 1999 interview) identifies as a 'gender terrorist' and 'pansexual'. Del was assigned female at birth in the USA in 1957 but has been living in England, at the time of our interviews, for the past 14 years. Following periods in which he identified variously as bisexual, and then as a sex positive queer dyke, he grew his beard, took testosterone (in that order) and started living as an FTM transgendered person some four years previously. In 1999 Del is identifying with the male pronoun and both as intersex and as pansexual.

In the past fifteen years, LaGrace has achieved a worldwide reputation as a photographer, particularly for his work within the lesbian S/M subculture (Grace, 1991; 1993) and, more recently, for his work with drag kings (Volcano and Halberstam, 1999). Other major projects have included Ars Poetica (1993), the Hermaphrodyke series (1995), and the Transgenital Landscape series (1998), published in *Sublime Mutations* (Volcano, 2000).

Figure 5.2 'Lesbian Cock', London, 1991 (Photographer and
© Del LaGrace Volcano)

Smyth (1996: 39) provides an excellent review of Del LaGrace's work up
to 1996, giving much of the flavour of LaGrace's earlier work, as follows:

Grace's images explode the idealizing, normative image of lesbian sex in a raw, difficult, fantastical
exposure of raunchiness ... Moving on from the celebration of femme/butch polarities, Grace began
to interpret the Daddy/Boy scene. *Lesbian Cock* 1991, for instance, presents two lesbians dressed in
leather and Muir caps, both sporting moustaches. One holds a lifelike dildo protruding from her
crutch. In this delicious parody of phallic power, these women are strong enough to show that they
are female, with breasts just perceptible. Their pose encapsulates the envy of the upfront cruising
style, the eroticization of the ass, casual sex, cottaging (looking for sex in public toilets), penetration
and the economic power and social privilege of the gay male. The image boasts the fun of a butch-
on-butch dyke camp that doesn't need to bind its breasts to impress.

For most of his adult life and work LaGrace has focused on the transgressive,
constantly falling foul of what he refers to as the 'gender police', initially those

214

'politically correct' elements within feminism and lesbianism, and, subsequently, with those more 'conventionally gendered' FTM transsexuals. In this sense, there has always been a 'transcending' motif to his life and work. However, since identifying as FTM transgendered, in the past four years, LaGrace's life and work provide us with especially significant and relevant material for sourcing a sociology of the intimate detail of transcending. In particular, unlike many 'transcending' transgender activists, LaGrace seeks to transcend the boundaries between the private and the public, both in his own life and in those of his 'subjects'. He is willing to share many of the details of his life as, for him, there is a political purpose informing his decision to be public. As he puts it: 'I allow myself to be seen because I can and so many can't.'

Here, we will focus on the emergence of LaGrace's gender identities within the interrelations between sex, sexuality and gender. Our intention is to illustrate an important variant of the transcending story – one in which there is a constant interplay between the 'attempt to get beyond the gendered and sexed practices of the social world, yet ... constantly harks back to the very categories it seeks to undo: male, female, gay, straight, bisexual' (Plummer, 1996: xvi).

Up until puberty, LaGrace experienced no particular gender conflicts when growing up. With puberty, however, came problems, mostly centred on his developing 'asymmetrical' body – one breast overdeveloped, while the other breast underdeveloped – and the growth of facial hair, which he plucked to avoid becoming that figure of curiosity: the bearded lady. Significantly, he has very few photographs taken of himself between the age of 13 and when he came out as a lesbian at 21, during which time he had identified as bisexual, having his first lesbian sexual encounter at 16. At 21, there followed some 17 years of living and photographing various aspects of the lesbian culture, most notably the lesbian s/m scene (Grace, 1991), after which LaGrace felt ready to develop further his own transgendering. By now he was well used to pushing the boundaries of sex, sexuality, and gender to their limits within lesbianism, and has continued to do so as he has pursued a polygendered, polysexual persona in his personal life and in his photographic work, during the past four years.

His body transgendering includes taking testosterone, growing a beard, and presenting male secondary characteristics. He has, however, kept his internal female organs and currently has no plans for a hysterectomy.

In the following passage, he comments on the significance for him of an intersex genital:

I started photographing Zach [FTM author of Nataf, 1996], as he was doing his transition. When I looked at his genitals, I thought I want that. You know that was part of my decision to take testosterone. I want those intersex genitals. That feels right. Not – I want a big penis. I wanted the intersex genital. I'd already had a big clitoris, comparatively speaking, and I wanted a bigger one. But it's not like a clitoris and it's not a cock. You know it's a different kind of genital altogether.

As regards sexual object choice (sexuality), Del is identifying as pansexual (at the time of our 1999 interview). He jokes that pansexuals adopt a libertine, 'polysexual' position that does not discriminate on the basis of gender or species. But his actual sex life is less radical. He's attracted to both gender variant bodies and gender variant identities in both men and women. His partners include transmen and butch dykes. Occasional object choices include androgynous people; very occasional object choices include 'extraordinarily' feminine women, but his preference is most marked for masculine women. While resenting the necessity to identify sexuality as masculine or feminine, he does regard his own sexuality as, in part, aggressive and selfish, which he identifies with men, and sees his sexuality as all of a piece with his masculine self-image and masculine sexual identification. His partners, however, do consider him as a very giving and considerate lover. In 1999, he is sure that 'heterosexuality absolutely does not work' for him.

His gender display depends upon the context. Since identifying with the male pronoun, growing a beard and taking testosterone he has no difficulty passing as male. In 1999, he wears a sports bra to conceal his breasts: 'Because the way I look and what they perceive my body should be, is not exactly the same thing', and for the most part presents as male.[6] During our interviews, for instance, he was favouring shorts, which exposed his hirsute legs, a t-shirt, and a padded gilet which concealed any semblance of breast development. Notwithstanding this display of gender, however, he would prefer to 'be accepted and respected for what I am, which is a hybrid gender, a kind of custom blend, if you like, of gender', and rues the lack of intersex visibility.

As regards his transgendered identity, he feels that to identify as FTM transgendered is not enough. It is too broad a categorization. Rather, he says:

I am everything. I'm omni-gendered, or polygendered, as much as I am polysexual. I have lived for 37 years believing myself to be only female in one sense, without realising that there is a possibility that I could also live as male. So, being a man, and only a man, is not any more an adequate decision than being a woman. Recently, I've wanted to be more proactive: in saying, yes, I am intersex. I don't even know if I have a right to call myself intersex. Like, what the hell am I?

LaGrace is more certain, however, of his political agenda:

That political agenda involves carving out a space for myself and for other people like me that are not conforming to a transsexual narrative ... I guess to promote understanding of things from female masculinity and that masculinity is something that someone who still identifies as female can possess. But also, you know, my main mission at the moment is to educate people around intersex issues ... And how wrong it is to make people choose between male and female when they clearly possess both. You don't have to be physiologically intersex to have those feelings. They could just be a feeling ... I really believe that we will have a society that is much more open and that you can be gender-less like Christie [see Chapter 4], if you like, or gender-full – like sometimes performing hyper

Figure 5.3   Del and 'Harry', San Francisco, 1996 (© Del LaGrace Volcano)

masculinity or hyper femininity or sometimes being androgynous. You know, I don't think gender is going to be of as much of an issue. I think it will be more of a pleasurable pastime. I mean, I hope so. I really hope so. I want people ... It's like when I say to people I'm a gender terrorist ... that I do mean it. It's a fine line I'm walking because I don't want to invalidate friends of mine like Jay Prosser [the FTM author of *Second Skins*, 1998] who are more conventionally gendered ... who I respect a great deal. So many people say that there has to be a right and wrong. Just like there has to be male and a female; a homosexual; a heterosexual. I want to blow that up and get people to accept that gender, as well a sexuality, is much more nuanced.

Plummer, writing on queer theory, has suggested that

what seems to be sought is a world of multiple gendered fluidities - a world at home in a postmodern cacaphony of multiplicity, pastiche and pluralities that mark the death of the meta-narratives of

217

gender which have dominated the modern world. The claim ... is to live 'outside of gender'. These are
the 'gender outlaws'. We shall have to see if this is possible. (1996: xvi)

Del LaGrace Volcano's life and work are proof, perhaps, that it is possible.
For how many of us it is possible, however, remains to be seen.

Methods, methodology and a tale of caution

Those of our readers who have grasped our theory and methodology will
appreciate that our life history data, like that drawn from our interviews with
Del LaGrace Volcano in the previous section, are a major source from which
we generate grounded conceptualizations and theorizations. We then use
selected material from such life history data to illustrate the conceptualizations and theorizations that have emerged from that life history data.

In addition, it needs to be said that out of respect for our informants we
make a practice of returning to our major informants, prior to publication,
to check for inaccuracies and final updates. Earlier in this chapter we drew
upon some of Stephen Whittle's reminiscences about the early days of the
trans movement in the UK, which we took initially from an email thread.
Whittle then amended what he had said in the light of a more leisurely and
reflective consideration. On other occasions, we note how informants say
we have 'got it right' but they wish to provide us with further material:
aspects of their lives that they have developed since we were last in contact
with them.

One major sissy maid informant (see Chapter 4), for instance, provided us
with some interesting new data describing how he would tightly gaff himself,
put on women's bikini bottoms and sun bathe and generally 'hang out' at
beaches frequented by gay males. Aware that gay men would be 'eyeing up'
each other's crotches, he took pleasure from the exposure of his flat 'sissy'
genital area.

He writes:

> In my real life here now, I go (in late summer only) to a known 'gay friendly' beach area two hours
> from where I live. There, I sunbathe in the bottoms of girl's bikinis (I have about six of them) and swim
> in the ocean in them also. I attract some gay guy's attention – but when they notice I am very well
> 'tucked' they seem to lose interest rapidly (which is great, 'cause I don't want it – I just think the swim-
> suits are cute!). Anyway, I do get (bottom only) 'girl's tan lines' from this. Since it is not on top, how-
> ever, there has not been any public embarrassment factor (at least yet).

Occasionally, however, an informant wishes to make substantial changes to
what we have written, not so much because we have 'got it wrong', but

because they have moved on in their theory and practice. This is what happened when we asked Del LaGrace Volcano for his comments on our first draft. Rather than substantially re-write the sections on Del, however, we prefer to use his case to underline the point that ALL presentations of life history material are frozen in time. The time-bound nature of this data does not matter to us, insofar as we are using it to illustrate our conceptual framework. However, our framework is, of course, designed to take account of the maximum range of diversity. In consequence, it is well capable of handling such 'updates' from informants. Most significantly, Del does not now identify as 'pansexual'. Indeed, Del now objects to this representation. In that sense, our use of Del's story to illustrate a particular set of interrelations between sex, sexuality and gender in one specific transcending trajectory has now been 'transcended', yet again.

It is instructive to draw upon Del's preferred amendments to the draft we sent him, drawing on our 1999 interviews with his preferred conceptualizations in 2005, shortly before this book went to press.

In 1999 Del is identifying as a 'gender terrorist and pansexual'. Now he identifies as a part-time gender terrorist but prefers the terms gender variant or gender queer to describe 'hermself'. Whereas six years ago, Del was identifying with the male pronoun and variously as intersex and pansexual, currently Del identifies primarily as a 'herm', as in 'hermaphrodyke' and as in her + him = herm.

Whereas, in 1999, he had said 'Heterosexuality absolutely does not work for me', this 'feels strange' to him now. He comments: 'For the past three years I have been involved with a woman who presents as quite feminine, although she is also a very successful drag king and when in drag passes as a better man than I do! The words seem very rigid reading them now.'

Having been with his current partner for three years, he has reconsidered how his attractions work. In particular, he finds especially problematic what we wrote about his 'pansexuality'. In part, this is because Del now identifies differently. In part, however, it is because he takes exception to how the tone of our writing on a past identification may be read by others. He finds the whole section on his pansexuality problematic now and adds: 'I am not so sure about stirring up the inter-species sex debate. It makes it too easy for people to dismiss what I am saying.'

In a particularly illuminating and detailed paragraph, Del adds:

I wouldn't say I identify as pansexual anymore. I wasn't aware at the time that for many people this term includes sex with animals and that is not the impression I'm wanting to give. They have enough ammo' without that. I would say I identify as 'gender queer' and 'gender variant'. I am also not necessarily a biological female. You could say I was assigned female at birth and went along with the assignation until I was 37 years old when I adjusted my physiology from F to I: female to intersex. According to the many medical examinations and tests I have, I have XX XO chromosomes and a high possibility of one ovo-teste on the right side. However, I am not interested in any more invasive surgery and this is what it would take to 'prove' medically if I am or am not intersex, according to strict definitions. 'G', the endocrinologist at UCL [University College, London] Intersex Clinic says it's all about how you define; for some I am and for some I'm not. My question would be, who do I give the power to define what I am? My answer is, to no one but myself.

As Strauss so aptly puts it:

The naming or identifying of things is, then, a continual problem, never really over and done with. By continual I do not mean continuous – one can lie in a hammock contentedly watching the moon rise and raising no questions about it, the world, or oneself. Nevertheless, some portion of one's classificatory terminology, the symbolic screen through which the world is organized, is constantly under strain – or just has been – or will be. (1977: 25)

Indeed, it necessarily must be so, given the very nature of action that always 'brings in its train' both the reconstruction of past experience and the emergence of new objects (ibid.: 25; Mead, 1934).

SIX   Conclusion

Then and now

In our opening chapter we documented the focus of 'The First National TV.TS Conference' held in the UK in 1974, which more or less coincided with our own entry into the research arena. The conference was entitled 'Transvestism and Transsexualism in Modern Society'. At the time, it was the first of its kind. Today, a similar conference would be more likely to be entitled 'Transgender in Postmodern Society'. It would justifiably proclaim itself an 'international' conference, and it would be just one of a number of similar annual or biennial events in the Euro-American world. Indeed, for the past decade or so, three rather different sorts of transgender conferences in the Euro-American world have taken place.

One tradition of conferences follows the original 1974 UK event almost identically. They are attended by a mix of medics, clinical psychologists, academics, and trans people. They incorporate social events for trans people and their partners. The emphasis at these conferences is on a genuine meeting of minds of sympathetic professionals and trans people with an interest in the 'serious' side of transgendering. At the same time, they can be used by trans people for their social function and as a base for having fun outside the more serious side of the programmes. The second tradition of transgender conferences focuses more firmly upon the 'serious' side of things. Events like that of the biennial HBIGDA (The Harry Benjamin International Gender Dysphoria Association) conference are more oriented towards the medical and psychological professions. In recent years, they have included increasing numbers of professionals who identify as trans. Finally, developments from the mid-1990s onwards have seen the rise in importance of transgender conferences favoured by cultural theorists, transcending transgendering activists, and social scientists favourably disposed towards transcending transactivisms.

Naturally enough, just as some self-identified trans people are professionally trained 'experts', so some medics are favourably disposed to the body modification projects espoused by some postmodernist theorists. There are psychiatrists and surgeons, for instance, who are favourably disposed to postmodern positions that approach sex reassignment surgery with a similar mindset to that which approaches body piercings and tattooings. For the most part, however, most professionals, and indeed most of their clients, subscribe to the dominant view that the hormonal and surgical alteration of the body is not a person's right but is only to be undertaken if authorized by an appropriate medical professional. Deference to experts is now more contested, perhaps, but in some quarters it is not so dissimilar to what it was 30 years ago. Transgender knowledge claims, generally, are now, perhaps, more widely contested than they were. Certainly, they are more debated. There is now, of course, a much wider range of literature and experience upon which to draw in any contested claim.

The original Euro-American pioneers of transgendering are now dead, in poor health or very old. Now it is possible to find many participants in the transgender community who have never heard of Virginia Prince, for example. Thirty years ago, that would have been most unlikely. However, recent years have seen a revisiting and reclaiming of these pioneers. Publications are now appearing, for instance, which seek to pay the pioneers the proper respect (Ekins and King, 2001b; 2005a; 2005b; Docter, 2004).

There is no doubt that the past three decades have seen major changes in many aspects of transgender, in theory and in practice, in 'lived experience' and in 'transgender studies'. However, it must be said that in other aspects, there has been little or no change.

Our approach to the diversity in transgender phenomena both 'then' and 'now' – specifically our focus on 'generic social processes' and grounded theory – is in important respects 'abstract of time and places' (Glaser, 1993: 1). This is because grounded theory is concerned principally with core problems and how they are processed. In large measure these are beyond personal prejudice, preference or fashion. To this end, we constructed a conceptual framework intended to enable sociological investigation of the maximum range of transgender diversity. As sociologists, we considered our material in terms of the social construction of realities with particular reference to the interrelations of sex, sexuality, and gender; of identities, communities and social worlds; and of discourse, knowledge and stories.

Furthermore, as Euro-American sociologists, as opposed to social anthropologists, our focus has been on transgender in the Euro-American context. More specifically, we found it instructive to re-frame the arena in terms of the narrative turn in social science and cultural studies – hence our conceptualization of our research arena in terms of tales and stories.

222

Transgendering takes its reference point and meaning from the particular arrangement between the sexes which in our culture is dominated by a bi-polar gender system. From the sociological point of view, it is this binary gender divide which provides the principal social structural determinant within which all gender relations are played out. Taking this binary gender divide as our starting point does not, of course, mean that we are committed to its maintenance. However, when the divide is taken as the starting point, we find it instructive to detail four major modes of transgendering in terms of migrating, oscillating, negating and transcending, and consider each mode in terms of the particular interrelations between the transgendering sub-processes of substituting, erasing, concealing, implying, and redefining. The major advantages of this approach are that it enables detailed investigation of the emergence and development, and of the ebb and flow, of alternative, and frequently competing, categories, discourses, identities and lifestyles – all conceptualized as emergents within the generic social process of transgendering.

Each of the preceding four chapters has focused, respectively, on each of the four modes of transgendering. However, this separation of modes for the purposes of clarity and exposition should not blind us to the importance of investigating their interrelations. A number of points might be made about these interrelations. One set of issues concerns how individuals live their lives in relation to the modes and their interrelations. Do they traverse the modes? How do they 'choose' between the modes? Do they combine the modes? And so on. A second set of issues concerns conceptual matters: in particular, how do meanings of objects, incidents, and lives shift and change as the apparently 'same' object, incident, or life is implicated within different sets of interrelations within different modes?

Individual transgendering trajectories may well traverse the modes many times. This is an empirical question. Indeed, researching life histories in the light of this traversing often proves particularly sensitising in regards to both the study of individual lives and the study of social change.

When we began our research, migrating and oscillating were the major 'choices' available to trans people. The goal of migration was assimilation; the high point of oscillating was often temporary 'passing'. In recent years, there has emerged what we consider to be a paradox of assimilation. In some ways assimilation is very much easier than it was 30 years ago. State of the art facial feminization surgery that alters bone structure can, for instance, feminize the face in a way not possible 30 years ago. We have one MTF informant who has 'chosen' her face from the web site of a celebrated US surgeon and is carefully setting aside savings to buy it. However, paradoxically, now that transgender is mainstream knowledge to many, it is less easy to assimilate and pass in many contexts. In the 1980s a 'woman' with an exposed cleavage may have been 'obviously' a woman. Now, we may not be so sure.

In general terms, the period of our research has seen a shift from priorities of assimilation and passing to a blurring of migrating and transcending. If we review how people live out the transgendering stories, we see many more trans people who are 'out' in considering themselves neither 'men' nor 'women' but somewhere in between. Many MTF trans people know, for sure, that they are not men; but they do not consider themselves 'women' in the same sense that birth-assigned girls have become women. Many MTF trans people consider themselves 'trans women', or 'women of transsexual experience', for instance. Chosen terminology varies, but the 'choice' of many, now, is to be 'out' as transsexual, transgender, or whatever. Other people, particularly many of the younger generation of 'out' FTM trans people, take a much more postmodern line and are freely playing with the signifiers of gender in more overtly innovative and experimental ways. Riki Anne Wilchins, gender revolutionary and anarchist in her own way in the 1990s, now looks to the transgendering young to further the revolution she, amongst others, originally spearheaded in the 1990s:

For Jesse, the dyke community he knows is mostly 'boys.' As he told me, the right word might be 'fags,' 'hets,' 'bi's, 'or something else related to sexual orientation, but among bio grrrls, T-boyz, andros, and tranny girls, that doesn't make sense 'because it requires silly things like gender.' (2002c: 292)

Wilchins continues: 'The identities you and I spent such time coming to grips with, coming out about, and defending at such great cost are not even an issue for these kids. They are beyond the boxes in which we have made our lives' (ibid.: 292).

However, it must be said that, contemporaneous to these developments, entirely 'old style' assimilation remains the preferred option of many. We contacted one of our informants from 30 years ago who we had not heard from for some 20 years. Now 70 years old, she was living her life in her reassigned role as an unassuming and unremarkable senior citizen. She had no contact with any trans people. She never reads the quality press and knew nothing of the UK Gender Recognition Act that enables her to be legally recognized in her chosen role. Only after we told her about the new Act, did she determine to get the documentation to authenticate her migration. For a short while she will revisit her migrating, before settling down, again, to her life of assimilation.

Despite the rise of the relatively 'out' contemporary 'girls just want to have fun' styles of MTF oscillating, 'old-style' secret oscillating still remains the only 'option' for many, particularly those from traditional and rural areas. We were recently asked to assist a television producer in her quest for Welsh-speaking cross-dressers who would be willing to appear on camera. None of our informants was willing to appear on the programme. And, of course, for every informant 'out' enough to talk to us or, indeed, to anyone about their oscillating, there are countless others who will carry their 'secret' to their graves. Significantly, despite the 'changes', we know of only one oscillator who publicly articulates a systematic story of regular and 'complete' oscillation in his work environment, outside the worlds of fashion and the performing arts. Transgender theorist and activist Miqqi Alicia (Michael) Gilbert specifically identifies as a cross-dresser. Sometimes Miqqi Alicia goes to work dressed as a man (as Michael), and sometimes as a woman (as Miqqi Alicia). Gilbert is a Canadian Professor of Philosophy with track tenure, but his/her 'achievement' is nonetheless remarkable for that (Gilbert, 2002a; 2002b).

There is now a growing, if small, body of research within different trans communities worldwide which provides empirical evidence as to whether participants within the researched communities are 'choosing' migrating, oscillating, negating or transcending options.

Mandy Wilson's findings in Perth, Australia, in the 1990s (Wilson, 2002), for example, are pertinent. Many of her informants flirted with postmodern fluid identities during the process of their transition – in their period of liminality, as she puts it. However, once they had transitioned, most of her informants sought to migrate rather than transcend in terms of their overall life-pattern. Jan Wickman (2001) considered similar tensions in the context of the transgender community in Finland. He indicated a complex picture within which his informants varied to the extent they embraced 'old-style' or contemporary 'solutions'. Darryl Hill found likewise in Ontario, Canada (2000). Perhaps the only useful generalization that can be made is that in the years since our research began, there is indeed a greater range of 'choices' to adopt, and a greater freedom to devise new 'choices'. Certainly, there is available a far greater range of sophisticated conceptualizations of transgender phenomena for individuals to identify with and add to, if they so choose (O'Keefe and Fox, 2003).

There is also emerging within transgender autobiographies a more sophisticated treatment of 'solutions' of who to come out to, with what, how, and when. The leading FTM activist and writer Jamison Green, in both his public talks and in his particularly fine and moving recent autobiography, makes much of the important distinction between 'privacy' and 'secrecy' in the process of his *Becoming a Visible Man* (Green, 2004). He argues for the importance of privacy, as and when it is desired and desirable. Secrecy, on the other hand, for Green, tends to be the mark of a denial of the past and, in general, undesirable, both to psyche and to society, more generally.

We may contrast this 'now' with the 'then' of Charlotte Bach, who as a trans person in the early 1970s felt the need to migrate in her personal life whilst putting forward a transcending trans theory of emergent evolution in her professional life. In Chapter 5, we left her biographer with the last word

225

on Dr Bach. According to Wheen (2002), her main achievement was her 'authenticity' as a woman in 'carrying her secret almost to the grave'.

There is, however, an alternative view of the meaning and significance of Bach's transgendering. Joebear Webb, who is making a film of the life and work of Charlotte Bach, redefines the 'then' in terms of the 'now'. Specifically, on the basis of a personal acquaintance with Bach, attendance at her classes, and a life-long interest in her life and work, Webb concludes:

> For me the significance of Charlotte Bach's transgender 'performance' is not the fact that it was for so many years so astonishingly successful, a fact I think you will agree is in itself trivial (in that it suggests merely that Charlotte Bach was a conman par excellence); but in the possibility that Charlotte Bach may also have been other than that: she may have been, as I think she consciously wanted us to believe she was: transcendent of gender, a specific indication of our future – a future in which, in terms of evolution, possibly the identity of the (individual?) human being is no longer rigidly gender-based. Thus in the tradition of the shaman, she may have been more of an avatur than a guru. With genetic engineering, such an indication no longer seems as absurd or far-fetched as it would have done four decades ago, when she developed her 'theory'. Just a thought, of course. But it's one that does genuinely spring out of a consideration of Charlotte Bach's life and experience and theorising. (personal communication, 2005)

In short, for Webb, Bach is both migrating and transcending. However, 35 years ago, there was no available 'paradigm shift' within which to work. For its time, Bach's traversing of the modes of migration was, perhaps, an appropriate 'evolutionary solution' to an ontogenetic and phylogenetic problem. However, nowadays, of course, there is an available paradigm shift within which to constitute and consolidate the definition of the transgendering situation. Indeed, Bach's dilemma and 'solution' highlight another aspect of the difference between 'then' and 'now'. Now many, arguably most, of the important 'transcending' theorists are self-identified trans people. Not only this, but increasing numbers of openly trans people are working as medics, sexologists, psychologists, psychotherapists and counsellors amongst other trans related professions. The times, they are, indeed, changing.

Conceptual matters

Our claim is not to be comprehensive in our consideration of the stories, themselves. Rather it is to provide a framework that might usefully be applied by others, to extend our arguments in terms of both breadth and depth. We do make the claim, for instance, that a consideration of transgendering in terms of the interrelations between the sub-processes of transgendering that we have identified enables a sensitivity to the detail of diversity that is notably lacking in much of the literature of transgender. The framework can, in principle, be applied with profit to any incident of transgendering wherever and however presented.

In this section, we detail two illustrations to indicate just how complex these interrelations are, in even the apparently most 'simple' transgendering incident. To give the flavour of what we have in mind we will focus first on 'gaffing' and then say a brief word about the acquisition of suntan lines.

Gaffing is a widespread practice in very different instances of MTF transgendering. It inhibits conventional genital response; it emasculates the body; and it provides an aspect of a blank canvas upon which to construct or reconstruct gender. For these reasons it provides a particularly suitable example to consider in terms of a study of the interrelations between sex, sexuality and gender.

It will be recalled from Chapter 4 that gaffing refers to various practices designed to conceal the male genitalia by pinning them flat. Sometimes it follows 'tucking', the practice of inserting the testicles inside the body. It might entail the wearing of a gaff to pin the genitals between the legs and under the bottom. Some people use surgical tape or elastoplast to keep the testicles and penis in place. Still others speak of gaffing when they wear a tight girdle or similar item of clothing, which compresses the genitalia against the front of the body. The purpose of gaffing in all these cases is to present a smooth genital area that conceals the presence of the male genitalia. The 'meaning' of gaffing, however, to those who gaff is likely to be very different.

Vicky is a pre-operative MTF transsexual who is still living with her wife but has recently met her first boyfriend, Sean. They are planning to spend their first night together in bed. Sean has learned that Vicky does not like his hands straying near her genital area and in deference to her pre-operative status avoids this area in their petting. Gaffing, for Vicky, is a practice which best helps her to disavow her male genitals. It conceals her male bulge, helps her to forget about its existence, and also denies the possibility of a male partner having access to it. She makes extra sure her gaffing is intact when she spends the night with Sean. It enables them both to engage in lovemaking without the obvious presence of two sets of male genitalia. In terms of our framework, Vicky is erasing in the service of substituting, but, particularly in a 'near-naked' setting, her gaffing is her 'best bet' migrating compromise pending reassignment surgery. Wearing feminine underwear over her gaff in bed helps her to redefine her absence of female genitalia during sex (sexuality) in terms of it being her 'time of the month', as she jokes to Sean. Thus does she disavow even her gaffing.

Vicky gaffs permanently, except when attending to personal hygiene, as an integral part of her body migrating. Tony, on the other hand, is a gay oscillating drag queen. As part of his stage act, he gaffs as part of his construction of a blank canvas upon which to 'perform' gender. He enjoys the attention his tight gaffing gains as he dances in front of his evening audience dressed only in a tight show girl costume. However, as soon as the show is over, he removes his gaff and later that night with his partner, both are free to enjoy his own and each other's erect penises. For Tony, gaffing is a professional requirement that gives him no particular pleasure, *per se*, although he does enjoy the attention it provokes in some of his audience, particularly that from 'transgender naïve' heterosexual women on hen nights.

As part of his performance of gender, Tony conceals principally in order to best perform temporary showgirl femininity. He is not particularly concerned to imply the presence of female genitalia, although this may be how his performance is read. Vicky, on the other hand, in one sense conceals in order to imply, but her concealing is carried out principally to erase, pending future substituting.

For both Vicky and Tony, gaffing is co-opted in the service of their migrating and oscillating, respectively. It is a relatively minor aspect of their transgendering. We might see it as an aspect of Vicky's maintenance of her identity as a migrating transsexual, rather than as an aspect of its formation or renewal. Certainly, neither Vicky nor Tony eroticize their gaffing. Indeed, gaffing became routinized rather quickly for them both, so much so that neither of them gives the matter much thought.

For Sissy Diana, by contrast, gaffing is a major preoccupation. In his personal schedule, he has written in his notebook: 'Wear a fresh gaff every day and night. I must note that each day and night I spend gaffed softens me more, addicting me to the simple security and comfort my sissy personality and sissy lifestyle offers me.' As we noted in Chapter 4, gaffs provide a major focus for many negating sissies. As Rose puts it in her article, 'The Social Implications of Gaffing: Effects of Foundation Garments and Fashion on the Sissy Male Psyche': 'Being gaffed, then, serves as a constant reminder to the sissy male that he is, indeed, a sissy. Every tug of the tight little garment, every glance down to see his smooth and girlish front makes it crystal clear what he is' (Rose, 1995b: 30). Furthermore, the intention is for gaffing to produce another 'side effect', as in the somewhat fanciful: 'While many sissies become impotent, some are still "fertile". But constant, tight, and restrictive gaffing causes most sissies to become infertile, as well as impotent. This keeps sissies where they should be – out of the sex and reproduction game entirely!' (ibid.: 32)

It is evident in such passages that gaffing practices and the gaff take on a very different meaning within this sissy maid context. When implicated in the service of the privileging of erasing in the service of negating, gaffs and gaffing are likely to be a major prop in identity formation, continuance and renewal. In addition, as we saw in Chapter 4, some negating sissies (paradoxically) variously eroticize gaffs and gaffing.

Gaffing makes for a relatively simple example of the very different interrelations between the various sub-processes in any incident of transgendering because of its elemental and potentially temporary nature. Moreover, were it psychologically possible, gaffs and gaffing can be dispensed with at any time. Yet, even with this 'simple' example we have done no more than hint at some of the many complexities entailed in paying the proper respect to diversities in transgender experience. As the transgendering becomes more permanent, all manner of additional problems are raised. What about, for instance, such semi-permanent matters as the MTF acquisition of suntan lines?

We saw in the last chapter how Sissy Bobbie enjoyed acquiring bikini bottom suntan lines, but because he sunbathed topless, he did not have to confront potentially embarrassing attention to his upper torso. Many of those who MTF transgender, however, are intrigued by the prospect of the acquisition of feminine suntan lines from wearing a bikini.

In the context of oscillating, for instance, such tan lines provide an excellent opportunity to examine the major tension in much oscillating: how to cross the binary in such a way that is as 'complete' as possible, but does not preclude the return to the 'other' side. Tanning lines from wearing a bikini might feature as a semi-permanent aspect of oscillating. In this context, it may provide a sought-after marker of the sub-process of 'implying'. But what is to be done when the oscillator returns to male mode and does not wish his oscillating to be revealed?

Different oscillating informants speak of different 'solutions' to this problem. Some trade off their pleasure gained from their tan lines by covering them up in public settings and denying themselves 'revealing' intimacies with partners until the tan lines have disappeared. Others spend time and effort trying to undo the lines by tanning the white areas with tanning lotions, visiting sun beds, and so on. For negating sissy maids, on the other hand, tan lines may be favoured as a semi-permanent marker of their identity as sissies. Conversely, a number of our migrating MTF informants consider that 'real' women sunbathe topless and seek to avoid tan lines on their upper torso. They take pleasure from the exposure of their naked breasts and lament what they consider to be the trivial pursuits of their oscillating and negating sisters and brothers. The complexities are endless.

Futures

We make no claim to futurology. However, we will close with some thoughts on the future of the 'three approaches' to transgender that we detailed in our opening chapter.

The significance and influence of the three approaches to transgender have waxed and waned since their inception both within and without the transgender community. We might expect this pattern to continue.

The first approach to transgender – that of Virginia Prince's 'transgenderist' – maintains the binary gender divide with the proviso that males can become women and (by implication) that females can become men. Males can renounce masculinity and embrace femininity. This approach provides a role model, an identity, a script and an ideology. It provides the rationale for an identity politics. These are the strengths of the approach.

It does these things, however, on the basis of a strict separation of sex and gender and the underplaying of sexuality (the erotic). Arguably, the gender theory it draws on is dated. Certainly, its models of masculinity and femininity often have a 1950s flavour to them. It is politically conservative – pass and 'be polite'. It is essentialist in its view of sex: gender can be changed but sex cannot be changed.

It would be a mistake, however, to assume that the approach will founder because of a *prima facie* outmodedness. Its clarity and seeming 'certainty' in its distinguishing of sex and gender and its underplaying of sexuality are likely to see the approach retaining its appeal. The approach's determined stance against the 'pathologizing' of transgender gives it further appeal to many.

The approach has, for instance, received an unexpected recent boost from an unlikely quarter. It finds itself an ally in what is arguably the most radical piece of transgender legislation yet passed by a Western legislature. The Gender Recognition Act (2004) recently passed by the UK Parliament allows transgendered individuals to legally 'change sex', not on the basis of genital reassignment (sex), but on the basis of role change (gender). Living in role for a specified period with a declaration of intent to live in the new role permanently, and with certification of 'gender confusion' from a qualified gender practitioner, enables biological males and females 'officially' to cross the binary divide on the basis of gender. The separation of gender from sex and sexuality that provides the foundation for this newly proposed legislation provides an unexpected endorsement of the contemporary viability of this approach.

The legislation does not endorse Virginia Prince's conceptualization of a male woman (or female man). Rather Prince's privileging of gender over sex is given what might be seen as a postmodern twist. The statute does not seek to ascertain the 'truth' of the 'sex' behind the gender. Rather, recognition of the change of 'gender' brings about a *de facto* change of 'sex' for all but the occasional exceptions detailed in the Statute. It is notable that Stephen Whittle and Christine Burns, two of the principal architects of this legislation within the UK transgender community, were honoured by Queen Elizabeth II in her New Year's Honours list for their contribution to gender issues, in effect for their service to the transgender community. Whittle received an

OBE (Officer of the Order of the British Empire) and Christine Burns, an MBE (Member of the Order of the British Empire). In striking contrast, those approaches to transgender that do not erase the significance of sexuality have, in the USA particularly, been seized upon by the Christian Right in their campaign to reverse legislation and case law that has been moving towards greater equal rights for transgendered people.

Whereas the focus of this first approach to transgender was initially on privacy, secrecy and discreetness, and had a middle-class bias, the second approach – that of the inclusive transgender community 'umbrella' approach – potentially encompasses the full range of transgendered people without regard to class, style of transgendering and, indeed, legality.

Rather than advocate one particular view on transgender, the aim, increasingly, has been to embrace all views in a spirit of acceptance and mutual support. This inclusive approach has provided a fertile resource for the development of alternative positions, some of which have involved organizing for greater acceptance in society, greater legal recognition, and so on. What would later be termed identity politics could establish itself within this growing 'transgender community'. It has provided a safe haven for the development of diverse ideas, alternative strategies, and the exploring of differences in a way denied by the rigidity of the first approach.

Moreover, the approach's flexibility meant that when new developments took place within the transgender world the tradition could embrace them. This was most noticeable throughout the 1990s when FTM transgender came to prominence and when a steadily increasing body of writings stressing the performativity and postmodern aspects of transgender came to the fore. It also enabled the tradition to include intersexed people when they wished to be included and those who wished to be 'ungendered'. Indeed, in some uses, lesbian and gay people were included within the community.

As we suggested in our initial delineation of the three approaches to transgender, as the 1990s progressed, overtly transgressive formulations of transgender tended to be linked with a more embracing usage of the umbrella sense of transgender. This led to a position where tolerance of transgender diversity became much more evident in transgender gatherings, in general, leaving a minority of community activists to variously campaign for equal rights, and an even smaller minority to develop transgender theory at the cutting edge of sex, sexuality and gender studies.

Moreover, the community increasingly embraced a wide range of professionals – surgeons, psychiatrists, psychologists and counsellors, speech therapists, and so on – all in broad agreement in their recognition of transgender diversity and their sensitivity to non-pathologizing discourses of transgender.

The strength of this second approach lies in its ability to accommodate change. The umbrella sense has shown itself to be sufficiently robust to withstand arguments about precisely who should and should not be included and by whom. In a sense, this usage has a 'banner' function. It is a grouping for social and political purposes. It includes subcultures and social worlds. It is encompassing and undercuts division.

The future of the third 'transgressive' and 'transcending' approach is inevitably tied up with the future of postmodernity and the way in which it is viewed. Opinion is divided as to whether the contemporary period is best understood in terms of late modernism or postmodernism. As we detailed in Chapter 5, one trend within this approach links its writings on transgender to theories of modernity – most notably, to grand narratives of Marxism and feminism (Feinberg, 1992; 1996; 1998). Another trend links its writings directly with postmodernism (Bornstein, 1994; Wilchins, 1997). Undoubtedly, the post-modern [pomo] trend has become more predominant, as is evidenced by such collections as Queen and Schimel's (1997) *Pomosexuals: Challenging Assumptions About Gender and Sexuality* and Nestle et al.'s (2002) *GenderQueer: Voices from Beyond the Sexual Binary*.

If the postmodern aesthetic – simulation, prefabrication, intertextuality, and bricolage – continues to spread roots, we might expect that the sex, sexuality and gender manifestations being developed within this 'transgressive' approach will gain increasing prominence. The 'periphery' minority position of this third approach might be expected to make its presence increasingly felt in mainstream society. In that case, it will transpire that its proponents are right when they argue that they are the harbingers of a new order. Modernity's stress upon 'science', progress, and rationality, as regards sex, sexuality and gender, will be increasingly undermined. The 'essentializing' of sex, so prominent in writers as diverse as Virginia Prince and Janice Raymond, will become untenable. 'Authenticity' will take on new meanings. Trans medical technology will become something to call upon for the purposes of 'optional' body modification, as opposed to 'diagnosis', treatment, or management of pathology or disorder.

There is, however, another aspect of postmodernism, less concerned with performativity, and more concerned with what Foucault refers to as the 'power/knowledge' couple. Categorizations of sex, sexuality and gender are both con-straining and enabling. Power/knowledge is variously diffused with complex interrelations and manifestations throughout social formations. Following this line of thinking entails proponents of the 'transgressive' approach resisting con-straining classifications, redefining classifications, and planning different strate-gies of resistance within different sites of power/knowledge.

Here we see the relevance of the approach's emphasis upon political com-mitment and the partisan. We might expect its proponents to draw on what-ever is at hand in the interests of their emancipation. Their future will depend on the success of their struggle set within the context of the future of the postmodern.

Notes

1 Telling Transgendering Tales

1 Routledge made the final decision on the title for *Blending Genders* in 1995. Routledge rejected 'A Reader in Transgender Studies', one of our suggested subtitles, on the grounds that it was not as suitable for marketing purposes as 'Social Aspects of Cross-Dressing and Sex-Changing', the subtitle they adopted. Similarly, when Susan Stryker proposed at the time of her GLQ Special Issue on 'Transgender' (Stryker, 1998) that it should be expanded into a 'Reader', 'Duke [the publishers] said they thought the journal volume would serve much the same purpose, and they didn't see any market for an additional, expanded, version' (Susan Stryker, personal communication, 2005). For an indication of how things have changed, in this regard, see the forthcoming *A Transgender Studies Reader*, edited by Susan Stryker and Stephen Whittle, to be published by Routledge, New York, in 2006.

2 David Valentine's (2002; 2003; 2004) recent anthropological work on the development of the term 'transgender' and the developing transgender community in the USA tends to lead to a conflation of our 'umbrella' and 'transgressive/transcending' approaches to transgender. Valentine's findings in the USA, may, or may not, be significant in the context of other research arenas. We consider it vitally important, however, to maintain the conceptual distinction between the two approaches to transgender, both for theoretical and strategic purposes. Our email discussion led us to the following 'conclusion' which Valentine summarizes thus (personal communication, 2005):

> Thank you very much for your clarifications. Let me try and clarify my own position on my argument. My sense is that the 'umbrella' sense arose quickly out of the activism that sprang up in the early 1990s in the US – perhaps, or perhaps not, inspired by what was happening in the UK. I think the 'transcending/transgressive' sense and the umbrella meaning are actually very closely related,

since the very idea of an umbrella was transgressive, and the umbrella meaning is also transcending of medical meanings. In the contemporary US, where 'TG' is seen by many of the more radical, transgressive and young gender variant folk as already co-opted, 'genderqueer' has come to take on the transgressive meanings of TG. (And, in turn, many people who understand themselves as TG in one way or another, or as specifically TS, see 'GQ' as an appropriation of their movement by gender variant gay men and lesbians who are 'on the fence.') In my field research, what I came across (and what I describe in Chapter 1 of my book ms) is a range of 'conflations' – or, I might rather say, as an anthropologist, complex and sometimes contradictory uses of the term. First, 'TG' is used as an umbrella most of all in 'institutional' contexts – especially social services, activist organizations, and, increasingly, in medical/public health settings, as well as legislative activism and (some) court cases. However, 'at the same time' precisely because of the lability of this collective sense, what frequently happens (especially in the medical literature) is that authors will speak of 'TG' but then go on to talk specifically about transexual [sic] people. My argument, in part, is that the theoretical and practical malleability of 'TG' in the umbrella sense enables it to be proposed as a unitary category, but it can then easily slip into meaning 'transexual' [sic] or 'TV' or anything else. It is partly for this reason that I find TG so interesting (though more especially what it does around the category 'homosexual', as you probably know from reading my ms). I think the difference between our analyses is that I am not trying to disaggregate these different meanings into distinct and categorical kinds of uses, but to look at how, in any social context, the meaning(s) of TG can shift and change – and what reasons there might be for such shifts and changes. I guess this is a function of our different disciplinary backgrounds!

3   The anecdote is engaging but apocryphal. The idea of the *New Directions in Sociological Theory* book emerged from meetings being held at Goldsmiths in 1970. According to Paul Filmer (personal communication, 2005) 'The "turn" to ethnomethodology began to constellate in the Spring term of 1970'. The contract for the book was signed in late 1970/early 1971. In January 1971, Filmer took up a visiting appointment at City College, New York, and taught also at the CUNY Graduate Center where Harold Garfinkel was a visiting fellow. Following a visit to Garfinkel in Los Angeles in the Summer of 1971, Filmer met most of the prominent thinkers who in their different ways were developing sociologies rooted in the critique of positivism. Filmer returned to London and Goldsmiths in the Autumn of 1971 and the book had just been published. Such 'reality' as there was in the anecdote was related to the fact that many of the major US sociologists involved in the sociological critique of positivism at the time (a number from California!) had attended the meetings of the Goldsmiths group, and no doubt contributed to the developing ideas for the book. Visitors from North America to Goldsmiths included, among others, Aaron Cicourel, Roy Turner, Peter McHugh, and Alan Blum.

4   John Money is rightly credited with the initial development of major conceptual distinctions between sex and gender, but often wrongly credited with the terminology of 'gender identity'. It was psychoanalysts Robert Stoller (1964) and Ralph Greenson (1964) who refined the concept of

gender with the term 'gender identity'. Meyerowitz (2002: 114–17) makes the fundamental points with splendid economy:

In explaining the sources of gender identity, Stoller attempted to bridge the gap between biological and environmental etiologies. More than many post-World War II psychoanalysts, he looked for a biological substrate of human behavior, and he reminded his readers that Freud, too, had written about the biological underpinnings of personality development. (2002: 115-16)

Later, Meyerowitz writes:

'As Stoller moved away from biology and toward psychology, John Money moved in the other direction. In the late 1960s and afterward he backed away partially from the environmental model that he and the Hampsons promoted in the late 1950s. He, too, adopted the term *gender identity*. (2002: 117)

We return to these matters, in a different context, in Chapter 2.

2 Migrating Stories

1 See Chapter 1, p. 24 and pp. 26–7 for details of the terminology of sex, sexuality, gender, and Gender used throughout this book.

2 On transgenderism and intersexuality in childhood and adolescence, see Cohen-Kettenis and Pfäfflin (2003); Di Ceglie (1998); and Zucker and Bradley (1995).

3 ICD refers to the *International Classification of Diseases*, now in its 10th revision, 2nd edition. The ICD-10 was endorsed by the Forty-Third World Health Assembly in May 1990 and came into use in WHO member states as from 1994. The DSM refers to *Diagnostic and Statistical Manual of Mental Disorders* now in its 4th edition (DSM-IV) published by the American Psychiatric Association, Washington, DC, 1994.

4 Benjamin was influential in the period surrounding the initial press coverage of Jorgensen's case. Interestingly, he arranged for Virginia Prince to visit Christine Jorgensen at the time of this initial press coverage (Richard Docter, personal communication, 2005). We also know from our own research interviews that those who were prepared to hormonally and surgically treat their transvestite/transsexual patients such as Benjamin in the USA, Bishop in the UK, and Hamburger's team in Denmark, had formed an informal network by the mid-1950s. It might be noted, too, that Jan Wålinder's (1967) study of transsexuals in Sweden had started in 1963. Benjamin's influence was making itself felt globally well before the establishment of the first Gender Identity Clinic in the USA in the mid-1960s.

5 See note 4, Chapter 1.

6 Writing of the two types of 'eonist', Ellis had noted that one type 'feels really to belong to' the opposite sex (1928: 36). Benjamin, while noting the similarity of this type to his conception of the transsexual, comments that:

'This reference to "feeling" here and in other places is of little scientific significance, as it is too vague, too subjective, and could vary in its meaning, not only from case to case, but also from mood to mood in the same individual' (1966: 33).

7   On the question of psychoanalysis and 'Research, Research Politics and Clinical Experience with Transsexual Patients', see the important exchange between Pfäfflin (2006) and Fonagy (2006).

8   One psychiatrist informant with extensive clinical experience of transgendered patients commented thus: 'Was the mother a dwarf? I hear these stories every day in the clinic: that 4, 5, 6, 7 or 8 year olds dress in their mother's clothes. These stereotypes usually collapse within a minute, and I am told they like to smell mother's wardrobe, that they may have used their mother's shawl or a similar item. Do you think Mother's bra fits an 8 year old?' When we put this point to Janice, she commented thus: 'So do adult women's bras, panties, girdles, dresses, stockings, and shoes fit 8-year-old boys perfectly? No. Does this prevent some 8-year-old boys from wearing them? I am very emphatic that I wore my mother's panties, bras, girdles, sanitary belts, stockings, dresses, shoes, necklaces, bracelets, and earrings at 8. They didn't always fit well, but that was hardly the point. In my case, smell was irrelevant.'

3 Oscillating Stories

1   Novic (2005) provides particularly detailed material for those researching the interrelations between sex, sexuality and gender in an oscillating trajectory.

2   It must be said that Freud did not have a high regard for Sadger's work. We thank Jutta Witzel for providing us with an English translation of Boehm (1923). Such was the power of the psychoanalytic 'definition of the situation' in those days, that Boehm is able to report a 'cure' of what looks like a 'moderately severe' case of transvestism in a matter of weeks. Now that transgender studies is becoming a globally recognized field of study, it is important that translation work is accelerated. In particular, we would like to see German-English translations of the important contemporary transgender work of Stefan Hirschauer, Gesa Lindemann, Annette Runt, and Manfred Steinkühler, to name but a few.

4 Negating Stories

1   Debra Rose considers the revised 2003 publication to be superior to the 1993 version in every way. In particular, the 2003 version is nearer to what she originally intended for the earlier publication.

2 A number of our sissy informants rate Girl-a-matic Corporation (2004) as their favourite site of this type. Home Page: http://www.geocities.com/WestHollywood/Heights/8036/ (accessed 25 July 2004).

5 Transcending Stories

1 Our account of the life and work of Charlotte Bach follows closely the popular accounts by Wheen (2002) and Wilson (1979; 1989). The psychology and sociology of the impostor are rarely thought to be relevant in the study of transgender. Study of the life and work of Bach suggests that they may well be very relevant. Intriguingly, the serious-minded Wilson thought it 'hilarious' when he learned of Bach's so-called 'true' sex after her death. Many of Bach's close followers were in a state of consternation about the revelation.

2 'The Transgender Alternative' first appeared as Holly (1991) 'The Transgender Alternative', *The TV-TS Tapestry*, 58: 31-3. In a revised form it entered the mainstream academic literature in Boswell (1997; 1998).

3 Wilchins spells 'transsexual' with one 's' as a 'way of asserting some small amount of control over a naming process that has always been out of my hands' (1997: 15). In this, she is following a number of her 'transexual' British predecessors (ibid.: 15), a number of whom still adopt this spelling.

4 We do, of course, take exception to Monro's comment that 'only post-structuralist and postmodernist approaches enable the inclusion and representation of the full range of gender diversity' (2005b: 14). Feminist thought in general, and postmodernist thought in particular, overlook the significance of the interactionist tradition in sociology for the study of sex, sexuality and gender. Intriguingly, one postmodernist feminist writer (Cahill, 1998: 308) influenced by queer theory has referred to our work as 'a "queer reinvention" of interaction theory' because (so she says) we argue 'that gender is not so much an identity formation as it is an ongoing process of performance and recognition or validation which occurs through interaction between the gendered self and its others'.

5 Jeffreys, like Raymond, always uses her preferred terms, as opposed to the preferred terms of the trans people she is writing about. The 'men' she refers to here are MTF transsexuals.

6 Del had the 'unwanted silicon implant' removed two years after our 1999 interview. He had been given the implant 27 years previously 'without (his) informed consent'. He now regards his breasts as 'small hermaphroditic breasts' and no longer feels the need to wear a sports bra.

Bibliography

Ailles, J. (2003) 'Pomosexual Play: Going Beyond the Binaristic Limits of Gender?' in J. Alexander and K. Yescavage (eds), *Bisexuality and Transgenderism: Intersexions of the Others*. New York: Haworth Press.

Aleksander, D. (1974) 'Outline Copy of Lecture', reported in The First National TV.TS Conference (1974) *Transvestism and Transsexualism in Modern Society*, sponsored by Leeds University TV.TS Group, Leeds, 15-17 March, pp. 11-12.

Allen, C. (1940) *The Sexual Perversions and Abnormalities*. Oxford: Oxford University Press.

Allen, C. (1949) *The Sexual Perversions and Abnormalities*, 2nd edn. Oxford: Oxford University Press.

Allen, C. (1954) 'Letter', *British Medical Journal*, 1 May, 1040.

Allen, C. (1962) *A Textbook of Psychosexual Disorders*. London: Oxford University Press.

Allen, C. (1969) *A Textbook of Psychosexual Disorders*, 2nd edn. London: Oxford University Press.

American Psychiatric Association (1980) *Diagnostic and Statistical Manual of Mental Disorders*, 3rd edn. Washington, DC: APA.

American Psychiatric Association (1994) *Diagnostic and Statistical Manual of Mental Disorders*, 4th edn. Washington, DC: APA.

American Society of Plastic Surgeons (2004) '2003 Cosmetic Surgery Gender Distribution (Male)', http://www.plasticsurgery.org/public_education/loader.cfm?url=/commonspot/security/getfile.cfm&Page ID=12553, (accessed 17 December, 2004).

Anders, C. (2002) *The Lazy Crossdresser*. Emeryville, CA: Greenery Press.

Andrei, C. (2002) *Transgender Underground*. London: Glitterbooks.

Anonymous (No date) *Non-Man* (no publishing details).

Anonymous (1957) 'Answer to Reader's Question', *The British Medical Journal*, 3 August, p. 309.

Armstrong, C. N. (1958) 'The Clinical Diagnosis of Sex', *Proceedings of the Royal Society of Medicine*, 51, 23-6.

Ayalon, D. (1999) *Eunuchs, Caliphs, and Sultans: A Study in Power Relationships*. Jerusalem: Magnes Press.

Bailey, J. M. (2003) *The Man Who Would Be Queen: The Science of Gender-Bending and Transsexualism*. Washington, DC: John Henry Press.

Baker, R. (1968) *Drag: A History of Female Impersonation on the Stage*. London: Triton Books.

Baker, R. (1994) *Drag: A History of Female Impersonation on the Stage*. 2nd edn. London: Cassell.

Barbier, P. (1996) *The World of the Castrati: The History of an Extraordinary Operatic Phenomenon*. London: Souvenir Press.

Beaumont Society (1975) Beaumont Society – Conference '75: A Study of Transvestism and Allied States in the Family and Society, Leicester University, 4–6 April.

Bebbington, P. (1975) 'The Use of Behaviour Therapy in the Treatment of Sexual Problems with Reference to Transvestism', paper presented at the Beaumont Society Conference '75, Leicester University, 4–6 April, pp. 33–8.

Bem, S. (1993) *The Lenses of Gender*. New Haven, CT: Yale University Press.

Benjamin, H. (1953) 'Transvestism and Transsexualism', *International Journal of Sexology*, 7 (1): 12–14.

Benjamin, H. (1954) 'Transsexualism and Transvestism as Psychosomatic and Somato-Psychic Syndromes', *American Journal of Psychotherapy*, 8 (2): 219–30.

Benjamin, H. (1961) '7 Kinds of Sex', *Sexology*, 27: 436–42.

Benjamin, H. (1964a) 'Clinical Aspects of Transsexualism in the Male and Female', *American Journal of Psychotherapy*, 18: 458–69.

Benjamin, H. (1964b) 'Nature and Management of Transsexualism with a Report on Thirty-One Operated Cases', *Western Journal of Surgery, Obstetrics, and Gynecology*, 72: 105–11.

Benjamin, H. (1966) *The Transsexual Phenomenon*. New York: Julian Press.

Benjamin, H. (1967a) 'Introduction', in C. Jorgensen, *Christine Jorgensen: A Personal Autobiography*. New York: Bantam Books.

Benjamin, H. (1967b) 'The Transsexual Phenomenon', *Transactions of the New York Academy of Sciences*, 29: 428–30.

Benjamin, H. (1969) 'Introduction', in R. Green and J. Money (eds), *Transsexualism and Sex Reassignment*. Baltimore, MD: Johns Hopkins University Press.

Benjamin, H. and Ihlenfeld, C. (1973) 'Transsexualism', *American Journal of Nursing*, 73: 457–61.

Bennett, P. (2003) *Abnormal and Clinical Psychology: An Introductory Textbook*. Maidenhead: Open University Press.

Blanchard, R. (1989a) 'The Classification and Labeling of Nonhomosexual Gender Dysphoria', *Archives of Sexual Behavior*, 18: 315–34.

Blanchard, R. (1989b) 'The Concept of Autogynephilia and the Typology of Male Gender Dysphoria', *Journal of Nervous and Mental Disease*, 177 (10): 616–23.

Blanchard, R. (1991) 'Clinical Observations and Systemic Studies of Autogynephilia' *Journal of Sex and Marital Therapy*, 17: 235–51.

Blanchard, R. (1993a) 'Varieties of Autogynephilia and their Relationship to Gender Dysphoria', *Archives of Sexual Behavior,* 22 (3): 241–51.

Blanchard, R. (1993b) 'The She-male Phenomenon and the Concept of Partial Autogynephilia', *Journal of Sex and Marital Therapy*, 19: 69–76.

Blanchard, R. (2000) 'Abstract of Autogynephilia and the Taxonomy of Gender Identity Disorders in Biological Males', unpublished paper presented at the Symposium on Phenomenology and Classification of Male-to-Female Transsexualism, the meeting of the International Academy of Sex Research, Paris, June, 2000.

Blanchard, R. (2005) 'Early History of the Concept of Autogynephilia', *Archives of Sexual Behavior*, 34 (4): 439–46.

Blumer, H. (1969) *Symbolic Interactionism: Perspective and Method*. Englewood Cliffs, NJ: Prentice-Hall.

Bode, H. (2003) 'Is Drag Subversive of Binary Gender Norms?' *Dialogue*, 1 (3): 19–26.

Boehm, F. (1923) 'Bemerkungen über Transvestitismus', *Internationale Zeitschrift für Psychoanalyse*, 9: 497–509.

Bolin, A. (1988) *In Search of Eve: Transsexual Rites of Passage*. New York: Bergin and Garvey.

Bolin, A. (1994) 'Transcending and Transgendering: Male-to-Female Transsexuals, Dichotomy and Diversity', in G. Herdt (ed.), *Third Sex, Third Gender: Beyond Sexual Dimorphism in Culture and History*. New York: Zone Books.

Bornstein, K. (1994) *Gender Outlaw: On Men, Women and the Rest of Us*. London: Routledge.

Bornstein, K. (1998) *My Gender Workbook*. New York: Routledge.

Boswell, H. (1991) 'The Transgender Alternative', *Chrysalis Quarterly*, 1 (2): 29–31. First published as Holly (1991) *The TV-TS Tapestry*, 58: 31–3.

Boswell, H. (1997) 'The Transgender Paradigm Shift Toward Free Expression', in B. Bullough, V. Bullough and J. Elias (eds), *Gender Blending*. New York: Prometheus Books, pp. 53-7.

Boswell, H. (1998) 'The Transgender Paradigm Shift Toward Free Expression', in D. Denny (ed.), *Current Concepts in Transgender Identity*. New York: Garland, pp. 55-62.

Boyd, H. (2003) *My Husband Betty: Love, Sex and Life with a Crossdresser*. New York: Thunder's Mouth Press.

Brake, M. (1976) 'I May Be Queer, But at Least I Am a Man', in D. L. Barker and S. Allen (eds), *Sexual Divisions and Society: Process and Change*. London: Tavistock.

Breen, D. (ed.), (1993) *The Gender Conundrum: Contemporary Psychoanalytic Perspectives on Femininity and Masculinity*. London: Routledge.

Brevard, A. (2001) *The Woman I Was Not Born To Be: A Transsexual Journey*. Philadelphia, PA: Temple University Press.

Brierley, H. (1979) *Transvestism: A Handbook with Case Studies for Psychologists, Psychiatrists and Counsellors*. Oxford: Pergamon.

Brubach, H. (1999) *Girlfriend: Men, Women and Drag*. New York: Random House.

Bruce, V. (1967) 'The Expression of Femininity in the Male', *Journal of Sex Research*, 3 (2): 129-39.

Bullough, B., Bullough, V.L. and Elias, J. (eds) (1997a) 'Introduction', in *Gender Blending*. New York: Prometheus Books, pp. 15-25.

Bullough, B., Bullough, V.L. and Elias, J. (eds) (1997b) *Gender Blending*. New York: Prometheus Books.

Bullough, V. L. (1974) 'Transvestites in the Middle Ages', *American Journal of Sociology*, 79 (6): 1381-94.

Bullough, V. L. (1975) 'Transsexualism in History', *Archives of Sexual Behaviour*, 4 (5): 561-71.

Bullough, V. L. and Bullough, B. (1993) *Cross Dressing, Sex, and Gender*. Pennsylvania, PA: University of Pennsylvania Press.

Bullough, V.L., Legg, W. D., Elcano, B. W., and Kepner, J. (1976) *An Annotated Bibliography of Homosexuality*, vol. 2. London: Garland Press.

Butler, J. (1990a) *Gender Trouble*. London: Routledge.

Butler, J. (1990b) 'Gender Trouble, Feminist Theory and Psychoanalytical Discourse', in L. J. Nicholson (ed.), *Feminism/Postmodernism*. London: Routledge.

Butler, J. (1993) *Bodies that Matter: On the Discursive Limits of 'Sex'*. London: Routledge.

Cahill, C. (1998) 'Nancy, Sean and Birdie Jo: Contested Convictions of Gender', *Journal of Gender Studies*, 7 (3): 307-17.

Cahill, S. E. (1989) 'Fashioning Males and Females: Appearance and the Social Reproduction of Gender', *Symbolic Interactionism*, 12 (2): 281-98.

Califia, P. (1997) *Sex Changes: The Politics of Transgenderism*. San Francisco: Cleis Press.

Castles, S. and Davidson, A. (2000) *Citizenship and Migration: Globalization and the Politics of Belonging*. London: Macmillan.

Castles, S. and Miller, M. J. (1998) *The Age of Migration*. 2nd edn. London: Macmillan.

Cauldwell, D. O. (1947a) *What Is Hermaphroditism?* Girard, KA: Haldeman-Julius Publications.

Cauldwell, D. O. (1947b) *Why Males Wear Female Attire*. Girard, KA: Haldeman-Julius Publications.

Cauldwell, D. O. (1949a) 'Psychopathia Transexualis', *Sexology*, 16: 274-80.

Cauldwell, D. O. (1949b) *What's Wrong with Transvestism?* Girard, KA: Haldeman-Julius Publications.

Cauldwell, D. O. (1950a) *Questions and Answers on the Sex Life and Sexual Problems of Transvestites*. Girard, KA: Haldeman-Julius Publications.

Cauldwell, D. O. (1950b) *Questions and Answers on the Sex Life and Sexual Problems of Trans-Sexuals*. Girard, KA: Haldeman-Julius Publications.

Cauldwell, D. O. (1951) *Sex Transmutation - Can One's Sex Be Changed?* Girard, KA: Haldeman-Julius Publications.

Chermayeff, C., David, J. and Richardson, N. (1995) *Drag Diaries*. San Francisco: Chronicle Books.

Christian Institute (2002) 'Transsexualism - Mind over Matter' http://www.christianpublications.co.uk/ html-publications/transsexualism.htm#seeking (accessed, 22 January 2005).

Closer (2004a) 'Nadia: "Why I Had My Sex Change"', *Closer*, 14–20 August, p. 1.

Closer (2004b) 'Nadia's Agony: "I've Lost My Virginity to a Love Cheat"', *Closer*, 30 October–5 November, p. 1.

Cohen, A. K. (1955) *Delinquent Boys: The Culture of the Gang.* New York: Free Press.

Cohen-Kettenis, P. and Pfäfflin, F. (2003) *Transgenderism and Intersexuality in Childhood and Adolescence: Making Choices.* Vol. 46, Developmental Clinical Psychology and Psychiatry Series, London: Sage.

Connell, R. W. (1995) *Masculinities.* Sydney: Allen and Unwin.

Connell, R. W. (2002) *Gender.* Cambridge: Polity Press.

Conrad, P. and Schneider, J. W. (1980) *Deviance and Medicalisation.* London: C. V. Mosby.

Conway, L. (2004) 'An Investigation into the Publication of J. Michael Bailey's Book on Transsexualism by the National Academies', http://ai.eecs.umich.edu/people/conway/TS/LynnsReviewOfBaileysBook.html (accessed 22 January 2005).

Coser, L. (1977) *Masters of Sociological Thought: Ideas in Historical and Social Context.* New York: Harcourt Brace Jovanovich.

Costa, M. A. (1962) *Reverse Sex.* London: A Challenge Publication.

Coulson, M. and Riddell, D. (1970) *Approaching Sociology: A Critical Introduction.* London: Routledge and Kegan Paul.

Cowell, R. (1954) *Roberta Cowell's Story.* London: Heinemann.

Cromwell, J. (1999) *Transmen and FTMs: Identities, Bodies, Genders and Sexualities.* Urbana, IL: University of Illinois Press.

Crowley, V. (2002) 'Drag Kings "Down Under": An Archive and Introspective of a Few Aussie Blokes', in D. J. Troka,, K. LeBesco, and J. B. Noble (eds), *The Drag King Anthology.* New York, Harrington Park Press. Simultaneously published in *Journal of Homosexuality*, 43 (3/4).

Crozier, I. (2000) 'Havelock Ellis, Eonism and the Patient's Discourse; or, Writing a Book about Sex', *History of Psychiatry*, 11: 125–54.

Demale Society (2003) 'The Demale Society Training Manual – Vol. 4' (Flyer), http://www.redlightnet.com/ princess/subscription/de04 (accessed 3 August 2003).

Demeyere, G. (1992) *Transvestism and its Wider Context: A Working Bibliography.* private publication, Demeyere, Wignegem.

Denny, D. (1994) *Gender Dysphoria: A Guide to Research.* New York: Garland Publishing Inc.

Denny, D. (1995) 'The Paradigm Shift is Here!' *Aegis News*, 4:1.

Denny, D. (1996) 'From the Editor', *Chrysalis: The Journal of Transgressive Gender Identities*, 2 (3): 3–4.

Dermen, S., Gamble, D., Hakeem, and five others [anon] (2002) 'Letter to the Editor', *The Daily Telegraph*, 15 July.

Devor, A. H. (2004) 'Reed Erickson and the Erickson Educational Foundation', http://web.uvic.ca/~erick123/ (accessed 30 December 2004).

Devor, H. (1997) *Female-to-Male Transsexuals in Society.* Bloomington, IN: Indiana University Press.

Diamond, M. (1965) 'A Critical Evaluation of the Ontogeny of Human Sexual Behaviour', *Quarterly Review of Biology*, 40 (2): 147–75.

Diamond. M. (2004) 'Sex, Gender, and Identity over the Years: A Changing Perspective', *Child and Adolescent Psychiatric Clinics of North America*, 13: 591–604.

Di Ceglie, D. (1998) 'Management and Therapeutic Aims in Working with Children and Adolescents with Gender Identity Disorders, and their Families', in D. Di Ceglie and D. Freedman (eds), *A Stranger in My Body: Atypical Gender Identity Development and Mental Health.* London: Karnac.

Docter, R. F. (2004) *From Man to Woman: The Transgender Journey of Virginia Prince.* Northridge, CA: Docter Press.

Eichler, M. (1980) *The Double Standard: A Feminist Critique of Feminist Social Science*. London: Croom Helm.

Ekins, R. (1978) 'G. H. Mead: Contributions to a Philosophy of Sociological Knowledge', PhD thesis, University of London.

Ekins, R. (1982) 'Male Transsexualism, Sociological Analysis and Some Problems of the Double Hermeneutic', paper presented to the Annual Conference of the British Sociological Association, Manchester, England.

Ekins, R. (1983) 'The Assignment of Motives as a Problem in the Double Hermeneutic: the Case of Transvestism and Transsexuality', paper presented to the Annual Conference of the Sociological Association of Ireland, Wexford, Ireland.

Ekins, R. (1984) 'Facets of Femaling in Some Relations Between Sex, Sexuality and Gender', paper presented to the Sociological Association of Ireland Annual Conference, Drogheda, Ireland.

Ekins, R. (1987) 'News from Around the World – In Their Own Words: Interview with Dr Richard Ekins of the Trans-Gender Archive, University of Ulster', *Renaissance News* I (5) 4–5 [The Chrysalis Interview].

Ekins, R. (1993) 'On Male Femaling: A Grounded Theory Approach to Cross-Dressing and Sex-Changing', *The Sociological Review*, 41 (1): 1–29.

Ekins, R. (1997) *Male Femaling: A Grounded Theory Approach to Cross-Dressing and Sex-Changing*. London: Routledge.

Ekins, R. (2002) 'The Case of the Girl-a-Matic Guides to Sissification', in A. Purnell (ed.), *Conference Report of the 7th International Gender Dysphoria Conference*. London: BM Gendys, pp. 22–30.

Ekins, R. (2003) 'Internet Erotica, Virtual Identity and the "Male Femaling" Gaze', paper presented at the 18th Harry Benjamin International Gender Dysphoria Symposium, Ghent, Belgium.

Ekins, R. (2005) 'Science, Politics and Clinical Intervention: Harry Benjamin, Transsexuality and the Problem of Heteronormativity', *Sexualities*, 8 (3): 306–28.

Ekins, R. and King, D. (eds), (1996a) *Blending Genders: Social Aspects of Cross-Dressing and Sex-Changing*. London and New York: Routledge.

Ekins, R. and King, D. (1996b) 'Is the Future Transgendered?', in A. Purnell (ed.), *Conference Report of the 4th International Gender Dysphoria Conference*. London: BM Gendys, pp. 97–103.

Ekins, R. and King, D. (1997) 'Blending Genders: Contributions to the Emerging Field of Transgender Studies', *International Journal of Transgenderism*, 1 (1), http://www.symposion.com/ijt/ijtc0101.htm (accessed 24 May 2006).

Ekins, R. and King, D. (1998) 'Blending Genders: Contributions to the Emerging Field of Transgender Studies', in D. Denny (ed.), *Current Concepts in Transgender Identity*. New York: Garland Press.

Ekins, R. and King, D. (1999) 'Towards a Sociology of Transgendered Bodies', *The Sociological Review*, 47: 580–602.

Ekins, R., and King, D. (2001a) 'David O. Cauldwell on Transsexualism, Transvestism and Related Topics: A Bibliography', *International Journal Transgenderism*, 5 (2), http://www.symposion.com/ijt/cauldwell06htm (accessed 24 May 2006).

Ekins, R. and King, D. (2001b) 'Pioneers of Transgendering: The Popular Sexology of David O. Cauldwell', *International Journal of Transgenderism*, 5 (3), http://www.symposion.com/cauldwell/cauldwell01.htm (accessed 24 May 2006).

Ekins, R. and King, D. (2001c) 'Tales of the Unexpected: Exploring Transgender Diversity through Personal Narrative', in F. Haynes and T. McKenna (eds), *Unseen Genders: Beyond the Binaries*. New York: Peter Lang.

Ekins, R. and King, D. (2001d) 'Transgendering, Migrating and Love of Oneself as a Woman: A Contribution to a Sociology of Autogynephilia', *International Journal of Transgenderism*, 5 (3), Symposion Publishing. http://www.symposion.com/ijt/ijtvo05no03_01.htm (accessed 24 May 2006).

Ekins, R. and King, D. (eds), (2005a) *Virginia Prince: Pioneer of Transgendering*. New York: Haworth Press.

Ekins, R. and King, D. (2005b) 'Virginia Prince: Transgender Pioneer', *International Journal of Transgenderism*. 8 (4).

Elan-Cane, C. (1992) 'I Am Living Proof of the Third Sex', *The Independent*, 12 May.

Elan-Cane, C. (1997) 'Prepared Speech for Cybergender Discussion', Transgender Film and Video Festival, London.

Elan-Cane, C. (1998) 'A World without Gender', talk given at the Third International Congress on Sex and Gender, Exeter College, Oxford.

Elan-Cane, C. (1999a) 'Christie Elan-Cane', in T. O'Keefe, *Sex, Gender and Sexuality: 21st Century Transformations*. London: Extraordinary People Press.

Elan-Cane, C. (1999b) 'A Life Without Gender in a Gendered Society', paper presented at the XVII Harry Benjamin International Gender Dysphoria Association Symposium, London.

Elan-Cane, C. (2000–1) 'The Fallacy of the Myth of Gender', in *Conference Report of the 6th International Gender Dysphoria Conference*. London: BM Gendys, pp. 78–82.

Ellis, H. H. (1913a) 'Sexo-aesthetic Inversion', *Alienist and Neurologist*, 34 (May): 156–67.

Ellis, H. H. (1913b) 'Sexo-aesthetic Inversion', *Alienist and Neurologist*, 34 (August): 249–79.

Ellis, H. H. (1914) *Man and Woman*, 5th edn. London: The Walter Scott Publishing Co., Ltd.

Ellis, H. H. (1920) 'Eonism', *Medical Review of Reviews*, (New York), 3–12.

Ellis, H. H. (1928) *Studies in the Psychology of Sex*, vol. 7. Philadelphia, PA: F.A. Davies.

Engels, F. (1884) *The Origin of the Family, Private Property and the State*, in (ed.), Eleanor Burke Leacock. (1972), New York: International Publishers.

Erickson, R. (1969) 'Foreword', in R. Green and J. Money (eds), *Transsexualism and Sex Reassignment*. Baltimore, MD: Johns Hopkins University Press.

Evangelical Alliance (2004) 'A Response by the Evangelical Alliance to the Lord Chancellor's Department's Invitation to Respond to the Government's Statement on its Policy Concerning Transsexual People', http://www.eauk.org/CONTENTMANAGER/Content/PoliticsandSociety/currentissues/Transsexual1.cfm (accessed 22 January 2005).

Faderman, L. (1981) *Surpassing the Love of Men*. London: Junction Books.

Fallowell, D. and Ashley, A. (1982) *April Ashley's Odyssey*. London: Jonathan Cape.

Farrer, P. (1987) *Men in Petticoats*. Liverpool: Karn Publications.

Farrer, P. (1996) 'In Female Attire: Male Experiences of Cross-dressing – Some Historical Fragments', in R. Ekins and D. King (eds), *Blending Genders: Social Aspects of Cross-Dressing and Sex-Changing*. London and New York: Routledge.

Feinberg, L. (1992) *Transgender Liberation: A Movement Whose Time Has Come*. New York: World View Forum.

Feinberg, L. (1996) *Transgender Warriors: Making History from Joan of Arc to Dennis Rodman*. Boston: Beacon Press.

Feinberg, L. (1998) *Trans Liberation*. Boston: Beacon Press.

Feinbloom, D. H. (1976) *Transvestites and Transsexuals: Mixed Views*. New York: Dell.

Filkin, Lord (2003) 'Government Announcement on Transsexual People', by Lord Filkin, Parliamentary Under-Secretary at the Department for Constitutional Affairs, 11 July 2003. http://www.dca.gov.uk/constitution/transsex/110703statement.htm (accessed 24 May 2006).

Filmer, P. (1971) 'On Harold Garfinkel's Ethnomethodology', in P. Filmer, M. Phillipson, D. Silverman, and D. Walsh (eds), *New Directions in Sociological Theory*. London: Collier-Macmillan.

Filmer, P., Phillipson, M., Silverman, D., and Walsh D. (eds) (1971) *New Directions in Sociological Theory*. London: Collier-Macmillan.

Fisk, N. (1973) 'Gender Dysphoria Syndrome. (The How, What and Why of a Disease)', in D. R. Laub and P. Gandy (eds), *Proceedings of the Second Interdisciplinary Symposium on Gender Dysphoria Syndrome*. Stanford, CA: University Medical Center, Stanford.

Fleischer, J. (1996) *The Drag Queens of New York: An Illustrated Field Guide*. London: Pandora.

Fleming, M., Steinman, C. and Bocknek, G. (1980) 'Methodological Problems in Assessing Sex Re-assignment Surgery: A Reply to Meyer and Reter', *Archives of Sexual Behavior*, 9 (5): 541–56.

Fonagy, P. (2006) 'Commentary', in P. Fonagy, W. Krause and M. Leuzinger-Bohleber (eds), *Identity, Gender, and Sexuality*, London: International Psychoanalytic Association Press, pp. 157–59.

Foucault, M. (1970) *The Order of Things: An Archaeology of the Human Sciences*. New York: Random House.

Foucault, M. (1972) *The Archaeology of Knowledge*. New York: Harper and Row.

Foucault, M. (1979) *The History of Sexuality*, vol. 1. London: Allen Lane.

Freedman, E. B. (1987) '"Uncontrolled Desires": The Response to the Sexual Psychopath, 1920–1960', *The Journal of American History*, 74: 83–106.

Freud, S. (1899) 'Letter to Wilhelm Fleiss', in J. M. Masson (ed.), *The Complete Letters of Sigmund Freud to Wilhelm Fleiss, 1887–1904*. Cambridge, MA: Harvard University Press.

Freud, S. (1905) 'Three Essays on the Theory of Sexuality', in *Standard edn. of the Complete Psychological Works of Sigmund Freud*, Vol. 7, pp. 130–243. London: The Hogarth Press.

Freud, S. (1913) 'On Psycho-Analysis', in *Standard edn. of the Complete Psychological Works of Sigmund Freud*, Vol. 12, pp. 205–11, London: The Hogarth Press.

Freud, S. (1918) 'The Taboo of Virginity', in *Standard edn. of the Complete Psychological Works of Sigmund Freud*, Vol. 11, pp. 189–208, London: The Hogarth Press.

Freud, S. (1930) *Civilization and its Discontents*, in *Standard edn. of the Complete Psychological Works of Sigmund Freud*, Vol. 21, pp. 57–145, London: The Hogarth Press.

Gagnon, J. and Simon, W. (eds) (1970) *The Sexual Scene*. New York: Transaction Books.

Gagnon, J. and Simon, W. (1973) *Sexual Conduct: The Social Sources of Human Sexuality*. Chicago: Aldine.

Garber, M. (1992) *Vested Interests: Cross-Dressing and Cultural Anxiety*. New York: Routledge.

Garfinkel, H. (1967) 'Passing and the Managed Achievement of Sex Status in an Intersexed Person, Part 1', in *Studies in Ethnomethodology*. Englewood Cliffs, NJ: Prentice Hall.

Giddens, A. (1976) *New Rules of Sociological Method*. London: Hutchinson.

Gilbert, M. ([1996] 2002a) 'Prof. Miqqi Goes to Work 1', *Transgender Tapestry*, 98 (Summer): 12–13.

Gilbert, M. ([1996] 2002b) 'Prof Miqqi Goes to Work 2', *Transgender Tapestry*, 99 (Fall): 24, 26.

Ginger (1980) *Female Mimics International* 2.

GIRES (2006a) 'Atypical Gender Development: A Review', *The International Journal of Transgenderism*, 9 (1): 29–44.

GIRES (2006b) 'Response to the Critiques of Atypical Gender Development: A Review', *The International Journal of Transgenderism*, 9 (1): 61–74.

Girl-a-matic Corporation (2004) Home Page, http://www.geocities.com/WestHollywood/Heights/8036/ (accessed 25 July 2004).

Glaser, B. G. (1978) *Theoretical Sensitivity: Advances in the Methodology of Grounded Theory*. Mill Valley, CA: Sociology Press.

Glaser, B. (1992) *Basics of Grounded Theory Analysis*. Mill Valley, CA: Sociology Press.

Glaser, B. (ed.) (1993) *Examples of Grounded Theory: A Reader*. Mill Valley, CA: Sociology Press.

Glaser, B. G. and Strauss, A. (1967) *The Discovery of Grounded Theory: Strategies for Qualitative Research*. Chicago: Aldine.

Glynn, J. D. and Harper, P. (1961) 'Behaviour Therapy in Transvestism', *The Lancet*, 18 March, p. 619.

Goffman, E. (1963) *Stigma: Notes on the Management of Spoiled Identity*. Englewood Cliffs, NJ: Prentice Hall.

Goffman, E. (1971) *The Presentation of Self in Everyday Life*. Harmondsworth: Penguin.

Goffman, E. (1979) *Gender Advertisements*. London: Macmillan.

Goode, E. (1969) 'Marijuana and the Politics of Reality', *Journal of Health and Social Behaviour*, 10: 83–94.

Gooren, L. (1998) BBC-TV *Heart of the Matter*.

Gorbutt, D. (1972) 'The "New" Sociology of Education', *Education for Teaching*, 89: 3–11.

Graburn, N. H. H. and Barthel-Bouchier, D. (2001) 'Relocating the Tourist', *International Sociology*, 16 (2): 147–58.

Grace, D. (1991) *Love Bites*. London: Gay Men's Press.

Grace, D. (1993) 'Lesbian Boys and Other Inverts', in V. Harwod, D. Oswell, K. Parkinson, and A. Ward (eds), *Pleasure Principles: Politics, Sexuality and Ethics*. London: Lawrence & Wishart.

Gray, J. (1992) *Men Are from Mars, Women Are from Venus: A Practical Guide for Improving Communication and Getting What You Want in Your Relationships*. New York: HarperCollins.

Green, J. (2004) *Becoming a Visible Man*. Nashville, TN: Vanderbilt University Press.

Green, R. (1985) 'Foreword', in B. W. Steiner (ed.), *Gender Dysphoria: Development, Research, Management*, New York: Plenum Press.

Green, R. and Money, J. (eds) (1969) *Transsexualism and Sex Reassignment*. Baltimore, MD: Johns Hopkins University Press.

Greenson, R. (1964) 'On Homosexuality and Gender Identity', *The International Journal of Psychoanalysis*, 45: 217–19.

Haberman, M. A. and Michael, R. P. (1979) 'Autocastration in Transsexualism', *American Journal of Psychiatry*, 136 (3): 347–8.

Haire, N. (1950) 'Change of Sex', *Journal of Sex Education*, 2 (5): 200–3.

Halberstam, J. (1994) 'F2M: The Making of Female Masculinity', in L. Doan (ed.), *The Lesbian Postmodern*. New York: Columbia University Press.

Halberstam, J. (1998) *Female Masculinity*. Durham, NC: Duke University Press.

Hamburger, C. (1953) 'The Desire for Change of Sex as Shown by Personal Letters from 465 Men and Women', *Acta Endocrinologica* 14: 361–75.

Hamburger, C. and Sprechler, M. (1951) 'The Influence of Steroid Hormones on the Hormonal Activity of the Adenohypophysis in Man', *Acta Endocrinologica*, 7: 167–95.

Hamburger, C., Sturup, G. and Dahl-Iversen, E. (1953) 'Transvestism: Hormonal, Psychiatric and Surgical Treatment', *Journal of the American Medical Association*, 152: 391–6.

Haynes, F. (2001) 'Introduction', in F. Haynes, and T. McKenna (eds), *Unseen Genders: Beyond the Binaries*. New York: Peter Lang.

Haynes, F. and McKenna, T. (eds) (2001) *Unseen Genders: Beyond the Binaries*. New York: Peter Lang.

Heat (2004) 'Nadia Loses a Stone in 4 Weeks!' *Heat*, 9–15 October, p. 1.

Henslin, J. and Sagarin, E. (eds), (1978) *The Sociology of Sex: An Introductory Reader*. New York: Schocken Books.

Hertoft, P. and Sørensen, T. (1979) 'Transsexuality: Some Remarks Based on Clinical Experience', in *Sex Hormones and Behaviour*. Oxford: Ciba Foundation Symposium 62 (new series), Excerpta Medica.

Hewitt, P. with Warren, J. (1995) *A Self-Made Man: The Diary of Man Born in a Woman's Body*, London: Headline.

Highboots, H. (1988) 'Fifteen General Rules for Sissies to Observe', *F.M.I. Female Mimics International*, Issue 43, 17 (5): 42–3.

Hill, D. B. (2000) 'Categories of Sex and Gender: Either/Or, Both/And, and Neither/Nor', *History and Philosophy of Psychology Bulletin*, 12 (2): 25–33.

Hirschfeld, M. (1923) 'Die intersexuelle Konstitution', *Jahrbuch für Sexuelle Zwischenstufen* 23: 3–27.

Hirschfeld, M. (1938) *Sexual Anomalies and Perversions*. London: Encyclopaedic Press.

Hirschfeld, M. (1991) *Transvestites: The Erotic Drive to Cross-Dress*. New York: Prometheus Books. Originally published in 1910 as *Die Transvestiten: Eine Untersuchung über den Erotischen Verkleidungstrieb*. Berlin, Pulvermacher. Translation by M. A. Lombardi-Nash.

Ihlenfeld, C. L. (1978) 'Dedication', *Archives of Sexual Behaviour*, 7 (4): 243–6.

James, A. (2004) 'Categorically Wrong: A Bailey-Blanchard-Lawrence Clearinghouse', http://www.tsroadmap.com/info/bailey-blanchard-lawrence.html (accessed 22 January 2005).

Jeffreys, S. (1996) 'Heterosexuality and the Desire for Gender', in D. Richardson (ed.), *Theorising Heterosexuality: Telling it Straight*. Buckingham: Open University Press.

Jeffreys, S. (2003) *Unpacking Queer Politics*. Cambridge: Polity Press.

Johnson, C. and Brown, C. with W. Nelson (1982) *The Gender Trap*. London: Proteus.

Johnson, J. (2004) 'Why We Love Nadia!' *Closer*, 14–20 August, p. 3.

Jorgensen, C. (1967) *Christine Jorgensen: A Personal Autobiography*. New York: P.S. Eriksson.

Joy and Marlene (No date, c.mid-1980s) *What Is Transgenderism?* Parow, South Africa: A Fanfare Publication.

Kane, S. (1998) *Samantha Kane: A Two-tiered Existence*. London: Writers and Artists.

Katz, J. (1976) *Gay American History*. New York: Thomas Y. Crowell.

Kelly, P. (ed.), (1987–90) *Chrysalis International*, Gender Transient Affinity Magazine, Freshwater, Isle of Wight.

Kessler, S. and McKenna, W. (1978) *Gender: An Ethnomethodological Approach*. New York: John Wiley & Sons, Ltd.

Kessler, S. and McKenna, W. (2000) 'Who Put the "Trans" in Transgender? Gender Theory and Everyday Life', *International Journal of Transgenderism*, 4 (3) http://www.symposion.com/ijt/gilbert/kessler.htm. (accessed 29 January, 2005).

King, D. (1981) 'Gender Confusions: Psychological and Psychiatric Conceptions of Transvestism and Transsexualism', in K. Plummer (ed.), *The Making of the Modern Homosexual*. London: Hutchinson.

King, D. (1984) 'Condition, Orientation, Role or False Consciousness? Models of Homosexuality and Transsexualism', *The Sociological Review*, 32 (1): 38–56.

King, D. (1986) 'The Transvestite and the Transsexual: A Case Study of Public Categories and Private Identities', PhD thesis, University of Essex.

King, D. (1987) 'Social Constructionism and Medical Knowledge: The Case of Transsexualism', *Sociology of Health and Illness*, 9 (1): 351–77.

King, D. (1993) *The Transvestite and the Transsexual: Public Categories and Private Identities*. Aldershot: Avebury.

Kirk, K. and Heath, E. (1984) *Men in Frocks*. London: Gay Men's Press.

Kirsty (2003) in *The Way Out Tranny Guide*, 11th edn. Enfield: Way Out Publishing.

Kockott, G. (2001) 'Sexual Disorders', in F. Henn, N. Sartorius, H. Helmchen and H. Lauter (eds), *Contemporary Psychiatry*. London: Springer.

Kosok, M. (1971) 'The Phenomenology of Fucking', *Telos*, 8: 64–76.

Krafft-Ebing, R. von (1901) *Psychopathia Sexualis*. 10th edn. London: Rebman.

Laub, D. R. and Gandy, P. (eds) (1973) *Proceedings of the Second Interdisciplinary Symposium on Gender Dysphoria Syndrome*. Stanford, CA: Stanford University Medical Center.

Lawrence, A. (1998) 'Men Trapped in Men's Bodies: An Introduction to the Concept of Autogynephilia', *Transgender Tapestry*, 85 (Winter): 65–8.

Lawrence, A. (1999a) 'Lessons from Autogynephiles: Eroticism, Motivation, and the Standards of Care', paper presented at the 16th Harry Benjamin International Gender Dysphoria Association Symposium, London.

Lawrence, A. (1999b) 'Men Trapped in Men's Bodies: Autogynephilic Eroticism as a Motive for Seeking Sex Reassignment', paper presented at the 16th Harry Benjamin International Gender Dysphoria Association Symposium, London.

Lawrence, A. (1999c) '28 Narratives about Autogynephilia', *Transsexual Women's Resources*. http://www.annelawrence.com/agnarratives.html (accessed 1 September 2000).

Lawrence, A. (1999d) '31 New Narratives about Autogynephilia plus Five Revealing Fantasy Narratives', *Transsexual Women's Resources*, http://www.annelawrence.com/31narratives.html (accessed 1 September 2000).

Lawrence, A. (1999e) 'Autogynephilia: Frequently-Asked Questions', *Transsexual Women's Resources*. http://www.annelawrence.com/agfaqs.html (accessed 1 September 2000).

Lawrence, A. (2000) 'Sexuality and Transsexuality: A New Introduction to the Concept of Autogynephilia', *Transsexual Women's Resources*, http://www.annelawrence.com/newintroagp.html (accessed 1 September 2000).

Lawrence, A. (2004) 'Autogynephilia: A Paraphilic Model of Gender Identity Disorder', *Journal of Gay and Lesbian Psychotherapy*, 8 (1/2): 68–87.

Lee, V. (ed.) (2003) *The Way Out Tranny Guide*, 11th edn. Enfield: Way Out Publishing.

Lee, V. (ed.) (2005) *The Way Out Tranny Guide*, 13th edn. Enfield: Way Out Publishing.

Leeds University TV.TS. Group (1974) *Transvestism and Transsexualism in Modern Society.* Conference Report, Leeds University TV.TS. Group.

Lenz, L. L. (1954) *Memoirs of a Sexologist: Discretion and Indiscretion.* New York: Cadillac Publishing.

Lorber, J. (2004) 'Preface', in S. Schacht and L. Underwood (eds), *The Drag Queen Anthology: The Absolutely Fabulous but Flawlessly Customary World of Female Impersonators.* New York: Harrington Park Press.

Lorelei (1995) *A Charm School for Sissy Maids.* Springfield, PA: Berkana Press.

Lowy, F. H. and Kolivakis, T. L. (1971) 'Autocastration by a Male Transsexual', *Canadian Psychiatric Association Journal*, 16 (5): 399-405.

MacCannell, D. (1999) *The Tourist: A New Theory of the Leisure Class.* Berkeley: University of California Press.

Mackenzie, G. O. (1994) *Transgender Nation.* Bowling Green, OH: Bowling Green University Popular Press.

Mahler, M., Pine, F. and Bergman, A. (1975) *The Psychological Birth of the Human Infant: Symbiosis and Individuation.* New York: Basic Books.

Marino, F. with Marks, S. and C. (1997) *His Majesty the Queen*, Ocala, FL: MSW Publishing.

Marshall, J. (1981) `Pansies, Perverts and Macho Men: Changing Conceptions of Male Homosexuality', in K. Plummer (ed.), *The Making of the Modern Homosexual.* London: Hutchinson.

Martino, M, with Harriett (1977) *Emergence: A Transsexual Autobiography.* New York: Crown Publishers.

McCloskey, D. N. (1999) *Crossing: A Memoir.* Chicago: University of Chicago Press.

McHugh P. (2004) 'Surgical Sex', *First Things*, 147 (November): 34-8. http://www.firstthings.com/ftissues/ft0411/articles/mchugh.htm (accessed 24 May 2006).

McNeill, S. (1982) 'Transsexualism ... Can Men Turn Men into Women?' in S. Friedman and G. Sarah (eds), *On the Problem of Men.* London: The Women's Press.

Mead, G. H. (1932) *The Philosophy of the Present.* La Salle, IL: Open Court Publishing Company.

Mead, G. H. (1934) *Mind, Self, and Society.* Chicago: The University of Chicago Press.

Mead, G. H. (1938) *The Philosophy of the Act.* Chicago: The University of Chicago Press.

Merton, R. (1971) 'Social Problems and Sociological Theory', in R. K. Merton and R. Nisbet (eds), *Contemporary Social Problems.* New York: Harcourt Brace Jovanovich.

Meyer, J. K. and Hoopes, J. E. (1974) 'The Gender Dysphoria Syndromes: A Position Statement on So-called Transsexualism', *Plastic and Reconstructive Surgery*, 54 (4): 444-51.

Meyer III, W. (Chairperson), et al. (2001) 'The Standards of Care for Gender Identity Disorders – Sixth Version', *The International Journal of Transgenderism*, 5,1, http://www.symposion.com/ijt/soc_2001/index.htm (accessed 31 December 2004).

Meyerowitz, J. (2002) *How Sex Changed: A History of Transsexuality in the United States.* Cambridge, MA: Harvard University Press.

Millie (1997) *'Millie': The Story of a Male Maid*, mimeo.

Mills, C. Wright (1940) 'Situated Actions and Vocabularies of Motive', in *Power, Politics and People: The Collected Essays of C. Wright Mills.* New York: Oxford University Press.

Money J., Hampson, J. G., and Hampson, J. L. (1957) 'Imprinting and the Establishment of Gender Role', *Archives of Neurology and Psychiatry* 77 (Mar.): 333-6.

Money, J. and Schwartz, F. (1969) 'Public Opinion and Social Issues in Transsexualism: A Case Study in Medical Sociology', in R. Green and J. Money (eds), *Transsexualism and Sex Reassignment.* Baltimore, MD: Johns Hopkins University Press.

Money, J. and Tucker, P. (1977) *Sexual Signatures: On Being a Man or a Woman.* London: Abacus.

Money, J. and Walker, P. A. (1977) 'Counselling the Transsexual', in J. Money and H. Musaph (eds), *Handbook of Sexology.* Amsterdam: Elsevier.

Monro, S. (2005a) 'Beyond Male and Female: Poststructuralism and the Spectrum of Gender', *International Journal of Transgenderism*, 8 (1): 4-22.

Monro, S. (2005b) *Gender Politics: Citizenship, Activism and Sexual Diversity.* London: Pluto Press.

Monro, S. and Warren, L. (2004) 'Transgendering Citizenship', *Sexualities*, 7 (3): 345–62.

Montmorency, D. (1970) *The Drag Scene: The Secrets of Female Impersonators*. London: Luxor Press.

Morris, G. (2005) 'A Brief History of Queer Cinema', http://www.greencine.com/static/primers/queer.jsp (assessed 24 May 2006).

Morris, J. (1974) *Conundrum*. London: Faber.

Namaste, V. (2000) *Invisible Lives: The Erasure of Transsexual and Transgendered People*. Chicago: University of Chicago Press.

Nataf, Z. (1996) *Lesbians Talk Transgender*. London: Scarlet Press.

Nestle, J., Howell, C. and Wilchins, R. (eds) (2002) *GenderQueer*. Los Angeles: Alyson Books.

Newton, E. (1972) *Mother Camp: Female Impersonators in America*. Chicago: University of Chicago Press.

Newton, E. (1979) *Mother Camp: Female Impersonators in America*. 2nd edn. Chicago: University of Chicago Press.

Novic, R. J. (2005) *Alice in Genderland*, New York: iUniverse, Inc.

Oakley, A. (1972) *Sex, Gender and Society*. London: Temple Smith.

O'Keefe, T. (2004) 'Equality for Normal, Heterosexual Transsexuals Only', in A. Purnell (ed.), *Conference Report of the 8th International Gender Dysphoria Conference*. London: BM Gendys, pp. 141–45.

O'Keefe, T. and Fox, K. (eds) (2003) *Finding the Real Me: True Tales of Sex and Gender Diversity*. San Francisco: Jossey-Bass.

Ostow, M. (1953) 'Transvestism', *Journal of the American Medical Association*, 152 (16): 1553.

Parkin, M. (1994) 'Mixed Feelings', *The Gurdian*, 4 March. [Appendix F(i) *The First National TV.TS Conference Report*, Leeds, p. 36].

Pauly, I. B. (1965) 'Male Psychosexual Inversion: Transsexualism', *Archives of General Psychiatry*, 13: 172–81.

Pepper, J. (1982) *A Man's Tale*. London: Quartet Books.

Person, E. S. (1999) *The Sexual Century*, New Haven: Yale University Press.

Person, E. and Oversey, L. (1974a) 'The Transsexual Syndrome in Males I: Primary Transsexualism', *American Journal of Psychotherapy*, 28 (1): 4–20.

Person, E. and Oversey, L. (1974b) 'The Transsexual Syndrome in Males II: Secondary Transsexualism', *American Journal of Psychotherapy*, 28 (2): 174–93.

Pfäfflin, F. (1997) 'Sex Reassignment, Harry Benjamin, and Some European Roots', *International Journal of Transgenderism* 1 (2), http://www.symposion.com/ijt/ijt.202.htm (accessed 24 May 2006).

Pfäfflin, F. (2006) 'Research, Research Politics and Clinical Experience with Transsexual Patients', in P. Fonagy, W. Krause and M. Leuzinger-Bohleber, *Identity, Gender, and Sexuality*, London: International Psychoanalytic Press, pp. 139–56.

Pfäfflin, F. and Coleman, E. (1997) 'Introduction', *International Journal of Transgenderism*, 1 (1), http://www.symposion.com/ijtintro.htm (accessed 1 September 2000).

Phillips, M. A. (1993) *Raised by Wolves: A Transsexual Diary*. California: Melanie Anne Phillips.

Phillips, M. A. (1994) 'Backword', in M. A. Phillips, *Raised by Wolves: A Transsexual Diary*, California: Melanie Anne Phillips.

Plummer, K. (1975) *Sexual Stigma: An Interactionist Account*. London: Routledge and Kegan Paul.

Plummer, K. (ed.) (1981) *The Making of the Modern Homosexual*. London: Hutchinson.

Plummer, K. (1982) 'Symbolic Interactionism and Sexual Conduct: An Emergent Perspective', in M. Brake (ed.), *Human Sexual Relations: Towards a Redefinition of Sexual Politics*. Harmondsworth: Penguin, pp. 223–41.

Plummer, K. (1995) *Telling Sexual Stories: Power, Change and Social Worlds*. London: Routledge.

Plummer, K. (1996) 'Foreword: Genders in Question', in R. Ekins and D. King (eds), *Blending Genders: Social Aspects of Cross-Dressing and Sex-Changing*. London: Routledge.

Press for Change (1996) *Transsexualism: The Current Medical Viewpoint*. London: Press for Change, http://www.pfc.org.uk/medical/mediview (accessed 24 May 2006).

Prince, C. V. (1957) 'Homosexuality, Transvestism and Transsexualism', *American Journal of Psychotherapy*, 11: 80–5.

Prince, V. (1960) 'In Memoriam', *Transvestia*, 1 (1): 45.

Prince, V. (1967) *The Transvestite and his Wife*. Los Angeles: Argyle.

Prince, V. (1969a) 'Change of Sex or Gender', *Transvestia*, 10 (60): 53–65. [Volume 9 appears on the front cover].

Prince, V. (1969b) 'Men Who Choose to be Women', *Sexology*, (February): 441–4.

Prince, V. (1971) *How to Be a Woman Though Male*. Los Angeles, CA: Chevalier Publications.

Prince, V. (1973) 'Sex vs Gender', in D. R. Laub and P. Gandy (eds), *Proceedings of the Second Interdisciplinary Symposium on Gender Dysphoria Syndrome*. Stanford, CA: Stanford University Medical Center.

Prince, V. (1976) *Understanding Cross Dressing*. Los Angeles: Chevalier.

Prince, V. (1977) 'Woman by Choice or Woman by Default?' *Transvestia*, 15 (89) 77–89.

Prince, V. (1978a) 'The "Transcendents" or "Trans" People', *Transvestia*, 16 (95): 81–92.

Prince, V. (1978b) 'Transsexuals and Pseudotranssexuals', *Archives of Sexual Behavior*, 7: 263–73.

Prince, V. (1979a) 'Charles to Virginia: Sex Research as a Personal Experience', in V. L. Bullough (ed.), *The Frontiers of Sex Research*. New York: Prometheus Books.

Prince, V. (1979b) 'The Life and Times of Virginia', *Transvestia*, 17 (100): 5–120. [This issue is wrongly dated 1977].

Prince, V. (1997a) 'My Accidental Career', in B. Bullough, V. L. Bullough, M. A. Fithian, W. H. Hartman, and R. S. Klein (eds), *How I Got into Sex*. New York: Prometheus Books.

Prince, V. (1997b) 'Seventy Years in the Trenches of the Gender Wars', in V. Bullough, B. Bullough, and J. Elias (eds), *Gender Blending*. New York: Prometheus Books, pp. 469–79.

Prosser, J. (1998) *Second Skins: The Body Narratives of Transsexuality*. New York: Columbia University Press.

Prus, R. (1987) 'Generic Social Processes: Maximising Conceptual Development in Ethnographic Research', *Journal of Contemporary Ethnography*, 16: 250–93.

Prus, R. (1997) *Subcultural Mosaics and Intersubjective Realities: An Ethnographic Research Agenda for Pragmatizing the Social Sciences*. Albany, NY: State University of New York Press.

Queen, C. and Schimel, L. (eds) (1997) *Pomosexuals: Challenging Assumptions about Gender and Sexuality*. San Francisco, CA: Cleis Press.

Ramet, S. (1996) *Gender Reversals and Gender Cultures*. London: Routledge.

Randell, J. B. (1959) 'Transvestism and Transsexualism: A Study of 50 Cases', *British Medical Journal*, 26 Dec.: 1448–52.

Randell, J. B. (1971) 'Indications for Sex Reassignment Surgery', *Archives of Sexual Behaviour*, 1 (2): 153–61.

Raymond, J. (1980) *The Transsexual Empire*. London: The Women's Press.

Raymond, J. (1994) *The Transsexual Empire*, 2nd edn. New York: The Teachers Press.

Rees, M. (1996) 'Becoming a Man: The Personal Account of a Female-to-Male Transsexual', in R. Ekins and D. King (eds), *Blending Genders: Social Aspects of Cross-Dressing and Sex-Changing*. London: Routledge.

Riddell, C. (1972) 'Transvestism and the Tyranny of Gender', paper presented to the National Deviancy Conference 10.

Riddell, C. (1996) 'Divided Sisterhood: A Critical Review of Janice Raymond's *The Transsexual Empire*', in R. Ekins and D. King (eds), *Blending Genders: Social Aspects of Cross-Dressing and Sex-Changing*. London and New York: Routledge.

Ringrose, K. (2003) *The Perfect Servant: Eunuchs and the Social Construction of Gender in Byzantium*. Chicago: University of Chicago Press.

Roberts, J. (1993) *A Who's Who in the Transgendered Community and International Resource Guide*. King of Prussia, PA: Creative Design Services.

Roberts, J. (1994) *A Who's Who & Resource Guide to the International Transgender Community*. King of Prussia, PA: Creative Design Services.

Roen, K. (2001a) '"Either/Or" and "Both/Neither": Discursive Tensions in Transgender Politics', *Signs: Journal of Women in Culture and Society*, 27 (2): 501–22.

Roen, K. (2001b) 'Transgender Theory and Embodiment: the Risk of Marginalisation', *Journal of Gender Studies*, 10 (3): 253–63.

Rojek, C. (1993) *Ways of Escape: Modern Transformations in Leisure and Travel*. Basingstoke: Macmillan.

Rose, D. (1993a) *Maid in Form 'A', 'B', & 'C'*. Capistrano Beach, CA: Sandy Thomas.

Rose, D. (1993b) *The Sissy Maid Academy*, vols 1 and 2. Capistrano Beach, CA: Sandy Thomas.

Rose, D. (1994–96) *The Sissy Maid Quarterly*, vols 1–5. Capistrano Beach, CA: Sandy Thomas.

Rose, D. (1994a) 'Top Drawer', *Sissy Maid Quarterly*, Number 1, pp. 36–7.

Rose, D. (1994b) 'The Maid's Room: We Test Rubber Sheets', *Sissy Maid Quarterly*, Number 2, pp. 27–30.

Rose, D. (1995a) 'Editorial', *Sissy Maid Quarterly*, Number 3, pp. 2–3.

Rose, D. (1995b) 'The Social Implications of Gaffing: Effect of Foundation Garments on the Sissy Male Psyche', *Sissy Maid Quarterly*, Number 3, pp. 29–33.

Rose, D. (1995c) *Where the Sissies Come From*. Capistrano Beach, CA: Sandy Thomas.

Rose, D. (1996) 'Cover Story: "He's Just Like a Girl"', *Sissy Maid Quarterly*, Number 5, pp. 6–7.

Rose, D. (2003) *Domestic Bliss: My Life as a Supermodel's Maid*, Books 1–3. Capistrano Beach, CA: Sandy Thomas.

Rowe, R. (1997) *Bert & Lori: The Autobiography of a Crossdresser*. New York: Prometheus Books.

Rubin, G. (1992) 'Of Catamites and Kings: Reflections on Butch, Gender and Boundaries', in J. Nestlé (ed.), *The Persistent Desire: A Femme-Butch Reader*. Boston: Alyson Publications.

RuPaul (1995) *Letting It All Hang Out: An Autobiography*. New York: Hyperion.

Sadock, B. J. and Sadock, V. A. (eds) (2000) *Kaplan and Sadock's Comprehensive Textbook on Psychiatry*, 7th edn. vol. 1. Philadelphia, PA: Lippincott, Williams and Wilkins.

Sadger, I. (1921) *Die Lehre von den Geschlechtverirrungen (Psychpathia sexualis) auf psychoanalytischer Grundlage*. Leipzig: Deuticke.

Sagarin, E. (1968) 'Ideology as a Factor in the Consideration of Deviance', *Journal of Sex Research*, 4 (2): 84–94.

Sagarin, E. (1969) *Odd Man In: Societies of Deviants in America*. Chicago: Quadrangle Books.

Sagarin, E. (1978) 'Transsexualism, Legitimation, Amplification and Exploitation of Deviance by Scientists and Mass Media', in C. Winick (ed.), *Deviance and Mass Media*. Beverly Hills, CA: Sage.

Schacht, S. P. (2000) 'Gay Female Impersonators and the Masculine Construction of "Other"', in P. Nardi (ed.), *Gay Masculinities*. London: Sage Publications, pp. 247–268.

Schacht, S. P. (2002) 'Four Renditions of Doing Female Drag: Feminine Appearing Conceptual Variations of a Masculine Theme', in P. Gagné and R. Tewkesbury (eds), *Gendered Sexualities, vol. 6 of Advances in Gender Research*. Boston: Elsevier Science Ltd, pp. 157–80.

Schacht, S. P. with Underwood, L. (eds) (2004) *The Drag Queen Anthology: The Absolutely Fabulous but Flawlessly Customary World of Female Impersonators*. Binghampton, NY: Harrington Park Press. Simultaneously published in *Journal of Homosexuality*, 46 (3/4).

Schutz, A. (1953) 'Common-Sense and Scientific Interpretation of Human Action', in A. Schutz, *Collected Papers*, vol. 1: *The Problem of Social Reality*, The Hague: Martinus Nijhoff, 1967.

Segal, L. (1994) *Straight Sex: The Politics of Pleasure*. London: Virago.

Senelick, L. (2000) *The Changing Room: Sex, Drag and the Theatre*. London: Routledge.

Shelly, C. (2002) *Silken Slavery*. London: Nexus.

Shively, M. G. and De Cecco, J. P. (1977) 'Components of Sexual Identity', *Journal of Homosexuality*, 3: 1, 41–8.

Sim, M. (1974) *Guide to Psychiatry*, 3rd edn. London: Churchill Livingstone.

Simmel, G. ([1908] 1971) 'The Stranger', in D. N. Levine (ed.) *George Simmel on Individuality and Social Forms*, Chicago: The University of Chicago Press, pp. 143–49.

Simmel, G. ([1917] 1950) *Fundamental Problems of Sociology (Individual and Society)*, trans. K. Wolf, in Wolff (ed.), *The Sociology of Georg Simmel*. New York: The Free Press, pp. 1–84.

Sissy Bobbi (1996) 'Report from the Academy', *Sissy Maid Quarterly*, Number 5, pp. 33-5.

Sissy Jennie (1994) 'A Sissy's World', *Sissy Maid Quarterly*, Number 2, pp. 16-21.

Sissy Times (1988) 'Editorial', reprinted in *F.M.I. Female Mimics International*, 43, 17 (5): 40.

SMQ (1994-96) *Sissy Maid Quarterly*, Numbers 1-5, Capistrano Beach. CA: A Sandy Thomas Publication, produced in conjunction with Rose Publications.

Smyth, C. (1996) *Damn Fine Art*. London: Cassell.

Smythe, S. (1993) 'She-Male Maid: Masturbation and the Male Maid – Practical Solutions', *Transformation*, 1: 46, 47, 50.

Socarides, C. (1969) 'The Desire for Sexual Transformation: A Psychiatric Evaluation of Transsexualism', *American Journal of Psychiatry*, 125 (10): 1419-25.

Socarides, C. (1975) *Beyond Sexual Freedom*. New York: Quadrangle.

Socarides, C. (1988) *The Preoedipal Origin and Psychoanalytic Therapy of Sexual Perversions*. Madison, CT: International Universities Press, Inc.

Sørensen, T. and Hertoft, P. (1980) 'Sexmodifying Operations on Transsexuals in Denmark in the Period 1950-1977', *Acta Psychiatrica Scandinavica*, 61: 56-66.

Spry, J. (1997) *Orlando's Sleep: An Autobiography of Gender*. Norwich, VT: New Victoria Publishers.

Star (2004) 'Nadia: "My Agony Over Secret Boyfriend"', *Star: The World's Greatest Celeb Weekly*, 1 November, p. 1.

Steiner, B. W. (ed.) (1985) *Gender Dysphoria: Development, Research, Management*. New York: Plenum.

Stekel, W. (1934) *Bi-Sexual Love*. New York: Physicians and Surgeons Book Co.

Stephanie (1994) 'Young LA Heiress, Who Could Easily Afford Any Number of Servants of Any Gender, Chooses a Sissy As Her Personal Maid', *Sissy Maid Quarterly*, Number 1, pp. 4-5.

Stoller, R. (1964) 'A Contribution to the Study of Gender Identity', *The International Journal of Psychoanalysis*, 45: 220-6.

Stoller, R. (1968) *Sex and Gender:* vol. 1 *The Development of Masculinity and Femininity*. New York: Science House.

Stoller, R. (1975) *The Transsexual Experiment*, London: Hogarth Press.

Stoller, R. (1977) 'Gender Identity', in B.B. Wolman (ed.), *International Encyclopedia of Psychiatry, Psychology, Psychoanalysis and Neurology*, vol. 5. New York: Van Nostrand for Aesculapius.

Stoller, R. (1982) 'Transvestism in Women', *Archives of Sexual Behavior*, 11 (2): 99-115.

Stone, S. (1991) 'The *Empire* Strikes Back: A Posttranssexual Manifesto', in K. Straub and J. Epstein (eds), *Body Guards: The Cultural Politics of Gender Ambiguity*. New York: Routledge.

Storr, A. (1964) *Sexual Deviation*. Harmondsworth: Penguin.

Straub, K. and Epstein, J. (eds) (1991) *Body Guards: The Cultural Politics of Gender Ambiguity*. New York: Routledge.

Strauss, A. L. (1977) *Mirrors and Masks*. London: Martin Robertson.

Strauss, A. L. (1993) *Continual Permutations of Action*. New York: Aldine de Gruyter.

Stryker, S. (1994) 'My Words to Victor Frankenstein Above the Village of Chamounix – Performing Transgender Rage', *GLQ*, 1 (3): 227-54.

Stryker, S. (ed.) (1998) *The Transgender Issue*, *GLQ* , 4 (2): 213-374.

Stryker, S. (2001) *Queer Pulp*. San Francisco: Chronicle Books.

Stryker, S. and Whittle, S. (eds) (forthcoming) *The Transgender Studies Reader.* New York: Routledge.

Stuart, K. (1983) *The Uninvited Dilemma: A Question of Gender*. Lake Oswego, OR: Metamorphous Press.

Sturup, G. K. (1969) 'Legal Problems Related to Transsexualism and Sex Reassignment in Denmark', in R. Green and J. Money (eds), *Transsexualism and Sex Reassignment.* Baltimore, MD: Johns Hopkins University Press.

Sullivan, N. (2003) *A Critical Introduction to Queer Theory*. Edinburgh: Edinburgh University Press.

Talmey, B. S. (1914) 'Transvestism', *New York Medical Journal*, 99: 362-8.

Taylor, V. with Rupp, L. (2004) 'Chicks with Dicks, Men in Dresses: What it Means to be a Drag Queen', in S. P. Schacht with L. Underwood (eds), *The Drag Queen Anthology: The Absolutely Fabulous But Flawlessly Customary World of Female Impersonators*, New York: Haworth, pp. 113-33.

Teh, Y. K. (2001) 'Mak Nyahs (Male Transsexuals) in Malaysia: The Influence of Culture and Religion on their Identity', *International Journal of Transgenderism*, 5 (3). http://www.symposion.com/ijt/ijtvo05 no03-04.htm

Teh, Y. K. (2002) *The Mak Nyahs: Malaysian Male to Female Transsexuals*. Singapore: Eastern Universities Press.

Telfer, J. B. (1885) *The Strange Career of the Chevalier D'Eon de Beaumont*. London: Longmans, Green.

Tewksbury, R. (1993) 'Men Performing as Women: Explorations in the World of Female Impersonators', *Sociological Spectrum*, 13: 465-86.

Tewksbury, R. (1994) 'Gender Construction and the Female Impersonator: The Process of Transforming "He" to "She"', *Deviant Behavior*, 15: 27-43.

Tewksbury, R. (1995) 'Constructing Women and their World: The Subculture of Female Impersonation', in N. Herman (ed.), *Deviance: A Symbolic Interactionist Approach*. Dix Hills, NY: General Hall.

Tewksbury, R. and Gagné, P. (1996) 'Transgenderists: Products of Non-Normative Intersections of Sex, Gender, and Sexuality', *Journal of Men's Studies*, 5: 105-25.

The First National TV.TS Conference (1974) *Transvestism and Transsexualism in Modern Society*, Sponsored by Leeds University TV.TS Group, Leeds, 15-17 March.

Thomas, S. (1991) *That 'A Girl*. Capistrano Beach, CA: Sandy Thomas Adv.

Thomas, S. ([1989] 1997) *Just Like a Woman*. Capistrano Beach, CA: Sandy Thomas Adv.

Thompson, R. with Sewell, K. (1995) *What Took You So Long?: A Girl's Journey to Manhood*. London: Penguin.

Transkids (2004), 'Welcome to the Transkids. us website', http://www.transkids.us/index.html (accessed 24th May 2006).

Tula (1982) *I Am a Woman*. London: Sphere Books.

Tully, B. (1992) *Accounting for Transsexualism and Transhomosexuality*. London: Whiting and Birch.

Turkle, S. (1997) 'Tiny Sex and Gender Trouble', in S. Kemp and J. Squires (eds), *Feminisms*, Oxford: Oxford University Press.

Underwood, P. (1974) *Danny La Rue: Life's a Drag*. London: Leslie Frewin.

Urry, J. (1990) *The Tourist Gaze*. London: Sage.

Valentine, D. (2002) ' "We're Not About Gender": The Uses of "Transgender" ', in Bill Leap and Ellen Lewin (eds), *Out in Theory: The Emergence of Lesbian and Gay Anthropology*. Urbana, IL: University of Illinois Press, pp. 222-45.

Valentine, D. (2003) 'The Calculus of Pain: Violence, Anthropological Ethics, and the Category Transgender', *Eithnos*, 68 (1): 27-45.

Valentine, D. (2004) 'Imagining Transgender: A Politics of Gender/Sexuality', [Forthcoming]

Vizetelly, E. A. (1895) *The True Story of the Chevalier d'Eon*. London: Tyleston and Edwards.

Volcano, D. (2000) *Sublime Mutations*. Tübingen: Konkursbuchverlag.

Volcano, D. and Halberstam, J. (1999) *The Drag King Book*. London: Serpent's Tale.

von Mahlsdorf, C. (1995) *I Am My Own Woman: The Outlaw Life of Charlotte von Mahlsdorf*. Pittsburgh: Cleis Press.

Wålinder, J. (1967) *Transsexualism: A Study of Forty-Three Cases*. Göteborg: Akademiförlaget-Gumperts.

Walker, K. M. and Fletcher, P. (1955) *Sex and Society*. London: Frederick Muller.

Walter, A. (ed.) (1980) *Come Together: The Years of Gay Liberation*. London: Gay Men's Press.

Wassersug, R. (2004) 'Eunuch Power in Old Byzantium', *The Gay and Lesbian Review*, 11 (3) 18-20.

Wassersug, R., Zelenietz, S.A. and Farrell Squire, G. (2004) 'New Age Eunuchs: Motivation and Rationale for Voluntary Castration', *Archives of Sexual Behavior*, 33 (5): 432-42.

Weeks, J. (1977) *Coming Out: Homosexual Politics in Britain from the 19th Century to the Present*. London: Quartet Books.

West, C. and Zimmerman, D. H. (1987) 'Doing Gender', *Gender and Society*, 1: 125-51.

Wheen, F. (2002) *Who Was Dr Charlotte Bach?* London: Short Books.

Whitehead, H. (1981) 'The Bow and the Burden Strap: A New Look at Institutionalised Homosexuality in Native America', in S.B. Ortner and H. Whitehead (eds), *Sexual Meanings*. Cambridge: Cambridge University Press.

Whittle, S. (1996a) 'Gender Fucking or Fucking Gender? Current Cultural Contributions to Theories of Gender Blending', in R. Ekins and D. King (eds), *Blending Genders: Social Aspects of Cross-Dressing and Sex-Changing*. London: Routledge.

Whittle, S. (1996b) 'The Trans-Cyberian Mailway', *Radical Deviance*, 2(2): 61–8.

Wickman, J. (2001) *Transgender Politics: The Construction and Deconstruction of Binary Gender in the Finnish Transgender Community*. Åbo: Åbo Akademi University Press.

Wiederman, G. H. (1953) 'Transvestism', *Journal of the American Medical Association,* 152 (12): 1167.

Wilchins, R. (1997) *Read My Lips: Sexual Subversion and the End of Gender*. Ithaca, New York: Firebrand Books.

Wilchins, R. (2002a) 'A Certain Kind of Freedom: Power and the Truth of Bodies – Four Essays on Gender', in J. Nestle, C. Howell and R. Wilchins (eds), *GenderQueer: Voices from Beyond the Sexual Binary*. Los Angeles: Alyson Books.

Wilchins, R. (2002b) 'A Continual Nonverbal Communication', in J. Nestle, C. Howell, and R. Wilchins (eds), *GenderQueer: Voices from Beyond the Sexual Binary*. Los Angeles: Alyson Books.

Wilchins, R. (2002c) 'Gender Rights Are Human Rights', in J. Nestle, C. Howell,. and R. Wilchins (eds) *GenderQueer: Voices from Beyond the Sexual Binary*. Los Angeles: Alyson Books.

Willox, A. (2002) 'Whose Drag Is It Anyway? Drag Kings and Monarchy in the UK', in D. J. Troka, K. LeBesco, and J. B. Noble (eds), *The Drag King Anthology*. New York, Harrington Park Press. Simultaneously published in *Journal of Homosexuality*, 43 (3/4).

Wilson, C. (1973) *Time Out*, 13–19 April.

Wilson, C. (1979) *Mysteries*. London: Panther Books.

Wilson, C. (1989) *The Misfits: A Study of Sexual Outsiders*. London: Grafton Books.

Wilson, M. (2002) '"I am the Prince of Pain, for I Am a Princess in the Brain": Liminal Transgender Identities, Narratives and the Elimination of Ambiguities', *Sexualities*, 5: 425–48.

Winter, S. (2002) 'Why Are There So Many Kathoey in Thailand?' http://web.hku.hk/~sjwinter/TransgenderASIA/papers_why_are_there_so_many_kathoey.htm (accessed 24th May 2006).

Winter, S. and Udomsak, N. (2002) 'Male, Female and Transgender: Stereotypes and Self in Thailand', *International Journal of Transgenderism*, 6 (1), http://www.symposion.com/ijt/ijtvo06no01_04.htm

Woodhouse, A. (1989a) 'Breaking the Rules or Bending Them? Transvestism, Femininity, and Feminism', *Women's Studies International Forum*, 12 (4): 417–23.

Woodhouse, A. (1989b) *Fantastic Women: Sex, Gender and Transvestism*. Basingstoke: Macmillan.

Young, M.F.D. (ed.) (1971) *Knowledge and Control: New Directions in the Sociology of Education*. London: Collier-Macmillan.

Zander, E. (2003) *Transactions*. Stockholm: Periskop Förlag.

Zerubavel, E. (1980) 'If Simmel Were a Fieldworker: On Formal Sociological Theory and Analytical Field Research', *Symbolic Interaction*, 3: 25–33.

Zimmerman, D. and Pollner, M. (1971) 'The Everyday World as a Phenomenon', in J. Douglas (ed.), *Understanding Everyday Life*. London: Routledge & Kegan Paul.

Zucker, K. J. and Bradley, S. J. (1995) *Gender Identity Disorder and Psychosexual Problems in Children and Adolescents*. New York: Guilford Press.

Index